YOU GOTTA WANNA

Somewhere I picked up a card with that slogan and it instantly rang bells with me. It was during my days at the car dealership that I realized that no matter how smart a salesman is, how good a family man, how hardworking—if he doesn't have the overwhelming desire to achieve, he won't be a good salesman. If you're trying to build your company, you need someone at the top who also has that intangible drive that springs from deep down—from the fire in the belly. You've gotta wanna succeed.

As for me, after a quarter of a century in business, after doing more than two hundred deals, after more success than I ever dreamed possible, I still wanna.

JIMMY
AN AUTOBIOGRAPHY

Jimmy Pattison
with Paul Grescoe

SEAL BOOKS
McClelland-Bantam, Inc.
Toronto

JIMMY: AN AUTOBIOGRAPHY
A Seal Book
Seal hardcover edition / October 1987
Seal paperback edition / October 1989

All rights reserved.
Copyright © 1987 by Jimmy Pattison
Cover photo copyright © 1989 by Brian Willer.
No part of this book may be reproduced or transmitted in any form or by any means, electronic or mechanical, including photocopying, recording, or by any information storage and retrieval system, without permission in writing from the publisher.
For information address: Seal Books.

Canadian Cataloguing in Publication Data
Pattison, Jim, 1928–
  Jimmy, an autobiography

Includes index.
ISBN 0-770-42252-7

1. Pattison, Jim, 1928– . 2. Businessmen—British Columbia—Biography. 3. Entrepreneur—Biography. 4. Jim Pattison Group—History. 5. Expo 86 (Vancouver, B.C.) I. Grescoe, Paul, 1939– II. Title.

HC112.5.P38A3 1987   338'.04'0924   C87-094846-6

Seal Books are published by McClelland-Bantam, Inc. Its trademark, consisting of the words "Seal Books" and the portrayal of a seal, is the property of McClelland-Bantam, Inc., 105 Bond Street, Toronto, Ontario M5B 1Y3, Canada. This trademark has been duly registered in the Trademarks Office of Canada. The trademark, consisting of the words "Bantam Books" and the portrayal of a rooster is the property of and is used with the consent of Bantam Books, 666 Fifth Avenue, New York, New York 10103. This trademark has been duly registered in the Trademarks Office of Canada and elsewhere.

PRINTED IN CANADA

COVER PRINTED IN U.S.A.

U   0 9 8 7 6 5 4 3 2 1

Contents

Prologue/1
Introduction/10
1. *Roots*/17
2. *Growing Up Fast*/30
3. *Getting Down to Business*/43
4. *The Bow Mac Years*/53
5. *In the Driver's Seat*/68
6. *News Talk*/82
7. *Taking Over*/92
8. *The Rise of Neonex International*/106
9. *Them Versus Us*/120
10. *Starting Over*/136
11. *My Life in Sport*/156
12. *My Life in Management*/172
13. *Liquid Assets*/192
14. *Maybe in Error, Never in Doubt*/205
15. *I Get Religion*/220
16. *"Park Your Cadillacs"*/240
17. *The Porn Debate*/256
18. *Expo*/272
19. *A Year to Remember*/297
20. *Back in the Deal Business*/310
21. *You Gotta Wanna*/322
Index/329

Prologue

It was 8:00 A.M. on a Sunday in early June 1985. I was alone in the boardroom at the Corporate Office of the Jim Pattison Group. For the next eight hours I would agonize over the toughest decision I'd had to make since I became chairman of Expo 86, the World Exposition in Vancouver. I'd accepted the unpaid position on a part-time basis in 1981. For the past year I had been at it full time. Now, with the opening of the world's fair only eleven months away, I had to decide whether to fire Expo's president, Mike Bartlett. It was the last thing I wanted to see happen. Mike was my responsibility, and I liked him personally. I'd recommended him and backed him when the B.C. government at first refused to ratify his hiring because he was an American and the government was sensitive about the financial deal we'd made with him. And I had supported him when the media got wind of his spending habits.

But I'd had it with Mike Bartlett—with him and with the arrogance of the whole Expo Corporation. Every day I was getting a string of complaints about how the exposition's top executives were ignoring community groups and snubbing small business. How Mike would stay holed up in his office, never getting out to talk to employees and hear their concerns. How he didn't have much time for the board of directors or government people. How most of the key managers he'd hired weren't working out; not one of the vice-presidents he chose would still be

1

with us at the end of Expo. I knew from personal experience that he wasn't controlling the corporation's costs: Expo Centre, the preview pavilion that had opened the month before, came in more than 50 per cent over budget.

Throughout that Sunday, I drew up a balance sheet on Mike Bartlett, an account of all his pluses and minuses. For a start, he certainly knew the amusement business—he'd been in it since his youth when he'd cooked hamburgers and painted roller coasters at theme parks. But one of his problems was that he'd come from a privately owned theme park and hadn't made a smooth transition to the demands of a public exposition. At one point, the media reported his policy that Expo wouldn't be letting visitors bring their own lunches on site—which caused a one-day controversy until the board of directors quickly reversed his decision. On the plus side, Mike had sure got the fair back on track; when he'd arrived, construction was four months behind schedule. But one thing that kept coming up was Mike's expensive personal tastes. He'd run Canada's Wonderland, a $120 million theme park north of Toronto, and took a cut in pay to become Expo president at $138,000 a year. Like most people in his business, he went first-class. Fresh flowers in his office every day, enormous expense accounts, and a $50,000 Mercedes Benz bought with public funds. When I spotted the car in the Expo parking lot, I made him sell it. Because I didn't want the public to lose any money, our company, Jim Pattison Leasing, offered the highest of three bids for the car and then swallowed a $7,000 loss in re-selling it. Mike also spent $9,017 on a meeting of his executives and marketing consultants at La Costa, a plush spa in southern California with a twenty-seven-hole golf course, twenty-five tennis courts, and four restaurants. I told him that he and his executives had to pay all their personal expenses from that trip—everything but their rooms and air fare.

The public heard about those two examples of Mike's lavish style. What they didn't know was that he set a tone of extravagance that was spreading throughout the entire Expo Corporation. By 4:00 P.M. that Sunday, I'd thought long enough. His balance sheet was negative. The next morning, I flew up to Kamloops with Expo director Ray Dagg to tell B.C. tourism minister Claude Richmond (minister responsible for the exposition, and my boss) that I wanted to fire Mike Bartlett. He agreed. I called a meeting of all Expo's directors except Mike and, despite the bad publicity the world's fair would reap, they unanimously voted to let him go.

Prologue

I phoned Mike in Toronto, where he was about to make a speech about Expo, and informed him it was all over, to come home. On board my boat the next day, as news helicopters from TV stations whirled overhead, Mike and I discussed his severance.

I agreed to act as interim president as well as chairman, although we never did hire another president. And as I began running the day-to-day operations of the fair, I came into even closer contact with many people on the government payroll who disgusted me with their callous disregard for taxpayers' money. I suffered culture shock coming from the atmosphere of private business, where every penny spent was the company's money—and I owned 100 per cent of the company. Now I was working in a public corporation where people never spent any of their own money: In the minds of many of them, government funds were really nobody's money.

I observed that attitude in federal and provincial Crown corporations, including Expo. But the worst were some of the men and women I dealt with in the federal government and in particular the external affairs department. When it comes to figuring out angles to beat the system and feathering of their own nests, they made used-car salesmen look like saints. I know: I've worked with both. I've kept notes of their senseless waste and indulgence just to remind myself of their attitude of incredible self-interest. Many millionaires don't live as well as a lot of these people do. They desired the best of everything, from expensive limousines and drivers to first-class travel and hotel suites and the finest of wines and liqueurs—you always knew where the best restaurants were by looking at their expense accounts. And they sometimes practised outright deceit, falsifying their expense accounts; we'd find that they were charging the public for meals with people they hadn't entertained, or they were on airplanes at the time they were supposed to have been dining in certain cities. The excesses occurred at every level: One commissioner general rented a house that cost the taxpayer $8,000 a month—almost $100,000 a year. Some of these people know every trick in the book. They're greedy, selfish, and unconscionable. If the ordinary Joe who pays his taxes and fights to survive within his family budget could see how some of them live, there'd be a revolution in this country. I have to confess that after watching how many bureaucrats spend the public's money, I've been rethinking my own position as a taxpayer. Knowing how some of the government people think, I have a new incentive to minimize my taxes as much as possible.

I realize that entertaining international dignitaries sometimes demands more than the routine level of hospitality. But it should always stay within the realm of reasonableness. During Expo, I went to one government luncheon for ninety people that was so outrageously lavish that I had to ask the organizer how much it cost. The price, per person, was $167. For lunch. Somebody in authority approved that amount, and somebody spent it. Of course, there are conscientious and decent bureaucrats in government—during Expo, the federal Customs people did their job especially well—but it's hard to remember that when you see the exorbitance that some of their colleagues are guilty of. The way these people threw money around at Expo set a terrible example to the participants from Third World countries and to our own young people working on the site. One commissioner general told me he'd been to 320 parties thrown by Expo participants, many of them black tie. Among the biggest offenders was the Ontario pavilion: I heard more young people on site and even commissioners talk about that province's extravagance and endless round of parties than they did about any other participant.

I became so concerned with what I was seeing that I approached British Columbia premier Bill Bennett—who knew exactly what I was talking about—and later had the opportunity to speak to Prime Minister Mulroney about it. (A year earlier, the federal government had learned of a blatant case of bureaucratic overspending when Auditor General Kenneth Dye pointed out that thirty-four memberships Canadian diplomats held in an exclusive Hong Kong yacht club had cost taxpayers $773,500; External Affairs officials said at the time that Hong Kong was considered "a hardship post".) I also told the prime minister he should make *more* political appointments in External Affairs, if they were the calibre of Joan Winser, Canada's consul general in Los Angeles. Compared to career diplomats, she was an absolute breath of fresh air in her experience outside the government and her understanding of reality. I pointed out to Brian Mulroney that it's far better to use people like her from the real world who care and who comprehend exactly how hard it is for the average person to make a living.

As models of how to conduct yourself at an international exposition, some of the best were from Communist nations, such as the Russians, the Chinese, and the Czechs. The Russians in particular had pride in their country and put on a good show, with the biggest foreign pavilion on site, yet never squandered their money on needless luxury. They were co-operative, decisive, and knew what they were there for; they came to work, not to party all night. After the fair, I wrote the president of their equivalent of the chamber of commerce to say that nobody had done a better job than the Russians. It just sickens me to compare their government representatives to some of ours—who are among the greediest people that I've ever known. With little or no regard for the public's money, they're a disgrace to Canada.

To counteract this kind of arrogance, I've always favoured full disclosure of every expenditure and every penny of revenue connected with Expo. Opening up the public accounts would discourage people who try to rip off the system, people who are supposed to be serving their country, not stealing from it. I agree with Iona Campagnolo who, as she stepped down as president of the Liberal Party of Canada, criticized her fellow party members about their years in power: "We got too used to the Jetstars, we got too used to the taxi chits, we got too used to the nice dinners and the good times, and we forgot that we are the servants of Canada."

Actually, I found most of the politicians I dealt with much more responsible about the public purse than the bureaucrats. What disappointed me right across the board, though, was that the ministers at both the provincial and federal levels didn't have as much control over their own departments as their deputy ministers. Even good ministers found it difficult to get things done that their deputies didn't want to do. Of all the politicians I knew, the aldermen of the city of Vancouver were absolutely the most conscientious about how they spent money. I was always fighting with them—many of them opposed the whole idea of Expo—but they ran far and away the most tight-fisted administration that I encountered in my years with the fair

Now all that's off my chest, I have to say that—despite six years of controversy—my Expo experience as a whole was positive and inspiring. The men and women who created the fair, the corporations that supported it financially, the fifteen thousand volunteers, the twenty-nine thousand people who worked on the site, the millions of Canadians who attended— they all did their country proud. Expo was an international success financially and culturally. The media called it the finest world's fair on this continent since Expo 67 in Montreal. And it came in on time, under budget, and with no scams.

Since it ended in mid-October, I've received more than my share of recognition for my role in the fair. In year-end editions, the press honoured me for what was really a tremendous team effort—*The Financial Post* hailed me as "Canada's Businessman of the Year" and *Maclean's* named me to its Honour Roll of a dozen Canadians who had made a difference in '86. But the most significant recognition of all was that I'd be made an officer of the Order of Canada.

Thanks to Expo, I became such a high-profile figure in British Columbia that key members of the cabinet and the press pushed hard for me to run for provincial premier. When Bill Bennett, the man who conceived Expo, announced in the summer of '86 that he was stepping down as premier, several influential Social Credit cabinet ministers came after me within days to be their candidate in the Socred leadership race. I received a lot of pressure—from the media and the public—to go for it. But after a very brief flirtation with the idea, I turned it down. After so long away from business, I wanted to get back to doing what I like to do best, and what I find the most fun in life: running the Jim Pattison Group. Over a quarter of a century, we've done more than two hundred deals and built the Group into the eighth-largest privately operated company in Canada. It's the only company among the top hundred in *The Financial Post* 500 owned by one person. I'm chairman, president, chief executive officer, and sole owner. And everybody still calls me Jimmy.

Fifty-eight years ago, I was born into a family that never had much money. I grew up on the lower-income East Side of Vancouver. And I grew up with cars: My father was the sales manager of a Packard dealership and I started selling used cars while I was still at university. In 1961 I opened my own General Motors franchise, where I earned a reputation as a hard-nosed automobile dealer. At least one of the stories people tell about me is true: I did fire the salesman who sold the fewest cars each month (I even had one salesman take saltpeter when his late-night fooling-around interfered with his work). By the late 1960s I was running a conglomerate of fifteen companies in transportation, communications, and consumer products. Most people didn't start taking me seriously until then—not until I had gone up against the Vancouver Establishment, survived when the bank cancelled my line of credit, and found myself operating a dominant Canadian sign company, Neon Products. Out of that company grew Neonex International, which in 1969 was on the verge of becoming the second-biggest company in B.C. and the twenty-fifth biggest in the country.

But, it's true: I still talked and dressed like a used-car salesman. Allan Fotheringham once wrote: "Jimmy Pattison . . . looks like Mickey Rooney's undernourished brother, dresses like

Nathan Detroit and thinks like J. Paul Getty." And, with a lot of the East Side still left in me, I made the mistake of trying to launch an unfriendly takeover of sixty-year-old Maple Leaf Mills of Toronto, one of Canada's major flour-milling and food-processing companies. In doing so Neonex went head to head against the powerful Eastern Establishment. They landed their blows anywhere they could and convinced the old boys' club of bankers to call my millions of dollars' worth of loans—*twice*. That wounded and crippled our entire corporation. They won. We lost.

But, we survived. Over the next decade and a half, I'd make more mistakes—jumping blindly into oil and gas, buying a World Hockey Association team, losing a fortune in the silver market before accidentally coming out on top. We came back to create a stronger corporation—strong enough to buy the international Orange Crush operations and turn Neonex into a private company, the Jim Pattison Group. In the summer of '85, as I was deep into some of the heaviest planning for Expo, the Toronto-Dominion Bank invited me on to its board of directors. Fifteen years had passed since the Canadian Imperial Bank of Commerce had called my loans during the Maple Leaf Mills takeover. I was pleased to accept the TD's invitation to become a director of one of Canada's Big Five banks.

By December 1986, the Group had seven thousand employees in thirty-nine companies operating in seven provinces, two states, and four countries on two continents. We had more than $800 million in assets and $1.5 billion a year in sales. We were bigger than the McDonald's Canadian chain of 509 restaurants. Among the corporate members of the Group:

AirBC, the country's largest commuter airline, which we were negotiating to sell to Air Canada early in 1987;

Ripley's Believe It or Not!, which runs the biggest chain of museum tourist attractions in the world, syndicates a cartoon feature published by three hundred newspapers internationally, has a globally syndicated TV series, and licenses its trademark for a variety of uses, including a bestselling board game;

The Jim Pattison Sign Company, the world's largest manufacturer of electric signs: Neon Products, Canada's largest sign-leasing company; Trans Ad, its largest transit-advertising company; and Claude Neon, at eighty-two one of the country's oldest sign companies;

The Jim Pattison Outdoor Group, the nation's leading Canadian-owned outdoor advertising company;

Beautiful British Columbia, Western Canada's largest (and

Canada's fifth-largest) paid-circulation magazine, with more than a million readers worldwide;

The nation's second-largest periodical, paperback, and magazine distributorship, with operations in Southern Ontario and throughout Northern and Western Canada;

Five radio stations and one TV station in B.C.;

Two GM and two Toyota auto dealerships (and a Nissan franchise being negotiated) in Greater Vancouver, and one Hyundai and two Toyota dealerships we were about to buy on Vancouver Island—making our Group the country's largest automotive dealer; and three car-leasing companies, including Western Canada's largest, and another that specializes in corporate leasing across Canada;

Overwaitea Foods, with forty-eight stores, B.C.'s fastest-growing chain of supermarkets; and Save-On-Foods, with nine discount one-stop-shopping supermarkets;

Fraser Valley Foods, B.C.'s biggest processor of agricultural products, which we were negotiating to sell to Pillsbury Foods;

The Canadian Fishing Company, which has a quarter of the national canned-salmon market under such brand names as Gold Seal and Ocean Spray; and

Great Pacific Capital SA, a Swiss company based in Geneva, which co-manages and participates in Eurocurrency underwritings for commercial and government issuers, and specializes in management and fiduciary services for individuals and institutions throughout the world.

In the final days of 1986, my life was hectic but happy. I had more time to spend with my wife of thirty-five years, Mary; I was back in business; and the University of British Columbia—which I'd left in 1950, only a few units short of my Commerce degree—had offered me an honorary degree in recognition of my role as chairman of Expo.

But some people had other ideas. A couple of years earlier, one of our Vancouver companies, Mainland Magazine Service, had been under attack by feminists and community leaders for distributing what was being described as pornography—magazines that had been legally allowed into the country yet still offended many members of the public. I'd taken steps that I believed would satisfy my critics. But when my honorary degree was announced, some students and women academics on the university's Senate protested (one woman senator resigned), saying I was profiting from the distribution of magazines that were degrading to women. They threatened to demonstrate at the

Convocation ceremonies in the spring. My presence there could disrupt a happy occasion for graduating students and their families.

Meanwhile, I also had to deal with a threat on my life. In late November, I received a letter saying that somebody was about to kill me, and for $2 million I could find out the name of that somebody. Later, a rock crashed through the bedroom window of our home. We received threatening phone calls. And police and security guards patrolling our house had just missed catching a prowler on the grounds. The police were taking it all seriously—armed plainclothes officers were with Mary and me, wherever we went, around the clock.

Life goes on. You go out and do your best. That was a lesson I learned from my dad when I was ten. My Sunday-school teacher, Mrs. Fisher, had asked me to play my trumpet for a little concert for our class of seven. Some older kids were going to be performing the same day for a major concert at church. I didn't bother practising since it didn't seem worthwhile—and besides, I didn't like to practise. But when I got to the church, I learned there'd been a mistake: I wasn't to play for the class concert, I was to perform for the whole congregation of about fifteen hundred people, my mother and father included. I was panicky. So before playing, I told the audience: "I want you to know that I don't play this very well. And I haven't practised. And I miss a lot of the high notes. But I'm going to play." And I was very bad, of course. When I got home, my dad took me aside and said: "There's a few things I want you to understand. One: When somebody asks you to do something, you do it. And you do it as graciously as you know how. Two: Get up there and don't make any apologies. Three: Do your best."

Introduction

I've had the roof cave in on me figuratively a couple of times in my business career, but never for real.

That is, not until April 23, 1988, when I was mingling with 370 staff and about 600 senior citizens as the preview of a spanking-new Save-On-Foods megastore in Burbabyu, B.C. Save-On and its parent, Overwaitea Foods, have become British Columbia's largest food chain by creating some of the most innovative supermarkets in Canada. This $5.4-million store was a tenant in a building just erected by a developer at the Metro Town shopping center in the Greater Vancouver municipality. Save-On's managers had decided to invite elderly shoppers to visit the day before the store opened to the general public. And then, about fifteen minutes after people began streaming through the aisles, it happened.

Helmut Buhrke was among the crowd who heard a loud snap. Helmut has been with me for twenty-one years, since the days when he was president of our Neonex Shelter housing company in Calgary. On this April Saturday, he was at the store in his role as Overwaitea's construction coordinator. Hearing the noise, he thought a light fixture had fallen down. But then, looking up at the ceiling above the deli section, he saw water gushing from a pipe connected to the sprinkler system. Seconds later, he spotted a big steel roof beam slowly begin to twist. He had the immediate presence of mind to race to Doug Townsend,

Introduction

Overwaitea's executive vice-president, and to say crisply "Evacuate!" While Doug began to spread the word to the staff to usher the customers quickly and quietly out of the store, Helmut ran to shut off the electrical power, gas, and water.

I was standing in the bulk-foods section when I saw the steel beam buckle. I wasn't particularly worried when word came to evacuate, so I was one of the last to leave. I've been in many hotels and office buildings when fire alarms went off, and there was never anything really wrong. But four and a half minutes after the Save-On staff started moving people out, the ceiling over the deli section collapsed with a roar, creating a hole half the size of a hockey rink. And twenty cars parked on the roof crashed onto the floor of the store.

I was about thirty feet away. Shaken but unhurt, I wondered if anybody was trapped under the jumble of concrete and steel. Fortunately, most of the staff and shoppers had left the building. But as it turned out, twenty-one people suffered injuries, most of them minor, although a company employee had a crushed pelvis.

A subsequent inquiry revealed that a support beam had been underdesigned and concluded that two consulting engineering firms of the landlords had made a series of assumptions and miscalculations that led to the roof's collapse. The owners later rebuilt the store to tougher specifications, and six months after the disaster Save-On moved back into the building.

It was a close call, but it was almost the only bad news the Jim Pattison Group faced during the year and a half since the first edition of this book was published. In that time, with annual sales of $1.897 billion, we've gone from being the sixty-first largest company in Canada (according to *Canadian Business*) to fifty-second overall. And when wholly-owned subsidiaries to foreign companies are excluded, we rank thirty-eighth.

For me personally, it's been a time of virtually continuous, continental and global trips in our Challenger 600 jet; lots of financial statements; and, lately, living on Eastern time, even when I'm at home on the West Coast (which means up at six and in bed no later than ten). In this period, I've been to the White House three times; at one luncheon, President Reagan, fresh from his historic meeting with Gorbachev, was sitting next to my wife Mary and told her all about his Moscow visit. I've also had the pleasure of dining with Dr. Armand Hammer, Ross Perot, and Boone Pickens, and media magnates Rupert Murdoch, Robert Maxwell, and Walter Annenberg. And during trips to Washington, it was good to renew the acquaintance of George Bush, whom I'd entertained on my boat during Expo 86.

For the Jim Pattison Group, these have been eighteen months of solid growth, new directions, and renewed expansion both in this country and in the United States, as we aim at doubling our size during the next five years.

In Canada, I was recently appointed to the board of directors of Innopac Inc. of Toronto, the diversified packaging corporation with annual sales of $252 million. We now have 21 per cent of Innopac, which has plants in Ontario, Quebec, and ten states. Meanwhile, we're also sitting a 9.9 per cent equity position in another major Canadian company.

South of the border we've taken position in four big corporations in recent months, just under the five per cent figure that requires public reporting. But while prices have remained too high for us to buy, the American business press did note in early 1989 that we—in affiliation with the Barbados-based Zeus Group—had sought the U.S. Federal Trade Commission's permission to acquire as much as 15 per cent of Whitman Corp., a $3.6 billion consumer-products company headquartered in Chicago. Whitman owns the Midas International muffler operation, Pepsi-Cola General Bottlers, supermarket-refrigeration-equipment maker Hussmann Corp., and Pet Inc., the most profitable food company in America.

As the debate on free trade began to heat up, we were quietly consolidating our position in the American and overseas money markets. In October 1987, *after* Black Monday on Wall Street. Rose Andersen celebrated her eighteenth year with me by setting up our New York office, Great Pacific Capital Inc. We are now in the risk-arbitrage business there and have opened a window on the American equity markets—with our eventual target the acquisition of a major U.S. corporation. We've also opened an office in Barbados, which undertakes worldwide equity investments and is also active in fixed-income investments, and we're planning another in London eventually. Meanwhile, our banklike finance company in Geneva, Great Pacific Capital SA, offers financial services to a wide international base of individuals and institutions as well as co-managing and participating in Eurocurrency underwritings for commercial and government issues. The Geneva operation has a new managing director, Claude Ruscheweyh, a former director and member of the board of management of Chase Manhattan Bank Switzerland.

We have been actively planning for both 1992, when the European Common Market becomes a fully integrated reality, and for the long-discussed North American free-trade agreement. In 1986, soon after Donald Macdonald brought down his Royal Commission report recommending free trade, we invited him to speak to our annual Partners in Pride Conference. As a fan of free trade ever since, I was disappointed at the destructive criticism levelled against the initiative during the '88 federal election campaign.

In the past year, as a member of the international council of advisors to the U.S. Information Agency, I was in Washington, D.C., twice to meet with high-level American government officials, including President Reagan. For my first meeting, I commissioned a national report on the mood of Canadians towards the U.S., including a look at our views on free trade. The report documented a series of national public-opinion polls showing Canadians about evenly divided on the merits of free trade. While those opposed were worrying whether our government programs would become much less independent and more in lockstep with the Americans, those in favor of free trade mostly feared the continuing, growing campaign of American protectionism.

The Jim Pattison Group is apolitical, but my view is that Canada can't afford *not* to be involved in a major bilateral trade agreement with the U.S. As figures in my report to the international council indicated, our two countries do almost $200 billion worth of trade together, and in recent years Canada has been enjoying an estimated $16–$20 billion trade surplus with the U.S. We're so financially intertwined with that country: in the last half-dozen years, our business with Americans had steadily increased from two-thirds of total Canadian trade in 1981 to more than three-quarters. At a time when Europeans are creating an economic fortress and Asians are discussing the same possibility, I don't understand why so many Canadians seemed so prepared to abandon the chance to do an end run around the protectionist sentiments of Americans—and, by doing that, to strengthen our presence in our single most important market.

What bothers me most is that some of us seem afraid to compete on a North American basis. I agree with Donald Macdonald's argument that "the Canadian nation is not a weak and fragile plant doomed to disappearance merely because we trade more freely with our American neighbours." Like a lot of other Canadian businesspeople, I've always welcomed the challenge and the opportunity that true bilateral trade would bring. I'm not saying that all of the Jim Pattison Group's companies would immediately benefit. In fact, I know some wouldn't because we recently commissioned Woods Gordon to analyze each one and determine the effects a Canada-U.S. agreement would have on its operations.

In some of our divisions, the trade deal will have no ramifications at all: Ripley's Believe It or Not!—the world's largest museum operation—has long been established across the continent and around the globe; the newsstand-distribution business, where our Group is the nation's biggest, already operates freely; and our six TV and radio stations in B.C. are unaffected because broadcasting is specifically exempt from the provisions of free trade. But as the largest Canadian automotive retailer, we will be affected by the deal's green light to allow used cars to move back and forth across the border. The current prohibition on this movement will be phased out by 1993. Used-car prices will then tend to seek a level between the two countries. And the cars in our leasing fleets will have to end up with a depreciated value competitive with their counterparts in the U.S. The deal will also influence the food business, with more selection in our supermarkets as Canada drops its high tariffs on a wide variety of prepared foods from the States. This may cause Overwaitea and Save-On-Foods to reconsider some of their buying relationships, particularly because our stores are B.C.-owned and their largest competitor has a firm base in the U.S. with strong contacts with suppliers in that market. Our major billboard and transit-advertising companies (Trans Ad has a 95 per cent market share in Canada) should benefit from free trade as more advertising is required to promote the sale of the increasing number of goods that will be available in this country. In the electrical-sign business, when we're the world's largest, the agreement will give us even more impetus to expand into the U.S. The tariffs on these signs, which are now higher coming into Canada than going into the U.S., will be removed gradually.

Overall, we decided that a free-trade environment would fit right in with the directions we're taking our Group in in the next twenty-five years. We are no longer concentrating only on Canadian expansion; with the opening of our New York office and the appointment of Les Landes as vice-president in charge of U.S. corporate development, we're actively seeking out American opportunities, large and small.

For instance, we have acquired the Oregon Sign Corp. of Portland, Oregon, and City Sign Co. Inc. of Tacoma, Washington—which followed our purchase of Heath Northwest Inc., a similar electrical-sign company based in Yakima, Washington. That gives us a good launching pad in the Pacific Northwest to tackle the

Introduction

huge, fragmented American sign market. We're also seriously considering automobile dealerships along the U.S. West Coast to make sure we have a continuous source of competitively priced used cars on both sides of the border. Meanwhile, with our office in Rockefeller Center as a listening post, we continue to look for the right opportunity to acquire a significant American company.

When I was asked in 1987 to participate in a very private financial conference sponsored by the Swiss Bank Corporation, I met the heads of multinational corporations, and among them was Martin Davis. Without a doubt, the chairman of Paramount Communications, Inc., formally Gulf & Western is one of the most impressive CEOs I've met in recent years. Paramount Communications, Inc. is the giant conglomerate that owns Madison Square Garden, the New York Knicks, the New York Rangers, the book publishers Simon & Schuster and Prentice-Hall, and Paramount Pictures. Martin Davis started his career as an office boy in Samuel Goldwyn's Hollywood studios and ended up as chief operating officer at Paramount. In the last few years, at Paramount Communications, Inc.'s helm, he has divested the corporation of sixty per cent of its diverse operations while acquiring more than $1.2 billion worth of new companies as he refocused Paramount Communications, Inc. on the areas of entertainment, publishing, and financial services. We hit it off right away. He's a doer, a driver, who's all business and cares deeply about his companies. He also has a strong moral sense that I appreciate. In 1987, I was invited on the board of directors of Paramount Communications, Inc.'s Canadian subsidiary, Famous Players, and a few months later on the Paramount Communications, Inc. board.

Beyond North America lies Margaret Thatcher's thriving Britain, now irrevocably linked with the other ECM countries in a unified market of 323 million people. I believe the integration of the Common Market creates opportunities the Jim Pattison Group can take advantage of. Which is why we've been discussing a London base that would initially be involved in arbitrage activities similar to those of our New York office.

Despite all this action outside of Canada, we are not ignoring our domestic divisions. Although our financial activities are focused in New York, Vancouver remains our operating base. John Withers has moved from Toronto, where he oversaw Ripley's and our outdoor-sign and transit-ad operations, to become executive vice-president of Jim Pattison Industries, our private company. He continues his previous responsibilities as well as assuming senior administrative duties in our Corporate Office, which include the general overseeing for our broadcast and publishing divisions.

Our Canadian divisions continue to grow, in most cases leading their fields. One of our smallest, the publishing group centred on *Beautiful British Columbia* magazine, recently acquired four publications, *B.C. Business*, *Alberta Business*, *Saskatchewan Business*, and *Manitoba Business*. Other divisions are adapting nicely to new conditions. It's true that I still have a soft spot for the Vancouver radio station whose cash flow helped me do my first takeover in 1967. So, despite its years of losses, we refused to sell CJOR, believing that a change of format and other factors could make it viable. We moved George Madden over from the Corporate Office to see how the AM talk-show station, which was older than I was, could survive in a crowded market. After months of study, consulting with North American broadcasting experts, George had to make the tough decision to let go most of the staff and redefine the station as CHRX, the city's first classic-rock station. It's too soon to tell, but along with its relatively new FM sister station—JR Country—CHRX should become profitable over the long haul.

And that's my focus for all of the companies of the Jim Pattison Group: quality assets and quality people managed for long-term growth. As a snappy corporate slogan, it may not bring down the house, but it sure expresses exactly what I believe as we build for the next quarter of a century.

JIMMY PATTISON
*Vancouver,
January 1989*

CHAPTER ONE

Roots

The Pattisons were never part of any Establishment. They were poor Irish Protestants who came to the United States in the great wave of migration during Ireland's potato famines in the nineteenth century. My father was born in 1894 in Crystal, North Dakota. His name was Chandos, but everyone called him Pat. When Dad was two, his father quietly went off to the Yukon gold rush and never came back. The Pattisons were always like that, my mother says: quiet, never made a big fuss about what they were doing. (She points out that I'm nothing like that—*my* "talker" developed early.) My dad's mother took him and his sister to live with their grandparents in Saskatchewan, in the farming community of Delisle, near Saskatoon. His mother later remarried a tall farmer named Harry Robertson. The family legend is that Harry could pitch a baseball so well that he could've had an American university athletic scholarship if his folks had let him go.

Any plans my dad had for a career were interrupted by the First World War. When Britain's Royal Flying Corps opened Canadian training schools in 1917, Pat Pattison—a short, stocky twenty-year-old—joined up with the idea of becoming a fighter pilot. By war's end about a quarter of the pilots in the Royal Air Force were Canadians, some of them heroes like Billy Bishop. My dad wasn't one of them: Trained to be a pilot, he never saw action. They rejected him for physical reasons—he didn't get dizzy in a test where he was supposed to lose his equilibrium. When the war ended, he was with the army of occupation in Cologne, Germany.

He came home to Luseland, Saskatchewan, a town of about four hundred, which was prospering amid the Marquis wheat fields about 175 miles southwest of Saskatoon. It was named for an Iowa entrepreneur who'd founded the Luse Land and Development Co. in 1904 to colonize three million acres of prairie ("Reap golden harvest at $1 per bushel from $15 land," the magazine ads promised in an early example of effective advertising). Long after my parents left Luseland, it would live in their memories. From my early childhood until the time I left home, everything was Luseland. Even when we moved to the West Coast, our house was always full of people from Luseland. And when I went back there to visit, I couldn't believe a town that small could generate all these people.

In Luseland, Dad began selling John Deere farm machinery for Lake and Clark, who also ran the local post office. One day at the post office he met Julia Allen, at twenty-three a slender, five-foot-two school teacher with a long, full face and a high brow. She came from the same kind of background he did, except she had lost a father and a mother. Her American parents had separated when she was seventeen months old, and she and an older sister were informally adopted by her father's sister, Annie Adams, in Delaware. My mother saw her own mother once in 1912 and not again until forty years later when I surprised her with the gift of a visit to her mother in New Haven, Connecticut.

In 1909 most of the Adams family of truck farmers migrated north to Major, near Luseland. The Adamses and their five sons were homesteading, growing grain and raising cattle and horses, and travelling in a rubber-tired buggy hitched to a long-legged ox. For the first three years they lived with my mother and a young married couple—ten people in all—in a two-room house built of sod laid like bricks. My mother remembers watching for three days a prairie fire heading towards their farm and, when it reached them, everybody beating it off with wet sacks until it jumped their house. Nearly eighty years later, she still shows visitors a little poem she likes, called "The Homesteader":

> He asked little of life—a house and a wife—
> Though the house was built of sod,
> He did his best, and left the rest,
> Content—in the hands of God.

Her stepfather, Henry Adams, had been what she calls "a shouting Methodist" down in the States; in Major he was a devout Christian who taught Sunday school and made a strong impression on her. Annie Adams, her stepmother, was mother to the whole community, an untrained nurse who'd treat kids suffering from pneumonia by putting onion poultices on their wrists and ankles. I'm not surprised that, with this upbringing, my mother has more backbone, more grit and determination, than anybody I know. She never gives up. She drove a car until she was eighty-four and she still plays the piano.

In 1924, after taking a teaching course at Normal School in Saskatoon, she moved to Luseland and taught intermediate grades until she fell in love with Pat Pattison and married him two years later. I was born October 1, 1928, James Allen, their only child. "I wasn't a family-bearing woman," my mother says; she'd lost one child before. I had blond hair, blue eyes, a round face—quite the stamp of my father, everybody said.

By this time, as Lake and Clark expanded to sell automobiles and service them at a one-pump garage, two brothers named McConica had a piece of the business. Not long after, the company became McConica Bros. & Pattison, with my dad as a partner. They sold Model Ts and eventually some of the newer General Motors cars. By the mid-1920s, Henry Ford's Tin Lizzie was selling throughout North America for $290. GM had introduced the idea of annual modifications to its popular models like the Pontiac Six, the best-selling six-cylinder car in America, and its stylish but still cheap $500 Buick. Canada's favourite car at the time was the McLaughlin-Buick, a joint venture with the McLaughlin Motor Car Co., which had become GM of Canada in 1918. My dad sold his company's first Pontiac, a beautiful robin's-egg blue model that my mother proudly drove out to the farmer who'd bought it.

Business was good until Canada began to feel the effects of the stock-market crash of 1929. When the first McConica answered the call of California as the Depression took hold, my parents rented his house. My dad worked at the post office and continued to sell cars with the remaining brother, watching the drought kill his customers' crops and the winds carry away their rich brown topsoil. Two-thirds of rural Saskatchewan went on relief. McConica Bros. & Pattison had a lot of money owing them out on those farms and could never collect. Always a drinker in those days, Dad took to drinking heavily now as his cashflow dried up along with the crops. He was gambling, too, playing poker Saturday nights in the pool room, and never winning. He left a lot of creditors behind when we moved to Prince Albert, Saskatchewan, where he sold Fords and kept drinking, hard. In our family annals, this period was a disaster. As my mother says now, the Lord had another plan for us.

In late '33, in desperation, my parents fled to Saskatoon to live near my dad's mother and stepfather. We rented two rooms in an attic, furnished only with a bed, couch, table, and stove. I can recall the landlady quietly filling our coal box so we could use our stove for heat. My strongest memory of those days is the time I won a two-dollar prize for being the best-dressed kid in a parade; I wore a fez with a tassle, and my tricycle was decorated with paper ribbons. Two dollars was a windfall at that time; our monthly rent was seven dollars. I never wore anything new; my mother made all my clothes out of castoffs from other families. More than 20 per cent of the population of Saskatoon was unemployed. The city gave families on relief free seeds and garden plots so they could feed themselves. People were living in tents and shacks on the city's outskirts; jobless single men were forced to spend the winter at the exhibition grounds in what the government described as a concentration camp under military discipline. Dad worked part time selling for a Jewish clothing firm, then joined his stepfather cleaning pianos, a job that sent him travelling around the province for a couple of months. They sold their own concoction, flakes to de-moth the felts in a piano. While he was away, my mother took a red satin dress she'd worn in happier days and made drapes out of it. When Dad returned, he told her the two little rooms looked like a palace to him. But when he lost his piano-cleaning job that bleak winter, he could no longer stand to be in those rooms with us every night.

Dad didn't have a dime to go to a show, so he used to go walking in the snow by himself. A block and a half from where we lived, on 19th Avenue, stood the Apostolic Church of Pentecost. One night, trudging by, he heard singing. An Irish-born travelling evangelist named C.K.S. Moffatt was holding a revival campaign. As my dad went inside the church to get out of the snow, he heard the preacher saying: "If you're in despair and you give your heart to God, then God can change your life. Come forward to the altar and give your heart to Christ." And he did.

He came home and told my mother that he'd been saved. At first she just didn't buy it. He told her that he'd seen an Indian woman and her children get the Holy Spirit and start talking in tongues; he was convinced that the kids weren't putting it on. Every night he went back to the church and my mother saw an instantaneous change in him. "It was like black became white," she remembers. He stopped drinking that night and, even though he was a heavy smoker, he quit within a few days. Finally, she agreed to go with him and became a member of the church. "We were both filled with the Holy Spirit and spoke in tongues," my mother recalls. I was baptized in that church in Saskatoon.

We became part of a Pentecostal movement that grew from nothing at the start of this century into the largest Protestant group in the world today. There are more than 51 million Pentecostal believers in 1,200 denominations. If you were to include the charismatic Christians of the main-line churches, you'd have to double that number. (I've read that 10 per cent of the world's Roman Catholics can be considered Catholic Pentecostals.) There's a lot of confusion about what Pentecostals believe. As I understand it, they're part of the Evangelical movement and, like the Evangelicals, they believe that the Scripture is divinely inspired; they believe in the resurrection of the body after death; they believe in the Virgin birth and the heavenly ascension of Christ and His eventual return to Earth. But one of the things that makes the Pentecostals distinctive is that they believe in the baptism of the Holy Spirit as a personal experience of God—and most also believe that speaking in tongues is an early sign of that experience.

That's probably the most misunderstood part of Pentecostalism. Yet speaking in tongues isn't a new idea; it's described in the Bible ("They were all filled with the Holy Ghost and spoke with other tongues as the Spirit gave them utterance," it says in Acts). My mother, who knows more about these things than I do, says one definition of it is "unlearned languages or religiously ecstatic speech in praise or prayer to God"; she likes to call it "heavenly language." I find the Pentecostalism I practise much freer and more spontaneous than some traditional religions. There's a lot of singing and hand-clapping—even applauding the Lord—and orchestras and choirs performing happy music, some of it with black roots. The people at the Pentecostal churches I attend seem to *enjoy* their God. I prefer a service with a little action, like the one I was at in Palm Springs not long ago. There were about fifty people gathered in a concrete-block warehouse with folding chairs—no church, no steeple, no pews. There were Mexican families in the congregation, being led by two black musicians playing piano and guitar, and a struggling young white preacher. The wind rattled the loading-dock doors during the service. To me, that's a Pentecostal church. It's not a place you go to see or be seen; you go there to worship the Lord in a personal way—and you can do that in somebody's house, in a tent, or in a warehouse.

Although I've never been a member of any one church since I was a teenager, I attend services regularly—every Sunday if I can. I don't like formal, organized Religion, including the old, dried-up formal Pentecostalism. I prefer a more individual expression of faith, where it's fun to go to church. I'm certainly no saint—in the words of Phil Gaglardi, who has been both a Pentecostal minister and a B.C. cabinet minister, "It's no good being so heavenly minded that you're no earthly good." There are people in the business community who think I am very religious and some people in the church who think I'm not at all religious in the traditional sense. They're both wrong. About age eighteen, at university, I had to decide whether I'd commit myself to my faith as an adult. I decided that there was no question that I believed in a supernatural God and that I cottoned to the Pentecostal experience and its tenets in general terms.

One of those tenets is a belief in divine healing. It's another badly misunderstood area of faith. Nearly forty years ago, in Vancouver, my mother experienced what she believes was healing by supernatural means. She'd been sick for years, off and on, while I was going to public school. This time, she'd been in bed for a couple of weeks with what was diagnosed as the start of gall-bladder trouble, with severe pains in her lower abdomen. Everything she ate disagreed with her; she couldn't even drink tea. Then a friend told her about an evangelist named Frank Proctor, a sugar-beet worker from Alberta who was holding healing services in town. My dad and I helped her into the house where Proctor was staying. We were surprised that he was so young (nineteen years old) and black. The evangelist placed a chair in the middle of the room, had her sit there, and asked the others to bow their heads while he prayed. "As you're being healed tomorrow, you'll feel like you're drinking a hot cup of tea all the way down your stomach." And the next morning I remember waking up and smelling the aroma of bacon and eggs. My room was off the kitchen and when I came in for breakfast, there was my mother at the stove; she hadn't had the strength to cook a meal in weeks. She says she experienced the healing sensation Frank Proctor had predicted, got up, felt well, and stayed up.

Even my mother says "that isn't a story you make anything out of," but it just added to my interest in the subject of divine healing. So when Oral Roberts came to Vancouver for a huge tent revival meeting about twenty-five years ago, I was curious about all the people who claimed they'd been healed by this popular American evangelist: curious enough to call the local ministerial association afterwards and ask them for the names of three Vancouver people who'd been healed—blind who could see, lame who could walk—so that I could authenticate their cases with their doctors. But they couldn't give me the names of any local people. I thought, *The man is a fraud.* Two months later, I was at the Statler Hotel in Los Angeles during a business trip when I spotted Oral Roberts eating alone in the dining room.

I introduced myself and said: "I was just at your tent meeting in Vancouver. Would you mind if I sat down with you and had dinner?" And it was during the meal that I told him: "I went to your meetings and I think you're a phony faith healer."

"What are you doing tonight?" Oral Roberts asked me.

"Nothing."

"You be at the Wilshire Boulevard door of the hotel at six-thirty and don't be late."

That evening a driver picked us up in a two-door Ford Victoria to take us to the tent in downtown Los Angeles where Oral was appearing. There were fourteen thousand people crammed into that tent. One of his assistants led me up on to the platform to sit with about a hundred local ministers. After Oral preached, people in the audience came on stage to be healed. He would pray for them, place his hands on them, and proclaim them healed. I was watching carefully when I saw a father walk up with identical twin sons, no older than seven. He said they had been deaf and dumb since birth. Now, kids that age are usually honest, so I observed them for about forty-five minutes as Oral prayed and then declared them healed. As they left the stage with their father, I leaped six feet down onto the sawdust floor, ran to the back of the tent, and followed them outside. A group of about fifteen people surrounded the boys, who were holding their hands over their ears. Were they trying to block out the incredible noise over the loudspeakers from the crowd inside the tent? Almost everybody was crying and wringing their hands. I approached a man who seemed to be under control.

"I'm the uncle," he told me.

"What religion are you?" I asked.

"We're Catholics."

"Give me your phone number." The family lived in Spokane, Washington.

I went back inside the tent for the rest of the service. Afterwards, Oral Roberts took me back to his hotel room and introduced me to Demos Shakarian, probably California's most successful dairyman, and founder of the Full Gospel Businessmen's Fellowship International, a group that reaches more than a billion people a year with what they describe as "the life-changing message of Christ's love." And Shakarian, this successful businessman, told me the convincing story of how his brother was once healed.

I didn't see Oral Roberts again until about eight years ago, but in the meantime—not long after his Los Angeles tent meeting—I called the twin boys' uncle and their parents in Spokane. I wanted to check out how real their healing was.

Well, the boys could hear now, they reported, and were slowly learning how to speak. I wasn't satisfied. They gave me the phone number of their family doctor, the man who had delivered the twins. Yes, he said, they'd been born deaf and dumb. After two years, I called again, to be told that the kids were in school and were speaking. And after another two years, the parents told me that their sons were perfectly normal.

I don't know if Oral Roberts—a Pentecostal preacher who belongs to the Methodist church—has ever helped to heal anybody else. What I do know is that those little boys were healed.

When I next met Oral, at the suggestion of a friend in Palm Springs, he didn't remember me. But we grew to be good friends, and I became convinced that he's sincere and believes passionately in what he's doing. That's more than I can say about many of the evangelists on television. I think that the fate of Jim and Tammy Faye Bakker of the PTL Club is probably the best thing that could have happened to the American syndicated televangelists. There are more than ninety of them with more than thirty-four million viewers—and the Pentecostals are the aggressive leaders in this movement. I'm delighted the heat's on this billion-dollar business. TV preachers who take viewers' money under false pretences should go to jail. Even though the PTL Club may have benefited some people, the Bakkers' $1.9 million salary and the millions they've spent maintaining their lifestyle are totally unjustified. I believe there should be full public disclosure with independent third-party verification: Televangelists should be held accountable for every cent of their money—not only should they justify what is spent on salaries and expenses but they should also supply a detailed breakdown of the costs of TV production and the percentage of donated funds that actually gets to the people they're supposed to be helping. In my opinion, no one should donate even five cents to any of them who refuses to do this. There are a couple of good models for the other evangelists to follow: In the United States, Billy Graham, who's above reproach in being completely open about how he handles donations; and in Canada, David Maines of television's "100 Huntley Street," who fully discloses his personal salary and the expenses of his ministry. If I had my way, I'd extend the requirement for complete public accountability to the mainline religions, like the Catholic and Anglican churches, and to any organizations raising money for charity. After all, the bulk of the money given to these groups comes from decent, hard-working people who really care and believe in the causes they support.

It's high time that Oral Roberts made full disclosure. I can't speak for Oral today, but I do know that in 1979 he didn't appear to be hiding anything. All of the money he raised went to Oral Roberts University on a 500-acre site in Tulsa, Oklahoma, the 777-bed City of Faith medical centre under construction on campus, and his missionary work. I know because I went to Tulsa and helped him clean up the difficulties he found himself in while the medical centre was being built. Then I played a role in reorganizing the financial affairs of his ministry. I was down there three and four days a week for more than three months. I called in his lawyers, accountants, government authorities, even members of his family, to find out everything about him. I learned, for instance, that he was drawing a total income of only $29,500. The one thing he had of his own was about a 25 per cent interest in his $200,000 mortgaged house in Palm Springs, the rest of which was also owned by three other people. After spending his whole life helping others, that was all he had to show for it in material terms, except for his furniture. A supporter of his—a fellow who felt that at Oral's age, he and his wife, Evelyn, should be living in their own home—bought out the partners in the house and paid off the mortgage.

Meanwhile, I told Oral: "You can't keep doing this. If you want to cut the overheads on the university, you've got to set the example." Local dealers had given him Mercedes and Cadillacs to drive, which I told him to give back. He turned in his corporate airplane. And he cut up all his credit cards in front of me, his family, his management team, and several members of his faculty. Then I brought in our vice-president of finance, Fred Vanstone, to sort out the university's problems. Fred eventually stayed in Tulsa to become Oral's chairman of the board. But although I encouraged Oral to offer public disclosure of his funds—and he was receptive to the proposal—some of his associates rejected the idea because televangelists weren't generally doing it.

As much as I like Oral Roberts, even I was skeptical in early 1987 when I first heard about his announcement on television that God had told him to raise the $8 million necessary to organize evangelical medical teams to work overseas. "And," God had said to him, "if you don't do it, I'm going to call you home." He even announced that he had been given a deadline by which he had to have the money from his supporters or die trying: March 31.

At the time, I told my wife: "Mary, Oral's pushing it too far this time." But when she and I went to see Oral, we came away convinced that he believes the Lord spoke to him and that he must obey—and he doesn't care who doubts his story.

Giving money to religious causes—the act of tithing—is a tenet of the church I wholeheartedly support. My parents, even though they didn't have much money, were good givers. Ever since I've been in business, I've tithed to religious groups of various faiths. I believe that people who have prospered from the system have a responsibility to return some of their profits to those who need help. (Yet a recent McMaster University study shows that 45 per cent of profitable Canadian firms with assets of more than $25 million do not give to charity.) The Jim Pattison Group averages thirty-one requests a day for money; Imperial Oil gets half that number. We give to a variety of charitable causes and public institutions, and to people we don't think the system looks after. Which is why we don't give to the United Way: It's a formal, organized charity and the Establishment companies take care of it. Besides, giving to the United Way is a very public act and I believe that true giving is done quietly, without seeking credit. As the Bible says: "Take heed that ye do not your alms before men, to be seen of them: otherwise ye have no reward of your Father which is in heaven. Therefore when thou doest thine alms, do not sound a trumpet before thee . . ."

One cause that I openly admit supporting is Israel, and the Jews' defence of their homeland. Because Pentecostals stress Bible teaching more than many other religions, Israel as the Promised Land is an important piece of geography to them. My father always taught me to favour the Jews (he used to pray for Israel and bought all his clothes from a Jewish tailor). In 1966, when my mother was sixty-five, she and a woman friend visited Israel and other Middle Eastern countries, even spending an evening in the home of a Palestinian Arab family. Four years later, she published a carefully researched, two-hundred-page book about ancient and modern Israel, entitled *Pillars of Time*. It includes a long discussion of the history of anti-Semitism, in which she writes: "Anti-Semites claim they are not against Jews as individuals, but against their claims to nationhood and rights. This reaction against Jewish freedom is unlike the old days of anti-Jewish feeling, which was mainly either business or church inspired. But today's brand is one similar to that in the days of Queen Esther in Persia. It is one which propounds the idea of a scapegoat. It is a subtle approach by which, when certain political parties acquire power, they seek to exterminate all Jews from the earth."

Her view is my view. In recent years, I've sponsored two dinners in Vancouver to bring together Jews and Christians, one for three hundred people and the other for a thousand. At the time, Vancouver was witnessing an anti-Semitic backlash in the wake of Israel's involvement in Lebanon. Alvin Narod, chairman of B.C. Place, a provincial Crown corporation, had told me he'd seen graffiti on the streets that said: "Kill the Jews." And Dan Pekarsky, the former president of First City Financial (who now operates the Canadian office of Rothschild Incorporated of New York), said the whole mood in North America was running against the Jews. I invited politicians and other decision-makers, along with Christian clergymen and lay people of all the major denominations, to sit down in understanding with leaders of the local Jewish community.

One of the most precious awards anyone has ever given me is an antiquity from Israel, a small clay jug dating back to before 1850 B.C., presented at a testimonial dinner in August 1986 by the United Israel Appeal of Canada.

Not long ago I went to Israel with a Christian minister; we were shown around by a third-generation Israeli and an Arab driver. I came away with the view that a guy like me, looking at that nation from the outside, really has no understanding of the complexities of its political problems. But I had one experience there that deepened my understanding of Christianity. I had the good fortune to view the Dead Sea Scrolls. These authentic Old Testament manuscripts, at least ten centuries older than any others ever found, fill in many of the gaps in the Bible. The story is that a Bedouin chasing a goat came upon them in a cave in the Judean Desert near the Dead Sea. That happened in 1947, the same year the United Nations agreed to the creation of a Jewish state in Palestine. It's hard to express the depth of emotion I felt as I looked at those weathered leather manuscripts. If there was ever a miracle to make you believe in God, it was the accidental discovery of these biblical scrolls during the birth of Israel.

After seeing the Dead Sea Scrolls, I left Israel with renewed belief in God. My faith has roots fifty years old in the Apostolic Church of Pentecost in Saskatoon. It has grown stronger as I have grown older and remains an important part of my life today.

CHAPTER TWO

Growing Up Fast

In the spring of 1935, during the thick of the Depression, my mother and I left Saskatoon to join my father on the West Coast. He'd gone ahead by train to de-moth pianos in British Columbia with my uncle Will Adams. We set out in a Chevy coupé owned by a fellow who drove us in return for our paying half the gas. His police dog, Chief, perched on the running board all the way over the Rockies. I was six, and Chief and I became good friends on that trip. During a stopover in Penticton, B.C., we were frolicking in a field when Chief attacked and killed a goat. When the goat's angry owner came to see how it had happened, I said: "Well, Chief bit him. And all I said was: 'Sic 'im.' " It cost my mother about $15 to pay off the farmer.

That summer I got to know my dad. We were moving from town to town in southern B.C. and he let me help him replacing piano-key felts. There were four men who have influenced my life deeply; three of them were successful businessmen. But of them all, my father—from humble circumstances, never a financial success—made the single biggest impact. For one thing, he was a people person, which made him a tremendous salesman as he canvassed door to door to find the fifty pianos in a town of three thousand people and convince their owners that the felts needed de-mothing. Then there was his quiet strength, his integrity. His handshake was his promise; his word was always good. My mother describes him as being brittle—he'd break up in anger over something I did but get over it in a hurry. And, boy, I always hated when he'd pull out a Bible to make a point with me, like "Honour thy father and mother." After his conversion, he became one of the most moral men I've ever known. I remember he once bought me a Mickey Mouse watch just over the border in Washington state. It cost $3.75 and he insisted on declaring it at Customs even though he knew there'd be duty. The duty was $2, which he didn't have, so we left my watch behind. What my dad taught me is that you declare at the border, you pay your income tax, and you settle your debts—no matter what. Even after going broke in Luseland, he refused to declare personal bankruptcy. Every month for years after we moved to the Coast, the Royal Bank would send us bills in blue envelopes for his Saskatchewan debts, which he'd pay off a little at a time. And it was a quarter of a century later, in 1956, when I lent him a Buick Roadmaster to drive back to Luseland where he settled the last of his debts—repaying shopkeepers or their remaining families for the meat and groceries and drugstore supplies he'd bought in the early years of the Depression.

My dad was never ambitious for money. The church became his life. The only night he didn't attend services was Monday, because he'd gone three times on Sunday. Every evening he would be down at the little Apostolic Church of the Pentecost—the Mission on East Hastings, Vancouver's Skid Row. It was a true rescue mission, gathering in the homeless and hungry. The nightly services were my parents' recreation. My mother would play the accordion and, because he loved to sing, my dad would lead the music for the street meetings near the mission. I can't remember a single Christmas that he didn't bring home old people living alone in downtown rooming-houses.

In the fall of '35, we moved into a couple of rooms on the third floor of a house on East 49th Avenue in Vancouver. It was the first of four rented places in the working-class East End where we lived as I grew up. There was never much cash around. My parents rented one house, which is still standing at 4893 Quebec Street, for $25 a month furnished. That's where I lost a dime in the snow on the way to the store to buy a quart of milk; money was so important to us then that my mom and I went out in the night with a flashlight to look for the dime. When our rent went up by $2.50 we were forced to move to 44 East 44th. That place was so old and cheap-looking that my mother and I were disgusted by it. But nobody had much money. By now, B.C.—which at the start of the 1930s had Canada's highest per-capita income ($4,339) —had an annual relief bill of more than $8 million. The year we arrived in Vancouver, the city was reeling after thousands of people on relief damaged the Hudson's Bay Company store and the mayor read the Riot Act. Somehow my dad got a job selling Fords at A.B. Balderston's downtown on West Georgia. He was enthusiastic and sincere, believing in what he sold, and shrewd enough to cater to women: he figured that when he got wives to the point of choosing the colour of the car, the sale would be made. I'd spend Saturdays with him. He adored cars and that's where I first fell in love with them, shining up their sleek bodies, polishing their hubcaps. At home, dinner-table conversation was always about cars, especially the classic, solid Packard, which my mother used to say was built like a train.

Although we were never very demonstrative, the three of us were close-knit. An only child, I was always surrounded by adults, and my mother says I grew up too fast. Thanks partly to her, I grew up feeling positive about myself and wanting to succeed. She influenced my later life in so many ways. One of her favourite lines, about loyalty, was from *The Three Musketeers:* "All for one, and one for all." She'd advise me: "Don't tell the other fellow everything you know because then he'll know what you know." My mother may not have been overly affectionate, but some of her friends thought she spoiled me, like the proverbial hen with one chick. As far as I was concerned, she was the family disciplinarian. Once she got something in her head, then you might as well toss in the towel. If vegetables were good for me, she'd poke carrots down my throat until I couldn't stand them. If she decided I shouldn't have any sugar, I'd have to rob a store to get sugar. She cooked good basic prairie fare and I still prefer it: roast beef, mashed potatoes with gravy, and plain vegetables. Even today one of my favourite foods is pork and beans with bread and butter. During the 1970s, when I was in New York trying to raise money to take over Maple Leaf Mills, my sophisti-

Growing Up Fast

cated financial friends would argue with me in fancy restaurants, trying to convince me not to order my steak burnt the way through. During Expo my standard lunch was a McDonald's milkshake and fries.

Because my birthday falls in October, I was too young to start school that first year in Vancouver. So my school-teacher mother instructed me with a Grade One correspondence course at night, or nine to three on the days I wasn't working with my dad. She was a good teacher: I got A-pluses in literature, language, writing, and drawing but only a B in arithmetic, which was not one of her strong subjects. When I went to General Brock Public School, I never got an A for good conduct. I'd finish my work fast, then distract the other kids. As the smallest kid in class, I was always getting into fights. Once I was having a fist fight on the street when a car with a chauffeur pulled up and a man stepped out and walked over to tell us to stop. He was Vancouver's mayor, Jack Cornett. One of the worst days of my young life was the time a bigger kid stole my marbles and, when I went after him, he beat me up under the school stairs. The principal strapped me after the fight, *then* I went home to get a spanking from my mother. Sometimes I'd get the strap three times a week, then have to come home and tell my mother, who'd give me a licking for getting a licking. After I started music lessons, she would discipline me to keep me practising. Recently when I was playing the organ on my boat, my mother told one of my guests: "I used the strap on Jimmy; his talent was developed by strap."

My mother, who played piano and accordion, decided I should take music lessons when I was eight. C.K.S. Moffatt, that Irish evangelist who'd changed my parents' life in Saskatoon, played trumpet. And when my mother saw me playing a kazoo in a school concert, she hired a music teacher to come to the house once a week to teach me trumpet. I hated practising the hour or more a day my mother demanded. So, when I had to play something difficult like "Carnival of Venice," I'd set the clock ahead to try to fool her. *Try*—I got a few lickings when she caught me at it. Within a couple of years I was confident enough to play on an amateur talent program on CJOR (a radio station I would have more than a passing interest in, years later). The announcer was Bill Reay, who went on to found 'OR's eventual rival, CKNW, and become the best-known radio man in Vancouver. His introduction: "Now we have a young fellow here, two and a half trumpets high."

¶ soon started playing in school bands, then in the Vancouver Junior Symphony and Arthur W. Delamont's world-famous Kitsilano Boys' Band. But mostly I played in church orchestras and out on the street three nights a week for the Pentecostal Mission's meetings. There'd be me, a grown-up playing guitar, and maybe some older fellow playing trumpet too. And I did that all through my teen years until I was married. In my twenties, I conducted a twenty-piece orchestra at the Apostolic church and later, at Glad Tidings Temple, a sixty-piece orchestra. As a conductor, I didn't care if the kids made mistakes as long as they participated. But I was firm in some things—everybody had to be on time. That probably went back to my teenage years when I was playing in Vancouver's junior symphony under a Russian conductor named Gregory Garbovitsky. I was doing the trumpet duet with another chap in Sibelius's *Finlandia*. Because we were at the back of the stage and there was about a 380-bar rest before the duet, I figured we had time to slip downstairs and have a malted milkshake. Service was a bit slow; when we showed up on stage again, there was a tremendous silence where the duet was supposed to be. Garbovitsky stopped everything and had the orchestra return to the point where we were to come in. And that was the end of my career in the symphony. About fifteen years ago, I quit playing trumpet altogether when my business was going sour. I didn't pick it up again until Expo when Claude Richmond, who was then the minister of tourism, would pull out his pocket cornet at various occasions. ("Don't give up your day job," I told him.) Mary saw that small cornet and bought me one for Christmas. I played it all summer long, for royalty and visiting dignitaries such as the prime minister of Czechoslovakia. Not long ago, when Mary spotted an even smaller pocket cornet in St. Moritz, Switzerland, I bought it and then gave it to Ray Smith, the chairman of MacMillan Bloedel, who'd been in the Kitsilano Boys' Band ahead of me. He was one of the finest trumpet-players in the country but gave it up about fifteen years ago. I gave the little cornet to him on the promise he'd practise and we'd play duets together.

When I was twelve, my mother told me to lay off trum-

Growing Up Fast

pet after I had operations for tonsilitis and appendicitis (I was so sick the doctor said he'd never been so glad to get an appendix out). I spotted an ad in the paper: "Learn to play the piano. 20 lessons, $40." I paid for the course myself, learned the chord system, and never took another lesson. The piano and then the organ became my only real relaxation away from work. Today in my home in Vancouver I have a regular piano, a player piano, and three organs; on my boat, a piano and an organ equipped with a synthesizer; and in my house in Palm Springs, California, a grand piano and a computerized Lowrey organ—one of only two in Southern California when I bought it in 1987. It's so sophisticated it can create seven million different combinations of sounds. It's fun for me to sit for hours playing gospel hymns like "Just a Closer Walk with Thee" or old chestnuts like "Bye Bye Blackbird," my guests singing along with me.

As a twelve-year-old, I'd earned the $40 for those piano lessons by doing the one thing I knew I liked, the one thing nobody had to discipline me to do—selling. From the first, I *wanted* to succeed at it—and to make money. I'd done the usual jobs kids do, like delivering newspapers and groceries, but I enjoyed selling most. My first product was garden seeds, when I was seven. One of the earliest lessons I learned was to consider what the customer wants. I would bring several packets of different seeds to a housewife's door and the first thing I'd ask her is: "What kind of vegetables do you like?" "I like beans," she might say. "Well," I'd reply, "I want to tell you, our particular beans may be different." The lady next door might be keen on carrots so I'd talk about the colour of our carrots. I wouldn't waste twenty minutes talking to someone about beans if she was crazy about carrots—beans were history; her neighbour liked them. By nine, I was selling magazines like *Ladies' Home Journal* door to door and did so well in competition with grown-up men that I won a contest for the highest sales of *The Saturday Evening Post*. Once in a *Post* circulation drive, I won a dog with a tail so long that an evangelist at our church cut it off for me. The fact that I was blue-eyed, freckled, and small for my age probably influenced my magazine career, but I was also putting into practice what I'd learned selling seeds.

My size may have helped get me a job at age fourteen as

a pageboy at the Hotel Georgia. It was 1942, the war was on, and with people pouring into the cities there was a lot of competition for the job at this first-rate downtown hotel. The head bellhop who hired me would make me do voice practice and showed me how to walk through the hotel lobby or into its very old and famous Windsor dining room and cry: "Call for Mr. ——. Call for Mr. ——." I'd carry a message on a silver tray and be wearing a typical Philip Morris pageboy outfit: red round hat, red suit with lots of braid. One of the regulars at the hotel was a boxer named Harvey Dubbs, who befriended me and even gave me his autographed picture ("To a real pal, Jimmy Pattison. From Sailor"). I loved that job. I'd work five days a week, from 4:30 to 8:30, and all day Saturday, bring a dinner my mother packed, and eat it in a lunchroom downstairs. All for $15 a month, plus tips and— even better—all the nickels that people left behind in the pay phones. That was the beginning of a habit I still have today. Peter C. Newman, the chronicler of the Establishment, talks about the time he was with me down in Palm Springs and I'd driven him in my Cadillac out to my Learjet at the airport. I'll let him tell the rest: "We gave our luggage to a waiting porter. As Jimmy and I were ambling towards the gates, he veered away and, to continue our conversation, I found myself walking beside him as we passed a long row of pay phones. In a ritual obviously evolved from long practice, Jimmy pulled open the change slot of every telephone. He scooped out whatever coins had been forgotten and never missed a beat as he continued towards his waiting jet. I was speechless."

As a pageboy, I used to see kids running into the hotel with a bundle of newspapers and then jumping on to the back of a waiting truck. They were swampers, and my worried mother didn't want me to take a part-time job as a swamper for the Vancouver *Province*. But I loved the excitement of hanging on the truck with one arm and flying around town, leaping off the rear deck, weaving through the traffic, and dumping the bundles at stores and news vendors'. Later on, during my college years, I drove those trucks. I was working for the *Province* on May 8, 1945, the day after the war in Europe ended. I got a phone call from my boss in the middle of the night and was out on the street at 5:30 that morning. You bought the papers for three cents each and sold them for a nickel. I decided to buy five hundred of them, $15 worth, and started peddling them at the busiest corner in town, Granville and Hastings. There was a great headline:

GERMANS LAY DOWN ARMS
Churchill, Truman
Proclaim Victory

Things went well until about 7:00 A.M., when I knew I was in trouble. Nobody was buying anymore and I'd sold only about 150 copies. What I hadn't thought of is that the radio was way ahead of the details in the papers; I was trying to sell old news. That was my first lesson about out-of-control inventories. Then I had a bright idea. I drove out to a subdivision of wartime houses in the suburb of Richmond and for the next two days went door to door selling those 350 copies—not as newspapers but as souvenir editions.

My childhood wasn't all business. I had some good friends in the East End, like Paul Lade, who grew up to become a Pentecostal minister, and his younger brother, David, a carpenter; I still consider both of them friends. We met at an Apostolic church when we were about seven. Typical boys, we climbed the fifty-foot cliffs of Little Mountain Park and put tacks on the chair of our Sunday-school teacher, Mrs. Fisher, who probably earned a special reward in heaven. We used to make bugs (what they now call soap-box cars) and I remember once convincing David to sell me four big bicycle wheels that his dad had given him. They were worth several dollars but I offered him fifty cents for all of them. Later, his father gave him heck for practically giving them away. David calls that my first deal. His father had a steady job as a painter for the old Spencer's department store; his folks would sometimes help mine out by inviting them over for dinner. I was always impressed that they had butter in the house and white cake for dessert every Sunday.

Yet I never felt poverty. I remember happiness. We didn't own anything, not even our furniture, but I had enough clothes and my dad always had a demonstrator car to drive. I recall times when I was about ten when our family would drive over to Shaughnessy and other good areas of town. What shocked me was that the kids there were wearing almost the same kind of clothes I was. I'd think: *They don't look much better than I do*. Later, there were other lessons. I'd just bought a brand-new CCM bicycle when a poor missionary from China came to speak at our church. My mother convinced me to give him my bike: "Jimmy, that poor man has to walk everywhere he goes in China." On Sunday mornings in my mid-teens, I'd drive my dad's demonstrator to pick up three or four carloads of kids from tenement houses with broken doors and smashed windows—kids with runny noses and sometimes no shoes. We'd pick them up just to get them off the street and into Sunday school. Then there were all those years I played my trumpet down on Skid Row, and after a Friday-evening service went with my friends for a middle-of-the-night steambath and breakfast on East Hastings. During Expo, when people started yelling at me to come to the Downtown East Side to see how the World's Fair was affecting residents there, I went, willingly. Nobody can tell me anything about that part of town; I was raised there.

For a few happy summers as a boy, I visited my mother's step-family in Major, Saskatchewan, near Luseland. I learned to ride horses on my uncle John Adams's farm and enjoyed staying with Uncle Elmer, who had a gas station and a Pontiac dealership in town. An outgoing, level-headed guy, Uncle Elmer liked cars. My mother says I'm more like him than I am either of my parents. Over the years, Saskatchewan continued to loom large in my life. When I was thirteen, my trumpet took me back there—and changed my whole life.

During the spring and summer of '42, I played solo trumpet throughout the province for five months at special Pentecostal services and at children's camps the church sponsored. I was biiled as "The Boy Wonder from Vancouver." It's a good thing there was no television in those days or I'd have been laughed off the stage. One camp was at 17 Mile Bridge, near Swift Current. The second night, the tents blew down in a big storm. The boys, trying to hold down the ropes, somehow ended up gathered around the girls' tent. That's when I met a girl from Moose Jaw named Mary Hudson. She had a good sense of humour, long black hair that brushed her shoulders, and a laughing face when she ran through the prairie sage and poplar hills of the camp. And, even though she was the same age as me, she was about a

Growing Up Fast

head taller. But she thought I was cute, with my curly blond hair. The camp minister, Norm Forge, warned Mary that her fondness for me was just puppy love. "But puppies have to grow up and get a licence," she replied. We quickly got into trouble. After lights out, you were supposed to be in bed, but I'd sneak over to the kitchen tent, borrow some muffins, and head up the hills to meet Mary for a nighttime picnic beneath the moon. When somebody finally told on us, I ran away with my friends Francis Snider and Russell Short and hid in the wheat fields. The camp leaders discovered us at three in the morning and threatened to send me back to my parents. When I did go home that summer, I announced to my mother: "I'm going to marry Mary Hudson."

We started to write to each other. Her father was a railway engineer, who, in England, as a young man missed his sailing on the *Titanic*. Her mother came from several generations of Ontario Canadians. Mary was the middle child of seven. She sometimes says that's why we managed to get on: In a family that size, she had to learn to give and take. In 1943, I was back in Saskatchewan, travelling with an evangelist preacher, Matt Strain, and his wife. In Saskatoon, the daughter of another preacher grabbed one of Mary's letters out of my hands and read it in front of me—which made me so mad that I went off to Moose Jaw and booked into a hotel with an older-looking friend I knew there. When my friend's mother phoned Mary's folks, Mr. Hudson told Mary to get me out of town. But she insisted on bringing me to the house. After her mother saw me, she laughed and said: "I thought this was a boyfriend. He's just a little kid."

Coming home on the train at the end of that summer, I sat beside the editor of *The Boissevain (Man.) Recorder*. W.V. Udall later wrote a letter to my dad that reveals something of the serious-minded, chatty (and car-loving) kid I was, even at thirteen: "In order to set your mind at rest in regards to my writing you, I am not in the market for a Pontiac nor a Packard car—new or second hand—this notwithstanding the fact that your son has informed me that both are first-class cars and good mileage per gallon is assured . . . all I wish to say to you is this—I do a lot of travelling both in Canada and the States, and consequently meet lots of people, many boys amongst them, and in all my travels I never met a more manly, better behaved, or more intelligent boy than your son. Consequently, I got a great kick out of the kid. . . . If I do not miss my guess this boy has a real future in front of him."

Mary and I didn't see each other again until we were eighteen. We wrote, though, and I sent her Christmas gifts— she still has the satin Chinese pyjamas I gave her one year. David and I were double-dating other girls, tearing around in my Austin with the fox-tails, necking down at Spanish Banks. But for all our carrying-on, neither of us ever smoked or drank, and I never got really serious about anyone but Mary.

In 1946 I drove out to Saskatchewan to play in Youth for Christ rallies and perform and even preach a little in Pentecostal youth services with Vern McClelland, a violinist friend. When I saw Mary in Moose Jaw, she thought I was too stuck on myself; we didn't hit it off at all. I left for Saskatoon where we were playing for a week in the same Apostolic church where my father had been saved. We decided to stay over to hear a Pentecostal group called the Musical Moors. The group's leader told me he wouldn't have bothered playing the church unless it guaranteed him $100 a week. I was devastated: It was a jolt for me to discover that some people in religion could put money ahead of their faith. Vern and I were happy if we earned our expenses. In fact, we'd run out of money in Saskatoon. Which is why I wired Mary for a loan. She was working as secretary to a CPR express agent, but as she was between paycheques, had to borrow the money for me from her father. After she wired the money to me, I came to see her again in Moose Jaw and we had a much better time on that second visit (oh, and I paid her back the money).

When I got back to Vancouver, I enrolled in Commerce at the University of British Columbia and sold used cars to my fellow students to earn spending money. I continued to write to Mary, and the next summer she came to Vancouver. She didn't tell me she was coming because, by now, I learned, she was engaged to someone else. David Lade bumped into her and called me to say Mary Hudson was in town and would be at the beach at English Bay that day. I went down to the Hudson dealership to borrow a brand-new Hudson, picked her up in this great-looking car that you stepped down into, drove her around Stanley Park, and, at Brockton Point, asked her to marry me. When Mary went home to tell her other boyfriend about my offer, he visited me in Vancouver.

Growing Up Fast

He demanded to know if I was sincere in my intentions. I played it very cool: "I like Mary but I'm not in a hurry to get married, I'm still in university." But the guy had forced my hand. After he left, I realized that I better do something that would tie Mary up, warehouse her for a little while. I bought a $1,000 diamond solitaire ring (not the top grade but a big one) for $50 down—that was all I had; I always spent everything I made. I phoned Mary to fly out the following weekend, and we became engaged. She took a lot of kidding about me from her family, who were big, strapping people. I was at my full adult height of five foot six and weighed one hundred pounds. Her mother warned her: "Mary, my girl, you're going to have to shake the sheets in the morning to find that boy."

On June 30, 1951, we were married in Moose Jaw, with the Reverend Norm Forge—our church-camp supervisor—proposing the toast to the bride. David Lade was my best man and a group of my practical-joker Vancouver friends was there, gunning for me. They'd tied tin cans to the back of a black Cadillac that my boss, Dan McLean, had lent me. But after the reception we eluded them in a car my dad had hidden at the back of the hotel and drove to the Saskatchewan Hotel in Regina where we registered under a fictitious name. After I drove part-way back to Moose Jaw, to trade cars with my father, Mary went to the drugstore. By sheer luck, my friends spotted her, kidnapped her, and kept her locked up in an implement warehouse in Moose Jaw. When I got back to find her gone, the hotel doorman told me, "Well, young fella, some of these girls get a little frightened and go home to Mother." I went to the train station and bus depot to see if she'd decided to leave. By now I was convinced she'd changed her mind about the marriage. I waited until 4:00 A.M. until I screwed up my courage to phone her parents. Mary answered. Now I was sure she'd run home to her mom. But she told me that David had just helped her escape from her captors and she was hiding out at her parents'. I drove up there with no lights, tooted my horn, she jumped in—and off we went on our honeymoon drive back to Vancouver with the $100 Mary's father gave us as a wedding gift. We hadn't been together on our first night, and on our second, when I couldn't find a place to stay, we ended up sleeping in the Cadillac on the side of the road. In a foretaste of things to come, the story made the pages of the Moose Jaw paper under the headline "Bride-Napping Fad." It was probably the only time the media hasn't mentioned us by name.

I'd promised Mary a lot of good times and no children for four years. James—Jimmy Jr.—was born eleven months and three weeks after we were married.

CHAPTER THREE

Getting Down to Business

The other vow I made to Mary was that I'd be a millionaire by the time I turned forty. We were starting from square one. I had no savings and still owed money on the engagement ring. Mary and I moved into a modest apartment building near downtown Vancouver at 12th and Granville. That was the first of two furnished suites we lived in until after Jimmy Jr. was born and we had a strong enough cashflow to rent a small house and buy a sectional suite with no down payment during Eaton's Trans-Canada Sale. Our deal from the start has been that she raises the children and I make the money. In 1951, I decided it was time to get serious about my end of the deal.

I figured I had a head start in my career. After all, I was in the car business—against the advice of my father, who didn't think it was a very high-class business to be in. But automobiles had been part of my life from the time I was three and my dad had let me steer the car from his lap. When other kids were playing football on Saturday afternoons, I'd be down at the three used-car lots where he worked over the years. I've always looked upon a car as something like a best friend. It's not a utility like a telephone, not just a means of transportation, but an integral part of me. My first was also one of the first two cars at John Oliver High

43

School, a '37 Austin two-seater that I bought for $357. Because I was fifteen, it was in my dad's name when we borrowed money from a finance company. Because I was so short, police would occasionally follow me home because they thought I'd stolen the family car. A year later, I was driving a '41 Ford. My first brand-new car, which I loved, was a sleek '48 two-tone brown Pontiac Silver Streak. That was the start of a long line of big General Motors cars I was loyal to over the years: among them a yellow '47 Buick Roadmaster convertible; a '55 Buick Special two-door hardtop with a continental-kit tire on the back; and a '60 white Cadillac convertible with its more restrained version of the famous tailfins. In 1973 I bought a custom-built, $32,000 Cadillac, as long and luxurious as they come, with twelve coats of powder-blue paint, a phone, colour TV, and refrigerated bar, a remote-control starter, and hubcaps wired with a burglar alarm. At my place in Palm Springs, for special occasions, I now keep a white '76 Cadillac Eldorado with six hundred miles on it; a limited-edition Bicentennial model, it's one of the final two hundred full-sized Cadillac convertibles ever produced. But I've always been most partial to the string of red Pontiac convertibles I had through the '60s and early '70s. My favourite car of all is the last of those ragtops to be built, a '75 Grand Ville Brougham that I drove at Expo, top down, throughout that sunny summer of 1986. I'd no sooner sell that car than I would my golden retriever.

My father, who wanted me to be a lawyer instead of a used-car salesman, always urged me to go to university. We compromised: I went to the University of British Columbia but I took Commerce—and sold cars. In my first real car deal, in 1945, I'd borrowed $350 from David Lade, who always saved everything he could from his job as a packer and shipper in a china store. I bought an old car, sold it fast, and paid him back within a week. During college I'd look for a used car in the classified ads every night, buy the junker for maybe $200, drive it out to the campus, sell it for $250 to a fellow student, and take the bus home that evening. Or I'd advertise the car in the student paper, *The Ubyssey*. It's what car dealers call curbing—literally, selling from the street curb instead of a lot. I'd always have two or three cars in my yard, one of them for my own use.

Getting Down to Business

In those days, my living expenses usually exceeded my income. I was driving the fancy Buick convertible, which would get me seven miles to the gallon. I had two or three girlfriends, one of them a hundred and fifty miles away in Seattle, Washington. I acted like a used-car salesman and dressed like one. Bright, fancy clothes—plaid jackets, nothing conservative. From the time I started selling cars at university, I spent my money on clothes and restaurants, cars, and trips to the B.C. Interior and sometimes Saskatchewan. David Lade, a carpenter by then, was a generous guy who financed some of my dates (many years later, I had a chance to repay him when he returned from missionary work and I endorsed a bank note for him so he could build a house). Together with David and another friend who was selling Fuller brushes, we borrowed money from the bank to keep going. Our friend knew an older man, a fellow Pentecostal who agreed to put up some bonds as collateral at the bank if we paid him a high interest fee each month. Later, I did manage to save $1,000 selling used cars and in 1949 gave it to my father towards the $1,500 he needed as a down payment to buy his first house.

To supplement my income through the first couple of years at university, I drove a delivery truck nights for the old *Vancouver News-Herald* and worked part of the summer of '48 as a pantryman on the CPR transcontinental trains. That's how I really got into the car business. I was on my second trip west when a flood washed out the bridge at North Bend, B.C., and the whole train crew was told to go to work on the Soo line out of Minneapolis. I didn't like the job—cracking ice, making salads, sweeping the dining car—so although I was almost broke I got off at Lytton, B.C. When I called home for money, my dad was disgusted that I'd quit my job; he offered no help. I waited in Lytton until I heard an east-bound train in the middle of the night. Jumping out of my hotel bed, I ran to the station and climbed on the flatcar of a freight train. As we wound along the edge of the canyons overlooking the Thompson River, I lay on that flatcar deck, spread-eagled, face-down—scared. Eventually the conductor, spotting me, took me into the caboose until we reached Kamloops. There, I headed for Calvary Temple, the Pentecostal church run by Phil Gaglardi, a bulldozer-operator–turned–preacher who had worked with my father in the Mission on

Skid Row. Four years after I saw him in Kamloops, the Reverend P.A. Gaglardi went into politics and became the controversial Social Credit highways minister, Flyin' Phil. That day in 1948, he gave me enough money to fly back to Vancouver on a float plane.

Broke, jobless, I decided to spend the rest of the summer doing what I liked: selling cars. For weeks I called on dozens of used-car lots trying to get a job; the operators all said I was too young and too short. Until a man named Fred Richmond, who made most of his money pumping gas, agreed to take me on as a lot boy to wash cars at $25 a week. Because there was only one salesman on that little cinder lot, I could fill in for him during mealtimes and earn $25 for every sale I made. My second week, I sold three of the seven cars they had on the lot during the salesmen's breaks. Richmond offered me a job selling full-time that summer.

The next summer, I was hired by Percy Bates at Kingsway Motors, Vancouver's biggest used-car dealer. By the end of the first month, I'd earned $1,000. From then on, I was their top salesman. My approach, which owed something to my father, was simple: hard work, sincerity, and honesty—always point out what's wrong as well as right with the car. "Now, for $395, this is good, but there's something here that isn't. You're going to have to understand that there are two bad tires on this car and the trunk leaks." Sometimes you have to decide what you think is right for the customer. "Well, I like this price," he'll say. "I don't think that's best for you," you say, "and here's why." And customers like to deal with sales people who have punch—enthusiasm, which can be loud or quiet.

One of my customers then was John McArthur, an elderly American who owned a motel near Hope, B.C. One day he stopped in front of Kingsway Motors in a pickup truck and asked to use the washroom. On his way out the door, I sold him a '47 Oldsmobile. After I delivered the car to him, he took a shine to me. McArthur drank like a fish but he was an interesting amateur inventor. Eventually he entrusted me with the formulae of some products he'd concocted, everything from piano polish and poultry bronchitis spray to applejack and tooth powder ("2 lbs. Precipitated Chalk, 2 oz. Iris Florentine, 2 drops Attar of Rose"). The product that excited me most was cellubile, an oil used in the petroleum industry that was McArthur's secret ingredient to make paint water-resistant. You were supposed to be able to paint in the rain, paint underwater with it. I went to Seattle to talk to the U.S. Navy about cellubile ("We'll paint every boat we have with this if it will do what you say," one naval guy told me) but after I put hundreds of hours into it, the deal never happened.

McArthur liked me so much that, even though he had children and a woman with a Deep-South drawl who lived with him, he made me his sole heir. Although I would have inherited more than $100,000, I didn't think it was a responsible thing to do. So, when I got a call one day to tell me John was in hospital dying, I took a lawyer friend named Roy Long Jr. to the hospital in Chilliwack to help me renounce the will. After McArthur died, his common-law wife came to see me when I was at Bowell McLean Motors. She was wearing a new fur coat, a broad-brimmed hat, and a big smile. "Jimmy," she said, "did you hear that John died? We just buried him. And now I'm looking for a new Cadillac." I sold her one.

I still remember that day I was driving to Chilliwack at eighty miles an hour, desperately trying to get there before John McArthur died, and Roy Long sitting beside me, remarking casually, "Look at the verdure on the mountains, Jimmy."

"What's verdure, Roy?"

"It's all the different shades of green."

G. Roy Long Jr. was a class guy. I met him at university when I was being rushed to join a fraternity. One of its members, a waiter I knew from the CPR dining cars, sponsored me. It was a big deal for a kid from the East End: Alpha Tau Omega was one of the oldest and largest frats in North America. In putting me in touch with people like Roy Long, who was president, that fraternity influenced my life. I'd never been exposed to people like the Longs before. It was my first real contact with anyone in the upper class. Roy had roots: He came from a fine Vancouver family; his father was part of the legal Establishment and a treasurer of the B.C. Liberal party. The family home, on several acres beside Deer Lake in Burnaby, was the nicest I'd ever seen. Roy was over six-foot-one, a Second World War veteran, six years older than me. He was a loving man, highly idealistic yet human and down to earth, and he took an older-brother's interest in me—to the point where we agreed to go into business together after he finished law school. Roy, Ralph Cattermole (a friend of Roy's who worked for the Army Pension Fund), and I put up $1,500 apiece. We called our company Oakridge Securities (Roy named it for the place in Tennessee where the atom bomb was created). We were babes in the woods, selling a few cars, financing a few appliances—and in 1950 getting involved in Operation Peru, the ambitious deal that cost me my university degree.

The scheme sounded wonderful. A fishing-supplier contact in Seatile, G.O. Basil Hackett, told us about a boat, M.S. *Victoria*, that could be leased to catch tuna off the coast of Peru. Roy and I began to research the field, learning that three Seattle companies might take up to a thousand tons of tuna per month from a reliable supplier. Roy would be president; Hackett, base superintendent (finance); and Dr. Harvey MacMillan, an American fisheries expert, field superintendent (production). In what amounts to my very first business prospectus, we explained the operation in inflated prose:

> The exploitation of the fishing potentialities are to be undertaken in a small but effective manner at the first: i.e. the M.S. *Victoria*, a charter boat at present in the Port of Miami, Florida, is to leave the United States on or about the 12th day of May and sail for Telera or Callao, Peru. The intended arrival date will be about the 22nd of May. Dr. MacMillan who will already have negotiated for a fishing fleet will come aboard and all should be ready to sail for the fishing grounds and set about their task. Once upon the fishing grounds the small individual fishing boats will leave the Mother ship (M.S. *Victoria*) and go about catching their quota . . .

"The future has not been left to chance," the prospectus promised. "We feel that effort is necessary but skill, integrity, and business sense are just as indispensable as the Tuna in Peru." It was all smoke and mirrors. What we didn't mention was money—about a quarter of a million dollars we needed to raise to lease the ship, outfit it with refrigeration, and pay the captain, crew, and Dr. MacMillan. In my first serious encounter with a bank manager, Oakridge Securities couldn't convince the Bank of Nova Scotia that this was a great investment. But in trying, and in doing the research for Operation Peru, I missed writing my third-year final exam in economics, which was my best subject. Although I thought I would pick the course up over the summer, I didn't.

Oakridge invested in another project that at least got off the ground. C-I-L (Canadian Industries Limited), the chemical and paint company, had moved into Vancouver and was trying to market a new product, polyethylene. Our idea was to become one of the Canadian pioneers in manufacturing plastic bags out of the stuff. Roy had a contact with a friendly manager at the Royal Bank who had known his father. To this day, neither Roy nor I can recall how much we borrowed, but it was just enough to buy one machine to make the bags and to pay $30 a month rent for a shop. Ralph Cattermole ran Pilgrim Products, with Roy helping out, even going down to the shop and stapling boxes. My interest in running a manufacturing business was pretty limited. I didn't get along with Cattermole, didn't like the way he was running things—didn't like being part of a three-way partnership—so I pulled out of Pilgrim after a couple of years. He and Roy remained partners until they had a falling-out; Cattermole got the company. Meanwhile, Roy and I had bought him out of Oakridge. The company soon became dormant as I got more heavily involved in the car business; I bought Roy out. He went on to become a partner in a firm of twelve lawyers. I don't see much of him anymore, but I still really love him.

In 1950, when I left university, my dad was furious, although I only learned that much later. "If you're not going to be a lawyer," he told me then, "you should be selling for Neon Products." Neon, which manufactured and leased electrical signs, was one of the most solid companies in B.C. Encouraged by my dad, I approached the sales manager for a job as salesman. He was a Pentecostal like me, but his reply was brief and pointed: "You're too young and you're too short, and that's it." It hurt. What I didn't know then is that Neon Products would figure so prominently in my life less than two decades later.

My father kept encouraging me to go back to my studies. I enjoyed university and the confidence it gave me, but aside from the lectures of an interesting economist named Dr. Crump, I felt I could learn more about life and people on the car lot than I could in the classroom. The year I married, I was working but still going to university three mornings a week, trying to pick up a few credits. As it turned out, I never did get my degree; I think I'm nine credits short. Everything else out in the real world was more interesting and fun.

What happened in that world shows exactly why timing is almost everything in life. I never use the word "luck" because I believe in most cases you make your own luck. But timing—being in the right place at the right moment—is critical. It was the summer of 1950, the year I first proposed to Mary in Vancouver. My dream at the time was to start my own used-car lot where I could work nights while I finished my education. I'd been curbing cars on my own for three years. The finance companies—which knew I could sell and knew my dad's good reputation in the business—were already backing me. They would put up 100 per cent of the wholesale price of a car I was buying. All of which meant that, because I knew the business, I wouldn't need any equity and I could hire a couple of salesmen and open a lot. I found one for lease on Kingsway, which in those days was Vancouver's used-car row. "Jimmy, I'm sorry," the owner said when I went to see him, "I just leased it." As I was walking out the door, he added, "By the way, the fellow I leased it to is looking for somebody to run it."

"What's his name?"

"Dan McLean. It's called Dan McLean Motor Company. Nash dealer."

I went straight to Dan McLean at his West Georgia dealership downtown. Reminding him that my father once ran a used-car lot for him and two other dealers, I applied for the job of running his new lot. "I'd like a deal where I could take maybe one university course in the daytime while I manage your used-car lot." He hired me, for $250 a month.

If anybody toughened me up, it was Dan McLean. Other than my father, he was the first man to make an immense impact on me. The McLeans were among the Old Boys of Vancouver; one brother ran B.C. Telephone Co., the other

Getting Down to Business 51

was a prominent eye specialist. The silver-haired Dan McLean was of the old school: Them and Us. "You're my servant, I'm your boss." His friends were at the Vancouver Club where he spent a lot of time, drinking. With everyone else, he was aloof. When he came to see me, it was, "Yes, Mr. McLean. No, sir, I'll let you know right away, sir." I reacted as if I was a private in the army and he was my general. Not once in all my years with him did we ever have breakfast, lunch, dinner, or even a coffee together, yet I admired and liked him enormously.

He left me to run that lot on my own. Whenever he came around to look in on me, I was always there, at ten in the morning or ten at night. I was happy because he was happy. By then, I *knew* I knew the car business. My strength was in closing a deal. I never let my three or four salesmen complete a sale; I'd have them bring the customers in and I'd ask: "Whose name would you like me to put this car in?"

"Just a minute," the husband might say, "I haven't made up my mind."

"Well, what is there left that you're concerned about?"

"I'm concerned about the colour."

"Okay, let's talk about the colour," I'd reply. "It's white, and you want black. That's the only thing you're concerned about?"

"Yes, the payments. I can only pay $75 a month, and I think this may be more."

"Well, let's talk about the colour first." I'd list the pluses and minuses, maybe ending with: "One thing is that white is much easier to keep clean, because the dirt and the dust don't show like they do on a black car. So the cost of keeping it clean is lower."

"I hadn't thought of that."

"Okay. Two: You can afford $75 a month and this car is $90 a month. We're short $15. Let's talk about your budget, where we can find $15. How much do you pay for rent on your house or your mortgage?" I'd start with that and go through most of the couple's expenses. "Well, look, we can get $10 a month out of your entertainment budget and we can cut down on your smoking by $5."

By this time, I would have the customer's trust, a quality a salesman has to transmit quickly and one that can't be taught.

"Now," I'd say, closing, sure of the sale because I'd waited for the right moment to ask for the order, "whose name do you want the car in?"

For the first time I was managing other people, hiring and firing, and holding weekly sales meetings to whip up their enthusiasm. I'd try to do something fresh every week, like a preacher delivering a different sermon. Once when everyone at the meeting seemed a little lethargic, I took a rock and tossed it through the plate-glass window. Everyone woke up. I had some successes, people like Wilson (Joe) Riley. He came from the small town of Powell River, B.C., but went to a good private school in Victoria. Aside from being a wonderful salesman, he was one of the best-looking guys I'd ever seen. Joe and I worked together for the next ten years and when he was let go after I left Dan McLean for the last time, we even curbed cars together briefly.

During my early days at the dealership, my uncle, Harold Robertson, encouraged me to take a Toastmasters speaking course. Not long ago I got a letter from a man who heard me give one of my first speeches at a Toastmasters meeting: "The young man came to the podium, stated he was Jim Pattison and that he had joined Toastmasters to improve his public-speaking technique. He intended to use this ability in furthering his future career. He wasn't particularly impressive! At this point the writer appraised the newcomer, and said to himself, 'The poor little chap, he'll probably never amount to anything!' "

If I couldn't make speeches, I could sell cars and manage salesmen. I was in business, where I belonged, and figured I was well on my way to my first million.

CHAPTER FOUR

The Bow Mac Years

In December 1950, just before Christmas, I decided I had to fire a salesman who wasn't performing well. He was married and about ten years older than me. I called him into my little office on the used-car lot and he sat across from me against the window wall.

"It isn't working out, Charlie," I told him. "I have to fire you."

"Jimmy, I feel terrible," he said, and started to cry.

I felt so bad that I cried with Charlie. But I fired him.

The story that gets told and re-told when journalists write about me is the one about my firing the salesman who turned over the fewest cars each month. That story is usually dredged up to show how ruthless or heartless I am. The story is true, but the real point of it—my motivation—is never examined.

I started doing it in '52, a year after Dan McLean sold his Nash operation and became a 50 per cent partner in a General Motors dealership with Mackenzie Bowell. The original firm was well-established: Mac Bowell and a partner had founded it in 1919. Mac, the grandson of our fifth prime minister, the Ontario Conservative Sir Mackenzie Bowell, joined forces with Dan McLean to sell new Buicks, Cadillacs, Pontiacs, and British Vauxhalls in the city centre as the

53

Bowell McLean Motor Company—or Bow Mac, as I rechristened it. Dan McLean brought me with him to Bow Mac to open a used-car lot on a separate site. Within eight months, I was also managing two more lots for them in other locations. The used-car business was just returning to pre-war conditions, when there had been plenty of product to sell; by 1952, independent dealerships were multiplying, with brightly lit lots and forceful salesmen. GM Canada was urging its new-car dealers to get back into the retail used-car trade they had deserted during the war. Bow Mac's own retail business was thriving.

At age twenty-six, I became general sales manager for the whole firm, and hired Joe Riley as my used-car manager. By then I understood what it takes to keep people motivated to sell cars—and exactly what you have to do if they can't be motivated. I was seeing nice guys come to work for me as car salesmen. They would struggle along in the business for three or four months, maybe as long as a year, just getting by. They didn't have that born drive of the true salesman. Keeping them on would not be doing the company a favour: They were holding down positions that could be better filled by others. But just as important, keeping them wouldn't be any great favour to them: They were never going to be successful at selling cars, so why shouldn't they cut their losses and become mechanics or teachers or something they'd be good at? I don't think anyone wins by staying at the bottom of the totem pole, by being mediocre. So sure, I would fire the low man at the end of every month. You sold the fewest cars? You were gone. Don't even come in Monday Turn in the keys Saturday night. It's over. Unless you'd been on holidays or had been sick—I wouldn't do it without a legitimate reason. Now, the important thing is that it would never come as any surprise to the salesmen: They knew the rules when they came to work for me. And it wasn't only the guy at the bottom who would go. The fifth- or sixth-best salesman might be fired because his general attitude was bad or he was starting to arrive late. It didn't matter if his sales were good, bad, or indifferent: If he came late more than once without a good excuse—like an accident on the Lion's Gate Bridge or a sick child—he wasn't going to work for Bow Mac. If he just liked sleeping in, bam! He was history.

Once, to illustrate my point and have some fun, my top

salesman and I made a deal that he would come late to a sales meeting. As usual, the minute the meeting started, I locked the door. Latecomers were out of luck. Within a few minutes, there was a terrible noise at the door. The blade of a McCulloch chainsaw ripped through the frame and carved out an opening that this salesman stepped through, determined to get into the meeting. It got everybody's attention.

In a business that's larger than life anyway, the Bow Mac sales meetings became legendary. By 1957, I had help in staging them from my advertising manager, one of the most colourful and enthusiastic characters I've ever known, Wilf Ray.

Wilf is a Lebanese Canadian, a couple of years older than me and just a little taller, with a big black moustache and thick head of hair, and the smooth baritone voice of a radio announcer—which he was: In the 1940s, at university, I used to listen to his popular "DX Prowl" while I was driving around at night. Forty years later, he's still on the air, with a weekly evangelical gospel-music program he's been producing and announcing for no fee on our radio stations, CJOR and CJJR, for more than two decades (he signs off with "It's been Jesus and yours truly, musically speaking"). Wilf is a showman. Going into real estate in '50, he had an illuminated wooden model of a three-storey house clamped to the top of his little Austin and he left it parked on downtown Theatre Row with his name and phone number prominently displayed. In six years, he sold four hundred houses at a time when he had only a thousand competitors in town. Mary and I went to Wilf's wedding, which was held on his front lawn. And then he and his bride—she was bedecked in $1 million worth of borrowed Russian diamonds—drove to the Pacific National Exhibition grounds with a sixty-car escort for a mock wedding before ten thousand people in a promotional stunt cooked up by a local jeweller. Wilf was soon driving big cars, with his name emblazoned on the side; we met when he bought an Oldsmobile from me at Bow Mac. In 1956, I asked his wife if she thought they could live on a salary instead of commission. Only when I had her approval did I call Wilf in to offer him the job as ad manager. During my days at Bow Mac, and for years after, he was my closest friend.

Wilf not only wrote, laid out, or voiced over more than four thousand print and television ads, as far as I was concerned, he was the best photographer in the world. During twenty-three years with me, he took tens of thousands of pictures and produced at least a thousand customized slide shows. Some of those shows were for the sales meetings that we held as often as three and four times a day. I might gather the salesmen in the morning to tell them we'd be having a contest: first one who sells a car, I'll give him a $100 bonus; three cars, I'll send him to Harrison Hot Springs for the weekend. For our weekly meetings, I might say, "Today, we're going to sell a hundred cars and to do that, we'll have to pull some rabbits out of the hat." And out Wilf would come, dressed up as a magician, yanking rabbits out of a top hat and letting them run all over the floor. At monthly meetings, top salesmen received trophy cups for their performance. And at annual meetings to launch the new models—where each department got its quotas for the year—there might be a golden cocker spaniel as a door prize and Wilf might kick off the season in football helmet, shoulder pads over pyjamas, and galoshes. Anything to create enthusiasm, to motivate.

Late one night, I told Wilf: "Look, I want something spectacular at the meeting tomorrow. Let's go for the gold."

"We might be able to get a beautiful girl to come in wearing a gold lamé bathing suit," Wilf suggested. One of the salesmen said he knew a pretty girl who'd be perfect. "I don't want her unless I can see her," Wilf said. "I guarantee she's great," the salesman assured him.

The next morning, as I waited in the wings, Wilf told the crowd of sales guys: "We're going for the gold this morning. And I want to introduce a young lady here who will emphasize that . . ."

There was deadly silence as she walked out, and then some snickering. Wilf turned around to see a beautiful girl in a golden swimsuit; she was eight months pregnant. By now one salesman was doubled up on the floor with laughter. I was speechless.

We were just as outrageous in attracting customers. Wilf would get on the public-address system and announce to all the people on the lot: "Congratulations to Mr. and Mrs. ——. They've just bought themselves a '57 Pontiac. They're taking advantage of the one-year Bow Mac guarantee." Inside, to promote station wagons, we'd re-create a whole woodland scene, with campers in a tent. Some Saturdays, we'd have a performing monkey in overalls as entertainment at our used-car Supermarket lot on West Broadway. Or we'd bring in the Levy brothers, hulking seven-foot-tall twins. In 1958, we staged the world's largest checker game. The lot was laid out as a giant checkerboard with two-foot squares. It was billed as a grudge match between Herb Capozzi, the manager of the B.C. Lions, and Cedric Tallis, manager of the semi-pro Vancouver Mounties baseball club. The human checkers were leggy models in red or black bathing suits. More than five thousand people showed up, stopping traffic on Broadway and buying plenty of cars.

We topped that the next year when we planned what people came to call "Pattison's Folly." It was going to be a big sign—it had to be, to compete with the booming Dueck Chevrolet Oldsmobile dealership down the road. But what Wilf Ray and I didn't realize was how huge the sign would be. By the time we were finished, it became the largest free-standing electrical sign in the world.

I had convinced Dan McLean to let me consolidate the three used-car lots into one, the Supermarket, on a rise of land overlooking the downtown on West Broadway. Together Wilf and I hatched the idea of creating a sign that would overshadow Dueck's two beautiful signs a couple of blocks away from us. At the time (1958) Dueck was the largest and most successful car dealer in the country. We'd been competing against them in this location for a few years when I decided that we had to go up against this institution with a landmark that would dominate the city.

Neon Products, the biggest and best electrical-sign company in Canada, was the obvious manufacturer. But even they had never handled a sign of the magnitude we were suggesting. Wilf and I planned it for months; it kept growing in size as we consulted with Neon's designers and engineers. The thing wound up costing $100,000—in 1959 dollars. Its statistics were impressive: It was more than ten storeys tall and took eight months to design and build, with about 120 people working on it. Contractors had to dynamite hardpan to dig a base sixteen feet square and twenty feet deep. They installed tons of reinforcing steel to strengthen the base before pouring more than half a million pounds of cement, enough to pave sixty driveways. The tower weighed twelve tons. Powered by a transformer big enough to light thirty-five houses, it had more than five and a half miles of wiring and thirty-five hundred lamps. And each of the six letters—BOW MAC—was ten to eleven feet tall and thirteen to fourteen wide. One writer called it "the tallest, most monstrous, most garish electric sign west of the Rockies." But you could see it ten miles away and it wound up being reproduced in B.C. schoolbooks as an example of the uses of electricity.

Two ladders were built in for maintenance crews to service the sign. The night of the unveiling, a radio reporter cut his forehead on his way up one of the ladders but continued to climb, blood streaming down his face, to broadcast in a Scottish accent from the top of the sign. That was a few years before Jack Webster became Canada's leading open-line radio host (and several years before he came to work for me at CJOR). To attract TV fans, we brought in two British comedians, Alan Mowbray and Frank Jenks, who were then appearing in a popular show called "Colonel Flack."

We advertised the event as our thousand-car month and, with two days to spare, turned over 1,046 cars, reportedly more than any other North American dealership had sold in a single month. We'd become B.C.'s heaviest car advertisers on the new medium of television, spending up to $75,000 a month. Our print advertising accelerated too: In 1951, our annual ad budget for used cars had been $3,410; by the end of the decade, we were spending $120,000.

"World Series Specials . . . Money-Back Guarantee . . . Brand New Tires and Batteries . . . 1/2-Hour Delivery"—those aggressive newspaper ads (which I did myself before Wilf joined me) came to the attention of an influential man in the East whom I rank among the four key people instrumental in my career.

E.J. (Jeff) Umphrey was vice-president of GM of Canada, in charge of sales and advertising. *The Financial Post* once described him as "one of the busiest men in Canada." In terms of his influence, I considered him Canada's single most powerful individual outside of the prime minister. Under his guidance, GM's market share in Canada was the best of any of its divisions around the world. His thirteen hundred dealers across the country either worshipped him or feared for their lives; he knew almost every one of them personally. Jeff Umphrey was one of the strongest personalities I've ever encountered. At first glance he looked more like a university president, but he was an absolute sledgehammer of a man. He had great presence: tall, wiry, with a protruding chin, eyes that pierced you from behind half-rimmed glasses, and a determined walk. Born on a Manitoba farm, he spoke in cultured tones, precisely and thoughtfully. Every business day, he asked his secretary to pick an interesting new word from the dictionary and explain its meaning to him so he could try to use it in every letter he wrote that day. Speaking to a GM sales rally in the Hotel Vancouver one spring, he relaxed his audience of dealers with jokes but also remarked: "We like to be wanted by our family and friends and business associates. We like to feel we're important. We like to think the part we're playing can't be played quite as successfully by anybody else. We don't like our talents to go begging for appreciation."

He first made me feel important one day in 1954 when I was having lunch in my car at a White Spot drive-in. Another car pulled up alongside me with the GM zone manager and Jeff Umphrey inside. The manager introduced me to Umphrey, who asked: "Are you the fellow who's made all these changes at Bowell McLean? I'm interested in the ad I saw in the paper this morning." And then he questioned me on why I had included different elements in the used-car ad. He must have been impressed, because he invited me back to his hotel room to discuss advertising in general—then asked me to send him all the ads I did for the next two years. He passed them on to other dealers as examples of good advertising. And later Umphrey got Dan McLean's approval to send me to a GM school in Detroit for three weeks to learn how to be a better dealer. I was there with thirty-eight other dealers from all over the world, including the man with the world's largest Cadillac dealership, from Saudi Arabia.

The year I met Jeff Umphrey, Bow Mac's sales were excellent. So I was surprised when Dan McLean didn't give me a Christmas bonus, money I'd spent ahead of time. I didn't say a word to Dan; if you have to ask people for money, you shouldn't be working for them. But because he didn't give me the bonus I believed I'd earned, I was ripe for the picking. Yet there wasn't a thought in my head of ever leaving the automobile business the day a guy named Ron

Brown came into the showroom the following spring. Brown, a regular customer for our Cadillacs, told me he'd noticed a big change in the company since I'd been around. "Would you be interested in coming with me, being my sales manager for Aristocratic Cookware?" It was a national door-to-door pots and pans sales operation.

"Mr. Brown, I wouldn't be interested at all in that. I love cars."

"How much money do you make a year?" he asked.

"This last year, I made $6,000."

"Well," he said, "the fellow I'm looking for, I'm willing to see that he makes $50,000."

"Mr. Brown, I just thought of somebody who might be interested."

"Well, whoever it is, tell him to be at the Vancouver Club at twelve o'clock two days from today."

I was there, and took the job as national sales manager for a minimum of one year, with no contract.

For three weeks every month that year, I was on the road. I enjoyed it, but Mary was a little upset by my absence. The first month, I went to Brantford, Ontario, and practised with the product so I could teach our salesmen how to sell. It was direct selling, cold calls, back to those days I went out with my dad de-mothing pianos, back to my career peddling garden seeds and *The Saturday Evening Post* door to door. I discovered a couple of important things. First of all, if I whistled cheerfully while I went up the stairs and knocked on the door, householders would open the door significantly more times than if I didn't. I also learned the percentages of the business. If I made thirty calls a night, I would be able to make three demonstrations of the product, and I'd make one sale—stainless steel cookware for $189, or $249 for the deluxe set—which would be good money for the night. And in friendlier rural areas, I could get more demonstrations per call than in the city.

Then, one evening when I was taking a plane back home from Ontario, I had my second important encounter with Jeff Umphrey. My first year with Aristocratic was almost up and I'd made an impressive $52,000. Sitting beside me in the plane, Umphrey asked: "How are you doing in the pots-and-pans business? Like it?"

"Love it."

"But you like cars better."

"Yeah, I really do."

"Jimmy, why don't you come back to the car business? I know Bowell McLean are thinking of making a change; you should go see Dan McLean. Will you phone him up tomorrow?"

The next day, I met Dan at the Vancouver Club and he doubled my old salary to $12,000 a year—$40,000 less than I was making in cookware. And there was no promise of any Christmas bonus.

But, I was back in cars. Business rolled in, and I did get bonuses. In my decade with Bow Mac, we became Canada's largest Pontiac-Buick-Cadillac dealer. I helped build up the leasing business from nothing to more than eleven hundred vehicles. And, along the way, I made lots of mistakes. One day, in the early 1950s, Dan McLean called me out to the back alley to look at a new car. "We have a chance to take on the distributorship. What do you think?" he asked me. It was a small car, the engine was in the wrong place, and it had no styling. I knew the car business inside out and Dan relied on me. I gave him my considered opinion: "Mr. McLean, it will never sell. I guarantee it." And that's how we lost the opportunity to be the sole distributor in B.C. for a German import called the Volkswagen Beetle. It cost us a fortune. A classic mistake.

One of my last big motivational sessions with the sales staff at Bow Mac was a one-day seminar in Harrison Hot Springs, a resort near Vancouver. We went by chartered bus, with an upright piano aboard and me on trumpet for the sing-song on the way up. When we arrived, the staff got play money to gamble with at roulette and craps, redeemable for prizes. I woke them up the next morning with a trumpet blast and for a full day we pursued the conference theme: "The Customer Is King." At the end, there was a prize for the employee with the best suggestion to improve customer relations. In its flavour, that 1959 seminar was a pretty accurate preview of the Partners In Pride managerial conferences I'd launch in my own company fifteen years later.

In 1960—a year after we'd set the North American record for monthly car sales—Dan McLean offered me a piece of the company. We were walking back from a GM luncheon at the Hotel Vancouver when he said: "Jimmy, Mac Bowell wants to sell out. What I'm thinking of doing is having

Peter Birks [Dan's son-in-law] buy 25 per cent of Mac's share and you buy 25 per cent. You don't have to put up any money: We could pay your 25 per cent out of the earnings of the company. And when I retire, I'll sell my half to you and Peter. So you and he would be partners."

Peter Birks was a nice fellow my age who worked for an associated finance company—co-owned by Mac, Dan, and Reg Ross—which handled a lot of the financing for Bow Mac's used cars. I told Dan: "I wouldn't be interested."

"Why?" Dan was astonished. "You could own up to half this company for nothing. You can pay for it out of the profits of the company."

"I like Peter, I've worked with him, I don't have anything against him. I just wouldn't be interested in going into business with him."

"Well, you think it over," Dan said.

We were walking by a BA service station when I replied: "I don't have to think it over." I would have gone into partnership with Dan McLean in a split second, but not with his son-in-law; I knew our personalities just wouldn't have clicked. I also realized at that moment that I was turning down a piece of one of the most valuable GM franchises in the country. The deal would have automatically made me a millionaire.

About a month later, I announced to McLean that I would be going into the car business for myself. I was giving him a year's notice. I'd give him everything I had in the meantime and he had the next twelve months to make plans. He agreed. A couple of weeks passed, then one afternoon he came into my office. He'd been at the Vancouver Club where he'd been drinking. He stood at my doorway. "Jimmy, we've decided that there's no reason for you to stay here anymore. We want you out of here today."

"Yes, sir."

He agreed that I could buy the white '60 Cadillac convertible that I was driving as a company car. I put my belongings in the car and drove home. Being told to go by Dan McLean was one of the worst experiences of my life. There are very few people in your life whom you really love; I'd loved this guy, given him ten years of good work, and he asked me to leave without a word of discussion. I felt enormously sad that our relationship, which had been so good, so

The Bow Mac Years

free of major arguments, would end on such a disappointing note. When I did apply for my own General Motors franchise soon after, Dan asked GM not to let me locate in Vancouver.

I saw him only twice after that. Once, eight years later when I was in the Vancouver Club and he asked what brought me down there. And then when I was getting strongly into the deal business, he stopped me on the street and said: "I like what you're doing."

Peter Birks, his son-in-law, subsequently got control of Bowell McLean and eventually went into receivership.

But on that day in 1960, I was out on the street.

Mary and I had three children by that time: Jimmy was eight, Mary Ann, five, and Cynthia (Cindy) was born in December. We'd changed addresses a couple of times during the Bow Mac years. When my parents moved out of their house in Gleneagles, a long way out in West Vancouver, we took over the payments. Mary hated the house because she felt trapped there on the edge of town, with me being at work twelve and more hours a day, and her depending on the sometimes unreliable junkers I'd get her for transportation. So, without telling Mary, I traded that house with a mailman for a smaller one on the waterfront in downtown West Vancouver. She didn't want to move in there, figuring the kids could either drown in the ocean in front of the place or get run over by a train on the railway line out back. And then in '59, when I found a bigger house, Mary had fallen in love with our waterfront view so much she didn't want to move this time either. The new place—on the slopes of West Vancouver's beautiful British Properties (the Guinness brewing family of Britain developed the land)—was a four-bedroom white clapboard with a view of the harbour. I didn't have any money for a down payment but promised the seller my estimated $5,000 Christmas bonus. By the time I left Bow Mac, I'd found some cash for landscaping but we lived with no drapes or carpets for two years.

Mary says I had a perfect record as a father: I never changed a diaper and never got up at night when the kids were crying. Mary raised the children. Like my mother, she was the house disciplinarian, but if there was a major problem, I'd sit down with the child and explain why I was about to administer a spanking. Even though I worked long hours, we all have some good memories of those growing-up days. The kids still laugh about how I'm not crazy about heights (I'd refused to go up the Space Needle in Seattle) and how they convinced me once to go on a roller-coaster, where they insist I slid down in my seat and screamed. Mary Ann talks about how she and I used to have wrestling matches against Mary and Jimmy Jr. and I'd call her a traitor when she deserted me to go on the winning team. Summers, we used to holiday at Kelowna, in B.C.'s Okanagan Valley, waterskiing with our good friends, the Frank Bakers; he was a trumpet-playing alderman and restaurant-owner in Vancouver. When Cindy was a teenager, our holidays had changed: She recalls horrible weekends touring all our Overwaitea stores in a motor home and having to count all of the competition's grocery buggies. The kids would go to Pentecostal summer camps; church was as much a way of life for us as it was for my folks. Later on, Jimmy Jr. played trumpet, Mary Ann vibraharp, and Cindy clarinet in the Glad Tidings Temple orchestra I led for a little while. Jimmy went to Europe with the Kitsilano Boys' Band I had played in as a teenager, and Mary Ann toured with a Glad Tidings gospel-rock band. Today, all our children and their spouses are firm believers in God.

The kids never got an allowance, but I paid them for doing specific chores. I even paid Mary Ann $25 for an A and $15 for a B in school. In their teen years, they all worked for my companies, typing, sweeping floors, washing cars. When Mary Ann worked at my car dealership, I told the accountant, Rose Andersen, to be tough on her. Rose made her cashier in the service department, the worst job of all, and told her: "You can't get mad at the customers, so if you have to cry, get to my office first." Though the kids grew up in the British Properties, they never felt particularly well-off; Jimmy remembers his classmates driving by in new cars their parents bought them while he was walking in the rain. Unlike their friends, the only private schools they attended were a Catholic school Mary Ann went to in Grade One and the tough Shawnigan Lake boarding school on Vancouver Island where Jimmy spent two of his high-school years when his marks were bad. He came back so independent that when we had a confrontation later over his long hair, he left home at nineteen. He was out with not a penny from us, though he did return for a time before leaving for good.

Aside from giving them summer work and financing their education, I promised the kids two things when they grew up: no jobs and no money. That way, there were no false expectations. Some people think I was being callous— even my mother said she'd be softer on them than me. I've heard stories about strangers being shocked just a few years ago to see the grown-up Mary Ann, Jimmy Pattison's daughter, on her hands and knees, scrubbing the floor of a 7-Eleven convenience store. Well, she was managing the store and she sure as hang should have been keeping it clean, one way or the other.

I had a good reason for making those promises to my children. It grew out of my days at Bowell McLean. For a long time, we were the only Cadillac dealer in town and, while either Mac or Dan dealt with the wealthy customers who bought Cadillacs, I usually served those people afterwards, delivering their new cars to their homes, making sure they were kept serviced. And a lot of the time I wound up dealing with their sons and daughters who were mostly my age. Look at most families of wealth and you'll find that generally the second generation doesn't have its values straight, doesn't respect the work ethic. That was the first time I really became exposed to rich kids—and I didn't like what I saw. They seemed to me to be arrogant, spoiled brats—demanding people who, because of an accident of birth, had a misplaced sense of their own worth. Those snotty kids treated me like their gardener, their servant. I determined then that if I ever made any money, and if I loved my children, I wouldn't shower them with an excess of money. I would let them make their own way in the world and let them have the satisfaction of providing the roof over their heads themselves. And if they were any good, they would rise to the top like cream. If they had problems, I would always give them advice. I could probably solve their problems quickly by tossing money at them, but they wouldn't learn about adversity that way, they wouldn't grow and mature. I decided instead to throw them in the water of life and let them swim—and the sooner they knew no help would be offered, the better and stronger swimmers they'd become.

Now, from the beginning, I always reserved the right to

help my children if they demonstrated good judgment, maturity, and balance. And in most cases they have. As adults, none of them has expected or asked anything from me. Their values are solid. Jimmy Jr. says things that remind me of my father: "If you're going to do something, do it as best you can." Mary Ann wrote me a letter not long ago thanking me for forcing her to find her own independence. And Cindy actually told a journalist recently: "The second generation never has the same work ethic."

In the case of my kids, the ethic may not be the same, but it's there. Cindy, the mother of twins, is a critical-care nurse. Mary Ann left the 7-Eleven job to sell life insurance and, more recently, to set up a business importing nannies with her professional-musician husband, who was a fellow manager at 7-Eleven. Jimmy became a partner in a truck-tire importing firm and then a video-games business before joining the Bank of British Columbia as a commercial account manager, lending money to business clients. In early 1987, when he was thirty-four, I offered my son a position as a trainee with Great Pacific Capital. He and his wife of six years have moved to Geneva. And Cindy's husband, Al, is now working for Jim Pattison Nissan.

To explain why I'd offered Jimmy and Al the jobs, I held a family meeting—our first one ever—in the Corporate Office boardroom. Mary was there, and my mother, and the three kids and their spouses. I chronicled the history of the company from the beginning and ran the company audio-visual to explain the scope of the Jim Pattison Group. I showed them a recent article in *The Financial Post Moneywise Magazine* that described me as one of the fifty richest people in Canada—the richest west of Toronto—and estimated my net worth as "probably close to $390 million." "I don't know if it's right or not," I told the family, "but this says I'm a rich guy." I also gave them copies of an article from *Fortune* which surveyed thirty multi-millionaires and found that six will give their children only minimal inheritances and almost half plan to leave at least as much to charity as to their heirs. H. Ross Perot, a Texas billionaire who sold Electronic Data Systems to General Motors, is quoted as saying: "If your kids grow up living in fairyland thinking that they're princes and princesses, you're going to curse their lives." After telling them what I thought of second-generation rich kids, I said: "Because I love my children, I didn't want to ruin them this way." Ruin them by giving them an unreasonable head start or raising false expectations that they'd have (in the words of one of *Fortune*'s multi-millionaires) "a lifetime supply of food stamps just because they came out of the right womb."

But now, I said, Jimmy and Al had both done their apprenticeships: They had solid marriages, they'd proven they could make it on their own, they were mature enough to know that life doesn't come on a silver platter. And they knew the value of money. "I've always had it in the back of mind to do this if the kids proved themselves," I said. Then we all went to the Terminal City Club for dinner.

When I said goodbye to Bow Mac in 1960, I was two years younger than Jimmy Jr. was when I offered him a job. At the time, I felt I had done my apprenticeship, and I'd better get moving if I was going to be a millionaire within the next eight years. In fact, I might have to revise my goal upwards, if I believed Dan McLean. I remember the early morning he called me up from the Vancouver Club to drive him home. We had just passed the corner of Granville and King Edward in the exclusive Shaughnessy district when he said: "Jimmy, being a millionaire is no good anymore. Today, you've got to be a two-millionaire."

CHAPTER FIVE

In the Driver's Seat

After a decade of managing dozens of employees, building up a successful business for somebody else, here I was back curbing cars. A long way from my promise to be a millionaire by forty. Well, the rest of Canada in 1960 was in big economic trouble too: The Conservative government of John Diefenbaker was heading for a minority and defeat as the country suffered a serious recession. The unemployment rate was at a post-war high—and among the jobless were Joe Riley, who was also fired by Bow Mac, and Jimmy Pattison. Going back to our roots, we bought some used cars together and for six weeks sold them out of my driveway in the British Properties. Then Alan Taylor came to see me. He was a stockbroker and just happened to be a good friend of a son-in-law of Dan McLean's. Taylor and two other partners had invested in an unsuccessful company called Westminster Savings and Loan, which sold savings certificates door to door. Would I go to work for them as general manager at $900 a month? Sure I would—on the clear understanding that I was about to apply for a GM dealership. Over about eight months, I built Westminster's sales staff from a couple to a couple of dozen, primed them with contests and other motivational incentives, and increased the sales volume sharply.

Meanwhile, I'd applied to General Motors of Canada for a local franchise. Instead, the company offered me dealerships in other cities in Western Canada and the East, everywhere but Vancouver. I explained that because my dad was quite ill with diabetes, I didn't want to leave the city. Eventually, I met with my old mentor, Jeff Umphrey. He decided—over the objections of Dan McLean and Dueck's—to let me take over a faltering eleven-year-old franchise, Marshall Pontiac Buick of Vancouver.

Now all I had to do was come up with the money. I'd developed a banker friend named Harold Nelson, the manager of a small Royal Bank branch on the exact West Broadway location where I'd started in the business, washing cars for Fred Richmond for $25 a week in 1948. Harold Nelson had given me an installment loan in 1951 and I used to stop in at his office when I was making my payments. Before long we'd developed enough of a relationship that we'd lunch together. Soon I was getting loans from him without having to bring in anybody as an endorser. When I joined Artistocratic Cookware, he warned me that I'd miss the car business terribly. So in May of 1961, he was sympathetic to my request for $40,000 to help finance a dealership selling Pontiacs, Buicks, Vauxhalls, and Tempests (Pontiac's new A-body compacts). My net worth was $22,000—$15,000 in cash-surrender value on my life-insurance policy and $7,000 equity in my house in the British Properties. That was it. At the time, Harold's branch could make discretionary loans up to a limit of only $7,500. Harold Nelson approached his supervisor, who rejected my application because of my youth. Harold agreed to take me to his boss, the man in charge of B.C. operations, who heard me out and then invited me back a second time to discuss more details of my bank plan. Finally, after I agreed to put up my house and life-insurance policy and 100 per cent of the shares of my new company—all that, as well as some personal guarantees—they gave me the $40,000. "But, you understand," they told Harold Nelson, "it's on your head." (Years later, I hired Harold to work for us; he's now retired in Dallas, where he manages more than $100 million U.S. for us.) And then GM, through its financing and management-assistance division called Motors Holding, lent me $190,000.

Nikita Khrushchev was preparing for a summit meeting with John F. Kennedy; Canada was imposing new restrictions on Japanese trade; and Saskatchewan premier Tommy Douglas was about to run for the leadership of the NDP. But as far as I was concerned, the biggest news in the *Province* on May 29, 1961, was the four full pages advertising the official opening of Jim Pattison Limited at Cambie and 18th. After I'd left Bow Mac, I helped get Wilf Ray, my advertising manager, a job with Ad-Pro in Toronto, writing sales-motivation material for GM salesmen across Canada. He came back to Vancouver on holiday to stage my opening. Among our guests were more than forty people from Bow Mac; in spite of a thick fog, they all showed up that evening. About the only other promotion I did was selling my first car—the white Cadillac convertible I'd bought from Dan McLean—to my old friend, Frank Baker, and having Wilf take a picture of the sale. The only incentive I offered customers was a no-risk, satisfaction-or-money-back guarantee—like a department store—on every product, from a sparkplug to a car. I spent less than $2,000 to put my name on the neon sign. I'd wanted to keep the Marshall name, which was respected for fairness, but Jeff Umphrey insisted I change it and after a big argument I agreed. By insisting, he changed my life because the company became so personalized, immediately identifiable with me as the owner.

There was no money to do anything fancier than put my name up on the old sign. Jim Pattison Ltd. had a two-car showroom. I went from having sold a thousand cars a month at Bow Mac to moving only twenty-five my first month in business. Marshall Pontiac had been run like a country club. To slash the overhead, I started firing staff. Several employees, unhappy at what I was doing, quit on their own. Among them was my accountant, who didn't like the heat I was putting on him. An Edmonton GM dealer named Hugh McCall, a friend I'd met while at Bow Mac, generously sent me his own accountant for several weeks to reorganize my accounts—at no charge, not even for hotel bills. (Football fans might remember McCall as a president of the Edmonton Eskimos.) Out of a staff of one hundred, I was soon left with fifty-seven, and then I began bringing in some of my own salesmen. One of them sold a lot of cars but would come to work absolutely beat from chasing women all night. I suggested he take saltpeter to slow down his sex drive—they used it in the Army, I told him. So he did, and it worked.

My first month, I lost $13,956 on net sales of $147,000. The second month, $12,000. Though I'd lost almost my whole net worth in the first two months, by the third I made a couple of thousand. Then I started to do well. Fast. Yet I continued to allow myself a salary of only $800 a month. And within nineteen months—putting into practice all the tricks I'd learned over ten years—I went from a losing operation to repaying General Motors every cent of their $190,000 *and* their effective rate of simple interest of 80 per cent. It was very expensive money. I'd made the fastest payout that Motors Holding ever had on their books in Canada.

When I exceeded GM's forecast for both volume and profitability in my first year, Jeff Umphrey sent me a note of congratulations, which ended: "Keep reaching, Jim. The stars are never beyond the touch of those who see them clearly."

One of my profit centres became car leasing. The only employee I took from Bow Mac was Bob Chant, who became my lease manager. At the time, Dueck Chevrolet Oldsmobile was the Canadian leader in leasing. Few other dealers across the country were paying much attention to the relatively new concept of leasing cars to corporate clients. I decided to make it a cornerstone of Jim Pattison Ltd. In late '61 I went to see Harold Nelson at the Royal about backing me in the lease business with a line of credit. The Bank Act didn't allow Harold to use the leased car as collateral, but he could lend me money if the bank took title or had first lien on it. "We'd have to have first claim on the car and Motors Holding would have second claim," he told me. Motors Holding told me they couldn't allow that—and nobody at GM Canada could approve such a change in policy.

It was a couple of days before Christmas. What the hang! I phoned the president of General Motors Acceptance Corporation in Toronto, Wilf Matthews. I spoke to him for more than an hour about what I wanted to do with the Royal. "The rules are made to be broken," he finally said. I got my line of credit. And during the '60s, I opened lease offices in Calgary and Toronto as our fleet became one of the biggest in Canada, with more than four thousand vehicles (including airplanes and cabin cruisers). In '63, in the largest Canadian car-lease deal outside of government, we arranged to supply Hertz with all of its cars across the country.

I was in Montreal that same year negotiating with a senior executive with Peterson, Howell and Heather, the largest leasing company in the world. We were at lunch in the Queen Elizabeth Hotel when he ordered a martini and I ordered ginger ale. He was offended: "I'm not prepared to talk to you about a deal unless you have a drink with me." I ordered a martini. That was the first time in my life I can ever recall tasting hard liquor. I was thirty-five. It tasted terrible; I didn't finish it. But the deal was done and ultimately his company bought a thousand cars from us.

The leasing business runs on slender margins (in '65, for example, a GM compact went for $49 a month). But leasing supplies you with used cars. And the key to success in the car business is to be able to handle and make money on all the used cars you can get. My philosophy has always been that I'm in the new-car business to buy and sell used cars. People can shop around and pick up a new Pontiac Acadian these days for about the same competitive price at any one of several dealerships across town. But what's a 1981 Cadillac worth? No two used cars are the same; the market fluctuates—and in normal times that's where the money is made. From the start, the leasing business gave us stable, steady earnings and control of our inventory. And we knew the secrets of the business. When a leased white car came back to us to sell as a used car, we'd make $100 more than we could on a black car. Leasing a car, we'd throw in power steering and electrically controlled windows for only $5 or $10 extra a month because we knew we could get $400 more for the car when we came to sell it.

I'm sold on leasing generally. Today, the Jim Pattison Sign Company owns and leases nearly forty thousand signs on maintenance contracts across Canada. This makes sense for our clients because they'd find it too expensive to service these sophisticated signs themselves. With leasing, we develop a relationship with our customer. If he buys a car from us, he may not necessarily come back to us the next time. But if he leases our car, he has to return and we get a chance to sell him again. In our Corporate Office, we lease our phones, our computers, even the engines on our Learjet. Because we get higher quality, better service—and regular upgrades—on products that need specialized attention and regular maintenance.

Not everything went smoothly for Jim Pattison Ltd. From the first, I had problems with the Pontiac-Buick wholesale managers in Vancouver, the company representatives who dealt with the dealers. We clashed over policy to the point where I refused to deal with them. At that point, GM sent in a twenty-six-year-old named Bill Sleeman. At first glance, he was a typical General Motors man: navy-blue suit, white shirt, hat on the head, around six feet tall. He was aggressive in a quiet way, poker-faced but pleasant. Bill had grown up in the paper-mill town of Fort Frances, Ontario, not far from the village of Sleeman (the place was named for his homesteading grandfather, who worked with the legendary editor of *The Winnipeg Free Press*, John Dafoe, to encourage immigration to Canada). Bill was always a jock: At the University of Manitoba, where he took political science and philosophy, he was active in everything from faculty football to handball and curling. He was in student government and, like me, got introduced to the Establishment through a fraternity. After a couple of years with Imperial Oil, selling to bulk agents in rural Manitoba, and a year in group-life insurance sales with Great West Life in Toronto, he joined GM at its Canadian headquarters in Oshawa, Ontario. As a junior in the distribution department—the department that acts as a liaison between the manufacturer and the regional zone officers across Canada—he came to the attention of Jeff Umphrey. The first time was when he drove Mrs. Umphrey to Toronto and charmed her along the way. The second was when he organized dealers to pick up their cars at the Oshawa plant during a Teamsters strike.

Bill Sleeman was in Kamloops, in the B.C. Interior, when he first heard about me. The former sales manager of Marshall Pontiac told him what a difficult guy I was to work for. In January '62, Bill moved to Vancouver to become the Pontiac-Buick wholesale manager. His first day, he remembers, a secretary asked if he'd started preparing his résumé yet. Why? he wondered. "Well," she said, "you've got Jimmy Pattison as a dealer. He just got the last two guys moved off the territory. You don't have a hope."

The next day, I was his first call. He came to do my annual budget and forecast—negotiations in which the factory and the dealer agree on the month-by-month budget and volume of cars. One of the problem areas was that GM had just introduced the small Pontiac Acadian and I refused to handle them. "I know you're going to want to talk about the Acadians," I told Bill. "But Volkswagen has all the market for small cars out here."

He was young, but smart. Instead of talking about Acadians, he dealt with the volume of Pontiacs and Buicks I wanted for the year. Explaining to me how the production lines worked in Oshawa, he said: "For every Acadian, there's only so many Pontiacs and Buicks I'm going to get. You'll get your fair share, but not as many as you want. I can't get you any more Pontiacs and I may even have to steal some from you because you won't sell Acadians."

Nobody had explained the situation to me quite like that before. "Bill, I want you over here next week for a sales meeting to tell the guys all about the Acadians."

Bill also convinced me to become part of GM's program to market used cars under the standard Goodwill dealership label. Corporate headquarters in Detroit couldn't understand why we were the first metropolitan GM dealer in Canada to refuse to join the program. The reason was simple: We offered a better warranty on our used cars than the Goodwill program did—six months instead of ninety days. "We have to have something that's better than the next guy, Bill. All your other Pontiac dealers are like sheep. Let's not talk about it."

Bill phoned Oshawa the next day to ask if there was anything to prevent a Goodwill used-car dealer from offering his own warranty as well as GM's. No problem, his boss said. Bill came back to me: "You're missing a marketing bet here, Jimmy. Your salesman can pull out the Goodwill warranty first and then pull out your special guarantee that's better than the ordinary vanilla warranty." Then he told me that GM was about to run a big used-car-dealer advertising program locally and our name wouldn't appear on it unless I signed up as a Goodwill dealer. Not only that, but he'd brought along some cans of paint to redo the faded old Goodwill sign that the former lot owner had left on the fence. I signed. I liked Bill Sleeman's style. That's why I went after him to work for me seven years later.

During those early days of my own business, I had two employees who made strong impressions on me. Among the original Marshall Pontiac employees who stayed on was Enzo Centrone, an Italian who was born in what's now Yugoslavia.

Enzo had been a bartender for American occupation troops in Trieste; he came to Canada in 1957, became a general mechanic, and then wound up as customer-relations representative in our lease business—the customers loved him—and eventually as service manager for Jim Pattison Lease. Enzo played a major part in building up the leasing company. Several years ago I asked him to work in the Corporate Office, doing everything from entertaining special clients and tending the bar on our boat to helping stage conferences. His only title today is "Enzo." He's the one employee still with me from my start in 1961—and every year on the anniversary of the opening of Jim Pattison Ltd., we try to get together for dinner, wherever I am in the world. He remains one of my best friends.

In 1963, a young married woman with two children came looking for a job with Jim Pattison Ltd. She was a miner's daughter, originally from Goldfields, Saskatchewan, who in her teens had taught Sunday school and done volunteer work at a hospital in Kimberley, B.C. Growing up with the dream of being a nurse, she moved to Vancouver and became a long-distance telephone supervisor instead. Looking for work that would allow her to be home days with her children, she joined us as a night switchboard operator—for fifty cents an hour. After she and her husband divorced, she married our lease manager, Bob Chant. Along the way, Maureen Chant went from attending the United Church as a child to accepting the Pentecostal faith as an adult.

I first paid attention to Maureen when I'd come in at night to prepare speeches for community groups and wind up practising them in front of her. Eventually she was promoted and became secretary to Wilf Ray in advertising and public relations. Impressed with her abilities, I asked Maureen if she'd be my secretary and offered to send her to school to improve her typing and shorthand if she would promise to stay with me five years. No, she'd rather pay for the lessons herself—she didn't want to commit for five years. She and Bob have since divorced, but Maureen Chant has been working with me for nearly a quarter of a century as one of the very few people who had the capability of growing with the company.

Maureen is attractive and pleasant—well-spoken and striking with her silver hair and elegantly tailored clothes. But she is a strong-willed woman (a plaque in her office reads: "Tough times never last, but tough people do!"). During our first fifteen years together, I don't think a day went by that we didn't have a spat over something. After she and I would argue with each other, she'd go into the washroom and cry, then come back and confront me again. The next minute, we'd be laughing together. Over the years, I gave her more and more responsibility and today she's my administrative assistant—my right arm. She has made a terrific contribution to our company. Maureen has always worked night and day, at least six days a week. She has done it all—typing up deals in a hotel room at four in the morning or making breakfast in the office after an all-night negotiating session; picking up the phone and sweet-talking an American airline into holding a plane for me for half an hour; taking an English lord on an informative car tour of all our companies in Vancouver. She likes people, knows them, and can anticipate trouble with them; sometimes, before anybody else has seen the signs, she'll tell me, "Jimmy, there's a problem coming up with this fellow." Along with all the usual work, like handling my special correspondence, she fields every complaint that comes into Corporate Office, from a guy whose lease car has broken down to a woman who is accusing the company of distributing pornography. She manages all my charitable donations. She planned and supervised the gutting and redesign of our offices while I was away at Expo. And she organizes our crucial quarterly divisional meetings and annual Partners in Pride management conferences. A local business magazine once recognized her as the top secretary in Vancouver; I consider her the best in Canada. I've heard more compliments about her than any other employee I've ever had.

Jim Pattison Ltd. was expanding quickly in the early '60s when I started looking for a bigger and better location for the dealership. I found a terrific spot on Cambie Street, just off West Broadway. I had the support of Bill Sleeman and GM's western regional manager. But Dueck's lobbied against me in Oshawa because the site was too close to their own turf. Early on Good Friday morning in 1963, I got a phone call at home from Jeff Umphrey. He'd never made a personal call to me like this before. "I'd like you to be in my suite at the Hotel Vancouver at ten o'clock this morning."

"Yes, sir."

I was out of bed and at the hotel at five to ten. I walked into his large suite and perched on a chesterfield. The place was packed with General Motors people. Jeff Umphrey looked at me with his steely eyes and spoke. "Jimmy, we don't want you to move to Cambie and Broadway. We want you to go to Main and Eighteenth. We want you to do it right now. And by the way, we don't want any competitive bids for the building. Dominion Construction is going to build it."

I was stunned. "Mr. Umphrey, I can't do that. There's never been a single successful retailer on Main Street. Never, ever. I know. I've lived on that street. There are Chinese vegetable gardens and slaughterhouses at one end of the street and junkyards at the other end.

"And besides, I'm not ready to move on it. I don't have the resources yet.

"And Marwell Construction is my best leasing customer and they're going to be very upset if there are no competitive bids."

"Well, Jimmy," Umphrey said. "I want you to do it. Now."

"What if I don't?"

"Then you have just one decision to make. Do you want to continue to be a General Motors dealer, or don't you?"

"I'll do it," I said, and left the room. A GM rep walked me to the elevator. "This is suicide," I told him.

"He's the boss."

"I know."

I drove to Main and 18th and shuddered at what I saw. There were old houses and the remnants of once-hopeful businesses. Dominion Stores, major Canadian food retailers, couldn't succeed with a supermarket on Main. Hamilton Harvey, big local retailers, went down in flames there. Nobody ever made it on Main Street. In forcing me to move there, Jeff Umphrey broke my heart.

The following Monday morning, I got a call from Clark Bentall, head of Dominion Construction: "Jeff Umphrey's called. Come down and see us."

"Look," I told Clark Bentall in his office. "I'm here 'cause I have to be, not 'cause I want to be. My best customer's Marwell, whom I love, and I don't know you people from Adam. I can't believe I gotta deal with you and there's no competitive bid. I don't like the land we're going to—I hate the location. Having said all that, here I am. Let's go."

Everything was already go. The Bentalls had optioned the land. I had to explain the lack of bids to my friends at Marwell Construction, who were sympathetic and remained my leasing clients. It was only years later, after he'd retired, that I asked Jeff Umphrey: "Why did you make me deal with Clark Bentall, with no competitive bids?"

"Oh," he said. "I had an IOU with him, and I just used you to pay it off."

Not long after he told me to move to Main Street, I had another call from Jeff Umphrey, asking me what I was doing the following weekend. He told me to bring Mary and come to Toronto, where he'd have us picked up and taken to his house in Oshawa. Even though I didn't have any spare cash for the airfare, I had to go. He obviously wanted to talk business. When we arrived, he announced that we were all going up to Lake Simcoe for the weekend. He had a house and a cabin cruiser there, but we never did go out on the boat. After dinner, he simply said: "Jimmy, play the organ." There was never any small talk with Jeff Umphrey. I sat down at the little organ in his house and played his requests: "The Old Rugged Cross," "Jeannie with the Light Brown Hair", and his favourite, "April in Portugal." I played song after song, for three solid hours. All the next day at the lake I spent wondering why he had brought me from Vancouver. But I left for home that night none the wiser—and to this day I'm still not sure why this powerful man had a kid car dealer, more than twenty years younger, fly across the country for the weekend.

Wilf Ray flew back from Toronto to help us launch Jim Pattison on Main in the fall of 1964. The opening party introduced the '65 Pontiacs and Buicks. Our guests saw the big motivational billboard in the service department: "Your BEST effort is important to our company's success!" And the not-so-subtle sign in the showroom: "Customers are the lifeblood of our business." We had the performing dogs from "The Littlest Hobo" TV show, Lance Harrison's Dixieland band, and my old friend Frank Baker as master of ceremonies—introducing top American executives of GM and Hertz, hot local football players Joe Kapp and Willie Fleming, and P.J.

Lipp, the jeweller who thirteeen years earlier had given me a lot of interest-free time to pay off Mary's $1,000 engagement ring.

My mother was a special guest, and the only sadness that evening was that my father wasn't there. He'd died the year before, at sixty-eight. A year after retirement, he fell ill while he was on the trip to Luseland to pay off all his old Depression debts. He'd never really recovered. I was with him in the hospital the Sunday morning he died. He got up in his bed, his legs over the side, coughed, and was gone. A couple of hours later, I went to church and played the organ during the service.

For the next two years, I cried every single day—in my car, going to work or coming home, it never failed. Every day, remembering my father, I wept.

As I predicted, Jim Pattison on Main was never the success it would have been if I could have built it in a better location. We had the odd good year with a decent profit, but we started off losing $40,000 a month and until recently had never consistently made any serious money there.

Some positive things happened. For two years running, I was invited to Detroit to be part of the President's Advisory Council, one of twenty GM dealers from among fifteen thousand in North America to be called on to discuss the business with the president and chairman of General Motors.

And Main Street did bring me some good people, who still work with me. Rose Andersen, a tall mother of two who'd worked for two other car dealers in Alberta and loved the wild characters in the business, came to be our accountant. We had one manager who dated the customers and bragged about it; at one meeting to discuss his problems, Rose said: "I'd like to suggest that we have him castrated; it would be easier and cheaper." She was soon corporate secretary for all my private companies and, when Neonex went private, moved to Corporate Office. Missing the excitement of the dealership, she'd step out in the hallway occasionally and start yelling: "Let's get some life in here." She's never taken much lip from me. Once, when she'd made an error and I asked her in mock anger: "How come you're so stupid?," she replied: "Look, Jim Pattison, I never said I was brilliant." If Maureen is at the front end of the business today, dealing with people, Rose Andersen is as important at the back end—running the cash, preparing our presentations to the bank, being corporate secretary, and dealing with all the financial people in our divisions.

My closest business associate outside the company soon became Don Selman, a chartered accountant who was a tax partner with Peat Marwick in Vancouver. One day, on my way to a Better Business Bureau meeting (I was vice-president), I came across a group of people in a boardroom. "What are you doing here?" I asked them bluntly. When they explained they were accountants doing an audit, I asked: "Well, who's a good tax guy?" They gave me the name of Don Selman, a slight redhead whom I came to have tremendous confidence in over twenty-five years. He was so good that when his firm later moved him to Montreal, I went to the senior partner in Toronto and had Don transferred back to Vancouver.

Harry Dunbar answered my Help Wanted ad for an accountant in 1966. A local boy, he'd become treasurer and administrator of Parsons Brown, part of the Continental Group of North American insurance companies. He was about thirty, the youngest officer in the whole Continental organization, when he faced an unwelcome transfer and responded to my ad. It attracted him with the promise of a company car. I made him secretary-treasurer of the car division and, week by week, he began to look after our minor companies too—including Oakridge Securities, which Roy Long and I had formed to catch tuna, and which was now doing some insuring and financing for the car company. One of Harry's chores was to keep track of our used-car inventory. At the end of each month, he'd count the cars and there'd usually be several missing. In those days, our salesmen were a bit wilder; it wasn't uncommon for them to lend one of our many used Pontiac two-door hardtops with bucket seats to a girlfriend. So Harry would post a notice on the office bulletin board which said that these missing cars had apparently been stolen, the theft would be reported to the police, and if anybody happened to know where they were, please notify Harry. They'd all come back, although occasionally we'd report one stolen and the police would pull over an innocent young girl who said that her boyfriend had lent the car to her.

Harry and Don Selman were helpful people to have around when I decided to expand our horizons beyond the car business. So was Wilf Ray, my friend and former advertising manager, who finally returned to work for me—lured away from Toronto by his first love, broadcasting. He just couldn't resist coming back to Vancouver when I decided to get into radio, and to get involved with characters like the controversial Pat Burns.

CHAPTER SIX

News Talk

"Honey," he'd tell a woman caller on his nightly phone-in show, "you're a little off your rocker." He'd involve an overseas telephone operator in a frank discussion of birth control when she didn't know she was on the air. His morning "World Edition" was a forerunner of CBC Radio's "As It Happens," a call-out show with him phoning around the world to everybody from American neo-Nazi leader George Lincoln Rockwell (whom he harangued as a lunatic) to a representative of the long-living Huntzerland tribe in the Himalayas. Pat Burns pioneered hot-line radio in Canada. And indirectly, his provocative programs helped me make my first move into the media world.

Pat was the sensation of Vancouver broadcasting in 1965. His "Hot Line" on CJOR was the highest-rated show in B.C. It took calls from anybody on any subject, from homosexuality to drug addiction to atheism—the wilder the better. *Maclean's* described his opinions at the time as "generally far to the left of centre," an appraisal that may surprise anybody who listens to Pat Burns now. But he'd run unsuccessfully as a candidate for the Liberals and the NDP, and in those days he supported medicare and the legal sale of heroin to addicts.

Until Burns came along, CJOR had been in terrible shape financially. Known mostly for its religious programs and racetrack coverage, the AM station had been near or at the bottom of the local ratings for fifteen years. Burns's success encouraged the owner of CJOR to hire other open-line hosts, who tried to be even more outrageous. One of them, Jim Crossen, would try stunts like broadcasting from a pot party or describing clinical details of lesbian sex.

All of this came to the attention of the Board of Broadcast Governors, which regulated Canadian radio. In '64 the Board criticized Pat Burns for his "wild opinionizations" and a year later it heard complaints from listeners about Jim Crossen. CJOR had gone out of control under the brief ownership of Marie Chandler. She was the elderly widow of the radio engineer who'd bought the station for $600 in 1926, two years after it went on the air. The day before the Board's 1965 licence-renewal hearings in Vancouver, Mrs. Chandler had fired Burns in a dispute over money.

(Pat Burns proved how popular he was when he hired the 2,900-seat Queen Elizabeth Theatre to tell his story about being fired, and ten thousand people—the biggest crowd in the theatre's history—showed up on a rainy night in March, tying up downtown traffic. Thousands were at the doors three and a half hours before the evening was to start. Despite everything, Burns stayed fired.)

Mrs. Chandler let Crossen go soon after she fired Burns. But it was too late. The Board said flatly: "The board has no confidence that CJOR Limited can, as a licensee, exercise sufficient supervision and direction of the station to ensure its operation in the public interest. . . ." It ordered the station sold—the first time in the history of Canadian broadcasting that a radio licence was lifted.

For a lot of reasons, I was definitely interested in taking a run at 'OR. My car dealership on Main Street—my mother hen—was sick; it wasn't making any money. GM had boxed me into a tight spot there, and its corporate policy wouldn't allow me to have more than one franchise. I had to grow in other directions. And broadcasting appealed to me. It wasn't as if I was buying something unknown like a cattle ranch or a coal mine. As a retail advertiser, I was familiar with radio, and knew that a well-run station could be a profitable business. CJOR's frequency was 600, electronically the best spot on the dial of the half-dozen private stations in the market. 'OR also held the Muzak franchise for Vancouver. There was even a bit of sentiment: I'd performed on the station's amateur hour when I was just two and a half trumpets high.

It must have taken me a month to get through to Mrs. Chandler. Her tough, middle-aged secretary, Dawn Draper, controlled access to her. I took Dawn out to lunch and dinner before convincing her to give me an appointment to meet her boss. If she hadn't taken a liking to me, my life wouldn't have turned out quite the way it has. When I finally did get to see Marie Chandler during the summer of '65, she invited me to her downtown West End apartment. She was always pouring me big tumblers of straight Scotch or rye which I'd accept to be sociable, but when she left the room, I'd dump out the open window or into her plants. What I soon discovered was that, at various times, more than twenty companies or individuals had been after the station. She'd already been negotiating deals to sell it to other people. Four station employees even had a signed preliminary agreement to buy it: manager John Donaldson, general sales manager Jerry Altman, news director Alex Young, and salesman Keith McMyn. Although they'd agreed to pay $459,000, they really had no way of raising the first $50,000 installment. Mrs. Chandler then offered the station to British Columbia Television, which owned a Vancouver TV station and—typical of the small, closed world of Canadian broadcasting—had direct or indirect corporate links to two other local radio stations. BCTV was prepared to pay $575,000 and actually began investing in CJOR through debentures, named new directors, and changed the station's bank. But when Mrs. Chandler heard that Ottawa might not approve of BCTV because of multiple-ownership concerns, she entertained an offer from Bill Bellman of CHQM, who merely wanted to move his station to 600 on the dial. Finally, when she heard that Bellman probably wouldn't be acceptable to the Board of Broadcast Governors, she agreed to talk to me.

Not that I had the money. But recently I'd met Ralph Cunningham, the financially sound, Establishment owner of a provincial chain of Cunningham Drug Stores and president of the Vancouver Board of Trade. He agreed to become my partner, which gave me both financial clout and credibility. Then, at the last minute, we cut in the four 'OR employees for a third of the action after Jerry Altman called me up to say: "You're fourth in line, and we're first in line, but you've got the money and we haven't; let's all be partners together." This was just a few days before the Board licence hearings. After thoroughly rehearsing answers to all the possible questions the Board might ask, we flew to Ottawa—where there were five other competitors for the station. Among them were Bill Bellman and BCTV. Just to make it interesting, one of the major shareholders of BCTV was J. Stuart McKay, who was married to the sister of my partner, Ralph Cunningham. Another BCTV shareholder was Peter Paul Saunders (who later ran Versatile Corporation); early on, during an Air Canada flight, he'd bet me a buck that I wouldn't get the licence. When BCTV made its high bid for 'OR, I'd mailed him the dollar. I was too hasty: In the fall of '65, we were awarded the licence for the station.

Afterwards, there was a little hitch when I was about to sign a final partnership agreement with the four station employees. Their lawyer, Fred Long (the brother of my old friend, Roy Long), advised them not to sign, pointing out they could keep their shares only as long as they continued to be employed at the station. Despite his advice, they signed. Two years later, I gained controlling interest when the Board approved my purchase of Ralph Cunningham's shares, and subsequently I bought out all four station employees.

The station had lost $462,000 the year we bought it; the BCTV debentures had to be repaid; and we had to deal with a bushel of lawsuits for alleged libel and wrongful dismissal. We needed help in turning CJOR around—and who better to turn to than Pat Burns? In '67, when I first approached him, he was back working in his hometown of Montreal, outraging all of French Canada with his open-line show on the English-language station CKGM. When he visited Vancouver, I took him out on the biggest yacht I could find and asked him back. Pat said he couldn't return as long as John Donaldson was still at 'OR as manager. I wasn't happy with Donaldson's performance anyway, so I fired him. (That's when I first met Jack Austin, who became the influential Liberal senator. Jack, a Vancouver lawyer, negotiated John Donaldson's severance settlement—and, even though he was tough on us, he and I became friends as a result of that encounter.) But when Pat found he couldn't legally free himself from his contract with CKGM, he stayed in Montreal. Two years later, he was infuriating French-speaking Quebeckers on the issue of English school rights—even leading a protest march. The day after Premier Daniel Johnson made an impassioned speech attacking Pat Burns as the voice of unreason, the premier died. Montreal's French press exploded in anger; one weekly had a photo of Pat in a rifle's crosshairs and headlines that said: "Johnson demanded the head of this agitator—will he be assassinated?" This time when I made Pat an offer, he was eager to accept. I'd already flown to Toronto to get approval for the move from the Board of Broadcast Governors' successor, the Canadian Radio-Television Commission. If I could control Pat Burns, I asked chairman Pierre Juneau, would the CRTC tolerate his return to Vancouver? Juneau said yes. Then I had Pat agree to certain conditions, which I promised him I would never reveal. We had a handshake deal, which he's honoured to this day.

Pat's return helped improve our ratings and cashflow position immediately, and so did the operating style of the station's new manager, Don Wall of Montreal, whom Pat had recommended. In what would become a pattern in other companies I later took over, I let Wall run the business himself on a day-to-day basis—with only a couple of exceptions. One was the re-hiring of Jack Webster, who had broken into radio with 'OR in 1953 after a successful career as the hard-hitting city editor of *The Vancouver Sun*. Jack was now doing a very popular open-line, investigative program called "City Mike" for our top-rated competitor, CKNW. But when 'NW refused to renew his contract at $100,000 a year, his lawyer called me. We did the deal over dinner at the posh William Tell Restaurant, sealing it with a handshake. After agreeing to the terms—$100,000, six weeks off in the summer, and a new studio—I turned to Jack's lawyer and said: "You write the contract. Anything you put in it is all right with me." That became a pattern, too, with people I trusted.

Jack Webster brought his audience with him and 'OR began to close the ratings gap with CKNW. He was at his best barking at federal politicians in his Scottish burr. Once, after being interviewed by Jack, Prime Minister Trudeau complained to an aide: "Why does that fellow Webster hate me? He shouts at me all the time." The aide said: "Don't be upset; he shouts at everybody." I thought the world of Jack. But then our management began to consider his audience too old and in 1978 refused to give in to his demand for sixteen weeks off at the same pay. They made a big mistake by refusing to renew his contract. We lost him to television. Our ratings began to slip and have never completely recovered. In a single day in 1981, the station had to lay off fifteen employees.

Over the years, we've tried other newspapermen on the air. To compete against Jack Webster when he was still at CKNW, we hired Jack Wasserman, the *Sun*'s top columnist and a good friend of mine. Recalling that experience later, Wasserman wrote: "[Pattison] has since gambled heavily in his efforts to knock off 'NW as No. 1 station in the market. His efforts included hiring a certain well-known columnist with no previous experience to go head-to-head against Webster. The columnist escaped with his life, but only barely."

Wasserman's successor at the *Sun*, Denny Boyd, also did a talk show at 'OR, and his experience in 1974 was no happier. His was called "The Female Forum," and its focus was sex. As Boyd would reminisce in his column: "Well, it was awful; just plain unremittingly awful. It was the wrong show in the wrong city in the wrong decade, hosted by a broadcasting rookie. . . ." Women who were upset by the frankness of the subject matter picketed my Corporate Office and others would freeze up Boyd's telephone lines by calling and leaving their phones off the hook. The station killed the show after three months.

But in its run after the ratings, CJOR has been an honest-to-goodness innovator in Canadian radio. It was the first in the country with a News Talk format—no music, just news, talk, and talk shows, twenty-four hours a day. The first to hire a former provincial ombudsman to handle citizens' complaints. And the first to hire a former provincial premier as an open-line host—the NDP's Dave Barrett. The station has always been politically non-partisan in its hiring: We've had a couple of federal Conservatives as open-liners, John Reynolds and Chuck Cook; and a Social Credit cabinet minister, Rafe Mair.

Getting into the broadcasting business eventually proved profitable. Under Marie Chandler, CJOR had the regional rights to Muzak, the recorded background music operation. I flew to New York in 1965 to convince Muzak's management to allow the station to retain the rights. Competing against seven others for the franchise, I was successful—and promptly bought out my 'OR partners' shares of Muzak. Nobody else at the station was interested in the environmental-music business. At the time, Muzak had only three hundred local contracts. I put one of our used-car salesmen in charge; he revived its fortunes and doubled the number of contracts within five years. It was so attractive at that point that Allan Waters pushed me hard to sell it to him. Waters controls CHUM Ltd. of Toronto, one of Canada's biggest broadcast holding companies, which then had the Muzak franchise in Ontario. By coincidence, I sat beside him on a plane to Vancouver and, within half an hour, he was asking me if I wanted to sell our Muzak rights. He started at $250,000, and I gave him a quick "No."

Somewhere over Winnipeg, he asked: "Jimmy, would you take half a million?"

"No, I have no intention of selling it, Allan."

As the plane was on its descent into Vancouver, he said: "I'll give you three-quarters of a million for Muzak."

"You've got yourself a deal." A few years earlier, I'd bought the business from my partners for $10,000.

A little later, I made another neat deal with Allan Waters, who ranks as one of the finest people I've done business with. It had its start one day in late 1969 when I got a phone call from Blair McAuley of Aikens McAuley, one of Winnipeg's leading law firms. CFRW, a Winnipeg AM and FM radio station with a lot of well-known local shareholders like the McAuleys and Purveses, was going bankrupt. It hadn't turned a profit since it opened six years before. "They went off the air today," the lawyer told me. "Maybe it's something you should look at."

I had to act fast. We had to get that station back on the air the very next morning so the government wouldn't cancel its licence for failing to operate.

I checked the airline schedule and then called five of our staff to grab a plane with me to Winnipeg that night. Before dawn, we were in the station: Wilf Ray, Maureen Chant, a CJOR employee named Jack Stewart, and one of our executives, Tiff Trimble. They had no permission to be there, but Tiff got a key after tracking down the announcer who'd made the final sign-off the day before. Maureen arranged to have the phones and hydro reconnected. All the news wires were down, so Wilf signed on with a newscast borrowed from the pages of several different papers he'd bought.

It was an incredible feat: The station had signed off, supposedly forever, at 5:00 P.M.; Blair McAuley had phoned me in Vancouver about four hours later; and first thing the next morning, CFRW was somehow on the air with a ghost staff, astonishing Winnipeg listeners. "Mystery Radio Station on the Air", one headline read.

That morning, I saw the lawyer for one of the major shareholders. Harry Dunbar went to the receiver, a crusty chartered accountant, to ask him not to pull the financial plug. CFRW, in receivership, was being offered for public tender. We were counting on the fact that, by acting fast, we'd be the only bidders at a bankruptcy hearing and be able to buy it for a song. If enough people got interested, it might have sold for as much as $750,000. No one bid against us; we paid $100,000. And it was only when I flew back to Vancouver that I called our bank from the airport to make sure I could arrange the financing; the B.C. manager, Doug Gardiner, gave me the okay over the phone.

Tiff Trimble took CFRW over, changed its sound from "good music" to hard rock, and turned it around financially within six months. It became Manitoba's top rock station. A couple of years later, Allan Waters bought it from me for $2.3 million. And I held on to the station's property near Portage and Main, which we just recently sold.

We've since bought more radio stations and a television station in B.C. and even had a run at buying *The Vancouver Sun*. Max Bell controlled *The Calgary Albertan* and the two daily papers in Victoria when he became partners with Victor Sifton of *The Winnipeg Free Press* to create the nine-paper FP Publications group. Before his death in '72, I approached Bell in Palm Springs to see if he was interested in selling the *Sun*. It was my home-town paper and it would have been a good investment. I recall an offer of about $38 million, but Max Bell told me it really wasn't for sale.

In 1983 we did get into the magazine-publishing business. The B.C. Ministry of Tourism decided to sell its glossy quarterly publication proclaiming the attractions and activities of the province. Competing against several other bidders, we bought *Beautiful British Columbia,* Western Canada's largest paid-circulation magazine, with a worldwide subscription base of more than 300,000. The company—operated by Audrey LaPointe, vice-president, managing director—also produces books and an annual gift catalogue featuring B.C. crafts.

Magazines, newspapers, radio—I've always had a soft spot for the media, from as far back as the days when I was tearing around town on the back of a newspaper-delivery truck. These days, I rely on the media for much of my general financial information. I have five television sets on one wall of my living-room. When I'm watching the news, they're usually all on together, with the sound running on one of them at a time. I don't watch TV for pleasure. And I've seen only two movies in my life: *Dr. Zhivago*, which Bob Bentall of Dominion Construction took me to see with a group of other people; and *The Godfather*, which I figured was research when I was about to meet some American businessmen with questionable connections. Although I never read fiction, I faithfully keep up with *Fortune*, *Forbes*, *Business Week*, and *Newsweek*. During Expo, I had no time for even newspapers so I saved the last year's worth of *The Globe and Mail* and *The Wall Street Journal*. They were lined up in piles along the length of the indoor swimming pool in my home. For weeks after the fair, I spent night after night reading every copy for its business news.

In the old days, one of my best friends was Jack Wasserman, who chronicled all my ups and downs in his *Sun* column. For years I had dinner with him once a week; we even played the penny stocks together. Jack died in 1977 and there's never been a journalist friend in my life to replace him. But I continue to respect most reporters. I can tell in a few minutes whether I'm dealing with amateurs or professionals by the amount of homework they've done. Generally, they've treated me fairly, even when I was at the eye of the hurricane at Expo.

In our own broadcast operations, I believe in allowing breadth of opinion and independence. You hire good people to go on the air and then give them the freedom to express their opinions responsibly and with good taste. I've had hundreds of letters over the years telling me we shouldn't allow the Pat Burnses or the Jack Websters on CJOR. When I hired Dave Barrett, Social Crediters confronted me: "Why are you promoting socialism when you're not a socialist? You can't do that! What kind of Socred are you?" (In fact, I don't belong to the party.) Or if one of our hosts features a psychic, bam!, within ten minutes we hear complaints from the Christian fundamentalists. But these are the public airwaves, we're using a frequency given to us by the CRTC, and I happen to believe that having a radio or television station is not a right but a privilege. Therefore, it's important to express all points of view, whether I agree with them or not. I don't believe in censorship; I do believe in freedom of speech with responsibility.

Today, CJOR doesn't loom very large in the Jim Pattison Group's scheme of things. Yet I continue to have a fondness for it, because twenty years ago it allowed me to make our move into the rarified world of takeovers and conglomerates and international finance—big business.

CHAPTER SEVEN

Taking Over

Even in the relatively tight business community in Vancouver in the 1960s, an upstart car dealer from the East End like me wasn't likely to be on a comfortable social footing with a well-placed drugstore magnate. Under normal circumstances, I'd never have met Ralph Cunningham, who was a financier and the owner of the flourishing Cunningham Drug Stores chain. He'd never have become my partner and given me the credibility I needed with the banks and the Board of Broadcast Governors to buy CJOR. And without the essential cashflow of that radio station, I could never have financed the takeover of Neon Products of Canada. Which turned out to be the most exciting deal of my young life.

Ralph Cunningham and I met through a unique international group that, out of choice, keeps a very low profile with the public. I've heard the Young Presidents' Organization described as everything from a secret society of capitalists to the best consulting service in the world. YPO turned my life around.

At the time I joined in 1964, the organization was only fourteen years old. Ray Hickok of Rochester, N.Y., launched it at twenty-seven after taking on the family business—the world's largest manufacturer of men's belts and jewellery—and realizing he could use the counsel of other entrepreneurial executives. YPO's purpose is "to help its members become better presidents through education and idea exchange." The concept really worked: It now has about a hundred chapters in fifty countries. But it's an exclusive club of no more than five thousand men and women. Members today must be presidents of corporations with gross annual revenue of at least $4 million U.S. and a minimum of fifty employees (or financial institutions with average assets of $80 million U.S., or service firms with annual fees or commissions of $2.5 million U.S.). They must have become presidents of their companies before age thirty-nine and—to keep the organization fresh—have to leave YPO on their fiftieth birthday. On average, 40 per cent of members own family businesses; 30 per cent have bought a company or were hired to run one; and the remaining 30 per cent are entrepreneurs like me who founded their own companies. There are no initiation fees, and individual chapters set their own annual dues, which seldom go above $1,000. Many presidents apply for membership, but relatively few are chosen. The major challenge is to get sponsored, survive the screening, and be accepted by other chapter members and YPO's New York headquarters. One reason for rejecting an applicant is that his or her specific type of business is already represented among members; competition would inhibit frank discussion that involved trade secrets.

YPO came to Canada in '55; among the members of the seven regional Canadian chapters are people of the calibre of George Cohon of McDonald's, Galen Weston of George Weston Ltd., and Ontario premier David Peterson. After hearing about the organization from a Toronto car-dealer member— Jack Carmichael of City Buick—I joined at the age of thirty-two, six months before my new GM dealership opened on Main Street. I'd asked a Vancouver car-dealer friend, Evan Wolfe, to sponsor me in YPO but he refused (Evan later became B.C.'s provincial secretary, my first boss when I became chairman of Expo 86). My sponsor was the landlord of my body shop, Abe Gray of Gray Beverages, Vancouver's major soft-drink distributor. Most of the local members were second-generation monied or had married into wealth, like Maurie Young of Finning Tractor, Frank Griffiths of Western Broadcasting, and Graham Dawson of Dawson Construction (and later Andrés Wines and Daon Development). I was very quiet at first. I listened. And learned.

YPO can be tremendously important for young executives with limited knowledge and few contacts. Describing its benefits, business writer Rod McQueen once wrote about my encounter with a Sudbury businessman, Peter Crossgrove: "[Crossgrove] was sitting disconsolately beside a phone at a YPO conference fifteen years ago when Jim Pattison of Vancouver, now chairman of Expo 86, happened along. Crossgrove had just hung up from his Royal Bank of Canada branch manager, who not only wouldn't approve a loan request but wouldn't let Crossgrove make a direct pitch to regional headquarters in Toronto. Pattison phoned a friend, Ted McDowell, now a vice-chairman at the Toronto-Dominion Bank, and McDowell quickly arranged for Crossgrove to get the money he needed. (As a result, Crossgrove switched both his personal and company business to the TD.)"

Our chapter held meetings in clubs and restaurants, in private homes, and on islands. We'd hear timely guest speakers or even be briefed by provincial cabinet members; every session was closed to the press. There'd be regional meetings of several chapters where I might be in charge of transportation or an audio-visual presentation. Some of my most crucial learning came at these gatherings and at what YPO calls its Universities for Presidents—international conferences, held three times a year around the world, which feature renowned speakers and experienced instructors with practical business skills. It was at a YPO meeting in Hawaii where—by chance, like Peter Crossgrove—I first considered the possibility of taking over Neon Products. And it was at a later YPO meeting in Arizona that I began to learn exactly how I could take Neon over.

By 1967, I desperately wanted to diversify, to build a Canadian growth company. I had a base: Combined, Jim Pattison on Main, our leasing company, CJOR, and the local Muzak franchise gave me a net worth of about $760,000. From the bank's point of view, the radio station in particular was a valuable property as a strong generator of cash; bankers generally don't consider car-dealerships' earnings as stable as broadcasting's.

I'd told stockbrokers to keep on the lookout for any companies that might be worth taking over. Then I attended

Taking Over

a YPO regional meeting in Maui. I was walking through the lounge of the Sheraton Hotel when I overheard a fellow tell some friends that Arthur Christopher (who owned the Vancouver-based Nelson Laundries chain) held control of Neon Products with only 2 per cent of the stock. Art's son, Gordon, was a member of my chapter of the Young Presidents' Organization. There I was in Hawaii and, by an accident of timing, I'd learned a key piece of information about a Vancouver company that had always fascinated me. I realized that if Christopher controlled Neon with such a tiny amount of stock, it was ripe for a takeover.

And it was one public company I would love to own. Although back in 1950 Neon refused to hire me because I was too young and too short, I knew it was the finest sign company in Canada. It manufactured neon signs and tubing in Vancouver and Toronto and leased its products across the country. Its subsidiary, Seaboard Advertising, was the major billboard company in Vancouver and Victoria. As a customer, I knew Neon; among other things, they'd built the world's largest electrical sign for me when I was managing Bow Mac. And, with our own car-lease company, I knew the beauty of the leasing business: Neon had $16.4 million worth of forward contracts committed over the next five years.

Back in Vancouver, I pored over Neon's annual reports. The company had always been a blue-blood operation. The first board of directors, back in 1928, included the likes of Gordon Farrell, president of B.C. Telephone; W.C. Woodward of the Vancouver department-store empire; J.P.D. Malkin, a turn-of-the-century wholesale food supplier (bought out by Weston's); and Harold E. Molson of the English side of the Montreal Molsons, who'd married a Malkin. In '67, Neon had six hundred employees; annual sales of about $8.5 million; profits of $664,000; and earnings of about 8 per cent on sales. At a time when cash was tight, it was in a terrifically liquid position: Management had used a loan from the Prudential Insurance Co. of America to retire most of the outstanding debt and double the capital. There was minor long-term debt of $3.7 million but Neon had $1 million in the bank, lots of unused credit with the bank, and cashflow of $3.8 million. A company with a steady stream of income and (according to my tax advisor, Don Selman) offering a lot of shelter against taxes.

All in all, Neon Products' solid assets and money management meant that, with proper handling, its earnings per share could be increased substantially. Earnings per share are that part of a company's profit allocated to each outstanding share of common stock. If a company earned ten million the previous year and had ten million shares outstanding, its earnings would be reported as $1 per share. And, as I'd discovered from my YPO seminars on mergers and acquisitions, earnings per share was the name of the game for big American conglomerates like Litton Industries and Jimmy Ling's LTV Corporation.

For a couple of years, I attended as many of these seminars as possible. The most interesting ones featured the number-two man at Boise Cascade Corporation, Bob Halliday. Boise Cascade was founded just before the First World War as a lumber company based in Boise, Idaho. That's what it remained until 1957 when a top Harvard Business School graduate, Robert Vail Hansberger, became chief executive officer. Hansberger started diversifying into pulp and paper, packaging, building materials, office supplies, housing, and urban development. The public company—by now a conglomerate—still operated out of Boise (population 73,000) but in a decade its sales had climbed from $35 million a year to nearly $1 billion. And its earnings per share had increased sevenfold. Executive vice-president Bob Halliday—Boston-born of Canadian parents, a Yale economics grad—was co-architect of its extraordinary expansion. At the YPO seminars, he lectured on ways of identifying appropriate companies to go after, structuring the takeovers for tax purposes, and dealing with the resulting people problems.

In the spring of '67, during a seminar at the Carefree Inn outside of Phoenix, I approached Bob Halliday. A big, bluff guy, he was sitting at poolside when I introduced myself and said I was about to go into the acquisitions business and build one of the first Canadian conglomerates. "I've picked out a company and I'd like you to look it over and give me some advice," I said. "Oh, and by the way, you see that fellow across the pool"—I pointed to Gordon Christopher—"he's the son of the chairman of the company I want to acquire."

Halliday looked over the figures I had on Neon Products and told me the company appeared interesting. We discussed my approach, he gave me some pointers on takeovers, and I went away believing I could make it happen.

Our next conversation was over the phone when I called him for the name of someone on Wall Street to help me raise money. "There are two people I recommend," he said. "One is an older guy at Lehman's—a real pro. And the other is Mike Dingman, a good, hard-working young man at Burnham's. If you put him on a project, he'll work his tail off and do it a lot cheaper too."

I related to the guy he described as a hustler: Mike Dingman at the New York investment banking firm of Burnham & Co.

Calling him, I said: "My name is Jim Pattison. You don't know me. I'm in YPO. I've been going to mergers and acquisitions courses for the last couple of years. One of the lecturers there was a guy I was very impressed with—Bob Halliday of Boise Cascade. I've just talked to him. He's given me your name as somebody who can help me. I want to build a Canadian conglomerate."

"Who are you?" Mike Dingman asked.

"Jim Pattison, a car dealer in Vancouver. The only thing I can tell you is that I've been on the advisory council of GM in Detroit for two years."

"Okay, I want to check you out," he said. Dingman's father was vice-chairman of American Telephone and Telegraph (AT&T) and had created the Communications Satellite Corporation. And Dingman senior was on the ComSat board with Fred Donner, who was GM's chairman in Detroit. Mike checked me out.

There have been four people who have shaped my life, influenced me in the most profound way: my father; Dan McLean of Bow Mac Motors; GM's Canadian vice-president, Jeff Umphrey; and Michael David Dingman, one of the brightest, most attractive, and most articulate people you could ever meet in American business. He was thirty-five, a general partner with a little office at Burnham & Co. (which later became the influential Drexel Burnham Lambert). Mike stands more than six-foot-four and comes from a well-to-do family. But we did have some things in common: He'd dropped out of college, too, after attending the University of Maryland for two years; and, like me, he was rapidly losing his hair. After college, he took a job sweeping floors in a Newark factory before selling automatic streetlight switches for Sigma Corporation near Boston. Although he was making $50,000 a year, it was too easy; at thirty-three, he threw himself into the investment banking world at Burnham's, taking a $30,000 cut in pay. By 1967, he was a rising star—and in years to come, he would do some of the biggest deals Wall Street has ever seen.

When Mike called me back, I invited him to Vancouver. He brought along a friend, a senior partner with Burnham's New York law firm, Mark Kaplan. A lawyer's son, Mark had grown up in the Bronx, attended public schools, and graduated from Columbia Law School. Where he was raised, if you owned a car dealership, you were considered a successful man. Brilliant and opinionated, Mark is more of a philosopher than the deal-making Mike Dingman.

On a late-summer day in 1967, they stepped off the plane and into my life. They were wearing bankers' clothes and they were smart. Wanting to impress them, I took them to the plush waterfront hotel, the Bayshore Inn, and then out on a charter boat for a harbour tour of the city they'd never seen. They met Don Selman, our accountant, and Harry Dunbar, our secretary-treasurer. I'd had Wilf Ray, our ad manager, create a slide show that summed up the Jimmy Pattison story. Driving down to the Bayshore, Wilf was still sorting slides in the middle of the Lion's Gate Bridge. It may have been corny and naive, but our little homemade show impressed Mike and Mark. Wilf narrated it in his buttersmooth tones:

MUSIC UP AND FADE
From New York, the World's Greatest City, two business executives left over the weekend to travel to the Nicest City on the North American Continent . . . Vancouver . . . to meet a man with mutual interests. A man who wholeheartedly believes in the American Way of Life. This film presentation was especially prepared for Michael Dingman and Mark Kaplan . . . so they might acquire a further insight into the Man . . . Jim Pattison.
MUSIC UP AND FADE

It pulled out all the stops, making our few companies sound like a mini-empire. We told them I worked seven days a week, stopping only on Sundays to take my family to church; that I was involved in the community as vice-president of the Better Business Bureau and a director of the Greater Vancouver Tourist Association; that I did volunteer work for the provincial Socreds and the federal Liberals; and that I had a wife and three kids and a German schnauzer, Herman ("Imported from New York, Herman took two months to housebreak and has never been seen outside of the Pattison home located in the British Properties in West Vancouver").

Mike and Mark said later they were influenced by my energy and willingness to take a risk; all I needed was some money and knowledge. After seeing our financial statements, they left with souvenir desktop totem poles in their suitcases and the resolve to help find me the cash to pursue Neon Products. Not long after, they asked me to meet the principals of Burnham & Co.: I.B. (Tubby) Burnham II, Mark Edersheim (who'd become vice-chairman of Drexel Burnham), and Alan Newmark, Mike's immediate boss, an outstanding lawyer and financier. All of them had monied friends and they convinced me to get financial backing for the takeover attempt from outside the banking community; they didn't trust commercial bankers as much as I did. Burnham itself would back me through an offshore vehicle called Worldwide Funds. And Tubby Burnham said he knew an influential Canadian who lived in New York, Paul Nathanson. The heir to the Famous Players movie-theatre fortune, Nathanson decided to invest and would later play a vital role in the takeover. Mike Dingman introduced me to Larry Hoguet, the heavy-set, cigar-smoking vice-president of finance for Engelhard Minerals and Chemicals of New Jersey, founded by American metals king Charles Engelhard. Hoguet, a nice man with good connections, was a commercial banker at a time when you reached that position with the right social background. I never did meet Charles Engelhard, had no idea of his history: for instance, that he'd imported gold in the form of jewellery from South Africa, an idea that his friend Ian Fleming would use in *Goldfinger*, modelling the nicer side of his villain on Engelhard. Eventually South Africa's Harry Oppenheimer became his partner, and Charles Engelhard became known as the world platinum king, his enormous empire extending over six continents. One of America's ten richest men—with villas in five countries and a stable of 250 race horses—he was an intimate friend of presidents Kennedy and Johnson. But about all I knew at the time was that a vice-president of one of his corporations was willing to invest in a car-dealer's attempt to take over a sign company in Vancouver, Canada.

From the start, I realized the takeover of Neon Products would have to be unfriendly. As I told *Vancouver Sun* reporter (now international trade minister) Pat Carney after the dust had settled: "These guys control the town. If I had said I'm a car dealer, and I want your company, I'd have been thrown out of their offices." The company's current board members were as Establishment as the original ones: Senator John Nichol, president of the National Liberal Foundation; D.P. Rogers, of the Toronto broadcasting Rogerses, a former president of Toronto's Union Gas; W.E. Thomson, chairman of Pemberton Securities; company president Harvey Smith, a veteran of two decades of steelmaking and dam-building with Kaiser Resources in the United States; chairman Art Christopher, a director of MacMillan Bloedel; local lawyer Charles Brazier, senior partner in Davis & Co., and a director of Pacific Western Airlines; Stan Whittle, who ran Neon in Ontario; two of the original directors, lawyer George E. Housser and Victoria businessman R.H.B. Ker; and—to keep it lively—Alan Eyre, president of the Dueck GM dealership that I'd been trying to top ever since I got into the car business.

Discovering the names of the shareholders was a little more difficult. I had Maureen Chant do a bit of detective work to find a shareholders' statement. Neon turned out to be the most widely held public company in the electrical-sign business. I already knew that the chairman, Christopher, held only 2 per cent. But he controlled a block of stock that included the holdings of the largest shareholder, his good friend William M. Anderson. The president of the Canadian Chamber of Commerce, Bill Anderson was also a partner in the same Vancouver accounting firm that audited Neon's books (which placed him in enough of a conflict-of-interest position that the Institute of Chartered Accountants later fined him $200 for professional misconduct). With Anderson's 7 per cent of the shares as well as other stock held by directors, Art Christopher commanded 15.8 per cent of Neon's common stock—which amounted to effective control of the company.

Taking Over

The takeover had to be done quietly, without revealing who was buying up the Neon stock. I had a $1 million line of credit with the Cambie and Broadway branch of the Royal Bank. That would be my pot to begin acquiring shares. Unfortunately, Art Christopher was a director of the bank and had his Nelson Laundries account at the same branch. So I couldn't tell Royal's manager, Ed Bowser, what I was doing. My credit line was supposed to finance the inventory for our car business. That September, a month before the new models would arrive, our used-car inventory was extremely low. Which meant that we didn't owe the bank much, if anything, and we could use our credit line to buy Neon shares without the Royal's knowing what securities we were buying.

During the next couple of months, I started buying stock for $7 a share through Mike Dingman at New York's Burnham & Co. and through the Toronto investment firm of T.A. Richardson. We kept bidding up the price, never buying more than three hundred to five hundred shares at a time, to avoid making the major stockholders suspicious. Nobody knew who was buying; the word out on the street was that it was either a mutual fund or a large conglomerate in Minneapolis. Apparently at one meeting of the Neon board, Senator Nichol asked why the stock was rising and none of the directors had an answer.

But as he looked over my monthly financial statements, the Royal's Bowser would spot a line that read: "Marketable securities." When he'd ask me what it meant, I refused to tell him. My accountants, Peat Marwick, offered to give Doug Gardiner, the Royal's head man in B.C., a letter that confirmed that these marketable securities were trading securities with a certain specified value—to assure the bank that they did represent a real asset. This didn't satisfy Bowser. So one Friday in early November, without warning, he sent me a letter that called my loan. Suddenly I had no line of credit. At our dealership I had all these new cars coming and no cash to finance the trade-ins. And now there was no more money for my takeover attempt.

The situation was desperate. I called Mike Dingman. "Dammit, Jimmy, they can't do that to you," he said. I flew to New York to consult with him and on Monday morning he took me in to see Tubby Burnham—who phoned Famous Players' Paul Nathanson for me: "Jimmy's got a problem in

Canada with the Royal Bank and we'd like to see if you can help him."

I've heard Paul Nathanson described as reclusive. He lived in Jacqueline Kennedy's apartment block on Fifth Avenue. After I got through the tight security, Nathanson answered the door to his darkly lit apartment in a dressing gown. He heard me out, then asked: "Have you ever heard of Lazarus Phillips? I'm going to phone him." Phillips was a prominent Jewish Liberal (he'd be named a senator a year later), a founder of the Phillips and Vineberg law firm in Montreal, and a confidant of the Bronfmans (he set up the wide-ranging Cemp Investments as a trust for the Bronfman children). Most important to me, Phillips was also a director of the Royal Bank of Canada. Now, in return for putting me together with Phillips, Paul Nathanson had a quid pro quo: He had me promise that I would go to work on the Liberal leadership campaign of Paul Martin. Lester Pearson was retiring as prime minister and Martin was a friend of Nathanson's. (And I did help out in his campaign on the West Coast.)

I flew to Montreal that night; nine o'clock the next morning, I was in Lazarus Phillips' office. He was a gracious man (I learned later he was a Talmudic scholar and an art collector) and I had a good introduction to him. He listened to me without saying a word. After ten minutes, he picked up the phone: "Earle, this is Lazarus Phillips. I'd like to see you right away."

W. Earle McLaughlin, the tough-talking chairman of the Royal, Canada's biggest bank. ("If the government had designed the Edsel," he once said, "they'd still be producing it.") We met. I told him that his people in Vancouver had taken away my $1 million line of credit.

"You've got it back right now," he said. "Don't worry about it." I would get a special $1 million loan that would let me continue buying Neon stock.

From Burnham to Nathanson to Phillips to McLaughlin. I was home Tuesday night, my credit line restored—as confirmed in a call from Doug Gardiner: "You've been down to see Mr. McLaughlin."

"Yes, I have."

"And we have instructions to give your line of credit back."

"Yes, I understand that."

"Well, you have it," Gardiner said. "Could I have the letter back, please?" I handed over the now-embarrassing letter from the Royal calling my loan.

Meanwhile, the Neon stock had reached $9 and we'd stopped buying. Although we had about 6 per cent of the outstanding shares, we needed at least 9 or 10 per cent more. If Art Christopher didn't sell his shares, I could be in a real bind: I'd be stuck with what I had, with no prospect for control, and it would take me a long time to get rid of my stock.

And then on Friday, November 10, I got a terrific surprise. T.A. Richardson in Toronto had a call from a stockholder who wanted to sell 175,000 shares. The caller was none other than Neon's chairman, Arthur Christopher, wanting to get rid of his control block. He had no idea whom he was selling to; and he didn't bother telling anybody else on his board what he was doing. But when we learned that Christopher wanted to sell, our people immediately approached Neon's president, Harvey Smith, with an offer to buy his 20,000 shares too. All of a sudden, the company was within our grasp.

That Friday moved faster—and slower—than any day I'd ever experienced. By now a Richardson representative from Toronto was in New York with Mike Dingman. While the two Western principals in the deal sat in Vancouver, the Eastern investment guys were working out the details at the other end of the continent. We began by offering Art Christopher $10 per share. Mike kept in constant touch by phone; the conversations went like this:

Mike: . . . I don't know whether Harvey Smith is in it [the share offering], but I made it clear to my guy that we wanted the company to remain as is, all we wanted was control of the board.

Me: Well, you see, Smith represented twenty thousand shares of this thing.

Mike: You want Smith in?

Me: We want Smith in. And this is an important thing. It's a key point as far as running the company. If Smith is out, we're looking for a new president.

Mike: Okay.

Me: Now, it seems to me the way for us to go is to bid Art Christopher ten dollars firm.
Mike: The broker says he won't take it.
Me: How does he know?
Mike: That's what he said. *[Pause]* He said he's absolutely convinced he won't take it.
Me: Well, there's only one thing to do . . . is try.
Mike: No, that's what in effect we did, Jimmy. You've really got to decide whether you want to go to ten and a half. . . . He came back and said eleven. He'd already been offered ten—period.
Me: Why don't you split it with him and go ten and a half?
Mike: Well, that's what I've been thinking of.
Me: Okay, if you've done that, I'd say go ten and a half and that's it. Take it or leave it . . .

Meanwhile, Mike was negotiating with Paul Nathanson, Engelhard's, and Worldwide Funds to get me enough cash to replace my lines of credit that I was using up on this takeover. I needed $550,000 for our car company and $500,000 to buy my third of the stock offering—as well as $75,000 to keep our business going. In one call, Mike told me: "I talked to Nathanson and he said he only has to make one phone call and you'll have your money. And he said, you know, it will take him a couple of minutes to do it . . . he's making the phone call. You'll get your money."

Finally I got the call I was waiting for:

Mike: Jimmy?
Me: Yeah?
Mike: You've got yourself a company.
Me: We've got ourself a deal, eh? *[Believe me, I was a hang of a lot more excited than I sounded.]*
Mike: You know what Christopher said when he heard it was you?
Me: No.
Mike: "Jesus Christ!" He said: "You know, the guy only lives two miles from me." And: "Where the hell is Jimmy getting all the money from?"

Taking Over

It was the first major hostile takeover in Western Canada, a classic out of the Eastern textbooks. Art Christopher had finally sold his block of 175,000 shares for $10.75 apiece—for a total of $1.88 million. I'd paid an average of just over $9 for all the shares I acquired over two months. My partners and I now controlled 20 per cent of Neon Products; we asked for, and got, control of the board. And afterwards, continuing to buy with borrowed money as the price fell back to $9, I soon became the largest single shareholder.

At a directors' meeting in November, Senator John Nichol resigned, protesting that Christopher shouldn't have sold his block without informing the other directors. I called a board meeting in January 1968, where Ker and Rogers resigned as directors for personal reasons. They were replaced by Mike Dingman and Larry Hoguet. I was named managing director, with the mandate to go after new companies. Art Christopher didn't like the idea: "I used to be chairman of a sign business," he told Pat Carney. "Now they want to make a conglomerate out of us." Some of my colleagues—including our secretary-treasurer, Harry Dunbar—had recommended that I get rid of Christopher and his old friend, Charlie Brazier. But they were conservative, well-spoken insiders in the Vancouver business community. And I was an outsider who'd come off the street wearing a plaid jacket and talking an aggressive game. In a decision that I'd come to regret a couple of years later, I kept them on the board.

CHAPTER EIGHT

The Rise of Neonex International

The 1960s were the go-go years of the conglomerates. In the United States, another Jimmy—Jimmy Ling—had turned $2,000 and a little electrician's shop into a $3.7 billion colossus called Ling-Temco-Vought Inc. America's fourteenth-largest industrial corporation, it had a higher public profile than other established conglomerates like Gulf & Western, ITT, and Litton Industries. A 1966 article in *Fortune* defined a conglomerate as a corporation involved in at least eight different businesses. Generally the term came to describe public corporations that had grown quickly in recent years by trading their stock to buy companies in fields outside their own. Of them all, Jimmy Ling's was the biggest: He'd combined the largest U.S. sporting-goods manufacturer, the third-largest meat packer, the sixth-largest steel company, and the eighth-largest defence contractor and airline—among a lot of others. They called him Jimmy Ling, the Merger King.

When I was getting into the game in 1968, I had no idea that North American conglomerates were about to lose their popular appeal as investment vehicles. Or that within two years Ling would be out of a job. Yet, even though I was starting from scratch, by '70 we'd create a Canadian conglomerate with more than four thousand employees and $159 million in annual sales. And I'd more than reach my goal of being a millionaire by forty.

There weren't many role models to follow in building a conglomerate in this country. Looking back on it now, I imagine that corporations like Anthes Imperial, Dylex (Diversified Industries), and Seaway Multi-Corp. qualified. But the only recent conglomerate of any consequence I knew of was Sogemines Limited of Montreal. Its name was an abbreviation of Société Générale des Mines, founded by a Belgium corporation with worldwide interests in resources, shipping, and banking. Sogemines became better-known by the name it took in '69: Genstar Corporation. Genstar—which (like me) never approved of the label "conglomerate"—began by manufacturing chemicals and cement, distributing steel and rubber, and operating tugboats and barges. It would open a real-estate wing that came to rank among Canada's biggest developers. Eventually, Genstar evolved into one of the most diversified conglomerates in the country.

Because Sogemines was the only real model for a Canadian conglomerate, we tried to learn a little from their experience. Don Selman, our accountant at Peat Marwick in Vancouver, was so good that we continued to use him even when his firm moved him to Montreal. Don consulted Warren Chippendale, a senior audit partner in the Montreal office of Coopers & Lybrand who handled the Sogemines account. Chippendale was an expert in a new variation on an accounting principle called "pooling of interests." And it was the revised principle that helped make conglomerates like Sogemines happen. I'd first heard about it from Bob Halliday of Boise Cascade during the mergers-and-acquisitions seminars he gave for the Young Presidents' Organization. Halliday was acknowledged as one of the North American pioneers in pooling of interests. In essence, the original concept was that, through an exchange of common shares, you'd merge your public company with another company of about the same size and in a similar business; you'd then re-state the past year's economic performance of your company based on the performance of the company you'd bought. And the balance sheets of the two companies would be added together, item by item. If you had chosen the right company to merge with, this accounting tactic could help increase your earnings per share— because you didn't have to increase the book value of your assets and so increase the depreciation charges. The conglomerates put pressure on their accountants to broaden the principle so that it was possible to merge with any company as long as common shares were exchanged. That meant that your earnings-per-share picture could improve dramatically.

In practice, here's how it worked: You own a company that made $1 million last year and broke even this year. Then, on the last day of your business year, you decide to buy another company, a bigger one, putting up the stock of your own company to acquire it. If you'd acquired a company that had lost, say, $10 million last year and made $10 million this year, you would combine the economic histories of that company with yours. Through the pooling-of-interests principle, your annual report would now show that *you'd* lost $9 million last year but earned $10 million this year. All of a sudden, it looked like your company had a terrific year, which made it an attractive prospect for investors. So you went after companies with a fast growth rate (the expression at the time was: "The company pools like a dream."). I spent a lot of time with Don Selman and his helpful and creative senior people in New York, who had the final say on what the accounting firm would put its signature on. Today, the practice of pooling of interests exists in a very restricted form in Canada. In the early '70s, it got a reputation as dirty pool, and the accounting profession went back to allowing only very limited use of it.

Before the takeover, Neon Products had been a conservatively run company with very little earnings growth—an ideal base for building a conglomerate. But first, I had to make some changes. It was a new era, needing new management. Within thirty days, I'd fired the president, Harvey Smith, and brought in a Neon executive vice-president from Toronto to run the sign company. Stan Whittle was originally from the West: Born in Victoria, he joined the Royal Bank at fifteen and Neon eight years later. He'd been with the company since 1943 and had worked in every department except the plant. Stan was a good people manager, the kind of guy who'd walk through the factory in his shirtsleeves every day and buy ten cases of cold beer for the workers at the end of a muggy shift.

In '68, to reflect the new corporate thrust, the company

The Rise of Neonex International

was renamed Neonex International Limited; Neon Products became one of its divisions. As we'd say ambitiously in our first annual report: "The word Neon is derived from the Greek—meaning 'new.' Neonex has as one of its major objectives the exploration and development of new horizons, new potentials and new ideas applied to established operations. The second syllable 'ex' in Neonex stands for expansion, both horizontally and vertically. 'International' is self-evident of our future aspirations."

On May 8—the day I'd opened the doors of my first business seven years earlier—I moved downtown from the car company into the handsome old Marine Building. Moving with me were Maureen Chant, Wilf Ray, Harry Dunbar, and Guy Lewall, who came from Neon Products to be a vice-president and secretary-treasurer. (A year later, we'd be around the corner, overlooking Vancouver harbour from the new Guinness Tower, where the Jim Pattison Group still is today.) In our first year, I became president of Neonex and continued the process of shedding the old directors and replacing them with our own people. By the end of '68, all but two of the previous board were gone. We'd kept Art Christopher as chairman and Charlie Brazier as a director because they were pillars of the local business Establishment and they'd provide some continuity. The new directors were: the trio of Americans who'd helped me stage the takeover, Mike Dingman, Larry Hoguet, and Bob Halliday; Harry Dunbar, whose title was now assistant to the president; Stuart Mitton, president of Overwaitea Ltd.; and Ross Turner, our new executive vice-president in charge of operations.

Those last two showed the direction Neonex was heading. Stu Mitton came on the board after we bought Overwaitea, a chain of fifty-one food stores outside of Metro Vancouver—the first acquisition that Neonex announced. And we'd gone after Ross Turner because of his reputation with BACM Limited, a fast-growing construction and concrete-products company in that pioneering Canadian conglomerate, Genstar. Turner—thirty-eight, six-foot-four—was an accountant before joining BACM in Winnipeg; in seven years he helped boost that company's annual sales sixfold to $100 million. He worked hard and people liked him. Eventually, when I became chairman of Neonex, he became our president and chief operating officer.

In the first year Neonex was in business, I approached more than two hundred Canadian companies about merging with us and bought thirteen of them, all but one privately owned. To let the world know we were in the market, we'd put out the word in the financial community: stockbrokers, chartered accountants, and a special group of "finders"—mergers-and-acquisitions experts who keep tabs on people who want to buy or sell companies. Although the Overwaitea deal was the first we made public, the one we closed first was the acquisition of Northern Paint in Winnipeg. Pemberton Securities led me to Art Laing and his forty-four-year-old company with a manufacturing plant, a dozen stores, and 850 dealers in Western Canada and Ontario—a nice consumer company with no debt and a good record of growth, which fit well with our plan to capitalize on poolings of interest. There was only one potential problem with Laing's company, which didn't materialize for eight years: It was heavily dependent on a major customer, Saskatoon's Federated Co-Op. I negotiated with Art Laing through one day and an evening. In what became a typical pattern, I made sure he didn't even take a break for dinner until we'd finished hammering out the deal. We acquired it for 280,000 shares of Neonex. Laing retired, but his second-in-command stayed on to run it; we always tried to keep the current management in place.

Overwaitea came to us through a Peat Marwick partner who knew the founder's daughter and controlling shareholder, an academic named Dr. Molly Kidd. The common stock was held by Stu Mitton, long-time food man, and by the chain's 375 employees. The company had been a good place to work ever since its founding in 1915 by Robert Kidd, a blender of Irish tea and a coffee roaster. Its name, an odd one for a food company, came from the fact that Kidd packaged every pound of tea with an extra two ounces—"overweight tea." Early on, the founder had allowed employees to own all the common shares. This enlightened policy had a negative side after his death: Because the managers felt they had to show a high rate of return on the employees' stock, they established a policy of no corporate borrowing, and that prevented any real growth. When we bought it, Overwaitea was free of debt. But, with only 3 per cent of the food business in B.C., it was David facing Safeway's Goliath. Its properties were located in small towns; some of the stores were no more than three thousand square feet; none was in a shopping mall. The management was conservative: Stu Mitton literally ran it out of his desk drawer, from an elastic-bound batch of filing cards with notes on sales and other figures. There were some pluses, too. Because the owners had left it alone, Overwaitea had developed a strong pool of independent managers. It had a higher return on sales than most food companies and enough of a profit to contribute to our earnings per share. And it was innovative: The year before, Overwaitea had introduced the concept of discount supermarkets to B.C. with a no-frills operation called Prairie Market.

We bounced the idea of buying the company off Mike Dingman and Bob Halliday and then negotiated at the Bayshore Inn with Dr. Kidd and her adviser, Jim Wilson of Peat Marwick in Montreal. It was a complicated deal. I traded Neonex stock for the common shares and all the equity held by the employees. But Dr. Kidd owned 54 per cent of the voting stock, the preferred shares, which we bought for cash. She had a niece she didn't get along with who held the other 46 per cent of the voting shares; the niece became our minority partner and it took us several years to buy her out. Overwaitea's final price tag, trading 1,003,820 shares of Neonex, was about $14 million. As it turned out, it was one of the best acquisitions we ever made.

Harry Dunbar and I began criss-crossing the continent in our search for suitable companies to buy. Harry himself looked at hundreds of them. On the taxi ride in from the Toronto airport, he used to detour through the streets under the expressways just to identify all the little companies that might be possibilities. He must have talked to the owners of every skirt and blouse manufacturer in the Toronto needle trade. They were cold calls, but nobody ever turned him away ("I'm not the slightest bit interested in selling," the owner would say, "but if I *were* . . ."). I was talking to anyone who might be of help in drumming up support for our stock. In a speech to the Boston Society of Security Analysts, where I was identified as James A. Pattison, I preached the strengths of Neonex and then managed to wave the Canadian flag while defending conglomerates: "Canada today needs larger companies, with all the benefits that accrue to large corporate enterprises, in order to compete with the foreign-controlled business giants which dominate Canada in almost every major field of our business activity. We need strong, Canadian companies that are tuned and geared to our Canadian ways of life . . . unless Canadian firms are allowed to continue to band together, more and more takeovers will continue to occur by the foreign-control giants from other countries, particularly from our good and friendly neighbour to the south."

We lived in planes and hotel rooms. I began to wear two watches, one of them with a double face, so I instantly knew the time on the West and East coasts and whatever other time zone I found myself in (I now also carry two pocket watches, one of them that tells time worldwide). And I learned how to travel light, taking only a briefcase and a carry-on bag. For the last twenty years, I've never carried any luggage that has to be checked, even when I went to Russia for ten days. Only one suit—on my back—which in recent years has been made of uncreasable ultra-suede, a sports shirt, a sweater for warmth on the plane, changes of socks and underclothes, and two ties, in case of a spill. And a batch of issues of *Fortune*, *Forbes*, and *Business Week*. We became masters of getting on flights at the last minute. You were nice to the ground crews, never trying to convince them how important it was to get aboard. Once, when Harry and I were trying to get home from New York via Toronto and Calgary, the plane had a mechanical problem that forced us to disembark in Toronto. I talked us on to a direct Air Canada flight to Vancouver. We loosened our collars and took off our shoes, pretending to be asleep. The passengers who were supposed to be in our seats had to sit in the small cocktail-lounge area at the front of the old DC-8. When we went to talk to them later, one said: "I've got a sneaking suspicion you're the sons of bitches who took our seats." It was on that same flight that we got paged to receive a message. Harry was going to be too late for a scheduled flight to go skiing with his family in Kelowna, so in Toronto I'd told him to call Maureen Chant and arrange a charter. Maureen—who can't be stopped—called Air Canada and convinced them to radio to our DC-8 that Harry's charter to Kelowna was all set.

By September of that first year, Neonex controlled four more companies: Reimer Express Lines, Imbrex Limited, UniverSport, and Acme Novelty. Acme, based in Edmonton,

The Rise of Neonex International

had $30 million a year in sales of fast-moving consumer goods. Run by the Van Dusen brothers, it had had a 300 per cent increase in sales in the five years before we bought it. Acme was built on a good sales gimmick: You had to have a special membership card to shop in its stores. Although anybody could have one, the card made you feel you were an insider, that you were getting things wholesale. The company did offer discount prices on thousands of items, from appliances and jewellery to padded toilet seats and monkey-pod wooden bowls. Although Acme cost us $14 million in Neonex shares, it was a good investment, making us a lot of money over the years. Eventually, though, changing market conditions and bad management decisions forced us to liquidate it.

It took me several months to buy Reimer Express Lines, a fine Winnipeg trucking company well-managed by a wonderful family, a very religious Mennonite father and his three sons. No deal before or since has taken me so much time and effort. I must have seen them fifteen times, even going to church with them before I won their confidence and they wanted to be part of Neonex. Their company operated mostly between the metropolitan areas of Eastern Canada and the major cities on the Prairies. President Don Reimer saw the chance of getting liquidity for members of the family as well as having the biggest trucking operation in Canada. We worked out the preliminary agreement in the Reimer living-room. It was four in the morning and we were still negotiating when I spotted a copy of *The Winnipeg Free Press* on the floor, with a story warning about the dangers of conglomerates. Although I was sure they'd read it by then, I carefully edged the paper under the chesterfield with my foot. The deal was done, for 230,000 shares of Neonex; part of the agreement was that Reimer Express would continue to tithe to whatever organizations the family wanted. When I got back to the Fort Garry Hotel, I told Wilf Ray: "Make sure it's on the Dow the minute the service opens." Making the deal public on the Dow Jones financial-news service would usually move the price of the stock up immediately. We soon acquired a small trucking firm in Vancouver, Hunt Transport, which extended the Reimer Express coverage to the West Coast. But the Reimers remained unhappy about selling their company and bought it back from us in '71. We did business together again six years later when I sold them Northern Paint.

Imbrex, Canada's biggest wholesaler of carpets and floor coverings, was also a reluctant seller. John Chaston, a vice-president with Pemberton Securities in Vancouver, had first approached Imbrex on his own, without consulting me, and without naming Neonex as a possible buyer. He assured Imbrex president Guy Godbout, a sophisticated Montrealer and a very proud Quebecker, that "there is no question about the financial capacity of our client." Godbout, hesitant at first, finally expressed interest. I followed up in a Montreal meeting with him (he suffered from narcolepsy and occasionally fell asleep while I was talking to him). I told Godbout that Imbrex shares were worth about $10—about double what they were then trading. He wouldn't take an offer of anything less than $12.50 to his directors. But he was obviously excited about my proposal. In a memo to his board (made public later in a court case involving several directors' roles in the takeover), he wrote that Neonex was building a conglomerate and "has substantial U.S. backing and a photostat of certain documentation will show you that its U.S. partners and directors are indeed substantial people with substantial firms." I took Godbout to New York to meet Mike Dingman, who helped me tell the story of how Neonex would soon be listed on the American Stock Exchange, as it was the following year. Although Godbout became enthused about the potential takeover, it came out in the court case that two of the directors—Trevor and Charles Jordan-Knox, brothers who ran Jordan Rugs in Vancouver—were unhappy. Charles Jordan-Knox told another director that I was a promoter, "not interested in management . . . he has never run anything."

Godbout had agreed that I could send in our financial people to size up Imbrex. There's no simple formula for determining a company's real value. You have to ask different questions for different situations. How much goodwill's on the balance sheet? What's the cashflow? Is it capital-intensive? What are the margins? Is it growing at 5 per cent per annum or 20 per cent? What market does it have—the Maritimes or a high-growth area like Toronto? What sort of competitors does it have? And what's the management like? In the case of Imbrex, which had annual sales of $28 million, everything looked fine. Guy Godbout had done a good job of building the company. The only real problem: Because Imbrex didn't manufacture its own carpets, it was dependent on a continuing relationship with its supplier, Harding Carpets. Their contract had a three-month cancellation clause. The court case revealed that the Imbrex directors wanted the company to trade shares in a merger with Harding instead of Neonex. Harding, however, would have none of it. At last Godbout agreed to sell to us for our offer of $12 a share, to be paid in Neonex stock. In one of the best responses to a share offering in recent market history, we got 96 per cent of the Imbrex shares. Soon after, we used Imbrex to buy UniverSport, a small Quebec sporting-goods manufacturer that we kept for three years.

By now we were seeing some action in the market. The Imbrex deal made our stock jump about 20 per cent in one hour. The value of Neonex as a public corporation was rising with every new acquisition and so were our earnings per share. On a poolings-of-interest basis, our internal growth rate at the end of our first year was 27 per cent and our earnings per share were sixty cents. The magic of this game is that because we were out there doing deals, the market began to anticipate our earnings growth and investors were prepared to pay multiples of fifteen to twenty. A multiple is another name for price/earnings ratio—the price of a stock divided by its earnings per share. The higher the multiple, the more investors pay and the more growth in earnings they're anticipating. With the kind of investor support we were getting, it essentially became cheaper and cheaper for us to buy more companies. For instance, when we acquired Overwaitea and Northern Paint in the second quarter of 1968, our high multiple—thirty and forty times eventual '68 earnings of sixty cents a share—helped us buy seven other companies at lower multiples in the next nine months.

Among them were three Alberta growth companies: Associated Helicopters of Edmonton, which did a lot of oil- and gas-pipeline work and fire-fighting for the provincial government; Provincial News of Edmonton, our first wholesale distributorship, which covered northern Alberta, Saskatchewan, Manitoba, the Yukon, and the Northwest Territories—an area larger than all of Western Europe; and United Trailer, Canada's biggest dealer in mobile homes, which specialized in making them for the resource industry. United brought us a good new associate who's still with us, Dan Johnsen, president of the mobile-home company. I negotiated the deal with him and Ted Riback, the principal owner. It was about 2:30 A.M. and we were still about half a million apart when Dan called me aside and said: "I think you're wrong about the company. It's like a rose and it's just starting to bloom." I pulled out my slide rule (this was before pocket calculators), slid it back and forth, and said, "Okay, you've got a deal." Dan later became president of our various shelter companies and ran Jim Pattison Developments, our real-estate holdings.

Through United Trailer, we went into a joint venture to develop mobile-home communities with Jack Poole, a fellow member of the Young Presidents' Organization, who ran Dawson Developments, Canada's major builder of resource towns for primary industry. Our ambitious five-year plan for Dawnex Properties Ltd. was to invest $20 million in creating and operating these communities in Ontario, Western Canada, and the states of Washington and Oregon. The venture never got off the ground.

At the time, we were financing acquisitions with $15 million U.S. worth of senior convertible subordinated notes from the Morgan Guaranty Bank of New York and a $20 million line of credit we'd negotiated with the Canadian Imperial Bank of Commerce. After our problems with the Royal over Neon Products, Canadian Imperial had become our prime bank, lending us $8 million for operations and $12 million for acquisitions.

Not all of our serious runs at companies met with success those first two years. I pursued a snowmobile manufacturer, Skiroule Limitée of Wickham, Quebec, with a vengeance. We even signed and announced a preliminary merger agreement offering a total of $26 million in cash and Neonex shares. One of the top three snowmobile-makers in Canada, the company was projecting sales of $12 million and a profit of $1 million in the current year. But it turned out that Skiroule was also negotiating with Coleman Company of Wichita, Kansas (the manufacturer of Coleman stoves and other camping supplies). At the last minute, just before we were to sign a definitive agreement, Skiroule's directors accepted a higher offer from Coleman. When they gave me the word, I was in a Montreal hotel room with Harry Dunbar, Ross Turner, Maureen Chant, Don Selman, and a local senior partner of Peat Marwick. Feeling depressed, everybody but Harry and I decided to leave immediately for dinner at Chez

The Rise of Neonex International

Bardet. They were well into their third course when we arrived at this classy restaurant. I was in no mood for the waiter who asked for my order.

"I would just like a piece of toast," I told him.

"Toast, m'sieu?"

"Yeah. And burn it on both sides, please."

Losing Skiroule to a U.S. company made me mad. I sent a telegram to Prime Minister Trudeau, telling him about the tax advantages that U.S. corporations then had over Canadian ones. In part, it read:

> In the past eighteen months, our company, Neonex International Ltd., has held preliminary discussions with over three hundred Canadian companies and has acquired sixteen of them. During this time the difficulty in competing to keep Canadian companies Canadian has become increasingly apparent to us. I speak of the current cost of borrowing money for the purchase of companies, where the cost of borrowing is deductible in the U.S. before taxes, while in Canada it is after taxes. Canadian companies, including our own, have felt the inequality of such legislation. In the past fourteen days alone, we have lost two transactions to U.S. companies—a $20 million bid for a Western Canadian firm, and the proposed $26 million acquisition of Skiroule Ltée. of Quebec . . . Unless Canadian companies are put on at least an equal footing with their American counterparts, the erosion of Canadian ownership will continue to take place.

Trudeau followed through. Don Selman and I later made a presentation on the problem to then finance minister Edgar Benson in Vancouver. I was one of many business people across the country protesting the inequity and, in the tax-reform measures of 1971, the laws on interest-deductibility were modified. Oh, and there was another interesting sequel to the Skiroule story. Losing our bid for the company proved to be a blessing in disguise. Coleman dropped tens of millions of dollars on Skiroule.

* * *

In 1969, we got some more help in buying companies when Bill Sleeman finally agreed to come and work for us. Bill and his wife, Bev, had moved to Toronto with General Motors two and a half years earlier. I'd given him a send-off party, telling him he had a job with me anytime. After we took over Neon Products, I asked him specifically if he'd manage our car dealership while I ran Neon. But he saw himself as a career man with GM—until the second-in-command, the man he most admired there, died in a plane crash. I called Bill the same day: "I have a feeling this might change your thinking about your future. I want to talk to you again." In Toronto a few weeks later, I promised: "This is the day I'm going to hire you." This time, when I offered him a job as my right-hand man, concentrating on acquisitions, he accepted.

A GM executive called me up later and said the corporation was disgusted that one of their dealers had taken one of their people "and we just want to know if you're going to hire anybody else from GM."

"You don't have to worry," I said. "There's nobody else I want."

It was the start of a close and valuable relationship that continues to this day. Bill and I aren't social friends, never visit each other for dinner— for one thing, he goes to bed at eight and gets up at four to run for seven miles and swim for half a mile. But he's become our number-two guy, as solid as a rock; there's no one I have deeper regard for. Bill came from the largest corporation in the world, a highly structured organization, to a chaotic little company that was growing in leaps and bounds. The first thing I did was to send him to a three-day seminar on mergers and acquisitions and then put him on an airplane. His job was to go after the smaller companies. A guy in Kansas City had invented a new type of photo-finishing. A snowmobile manufacturer in Quebec looked interesting. Dry cleaners. News distributors. A lot of companies in small towns in Western Canada and the American Midwest. In the first nine months of '69, Bill negotiated three acquisitions that helped Neonex begin billing itself as the leading consumer services and transportation company in Canada. He brought us the TVS Group of Vancouver, one of Canada's largest suppliers of closed-circuit TV systems for industrial and educational markets; Otto Manufacturing Enterprises, one of the largest camping-trailer manufacturers; and Triple E Manufacturing, which made travel trailers at Winkler, Manitoba. We'd already bought Travelaire Trailer Manufacturing, with plants in Red Deer, Alberta, and Arnprior, Ontario.

Almost the day Bill Sleeman arrived, we took our car-leasing company public as Great Pacific Industries. In those days, you could take a hot-dog stand public. Great Pacific traded stock to acquire Fabco Leasing, which leased industrial bunkhouses, and a Vancouver hotel, the Doric Howe. Nine months after joining me, Bill became president of Great Pacific and later merged Fabco with Porta-Built Industries, an Edmonton manufacturer of pre-fab, custom-made industrial buildings. Largely because of Porta-Built, Great Pacific's earnings skyrocketed during Bill's first year in charge.

In the fall of '69, Neonex and Great Pacific were flying so high that we decided to get one of the first Learjets in Canada, a Lear 24 with an eight-track tape deck aboard. Sometimes while we were playing songs with a beat, our staff pilot would tip the wings back and forth in time to the music. All the songs were happy for Neonex International, which had become a darling of the media and the financial community. The research department of the Montreal investment firm of Greenshields Inc. issued a bulletin recommending our stock highly. *The Globe and Mail* assigned two reporters to do a major feature story on us. And *Time*'s Canadian edition ran an admiring article which said: "After a short, hectic eighteen months, Pattison and Neonex are pausing for breath, but almost imperceptibly. 'Every time I get to the top of a hill, I set my sights on another,' Pattison says."

The next hill in sight was Maple Leaf Mills, and I didn't know how high and mighty it would be.

CHAPTER NINE

Them Versus Us

Toronto was cold that December, in more ways than one. It was my first foray into the minefields of the Toronto Establishment. I would learn about power: the overwhelming strength and influence of the East's old monied families and the dominance of what was then the exclusive Eastern club of Canada's Big Five banks. Our battle for Maple Leaf Mills Limited of Toronto would bring Neonex International to its knees. It would lead to a series of lawsuits that would take thirteen years to settle. It would change my life.

For nearly sixty years, Maple Leaf Mills had been feeding Canadians. It was the country's major flour miller and one of the largest food-processing and agricultural operations. Families across Canada grew up on its Purity flour, Monarch cake mixes, and Red River cereal. We fed our cats and dogs its Master pet foods; we dined on chicken from its Sky Line Farms. We bought bread from its McGavin Toastmaster and Canada Bread companies and spread the slices with margarine made from Maple Leaf's vegetable oils. More recently, we were growing our lawns and gardens with its Steele-Briggs and Rennies seeds. It produced and sold much of Canada's livestock and poultry feed and was a massive merchandiser of grains and oils around the world; currently, it had a big wheat contract with Russia and delivered flour to

Cuba. The public company's annual sales at the beginning of 1969 were about what Neonex's would be by the end of the year: $150 million.

Maple Leaf was controlled by two multi-millionaires who never got along: a Canadian, Jack Leitch, and an American with a Canadian background, Bruce Norris. Although their fathers had built the business as partners and friends, the sons were as different as day and night in style and interests. John Daniel Leitch was part of Toronto's horsey set, a conservative and proper businessman as chairman of Maple Leaf Mills and president of Upper Lakes Shipping, one of the key eastern shipping lines. He held important directorships: Dominion Foundries and Steel (Dofasco), Canada Life, Massey-Ferguson, American Airlines, and the Canadian Imperial Bank of Commerce—my bank. In *The Canadian Establishment*, Peter Newman estimated that Leitch had assets of more than $50 million. Bruce Norris, who lived in Chicago, was the big, boisterous owner of the Detroit Red Wings of the National Hockey League. He came from a colourful family: His late half-brother, Jim Norris, had owned the Chicago Black Hawks and controlled much of professional boxing during the '50s. Where Jack Leitch had horses, Bruce Norris kept a cheetah as a pet. Among his worldwide holdings, Norris had a ranch in Africa where he raised purebred Brahma cattle. He was worth an estimated $200 million in '69.

And he seemed to be in a position where he called the shots for Leitch. Or so we thought. Norris owned Norris Grain Company of Illinois and its subsidiary, Norris Grain Company of Winnipeg. Norris Winnipeg owned nearly two-thirds of Upper Lakes Shipping—which meant that Bruce Norris had firm control of a business that Jack Leitch loved and that he actively disliked. He especially disliked the shipyard operations that Upper Lakes ran and the unions in the shipping business. Their relationship was strained; as Norris once told Leitch, "You keep this job only at my pleasure." Yet he wouldn't sell out his shares to his one-third partner because he believed Leitch had tried to depress the company's earnings so he could buy Norris out at a bargain price.

They were unwilling shareholders in Maple Leaf, too: Upper Lakes owned 28 per cent, Norris Grain Illinois 10.5 per cent, and Leitch Transport 14 per cent. We learned most of this from one of our active American directors, Mike

Dingman, who'd met Bruce Norris three years before. Keeping an eye on Maple Leaf, Mike first approached representatives of Norris early in '69 to see if his shares were for sale. The company fascinated us. Our director, Bob Halliday, was always saying we should be going after companies with assets, not just high-multiple service industries. Maple Leaf was heavy in assets, some of them undervalued. It had substantial working capital of $19.3 million and a strong cashflow. And it had a great capacity to borrow with generous lines of credit at special rates. By capitalizing on its base, we thought we could create a tremendous Canadian growth company.

Meanwhile, I'd met Maple Leaf's president, G.M. MacLachlan, and kept him current about Neonex by sending him regular reports of our acquisitions. When Norris finally expressed interest in talking to me, Mike Dingman arranged for me to meet him in late October. Bruce Norris was an incredible character. He never did business during the normal working hours. Over the next few months, I sat up many nights with him in jazz clubs and restaurants in New York. A bachelor, he always had beautiful women hanging on him. Late one night he took me along on a visit to one of his girlfriends, Cynthia, who lived in an apartment where she sat fish. Every wall in every room was lined with aquariums holding the tropical fish Cynthia looked after for people away on holiday. And every inch of the floor was covered in animal rugs; I had to keep stepping around the stuffed heads of lions and tigers. Another night, going for dinner, we encountered an angry man coming out of the restaurant with his girlfriend. Bruce told the fellow he wasn't being nice to the woman. "Mind your own business," he warned Bruce, who then put the guy on the pavement. He really thumped him with his huge hands, and then just stepped into the restaurant for dinner.

At our first meeting, Mike Dingman let Bruce know we'd be interested in buying his shares—for cash, if he wanted. In the next month, Bruce decided he'd prefer to trade shares with Neonex instead, mostly for tax reasons although he liked Maple Leaf and could continue participating in it by taking shares in our company. Originally he valued his Maple Leaf shares at $35 apiece; he finally agreed on $30. Norris and his lawyer, Robert Vincent, made it clear that they were interested in selling the Norris Illinois shares of Maple Leaf only if it could be done largely tax-free. To accomplish this, they proposed two separate deals.

The *principal* Norris agreement was to sell to Neonex all of the outstanding capital stock of Norris Winnipeg in exchange for 27 per cent of Neonex outstanding common shares. This exchange would be free of tax in the United States. The deal would make Bruce Norris the largest single shareholder and me a junior partner in Neonex. I considered it a fair tradeoff; I'd rather own a small piece of a major company than 100 per cent of a minor one. The key was getting results—moving the stock prices up and making Neonex a success. This principal agreement gave Neonex 66 per cent of Upper Lakes and its 28 per cent of Maple Leaf. But it also gave us Norris Winnipeg's shares of Dofasco, the Hamilton, Ontario, steelmaker. These were blue-chip securities worth about $7 million, which we intended to use to help finance the Maple Leaf acquisition.

The Norris *option* agreement gave Neonex an option to buy from Norris Illinois its 10.5 per cent of Maple Leaf shares for $4.3 million. This option would cost us $856,000.

We signed these agreements Tuesday, December 16, at a meeting in Bruce's boardroom on New York's Madison Avenue. We then had 38 per cent of Maple Leaf. Now, the only problem was to tell his partner, Jack Leitch, and offer to buy his shares. Bruce had made us promise that we'd offer Leitch the same terms and conditions we had given him. That afternoon our whole entourage—Mike Dingman, Guy Lewall, Don Selman, Wilf Ray, and Maureen Chant—flew with Norris, Bob Vincent, and me to Toronto on our Learjet. During the flight, Norris kept saying how great it was to be partners with young people who were about to take on the Establishment. Vincent warned me that the only way to deal with Leitch was to be tough, to grind him down. In Toronto we met first with a director of Maple Leaf, Frank Logan, who was with a brokerage firm, Dominion Securities. We were covering ourselves: If Jack Leitch didn't accept the same terms as Norris, we wouldn't be able to get 51 per cent control of Maple Leaf and would have to work through a broker to buy the additional shares. In the trade, it's called a tender offer—a public offer to buy Maple Leaf stock within a specified time period. Our offer was code-named TenderLeaf.

Then Bruce Norris took me to see Leitch at his office; we

entered through a freight elevator so Leitch wouldn't spot me coming in. After spending the first fifteen minutes alone with him, Bruce introduced me and Mike Dingman to Leitch and his lawyer, Jim Lewtas. Leitch was as chilly as the weather outside: "Neonex. I've never heard of it. What is it—a contraceptive?" I explained what the company was all about and offered to give him the Upper Lakes stock and get his piece of Maple Leaf on the same conditions we'd given Norris. Leitch said it seemed like the minnow was trying to swallow the whale. He told me he'd think about it; we'd meet in the morning; and now he had to leave for dinner with the American ambassador. The next day, Wednesday, Leitch said he wasn't interested in any deal with us except to acquire our shares of Upper Lakes. But by Thursday, we knew we were too far apart on the value of those shares. No deal.

That day Wilf Ray put out a press release announcing we'd entered into an agreement with Norris. And we were all primed to mail out a tender offer to get the shares we still needed to gain 51 per cent control. The only hitch was that if we offered $25 per share to the stockholders, and someone else offered more than that, we were legally locked in and couldn't compete on the open market. And Thursday night, just before the brokers were to put the offer in the mail, we had a phone call from a friend who didn't want to be identified. Someone else was going after Maple Leaf, he said. Molson's.

Molson Industries Ltd. of Toronto was an immense conglomerate created from the fortunes of the brewery founded in Montreal a couple of centuries ago. The Molsons had built the first railway in North America, the first steamboat in Canada. They had their own 125-branch bank that printed its own money until it merged with the Bank of Montreal. Molson companies now were in construction, warehousing and trucking, diversified equipment manufacturing, furniture-making, and office equipment and forms. And Molson's owned the biggest brewery in the country. The new president of this empire was Donald G. (Bud) Willmot, who shared Jack Leitch's love of horses at his Kinghaven Farms. ("I don't like the term 'Establishment,' " Willmot once said. "It does exist, however, but it's made up of responsible people who do great things for Canada.") On the day of our second meeting with Jack Leitch, Bud Willmot had called him to renew a year-old offer to buy

Maple Leaf. Leitch was definitely interested. But even with his shares, Molson's would have to buy publicly held stock to counter our 38 per cent block. As Sandy Ross would write in his *Financial Post* column: "Jimmy Pattison vs Molson's! This is not to be believed! It's like the Bowery Boys vs the Chase Manhattan Bank."

On Friday, December 19, Ross was with us in a ninth-floor suite of Toronto's Royal York Hotel after we decided to pull our tender offer and go on to the open market for the 13 per cent more shares we required for control. As he described the scene, I was "barking orders, listening hard, grabbing telephones, huddling with lawyers and brokers, yelling in that urgent, high-pitched voice. It was nearly noon, and for the past few hours Jimmy Pattison had known he was involved in the biggest fight of his incredible career." He had it right. We couldn't convince any brokers in Toronto to act for us and buy the stock, so I called Bob Wyman of Pemberton's in Vancouver. Bob and one of his brokers flew all night to be on the floor of the Toronto Stock Exchange the next morning. The opening trade for Maple Leaf was $25¼, a gain of $7¾ from Thursday's closing price. Within forty minutes, 100,000 shares had been traded and the price leaped to $30. Then the exchange suspended trading because of a pending announcement, which was that Molson's intended to offer one of its Class A common shares plus $5 cash for each common share of Maple Leaf. Leitch announced his support of the offer. At 2:04 P.M., we were back trading from our war room in the Royal York. By 3:15, I knew we'd won: Molson's had acquired only 10 per cent of the stock while we got 14 per cent—giving us more than 51 per cent control of Maple Leaf.

The next day's headlines shouted: "Molson Takeover Bid Foiled" and "Neonex Victorious in Battle of Giants." We'd won that battle. But as it turned out, the war raged on. Upper Lakes Shipping wired us immediately that its directors would be meeting on Monday, December 22, to determine who would get the company's 28 per cent worth of Maple Leaf shares: Neonex or Molson's. There was no doubt which way their sympathies would lean. As well as Leitch, the Upper Lakes board included H. H. Bawden, who was a big shareholder and a director of Molson's. If the board rejected Neonex, we'd be left with only 24.5 per cent of Maple Leaf and Molson's would become the controlling shareholder with

38 per cent. Both sides were invited to make competing bids to the Upper Lakes directors.

After flying home for the weekend, I arrived back in Toronto Sunday afternoon as our lawyers were preparing a strategy to sidetrack this bidding war. We were working with two lawyers: Bob Davies, a partner in Davies Ward & Beck of Toronto, and Sam Pryor, our New York attorney, who'd just stage-managed America's largest corporate takeover, General Electric's billion-dollar acquisition of Utah Mining. Monday morning, Pryor and Davies attended the Upper Lakes board meeting along with Molson's legal counsel. The atmosphere was tense, hostile. Jim Lewtas, Jack Leitch's lawyer, told both sides to bring back their written bids for the Maple Leaf stock by that evening. We set our bid price at $30¼ per Maple Leaf share, just slightly higher than we thought Molson's might offer. At about 11:00 P.M., after both bidders had made their case, a nervous and upset Jim Lewtas emerged from the meeting to announce that the board had accepted the Neonex offer.

But what Lewtas didn't realize was that our written bid, which Sam Pryor read to the directors, had a catch: "To comply with the foregoing it shall be a condition precedent to the closing that the necessary approval of the noteholders is obtained and that the shareholders of the company approve the sale and delivery of the shares." In effect, we were saying that the whole process was meaningless without the approval of the majority Upper Lakes shareholder, Bruce Norris. Our lawyers had built in that conditional clause for two reasons. One was to use it as a platform to point out to the Upper Lakes directors that they were trying to sell a principal asset of the company against the express wishes of the major shareholder—and Norris certainly wouldn't approve their selling Maple Leaf stock to Molson's. And the second reason was to buy time for ourselves while getting Molson's out of the way. But, even though Pryor read the key clause slowly, the board didn't respond to it.

Early the next morning, an associate of Jim Lewtas came across that clause (as I learned in a later court case) and told him: "That son-of-a-bitch Pryor pulled a fast one on us." Lewtas then called me to say the Neonex offer should never have been accepted. Now the directors were going to consider alternative offers at a board meeting being held that

Tuesday morning. This time, I joined our lawyers at the Upper Lakes offices. Sitting outside the boardroom, I could hear a lot of angry voices. And when Jim Lewtas came out during a break, I seized my chance. Approaching him at a water fountain, I said: "There's a better way of dealing with this problem than fighting like this. I've got some thoughts I'd like to discuss with you and Jack."

The three of us went downstairs to Jack Leitch's office. It took only a matter of minutes for them to agree to the fundamentals of the eventual deal. Leitch owned Dofasco stock worth $13.5 million; he'd give it to Upper Lakes and in return he'd get the 28 per cent block of Maple Leaf that Upper Lakes owned. Neonex would then buy that 28 per cent block from Leitch for $3 million cash and the two-thirds control of Upper Lakes that Neonex would be getting from Norris. Leitch would give us the option to buy his own 14 per cent Maple Leaf shares. The option would cost us $1.15 million and the total share price would be $5.7 million. The result: Jack Leitch would control his own shipping line and we'd control Maple Leaf.

We signed the agreement two days before Christmas. That should have been that. But a week earlier, when Leitch didn't think he would ever do a deal with us, he'd visited an influential friend of his, Neil McKinnon, chairman of the Canadian Imperial Bank of Commerce. McKinnon had a reputation as a cold-eyed autocrat. It was his bank, of course, that controlled Neonex's $20 million line of credit. And he hadn't known in advance that we were attempting to take over Maple Leaf.

In those days, I just didn't appreciate how the Canadian banking system really worked. As far as I was concerned, the Canadian Imperial Bank of Commerce was in Vancouver. I didn't know anyone in Toronto. So I'd told Peter Pousette, who ran the Commerce in B.C., about my planned takeover. He advised me that it would be wrong to put the bank in the middle between me and one of its prime customers in an unfriendly takeover. Jack Leitch was not only chairman of Maple Leaf, he was also vice-president and a director of the bank. So we bypassed the Commerce head office entirely and went to Marine Midland Grace Trust Company in New York for a loan; at no time did we break any of our loan agreements with the Commerce. Only in the aftermath of Maple Leaf did I realize that, if you're doing a deal of any size, the bankers who grant the credit—the people in head office, as well as in the regions—should know you personally as a customer.

On December 17, as I heard later, Leitch met at the Toronto Club with Neil McKinnon. Whatever Leitch told McKinnon about me that afternoon, the outcome was dramatic. On the day we were closing the deal with Jack Leitch, two days before Christmas, the bank asked for a meeting with Mike Dingman. Throughout the Maple Leaf negotiations, Mike had been dealing with the Commerce's assistant general manager, Don Fullerton (R. Donald Fullerton is now chairman and CEO). Mike recalls that the day was cold—ten below—and that his meeting with Fullerton was the coldest he's ever had in his career.

Peering frostily at him over his glasses, Fullerton said: "Mr. Dingman [not "Mike"], the Canadian Imperial Bank of Commerce has lost confidence in the management of Neonex and in all of the companies Jim Pattison represents and in Jim Pattison personally."

"Don," Mike said, "what the hell do you mean by that?"

"We've lost confidence and we want your loans out of this bank as soon as practical . . . within sixty days."

"That's the worst thing I've ever heard," Mike told him. "You can't do that."

But Fullerton could. When I met with him about five that evening, he told me they were not only pulling Neonex's loans but would also cancel Maple Leaf's $46 million credit line if we took over Maple Leaf. The official reason: I hadn't informed them of our takeover plans. He was surprised when I let him know that we'd just signed an agreement with Leitch, which I thought would make him reconsider his decision. But as I left his office at ten to six (the time is frozen in my memory) Fullerton gave me no assurances anything would change. However, he'd discuss it with his superiors and we'd discuss it the following week.

I flew home to Vancouver for a restrained Christmas (at one point during our negotiations with Bruce Norris in New York, I'd asked accountant Don Selman if he'd try to find a Christmas gift for my children; he returned from F.A.O. Schwarz with an electronic stock-market game).

Between Christmas and New Year's, I was back in Toronto. Don Fullerton confirmed what I'd feared: All Neonex and Maple Leaf credit was frozen. We would have to make other banking arrangements. Afterwards, a high-ranking executive in the bank confessed privately to me: "Jimmy, I never believed what could happen in this country until I saw what happened to you." At the time, we were lunching in the Toronto Club, where Jack Leitch and Neil McKinnon had decided my fate. The bank official pointed and said: "See that spot over there? That's where it all happened, right over there. It was the old boys' school that put you down, Jimmy. You never had a chance."

We did have another limited, and non-Canadian, source of funds. After we'd decided not to approach the Commerce in Toronto about the takeover, Neonex went to New York to finance some of the buying of Maple Leaf. We got a $10.7 million (U.S.) loan from the Marine Midland in New York, which had a good relationship with Mike Dingman. But we'd intended to repay that loan quickly with our credit from the Commerce. Desperate, I tried to get an appointment with the Commerce chairman. I'd bought a new suit with a vest; Jim Lewtas, Leitch's lawyer, had warned me: "Don't you go see Neil McKinnon without getting a three-piece suit." For two weeks, I sat in the Royal York while McKinnon refused to see me. (But in a wonderfully kind gesture that meant such a lot to me, Russ Harrison—the bank's new general manager and later its chairman—came down to the hotel one Saturday with his wife, Nancy, and had tea with me.) Bruce Norris was a friend of McKinnon's and at one point, he and Mike did get in to meet Commerce president Larry Greenwood. His advice was blunt: Get rid of Jimmy Pattison as chief executive officer of Neonex.

Mike and I began making the humbling rounds of major Canadian banks to see if we could find new lines of credit. We called on the Bank of Montreal, the Royal, and the Nova Scotia, whose president, Art Crockett, levelled with us: "You fellows are wasting your time." In effect, he told us that we wouldn't get any major Canadian bank to take over our loan.

Two decades ago, the big Canadian banks were a lot less competitive than they are now. A company our size had virtually nowhere else to go to borrow at reasonable rates. Ottawa had only recently revised the federal Bank Act, which would help clear the way for new banks. The regional institutions, like the Bank of British Columbia, were just getting off the ground. And there were only a few of the roughly sixty foreign banks we now have in Canada. Today, with the existing competition, the big banks can't wield the same iron-fisted control that they did with us in 1969.

All but one of them. There was a crack in the armour when Mike, Bob Halliday, and I met with Dick Thomson, the tall, thirty-six-year-old assistant to the president of the Toronto Dominion. Mike's background on Wall Street obviously helped us, and so did Bob's connection with Boise Cascade because the large American conglomerate dealt with the bank. The TD, which was one of three banks sharing Maple Leaf's accounts, came through at a critical time. We met in the Toronto head office after hours one evening. Thomson was keen-minded and thorough, but he made a fairly fast decision. He took a chance and extended a $2.5 million credit line to Neonex. Not a penny more. It wasn't enough, but a start, to help us at least make our payrolls. "Dick," Mike told him, "you're a prince of a man. Because the rest of the banks are literally killing Jimmy." Thomson would go on to be the innovative chairman of the Toronto Dominion (which *Toronto Life* recently said "is acknowledged to be the best-run bank in the country" and "also the leader in profitability"). Under his direction, it became Canada's major bank in financing takeovers and the first to offer unsecured, cashflow lending of the kind it advanced us. Today it's one of only two banks in North America with a triple-A rating.

Meanwhile, in February 1970, Larry Greenwood of the Commerce wrote me to say I should definitely make other banking arrangements. Instead, I requested a meeting with the bank. And I walked in carrying a Telex from a London-based bank that confirmed its willingness to lend us $20 million. Through Mike Dingman's investment-banking network, we'd gone offshore to find a foreign institution that would finance Neonex. The Western American Bank was a combination of Hambros Bank (one of Britain's largest merchant-banking operations), Wells Fargo, and two other American banks. But its loan would be expensive money— about 13 per cent financing because of Canadian withholding taxes. Not only was the interest usurious, the Western Amer

Them Versus Us

ican was also demanding warrants, which were a potential dilution to the equity in the corporation.

We'd paid the London bank a stand-by fee of about $30,000 to reserve the funds for a few days and now our American lawyer, Sam Pryor, had to file a 10-K (the full-disclosure form that the U.S. Securities Exchange Commission requires from every company listed on American stock exchanges). It was at that point I decided I'd had it. The Commerce could do what it wanted to me. I was prepared to go right to the wall. So on the afternoon of February 24, in I walked to my meeting with Greenwood. He sat behind his desk and lined up along one side of the office were three bank officers.

"Gentlemen," I told them, "you called our loan and we've now got the ability to pay you. But I've decided that it's wrong for a Western Canadian company that has broken no loan agreements to turn around and dilute its ownership unnecessarily to foreigners and to be penalized with an enormously high rate of interest. Here is the Telex that says we have the money. But we are not taking this deal. I'm going home to Vancouver tonight. And when I get there, I'm calling a press conference to announce that the 10-K is going to disclose that we have no lines of credit but we had to get a loan from the Western European Bank. I'm going to disclose this whole situation from start to finish. I started as a used-car salesman and I'm prepared to go back and be a used-car salesman again.

"I'm catching the 7:30 plane and meanwhile I'll be at the Skyline Hotel with my lawyer, Sam Pryor."

"Jimmy," Larry Greenwood said, "we'll call you by six o'clock."

Before I left for Vancouver, he called: "We've decided to extend all your lines of credit for six months."

While the Commerce was not willing to withdraw its letter requesting repayment of the loans to Neonex and Maple Leaf as soon as practical, it did allow Neonex to have a credit position with the bank of $10 million for the next six months (which was $600,000 higher than the current outstanding loan we had). It also agreed not to put any pressure on Maple Leaf nor to call the personal loan I had with the Commerce for my privately held companies.

* * *

The heat was off, temporarily. We could continue operating Neonex. And Maple Leaf would carry on as normal. The truth was, we had little day-to-day control over Maple Leaf. We'd asked for the resignations of several of its directors and replaced them with our people: Bruce Norris, Mike Dingman, Bob Halliday, Larry Hoguet, Ross Turner, and Harry Dunbar. Yet although I was chairman, the management running Maple Leaf remained the same.

There was another important reason for our lame-duck approach to the company: We wouldn't have true control of Maple Leaf until at least September 30, 1970. When we'd signed the principal agreement with Bruce Norris, he asked that the closing date be allowed to float until he received a ruling from U.S. tax officials that his deal with us was tax-free. The earliest he thought he'd hear from them was the end of September. Then, when we signed the agreement with Jack Leitch, Norris had given us a letter that said he would use his "best efforts" to ensure two things: that Upper Lakes shares owned by Norris Winnipeg would be delivered to Neonex, which could then deliver them to Leitch; and that the Dofasco shares owned by Norris Winnipeg would be delivered to Neonex, which could then sell them to finance the Maple Leaf takeover.

In our deal with Leitch, the closing date could be no later than September 30—the same day we were hoping to close with Norris. At first, we saw no problems in getting the Upper Lakes and Dofasco shares from Norris. He was so co-operative that in March he even advanced Neonex a loan of $1 million to meet our payroll (we repaid it within ninety days). But as the months progressed, and investors saw Neonex in a holding action, our shares began to plummet on the stock market. *Investor's Digest of Canada* compared me to Jimmy Ling, America's conglomerate king, who had just been thrown out of his own corporation. "Apart from the mediocre earnings outlook [for Neonex]," the *Digest* said, "general enthusiasm for Mr. Pattison as an entrepreneur is waning." Between December '69 and September '70, our shares fell to $3¾ from $9⅝. Suddenly, the stock that Norris would hold in Neonex, once the deal went through, was worth only a third of what it had been when we signed the agreement. There was one other thing bothering Bruce Norris: He felt that his old enemy, Jack Leitch, would come out of the deal better than he would.

Them Versus Us 133

In early August, I started to hear disturbing news from the Norris people. For one thing, they said, their Upper Lakes shares were pledged as collateral with the Bank of Montreal and they couldn't deliver them to us free and clear by the end of September. In later meetings, I learned that Norris's Dofasco shares and Maple Leaf stock were pledged with the First National Bank of Chicago and couldn't be delivered by the closing date either. Bob Vincent told me that Norris had lost between $50 million and $60 million in the stock market; because of that, the Dofasco shares were pledged so firmly that they were "in the lowest, lowest vault" of the Chicago bank. These shares were absolutely crucial: Without them, we couldn't complete our deal with Jack Leitch. We insisted on hearing from the bank itself if the Dofasco stock could be cleared as collateral and delivered to us. Bruce agreed, but just as I was meeting Leitch in Toronto to bring him up to date, the phone rang. It was Bob Vincent: The meeting with the bank was called off because the Norris people didn't have all their financial information ready. We never did see the bank people and, as the bank would confirm in court years later, Norris was "not short [of] collateral" and the bank actually would have been prepared to release his Dofasco and Maple Leaf shares on the closing date. Norris had completely invented the story about his financial problems in an effort to force Neonex to renegotiate the Leitch agreement on terms less favourable to Leitch.

On September 30, our lawyer, Sam Pryor, met Norris's, Bob Vincent, in Toronto for what was supposed to be the closing. It didn't happen. Vincent said that he interpreted a clause in our agreement to mean that Norris had another sixty days to deliver the vital Dofasco shares. Pryor disagreed, believing that Norris was really in financial difficulties. The deal was off. That same day, we told Jack Leitch that we could not consummate our agreement with him. We put out a brief press release announcing that "Neonex was unable yesterday to complete the acquisition of shares of Maple Leaf Mills Limited from Leitch Transport Limited, because Norris Grain Company failed to deliver certain securities which Neonex had agreed to acquire from it."

For the next few weeks I lived in Toronto, feverishly trying to restructure the deal. Jack Leitch was co-operative, but we couldn't put the pieces back together with Bruce Norris. Maple Leaf Mills had slipped from our grasp.

The resulting lawsuits wouldn't be finally resolved until 1982. We launched the first action in 1971 against Norris, claiming $32 million in damages for breach of contract. He counter-sued, claiming $2 million in specific damages and, because our press release blamed him for killing the whole deal, $50 million for defamation. Leitch launched his own suit against Neonex for breach of contract.

Trying to avoid the legal battles was consuming my time and energy. As I admitted to a gathering of Neonex presidents in early '72, "My number-one concern today is Maple Leaf. And I don't know the solution to it. It's gotta be settled out of court. The complexities of this thing are enormous. I gave a year of my life—*totally*—to solve that problem and was unsuccessful. But we're about to start again and try to find a solution to this Maple Leaf problem."

In our suit against Norris, we went up against one of the most celebrated lawyers in North America: Joe Flom. A takeover specialist, Flom has been called "the greatest legal entrepreneur of the century," and his New York law firm—Skadden, Arps, Slate, Meagher & Flom—is among the fifty highest-grossing in the United States. By that time, I'd asked New York lawyer Mark Kaplan to be a Neonex director. And my friend Mark, who'd helped us take over Neon Products in 1967, was instrumental in resolving our dispute with Norris out of court. He called Flom up and said: "How do we settle things?" Things had been tense from the start: Lawyer Bob Vincent threw an iron pole at the process-server delivering his subpoena. During the negotiations, Mark moved from room to room as a peace-maker. Under the terms of the 1975 settlement, Norris—who was then taking Maple Leaf Mills private—bought all of the Neonex-held shares of Maple Leaf for $7.3 million. He dropped his defamation action against us. (Norris's involvement with Maple Leaf ended in 1980 when Canadian Pacific Enterprises bought it through its $122 million acquisition of Maple Leaf's holding company, Norin Corporation. Norris died in 1986.)

Leitch's suit against Neonex ended less amicably. We spent hundreds of thousands of dollars in legal fees and I passed nine weeks of my life in a Toronto courtroom during the fall of '77 as we relived the Maple Leaf takeover attempt. The case was complicated by the fact that three of the key lawyers involved in setting up the deal died before it came to court: our Toronto lawyer, Bob Davies; Jim Lewtas, who acted for Jack Leitch; and Bob Vincent. In March 1978, the judge decided that we had technically breached our contract with Jack Leitch and awarded him a surprising $9.6 million in damages. Both sides appealed, Leitch because he believed that inflation had depressed the value of the dollar in the years since the deal fell apart in 1970. Well, he did get another half a million for inflation, but the appeal court also decided that he'd received too much in the overall settlement and reduced it by more than half to $4.1 million.

Under our out-of-court settlement with Norris, he owed Neonex half that $4.1 million plus court costs. We advanced the whole amount of the settlement to Leitch and took a promissory note from Norris for his share. He ultimately paid us everything, but the final $60,000 for court costs didn't arrive until 1982—thirteen years after we'd first gone after Maple Leaf.

By far the worst fallout from the failure of the Maple Leaf takeover was the effect it had on our relationship with the Canadian Imperial Bank of Commerce. We'd established a truce with the Commerce from the time it first called our loan until September 30, 1970, the day we refused to close with Bruce Norris. But when we lost Maple Leaf, the bank cancelled our loan again. As 1971 began, Neonex was facing the bleak prospect of trying to operate without any of its major lines of credit. I was facing the blackest period of my career; nothing would ever be quite the same again.

CHAPTER TEN

Starting Over

This is how bad it got: At one point during the aftermath of Maple Leaf Mills, Maureen Chant came into my office and announced: "Jimmy, you haven't got $800 to give Mary for housekeeping." That was the money my wife had every month to run the house. And my personal cashflow situation then was so bad that I couldn't even write her a cheque. At the time, I had $17,000 of my own funds tied up in a proposed Alaskan oil-drilling venture. I called the fellow doing the deal and asked him what had happened to the money. When he said it was still sitting in a trust fund and did I want it back, I took it—so that, among other things, Mary could feed the family that month. She didn't know I was so hard-pressed for cash; I felt there was no sense in both of us worrying about it. I've always tried to keep my family and my business lives separate. Over the years, I haven't always been successful in isolating Mary from the rocky roads I've travelled—sometimes the crisis has been too big and public. So, although I've never discussed financial strategies with her, I have shared the fact that things were not going well.

As they weren't at the start of the '70s. Neonex was in deep trouble. Before too long, we'd lose one of our most important directors and battle a revolt by two other directors attempting a palace coup. We'd have to absorb a big loss in liquidating Imbrex, the national floor-coverings wholesaler. Our second public company, Great Pacific Industries, would be financially battered and face a shareholders' rebellion. And investors would become disenchanted with Neonex, along with all the conglomerates. As *The Toronto Star* reported in May 1970: "With the stock market slump last spring, the conglomerate bubble burst. Conglomerate stocks took a drubbing. While other stocks dipped maybe 20 to 30 per cent, conglomerate shares plummeted as much as 80 and even 90 per cent. . . . With their shares at bargain basement prices, conglomerates now don't find it so easy to show the rapid-fire growth, often evolved greatly through accounting legerdemain, that awed investors in the first place. . . . On the Canadian scene, companies considered to fall into the conglomerate category include Neonex International . . ."

Throughout North America, the bloom was off the conglomerate rose. Analysts now date the beginning of the problems back to 1968 when a major American conglomerate, Litton Industries, reported the first decline in its quarterly earnings in fourteen years. A year later, Jimmy Ling took over Jones & Laughlin Steel, his largest acquisition—and his downfall. The steel company began draining its parent corporation's finances; the U.S. government filed an antitrust suit against Ling; and in a subsequent boardroom battle, he was toppled as chairman of the continent's leading conglomerate, Ling-Temco-Vought. Because people began to shy away from conglomerate stock, LTV's troubles had an indirect but real effect on Neonex. And so did the actions of the notorious Bernie Cornfeld, who'd created the world's biggest group of mutual funds in his Investors Overseas Services Group. Some of his fund managers had been buying a lot of Neonex shares. Then when IOS fell apart in 1970 and Cornfeld went to jail, they dumped our stock, which put even more pressure on Neonex. From a high of $45 before a two-for-one split, our share price fell to a low of 80 cents.

I couldn't take any comfort from the fact that, during the early 1970s, Neonex was mirroring the economic uncertainties of the whole country. Soon double-digit inflation and unemployment would get a hammerlock on Canada; by '74, we'd have the second-worst strike record in the western world (after Italy) and our Gross National Product would actually decline for the first time in a decade.

And all the mistakes I'd made with Neonex showed up.

The game was over. At the age of forty-two, I should have been capitalizing on the success of my thirties. But my credibility was shot. Neonex had enormous lawsuits hanging around its neck. I was broke; my personal loans of $700,000 were called, and the bank wanted repayment of many thousands of dollars a month. Neonex had no money to make acquisitions. To comply with the bank's directives, we were forced to reduce inventories of several of our companies. We had food stores under construction that couldn't be completed. I sold our Learjet and even returned paintings that hung on my office walls.

Through all of this, Mary supported me with her quiet strength. Her philosophy is "What will be, will be." She always had confidence that if I plunged to the bottom financially, I'd soon be back on top again. Even though I didn't spell out my feelings during this crisis, she knew I'd hit bottom. There was many a night when I was up at 4:00 A.M., unable to sleep, wondering how to survive the calling of my personal and corporate bank loans. I would sit in the dark in the den, looking out at the lights of the city, dim in the winter rain. The weather was bad, business was bad, and my friends were becoming fewer and fewer. It was during one of those sleepless nights that I had the idea of approaching the small, new Bank of British Columbia.

Albert Hall, its chairman, saved my tail. After hearing my whole story, he lent me $300,000 for one of my private companies, Jim Pattison Enterprises, a loan that allowed me to take it out of the Commerce. It was the first of the credit lines I was able to switch to another bank. That's why, when Edgar Kaiser (who was Bank of B.C. chairman a couple of years ago) approached me for several million dollars to help refinance the bank, I gave him the money. Throughout the '70s and '80s, I continued to support that bank, giving it our leasing- and car-company business and eventually the accounts of one of our food companies and AirBC. At the peak, we had more than $30 million in accounts with the Bank of B.C. And when the bank got into trouble, we kept $5 million in cash and deposits there and bought its stock.

In those early post-Maple Leaf days, the Mercantile Bank gave us a small line of credit for another one of my private companies. But the general attitude of the major banks towards Neonex was enough to make Mike Dingman resign from our board of directors. Mike Dingman, who was the key player in helping make it possible for us to create Neonex International, said he was through with Canada. "Jimmy," he said, "I'm glad I'm American. They don't play by the Marquis of Queensberry rules up here; they get in blood fights." And years later, he described how he felt returning to the States under those circumstances: "I went back with my tail between my legs." He went back to found his own conglomerate, Wheelabrator-Frye, in the lenient tax state of New Hampshire, and built it into a corporation with annual sales of $1.5 billion. I missed his strong contributions to our board and I missed him as a friend. The loss of Mike Dingman was a bigger blow to me personally than the bank's calling of our loans.

Meanwhile, I was still trying to change the minds of the Eastern bankers who held our fate in their hands. Looking for some legal help, I went to Doug Brown, one of Vancouver's most distinguished lawyers. I asked him to write carefully worded letters to both the Commerce and the Toronto-Dominion that would support our case for continued lines of credit. Brown (the uncle of Peter Brown, who's now the very attractive chairman of Vancouver's Canarim Investment Corporation) prepared a couple of vital letters which I was exceedingly grateful for, even if he did bill us $22,000 for them. I also approached a man for whom I had the highest respect, J.V. Clyne, the chairman and chief executive officer of B.C.'s largest public company, MacMillan Bloedel. Jack Clyne, who ran the giant forest-products company after being a judge of the B.C. Supreme Court, was a director and a member of the executive committee of the Commerce. In 1970, when my back was against the wall and he really didn't know me from Adam, he listened to me. He felt Neil McKinnon hadn't treated us properly and helped me draft an important letter along with his vice-chairman, George Currie, a former vice-president of the Commerce. To have them in my corner during my darkest moment gave me tremendous heart.

I began meeting every Monday night with the B.C. manager of the Commerce, Peter Pousette, who'd advised me not to approach his head office when I was going after Maple Leaf. We became good friends over weekly dinners where I reported our financial progress to him. Neonex had no formal lines of credit, but eventually, over a period of eighteen months, the Commerce decided to let us maintain our $10 million loan on a day-to-day basis—and on the strict condition that we never exceeded that limit.

During that same year and a half, I got friendlier with the Toronto-Dominion, which had given us a vital $2.5 million line of credit when the Commerce cut us off the first time. I kept the TD informed about our activities and tried to demonstrate to its top people that Neonex was a legitimate, viable company. It wasn't always easy. My public profile across the country continued to suffer as deals fell apart. In June '70, for example, *The Toronto Star* ran a headline on its business pages, "Trailer Park Project Flops," over a story detailing how our joint venture to develop mobile-home communities with Jack Poole of Dawson Developments had died after only nine months.

Fortunately, the media didn't know anything about the internal problems we were facing. In 1970 I came close to being tossed out on my ear as chairman. The instigators of the mutiny were those two directors from the old Neon Products days, Art Christopher and Charlie Brazier—the pair of Establishment types whom some of my associates warned me about. As it turned out, I'd made a mistake keeping them on the board instead of cleaning them out with all the rest. One day Christopher and Brazier came into my office and demanded my resignation. I'd lost the confidence of the banks, they told me, and they wanted me out of the company. They caught me when I was leaving on a trip, so— buying a few days' time—I asked them to think things over. We met the following Saturday in the Neonex boardroom, where I went to the blackboard and tried to show them I was close to solving our problems with the banks. "We're not interested," they said. They wanted nothing less than my resignation. The moment I was down, they were at my throat. Because of the current makeup of the board, I knew I could be beat. On my side for sure were my supporters, Bob Halliday and Harry Dunbar. We felt that, with the decline of the stock and the difficulties with the bank, Stu Mitton, Overwaitea's president, and Ross Turner, Neonex's president and chief operating officer, might side with Christopher and Brazier.

Somehow I had to fight them off. To plan the counter-attack, I set up a war room with Bill Sleeman, Maureen Chant, and my lawyers in a suite at the Bayshore Inn. Now, I knew that on the coming Monday, Charlie Brazier (senior partner in the Davis & Co. law firm) had one of his biggest clients arriving in Vancouver from Germany. There was no way Brazier could be out of town. Waiting until the last minute I could legally inform him and Christopher, I called a board meeting for that Monday in Toronto. Then I had a Learjet pick up Bob Halliday in Boise, Idaho, and take him to Toronto. Neither Brazier nor Christopher made it to the meeting at the Royal York Hotel. It was apparent that I had the balance of power. The leaders of the revolt, Christopher and Brazier, publicly resigned by telegram. Ross Turner had resigned before the meeting. Afterwards, Ross did well for himself, returning to Genstar, eventually rotating in the position of chief executive officer with Angus MacNaughton. In 1987, after Imasco took over Genstar, the two men started running a California venture-capital firm, Sutter Hill Ventures, partly financed by Imasco. I've seen Ross several times since, most recently when he spoke on my behalf when the University of Manitoba's Faculty of Management gave me its International Distinguished Entrepreneur Award.

For that critical board meeting in Toronto, I'd brought along two people who were elected as new directors: Lawrence (Bud) Eberhardt, who was a vice-president of Neonex, and our lawyer, Don Easton, a partner with Harper, Gilmour, Grey & Company in Vancouver. I'd got to know Don at Bow Mac, when he defended a guy suing us over a used car; I was so impressed that Don won the case even though he shouldn't have that I retained him as our lawyer. Don created the legal entity of my very first company, and to this day he's our official corporate lawyer and my close friend and trusted confidant. (He's only one of several lawyers we use, including Morley Koffman, a well-respected senior partner with Freeman and Co., a leading expert in mergers and acquisitions.) Don and Bud Eberhardt were later joined on the board by Mark Kaplan, who by then was a senior partner with Burnham & Co.; Russell Dunn, president of Eurocan Pulp and Paper Co. in Vancouver; and John Thompson, chairman of the board of Crush International in Toronto. I'd come to know Thompson a couple of years earlier when I first talked to him about buying his company (he wasn't interested).

Now that I was back in control of the board, I could concentrate on rebuilding Neonex International. There was a lot of work to do. Imbrex, the Montreal-based floor-covering company we'd bought in 1968, was in desperate straits. Our worst fear was realized: Harding Carpets, the supplier Imbrex depended on, had pulled out of the relationship on January 1, 1969, leaving us to find another carpet manufacturer. It was my mistake because I didn't do my homework. I should have talked to the Harding's people before I went into the deal. But Guy Godbout, the Imbrex president, convinced me it was better not to see them until afterwards. He assured me that Harding's would not go into its own distribution business, that they needed us more than we needed them. What I found out later is that relations between him and Harding's had been turning sour. When the carpet company sent us a letter saying goodbye, I told Godbout: "Don't worry about it. We'll stick with it." He found another American supplier, Bigelow-Sanford Inc. of New York, which was owned by the S&H grocery green-stamp people. Together as fifty-fifty partners, we got a $1.4 million federal Regional Economic Expansion grant and opened a $7 million factory in Ste. Agathe, Quebec. Bigelow started making a new line of tufted carpets and Imbrex marketed them. After that, everything began to deteriorate. Our deal with Bigelow was unsatisfactory from the first because they wanted control of the mill and always seemed like a reluctant partner. And to make matters worse, Harding's did go head to head against us, opening big distribution plants. The competition was aggressive: In '70 our sales tumbled to $19 million from $27 million and we started closing warehouses. That year our pre-tax operating loss was $3 million. In May '71, cutting our losses, we sold our American partners half of Bigelow Canada and later all of the carpet inventory, everything except Imbrex Atlantic, a company that continued to run profitably until we sold it in 1975. But in liquidating the main Imbrex operations, we wrote off about $1.4 million. As I told shareholders at the next Neonex annual meeting, "so much for the floor-covering business."

The problems we were having with Neonex were being echoed over at the other public company, Great Pacific Industries. At one point, we just about lost control of GPI. Bill Sleeman's first year running it went well. It was deeply

Starting Over

involved in the manufacture and leasing of industrial buildings primarily for petroleum companies exploring the North Slope oil fields of Alaska as well as the Canadian Arctic and Alberta. One division, Fabco Leasing, leased buildings made by Fabtec Structures, of which we owned 30 per cent. In 1970 Bill had bought a company in the same manufacturing business, Porta-Built Industries of Edmonton, which contributed significantly to GPI's earnings per share. But the next year was a bad one as the stock market fell, conglomerates lost favour, and the shares—which were issued at $2 and had nearly reached the double digits—thudded below a dollar. My piece of GPI had started out at 80 per cent. Now it was diluted down to 37 per cent because we'd traded stock to people whose companies we bought. Among those people were Marcel Prefontaine, who'd owned one of our stranger acquisitions, the Doric Howe Motor Hotel in Vancouver. Prefontaine was pushing us now to keep our promise to refurbish the hotel at a cost of a couple of hundred thousand dollars. To raise the money for the renovations, it became apparent we'd have to do a secondary underwriting of $1.5 million in convertible debentures.

A new company like GPI would have a hard time borrowing long-term funds through bonds, which are generally secured by assets, or through ordinary debentures, which are unsecured. Debentures can be compared to promissory notes because they're issued for a fixed period and draw a fixed rate of interest. Convertible debentures are something between stocks and bonds: They allow lenders, if they want, to become investors by converting their debt security into common shares at a price pegged above the market price at the time of issue. So, if a company does well, these lenders can profit along with the holders of its common stock.

When Pemberton Securities in Vancouver wasn't excited about doing an underwriting of convertible debentures, I lined Bill Sleeman up with large stockbrokers in Toronto and New York. He went on the road with Wilf Ray (by now our communications director) and a corporate audio-visual show. Bill's best bite was Morgan Guaranty in New York, which had done some financing for Neonex. He left with a handshake agreement from a senior vice-president that Morgan Guaranty would do this convertible-debenture underwriting after it looked over GPI's balance sheet. But when the V/P's assistant, the son of India's finance minister, didn't like what he saw, the bank turned us down. We decided to try Pemberton's again. This time they agreed to the underwriting, but only for $1 million at an 8 per cent interest rate. The deal was all set to go in principle when Bill got a call to see Pemberton chairman John Chaston. He told Bill that Pemberton's couldn't do the underwriting after all. Their retail salespeople didn't feel they could place more than $700,000 to $800,000 and even that much was a problem at 8 per cent. Bill (whose heart was in his shoes) shot back: "You could do seven or eight hundred thousand [dollars] and the interest rate is too low. So what would it take?" Chaston was caught: "Well, we could do a debenture of seven hundred thousand dollars at nine and one-quarter per cent." After commissions, that gave us about $640,000 to finance, among other things, the Doric Howe renovations that Marcel Prefontaine was demanding.

But that didn't satisfy Prefontaine for long. There had been a pause in oil exploration, and with its main customers on hold, Porta-Built began to lose money; Prefontaine's shares were quickly losing value. One of the five key shareholders in Porta-Built was Doug McNab, a boyhood friend of Prefontaine's. Realizing that we had only 37 per cent of Great Pacific Industries, Prefontaine knew that he and the Porta-Built people had enough GPI stock combined to lead a revolt and make him president. We would lose any control of the company. When one of the shareholders cracked and told Bill about the plan, we called a meeting at the Château Lacombe in Edmonton and announced to the Porta-Built bunch that we knew all about it. We were determined to keep control of the company. After almost a day of trying to convince them we could do a better job of operating GPI than Prefontaine, Bill had a private meeting with Doug McNab, who held most of the non-Pattison stock. McNab admitted we would be better operators but Prefontaine was his friend. "Well, Doug," said Bill, "your net worth is in that stock. If your friendship is more important. . ." McNab said he'd commit to us if we agreed to a meeting with Prefontaine where we'd all try to persuade him to change his mind. We met, but Prefontaine wouldn't budge. When he finally realized that McNab and the others were leaning towards us, he walked out of the meeting and asked if anybody else was joining him. No one was. For the second time, I'd been a whisker away from losing a company.

Starting Over

* * *

By 1972, knowing that we were still in trouble, I called all my top operations people together for what amounted to a corporate pep rally at the hotel in Harrison Hot Springs, B.C. They came from across Canada for an afternoon meeting where I presented them with what I called "a little philosophy." My speech was also a taste of the management style I'd be using from then on. Presidents of all the Neonex companies sat around a table, sipped ice water from pitchers, and listened to me talk enthusiastically about the reality of the long road ahead. The subject matter was different, my approach was a little smoother, but it was the same psychology I'd used twenty years earlier to motivate our car salesmen:

"I've told you that we're gonna start analysing your [financial] statements in our Corporate Office. If you've made a mistake and you've got trouble—and there's nothing wrong with that, we're not critical of mistakes, we just want to know about 'em, quick—just pick up the phone and say, 'I've got a problem.' And then we can decide which direction to head. If you've got a problem, don't try to hide it. Come and lay it on the table and tell us.

"We aren't gonna suffer fools gladly. And we have been tolerant in the past, on a few occasions. But we don't intend to be anymore. People are gonna come through for us. You know, this starts from Jimmy down. We all gotta produce—*I've* gotta produce, everybody around me has to produce. And there's no exception to the rule. The day we don't produce, then somebody else better come and do it for us and do a better job. I am totally committed to the owners of this company, which are the shareholders, and that means we've gotta make money. We've gotta get the credibility and the confidence of the investor and the investment community back into this company. And the only way we're gonna do that is not with fancy PR statements—they have their place, not fancy ones but realistic ones. Corporate image has its place, but the only thing that's gonna count is solid earnings, quarter by quarter by quarter. [I slammed the table on each "quarter" for effect.]

"And we've gotta demonstrate that we made twenty-seven cents a share in 1970, and that we're gonna make forty cents a share in '71, fifty cents in '72, and sixty cents in '73—whatever the figures are, what I'm saying is growth per share. Now, anything that is *not* in congress with the growth per share of this company is not the company policy. It's just that simple. Unless it's gonna help that objective, we're not interested. We're not interested in doubling the size of the company for the sake of having more sales. We're not interested in doubling the earnings of the company for the sake of doubling the earnings. We're only interested in what it's gonna do for the share growth of this company. Now that's the policy, that's the philosophy, and I personally am totally dedicated to it. . . .

"Mistakes we're gonna continue to make, but we're gonna continue to give this thing everything we've got to get back up there where we were. I don't expect to see the stock back up to twenty [dollars] for some period of time. But I'll tell ya, I *do* expect to see that stock at twenty. It's gonna be down the road a ways, but we're gonna have to have earnings of a buck and a quarter a share and a compound growth rate of 15 per cent per annum for five years to do it. . . . So never mind acquisitions. This company is gonna grow and produce earnings per share on internal growth. If we never make an acquisition, our earnings growth is gonna continue to grow.

"But one of the important functions of a central office is acquisitions. And that is one thing we do know something about. We've probably had more experience with it than anybody in Canada. Now, we've played it pretty cool for the last year and a half or two years but I'll tell ya, we're back on the track and we're starting to look at one and two and three deals a day again for the first time in what?—two years, Harry? [Harry Dunbar agreed.] And the phone's starting to ring. And in a month's time we're gonna make an announcement. We're in Oregon. [A month later, we'd be establishing a travel-trailer manufacturing plant in McMinnville, Oregon, and setting up an American dealer organization.] And I'd say within seven days, there's a possibility we'll make an acquisition in Vancouver. And if we make that critical acquisition, it's gonna be good for the company. [It took several weeks, but we bought EDP Industries, a Vancouver-based computer data-processing company.]

"So we really mean business. There's no foolin' with us. We're out to win and we're out to perform.

"And I'm also saying here today we don't think we know all the answers. I'm satisfied that you guys here around this table can help us improve what we're doing, straighten us out where we're doing things wrong, correct us in some things that our judgments are wrong on. Just because we happen to be sitting in Vancouver doesn't mean to say we've got the answers. Because we don't have the answers. And we welcome criticism. We welcome you coming in and raising hell with us—providing you've done your homework. We want help—and we've got talent around here and we want to use it.

"Okay. I told you where I think the opportunities lie in the future in this company. One thing we must not have are financial surprises. We can't find that we've got half-a-million-dollar bad debt on our hands, like we had with Imbrex. Probably the best money we ever spent was on Imbrex, because we learned so much over Imbrex, we will have made so much money in the next twenty years over everything we did wrong with Imbrex, that I'm satisfied that it's the best thing that ever happened to us. But we can't stand financial surprises. Bad inventories, where we wake up one morning and somebody tells us we've got a million-six tied up in tent trailers up in Edmonton—like, two years' supply because somebody forgot to shut off the production line. Those kind of surprises we won't tolerate. We must not have them and we won't accept them. And the people involved in these decisions—we won't accept *them*.

"The other thing is that every operating guy in our company has got to be on the incentive system. . . . Now, I've started on this once before but it never got off the ground because the concept was wrong. Anyway, we're coming back at it again. So that if a guy like Rex Kaufman [of Associated Helicopters] can triple the earnings in his company, then he should participate directly in the results of what he contributes to our earnings.

"The stock market—you know, you don't really have any control over that. If I go out and screw the company up and make a Maple Leaf deal, or go out and buy Imbrex and don't look after it, we can't really hang you with that. But we're hanging the guys at the Corporate Office for that because we're saying to them: 'Okay, you guys, how you win is with the stock.' But we're saying to the operating guys that we've gotta look at things on the basis of your performance. We haven't got a firm view on this because it's as complex as the pension plan. But we are open to ideas. The chief operating officers of the profit centres must and will participate in the performance of their companies in 1972 on some basis." (And they did.)

It was 1973. The NDP government had been in power in B.C. for a year after ending W.A.C. Bennett's two decades of Social Credit government. Premier Dave Barrett was reshaping the province. And we were trying to revitalize our companies with just as much energy. Bill Sleeman was back in our Corporate Office after Great Pacific Industries sold the Doric Howe Motor Hotel for a profit of $1.1 million and sold Porta-Built and Fabco to Neonex. GPI then concentrated on the successful vehicle-leasing business it had started with. Bill came back to a corporation that was just starting to see some light at the end of a very long tunnel. He, Stan Whittle, and Bud Eberhardt were group vice-presidents; Harry Dunbar was vice-president, corporate development; Guy Lewall was vice-president and secretary-treasurer; and Fred Vanstone was vice-president, finance and administration. I'd found Fred at the Bank of B.C., where he was the talented and likeable assistant to Albert Hall, the chairman who'd given me the timely $300,000 line of credit. Fred Vanstone had also worked for the Toronto-Dominion Bank, which was now an important factor for Neonex. After months of courtship, they'd agreed to become our bankers and Ed Lawrence, the TD's vice-president, credit, came on the Neonex board.

By being cautious, holding back on acquisitions, and focusing on what we had, we were slowly regaining financial credibility. As I'd tell *Business Week:* "Before, when we acquired a company, we had a philosophy of 'we acquired it, you run it.' Now, that has changed to 'we acquired it, so let's run it together.'" At Neonex we attracted directors of the calibre of Ed Lawrence and Jack Thompson, the Crush International chairman. Directors of Great Pacific Industries included Bob Wyman, senior vice-president of Pemberton Securities (later Pemberton's chairman and the chancellor of the University of British Columbia), and Sir Michael Butler, of the Vancouver legal firm of Farris, Farris, Vaughan, Wills & Murphy (Sir Michael, formerly of Toronto, had some expertise in the takeover business). Even the Canadian Imperial Bank of Commerce was coming 'round. I got to know

Earl Maxwell, the Commerce's general manager of credit. And our relations warmed up even more after the chairman, Neil McKinnon, was deposed in 1973. I saw some irony in what happened to McKinnon: One of the bank's directors who was instrumental in forcing him to resign was none other than Jack Leitch—who'd reportedly gone to McKinnon for his help during our Maple Leaf takeover attempt when the Commerce called our loan. Leitch was chairman of a committee of directors set up to define the powers of the Commerce executives. The dissident directors were upset because of the bank's relatively low earnings. In recommending that the chairman be limited to chairing board meetings and consulting to the president, the committee was attacking McKinnon's own dictatorial way of running the bank. He took early retirement; Two years later, he drowned in a snorkeling accident. After Neil McKinnon left, the Commerce actually wanted to revive our financial relationship. I continued on good terms with Russ Harrison, who became president and in '76 chairman and CEO. And in later years we placed some of our companies with the Commerce, eventually re-establishing a $40 million line of credit. (During Expo, Russ told me during a dinner of Commerce directors: "You're the only person I can remember whose loans we called and yet always stayed good friends with.")

But in 1973, even with the TD behind us and the Commerce about to do business with us again, we weren't out of the woods. Three of our operations were in trouble. In at least one case, the problem was out of our control. When the Arab petroleum-producing countries curtailed oil production after Egypt's Yom Kippur War with Israel, North America faced an energy crisis. That had a sudden and dramatic effect on Neonex's recreational-vehicle business. In a few years of rapid expansion, we had bought or opened seven RV factories in Canada and the United States. But as gas prices climbed from $3 a barrel to $10, people stopped driving big leisure vehicles such as motor homes. Within a year our profits had fallen by 80 per cent. We cut production at our RV plant in the City of Industry, California, and a travel trailer plant in McMinnville, Oregon, and sold our RV plants in Red Deer, Alberta; Winkler, Manitoba; and Woodstock, Ontario. Our total investment in the industry was down by about half.

In a speech to shareholders in 1974, I also blamed the economic uncertainties created by the energy crisis for our decision to get out of a Neonex investment in an American franchise of Pop Shoppes. That wasn't the only reason. Harry Dunbar brought this deal to us and we liked the concept. Originally developed by a couple of London, Ontario, men, Pop Shoppes produced and distributed low-priced soft drinks directly to the consumer through franchised retail outlets in North America. Because distribution is always a major cost in that business, the idea of having the customer come to the store seemed like a good one. We bought the franchise for Texas, Hawaii, and California, where we opened our first store in Fresno in '73. That was before I was exposed to Pop Shoppes' top management. Within a month of seeing how they ran things day to day, I decided to pull the plug. We sold out to an American. The only moral of the story is that when you make a mistake—and we made a mistake in the Pop Shoppes deal—recognize it and get the hang out right away. That was our first leap into the soft-drink market, but not our last.

For more than four years, Acme Novelty had been making a lot of money for Neonex. But by '73, we were starting to see signs that Acme Merchandise Distributors (as it was now called) was starting to slip. Although sales were higher, so were operating costs. Management had made several mistakes. Acme was growing too fast; we'd quadrupled the number of stores to thirty-six. We had also dropped the idea of a special membership card for customers, which suggested exclusivity. In the early days, staff would move into a place like Winnipeg and, while our store was being built, go around to businesses and factories and tell the general managers: "This wholesale merchandising firm is opening up and we'd like to give your employees the opportunity to shop there with their own card." Instead, Acme become a catalogue-shopping operation in the image of Consumers Distributing, which was doing well in Ontario. We didn't do well there: In '74, we sold five of our Ontario stores. At the same time, we were building a major distribution centre in Edmonton. Centralizing distribution led to delays and classic errors, like sending a semi-trailer load of salt-water fishing equipment to Regina and Winnipeg. In some of our satellite stores, we might have only 250 items in stock out of 2,700 in the catalogue. I say "we," but ultimately I have to take responsibility. I hired one president, an industrial accountant who'd been vice-president of finance, and I hired his replacement, a Toronto management consultant whom we'd called in to recommend changes in the operation; instead of the company's fortunes improving, they kept getting worse. On at least two occasions, to keep Acme afloat Neonex had to advance what at the time was big money, once as much as $2 million. Our troubles continued. Discount stores like Woolco and K-Mart were opening and, as inflation climbed, catalogue sales were declining all over Canada; Eaton's was about to drop its 18-million–circulation catalogue. By the time we shut down in early '76, Acme had only thirteen stores left. We kept two subsidiaries, Bazaar & Novelty in the East and Acme Amusements in the West, which merchandised carnival goods, bingo supplies, and novelties.

Overall, the business had earned good money in its best years and, when it closed, gave us three people who made sizeable contributions to the parent company: Iain Harris, who became president of AirBC; Don Connors, head of the Jim Pattison Automotive Group; and John Seebach, head of the Jim Pattison News Group. They were all strong managers and, after Acme, I asked them to work at other Neonex operations.

A lot of other people lost their jobs. Closing down a company is never easy, but the reality is that no company can survive if it doesn't make money. Banks don't lend money to unhealthy companies. I have no hesitation in shutting down one ailing business to help save the thousands of jobs that people hold in all our other businesses. If I had cancer of the arm, I'd chop off my arm to save the rest of my body. When I opened my first car dealership, I had to reduce the staff by half or I never would have survived—and all hundred of the original employees would have lost their jobs. So to save fifty, I let fifty go. The company became healthy, we built on it, and today we employ seven thousand people. You either fix an uneconomic operation or shut it down. We tried to fix Acme twice, with new management, and failed both times. Now, sometimes you can sell pieces of a company, as we did with Imbrex, and keep people employed. We sold part of that floor-coverings company to Rudy Goulet, who was vice-president of marketing for Bigelow Canada. Some of the two hundred jobs were saved. But some businesses—again, like Acme—are overtaken by events. Sure, we made mistakes with that company, but we struggled to save it for years. Inflation, competition, and a change in buying habits all combined against Acme. Times change. If, at the turn of the century, there are two hundred people making buggy whips in factories in Ontario and the age of the automobile arrives, what do you do with those people? They may have been working there all their lives, but suddenly it's over. In the 1950s, when Packard stopped making cars, my dad lost his job with the Consolidated Motor Company in Vancouver. At age sixty-one, after twenty-one years with Consolidated, he got three months' severance pay—$1,200. But the reality was that Packard could no longer compete.

To jump ahead in time: The Jim Pattison Group faced one of those do-or-die decisions in 1985 when Vanguard Manufacturing in Winfield, B.C., was no longer competitive. We'd owned the company for nine of the twenty-five years it had been operating. Now it was losing money. For years, Vanguard had been the absolute leader in the field of quality recreational vehicles. But when RV manufacturers in Manitoba and Ontario were consistently selling at lower prices, we asked the unions at Vanguard for concessions in their contracts that would allow us to compete. We wanted to hire new people at lower wages and to contract out the fibreglass manufacturing. The unions told us to jump in the lake. My mind was on Expo at the time, but we warned them that, even though we wanted to stay in business, if we didn't get flexibility in their contracts, we would pull out. They didn't believe us. And after we sold Vanguard to a company that moved it to North Battleford, Saskatchewan—and ended three hundred jobs in B.C.—the unions came back to us and said they'd now take our deal. It was too late. There's no security for anybody in a company that continues to lose money.

By the mid-1970s, most of the other Neonex companies were making money. Overwaitea Foods was renovating two stores and building four new supermarkets and a central distribution warehouse. The Neonex shelter division—by now building and leasing both pre-fab industrial and residential structures—was recording strong profits. Provincial News was prospering, along with a 1972 acquisition, Mountain City News of Hamilton, a wholesale news distributor serving Southern Ontario.

As for the companies I held privately, CFRW in Winnipeg was gone, sold to Allan Waters, but CJOR in Vancouver was healthy and our second General Motors dealership was performing well in its fourth year. It's interesting how we picked up the Courtesy Chevrolet dealership in Burnaby, a Greater Vancouver municipality. In 1971 we wound up buying the location from Dueck Chevrolet Oldsmobile, my old competitors during the Bow Mac days. Dueck, the largest Chevrolet dealer in Canada, had been operating it as a second outlet for used and leased cars. General Motors didn't permit an individual dealer to have more than one dealership. But because Jim Pattison on Main sold Pontiacs and Buicks, General Motors allowed us to open Burnaby as a Chevrolet-Olds franchise.

Another company we'd acquired privately during those years of recovery was performing well. When we bought it in 1972, EDP Industries was a Vancouver-based computer business, with operations in Ottawa, Toronto, and Detroit, which was developing its own programs and doing data-processing for smaller companies. It had an Establishment board, including Alan Eyre, president of Dueck Chevrolet, and Dr. Gordon Shrum, former chairman of B.C. Hydro. But the public company was almost bankrupt when Bill Wood, its president and a fellow member of the Young Presidents' Organization, came to ask our help in rescuing it. The only way to save it was to put up $300,000 for 92 per cent of it, in the form of Treasury stock. We bought it at 8.7 cents a share; afterwards, as the stock rose to $1, shareholders had the chance to sell. EDP came with several million dollars' worth of tax losses to carry forward, which meant that we got the business for virtually nothing. Ed Pyrik, who'd been a vice-president of finance with us, began running the company and slashed expenses, in part by selling all the operations but Vancouver. Later, we began to wonder how we could take it private. There were hundreds of shareholders who had invested before we came on the scene. For instance, an average shareholder who might have invested a total of about $2,200 in shares now found that all of them together were worth only about $26. We couldn't see making these shareholders an offer—why would they even bother to take virtually worthless stock out of their safety-deposit box? Somehow we had to get the number of shareholders down to a manageable level. Then, while Harry Dunbar was attending a San Francisco seminar on mergers and acquisitions, a lecturer told him how he'd consolidated the shares of one company at a ratio of 5 to 1, which was enough of a multiple to create a lot of fractional shareholders who were paid off in cash. Going through our shareholder list, Harry concluded that to leave us with only seven shareholders, we'd have to consolidate at the incredible ratio of 40,000 to 1. In other words, we'd offer to exchange one new share for 40,000 old ones; shareholders who didn't have that many would have to accept cash instead—at 5.7 cents per share. Not consolidation with that high a ratio of shares had ever been done in Western Canada. But we did it and, after paying off the shareholders, we owned 100 per cent of the company.

We also made a couple of memorable mistakes in the mid-1970s. One was mine alone. In '74 a Vancouver writer named Tom Ardies came to me with a proposal to finance a book about a Nazi war criminal I'd never heard of. At the time Tom was the son-in-law of an old friend of mine, Frank Bernard, who was the local vice-consul for Spain. It sounded like a fascinating deal and Frank recommended it highly. Tom Ardies, it turned out, teamed up with a former safe-cracker and jewel thief named Bobby Wilson, a Canadian who claimed to have good contacts in South America where the Nazi was living. I was part of a group of at least ten local people to front them $20,000 to buy the rights to the story and $5,000 for expenses. Then my friend Jack Wasserman, the *Vancouver Sun* columnist, came to me and asked: "Do you know who this Gestapo killer is?" After Jack explained, I immediately walked away from the deal. Tom never did follow through with the book. Bobby Wilson did, though: He made several trips to Bolivia and, based on the subject's thousand-page scrapbook of the Second World War and a long taped interview, wrote *The Confessions of Klaus Barbie, The Butcher of Lyon*.

The other unforgettable error wasn't mine alone. It involved another company that we bought privately. But unlike Courtesy Chevrolet and EDP Industries, it failed miserably. If we had good people to guide us through the computer industry, and understood the automobile field almost instinctively, this new acquisition was in a business that my executives and I knew absolutely nothing about: professional hockey.

CHAPTER ELEVEN

My Life in Sport

In hindsight, it was a big mistake. At the time it looked like a swell idea and our second-in-command, Bill Sleeman, was pushing me into it. Bill is a sports nut; I like to say he was the only reason I ever got involved in the unlikely world of major-league hockey. I'm not a jock. I played tennis for fun in my younger days, and I bowled, and these days I try to swim every day in my wave-action pool at home. Though I belong to a golf club in Palm Springs, I've only golfed twice in my life. Never really played hockey, though the sport always intrigued me. Growing up, I used to listen to Foster Hewitt's dramatic reporting of "Hockey Night in Canada" on radio and, until I became a businessman, I watched the National Hockey League on TV. During the Maple Leaf Mills crisis, I had a front-row seat in the life of Bruce Norris, the Detroit Red Wings' owner and NHL chairman. We even tried to buy the Toronto Maple Leafs and the Vancouver Canucks because NHL teams were so lucrative at the time. So when the chance came to acquire what sounded like a bargain-priced franchise of the one-year-old World Hockey Association, we were ripe and ready.

Hockey is only one of the sports we've flirted with financially over the years. We've contemplated buying a piece of the B.C. Lions of the Canadian Football League and briefly held the option for a World Football League franchise. In '78, when the Lions looked like they were about to fold, a sportsman friend of mine, Herb Capozzi (a former CFL lineman), tried to put together a private group to buy the team. We would have been bidding against Herb in what we decided would be a worthwhile community involvement. But the directors of the Lions managed to get a debenture that kept the club afloat without us. Then when Johnny Bassett Jr., the Toronto sports entrepreneur, was trying to promote the American-based World Football League, he gave us the option to have the Vancouver franchise—but that was an option that the Canadian government wasn't keen to have anyone pick up. We've had several runs at major-league baseball, going after the Cleveland Indians, Minnesota Twins, and San Francisco Giants. Meantime, we owned the minor-league Vancouver Canadians in the hope of someday attracting a big-league club to our home town. But if we've earned any scars in the sports arena, it was as owners of a luckless WHA club called the Vancouver Blazers, which became the Calgary Cowboys.

My appetite for pro hockey had already been whetted a couple of times at the start of the '70s. Both episodes involved people who went to prison for fraud.

Stafford Smythe was interested in selling the Toronto Maple Leafs, the legendary team founded by his father, Conn. I sent Harry Dunbar, my assistant, to talk to Smythe. The negotiations were serious, reaching the point where we had an agreement in principle to buy the team—for about $10 million, I recall—subject to our auditors checking the books. Well, when Peat Marwick's people looked things over, they came back to us with concerns about improprieties in the accounts. If we'd done the deal, we would have bought shares in the company. To avoid any trouble, we just backed away quietly. Smythe died soon after, and in '72 his partner, Harold Ballard, went to prison for defrauding his company, Maple Leaf Gardens, of $82,000 and participating in the theft of $123,000.

About the same time that we were considering the Leafs, we were looking at the Vancouver Canucks. Medicor, a Minneapolis-based conglomerate, controlled Northwest Sports Enterprises Inc., which was the parent company of the Canucks. Medicor's president, Tom Scallen, had recently been charged with theft of $3 million and issuing a false prospectus, in transferring funds from Northwest to Medicor. Even the judge in the case accepted the fact that Tom didn't intend "to permanently deprive Northwest of the money." I knew Tom as a fellow member of the Young Presidents' Organization. On first hearing of the charges, I told him we'd be interested in acquiring control of Northwest. He wanted to keep the team. In '73, he was convicted and sentenced to concurrent four-year prison terms on each charge. I felt sorry for him. When he was in the process of asking leave to appeal to the Supreme Court of Canada, I guaranteed his $100,000 bail (reportedly the highest bail ever requested in B.C. at that time and the first time anyone in B.C. had been granted bail before such leave was actually approved). While Tom was serving a third of his reduced sentence of two years, I went to see him at B.C.'s Agassiz Mountain Prison on a couple of occasions—until he informed me that I was using up his wife's visiting time. One day in '74, during the Russia-Canada hockey series, he called me from the prison kitchen to ask if I could get four tickets to the game in Vancouver. "It'll do me a lot of good with the guards in the kitchen if I can get them tickets." I got them tickets.

I had a second chance to buy the Canucks. In 1973, before Tom Scallen went to prison, we wound up together on a YPO cruise in the Mediterranean aboard the *Queen Elizabeth II*. We were sitting up late one night when he said, "Jimmy, I'll sell you the Canucks for $13 million." But that was too rich for me. So I got off the ship at Lisbon, caught a plane to Vancouver, and bought the Blazers instead.

From the start, it was a pretty improbable deal. As *The Complete Encyclopedia of Hockey* puts it, "many would say the WHA was nothing more than a carpet-bagging league, constantly on the prowl searching for gullible owners in new cities populated by naive fans." The league was founded by a couple of Californians, one of them a Los Angeles lawyer and entrepreneur named Gary Davidson. He'd never even seen a hockey game when his partner-to-be, Dennis Murphy, approached him in 1971 to consider starting a second major league. The two of them were professional league-launchers. Murphy had dreamed up the American Basketball Association to compete with the National Basketball Association.

My Life in Sport

Davidson, who'd also been involved in the ABA, would go on to help create the World Football League, which survived only briefly up against the rival National and American Football leagues. Davidson was impressed by the NHL's success. By the fact that it was grossing $50 million a year and playing to nearly 90 per cent capacity—even after expanding to fourteen franchises, some of them moneymakers from Day One. Not only that, he figured it wouldn't take much to lure away the league's players because they were the lowest-paid in professional sport, earning an average of only $25,000 a season. He was right: when the WHA began in 1972, it had robbed the NHL of many well-established players and one superstar. Surprising everybody, Bobby Hull left the Chicago Black Hawks to sign a $2.75 million contract to coach and play for the Winnipeg Jets—for $1 million up front.

As founders, Davidson, Murphy, and a lawyer friend named Don Regan decided they would ask $25,000 for each WHA franchise. It was a steal compared to the minimum $6 million for a new NHL franchise or the $13 million Scallen wanted for the Canucks. The league's original slogan was "Comin' on strong!" In the opening season, twelve franchises, four of them Canadian, ambitiously drafted more than a thousand players. Setting the zany tone of the league, Scotty Munro of the Calgary Broncos selected a European named Alexei Kosygin, who happened to be the Soviet premier. The Broncos didn't even survive the start of the season; Calgary and Miami backed out, to be replaced by Chicago and Cleveland. Among the original teams was the Philadelphia Blazers, which established two milestones. One of its centres, André Lacroix, captured the league's first scoring championship. Another centre, Derek Sanderson, signed a ten-year deal for an estimated $2.325 million but his contract was bought out for an outrageous $1 million after he played only eight games, badly. The Blazers were a classic hard-luck team. Not only did Sanderson make an expensive departure, but goalie Bernie Parent also deserted them that first season, taking about $200,000 of his contracted $750,000 with him. Playing coach Johnny McKenzie missed the first eighteen games of the year after fracturing his arm in training camp (his former team, the NHL Boston Bruins, once told "Pie" McKenzie to stop riding in rodeos during the summer and find safer work; he got a job in a winery). And at the grand opening in Philadelphia, the ice-sweeping machine crashed through the ice, cancelling the first game; angry fans pelted officials with 7,500 souvenir pucks.

We had more than passing interest in the fortunes of the Philadelphia Blazers. In 1973, business associates were suggesting we buy one of the floundering American clubs, such as Philadelphia, and move it to Vancouver. A new team, the Toronto Toros, had joined the WHA and we knew the reputation of some of its backers, including Johnny Bassett and John Craig Eaton. Despite first-year growing pains, the Toronto franchise-holders said, the league was on the verge of having credibility. The New England Whalers were owned in part by Aetna Life; the Cleveland Crusaders by Nick Mileti, who had a chain of radio stations; the Edmonton Oilers by Dr. Charles Allard of Allarco Developments; and the Winnipeg Jets by a responsible group led by financially independent Ben Hatskin, who operated the local junior team.

In early May, we heard reporters' talk of a WHA franchise coming to Vancouver. I asked Maureen Chant to call Ben Hatskin, the league's chairman; she located him in Houston where the Jets were playing in a semi-final.

"You probably haven't heard of me, but my name is Jimmy Pattison and I hear there may be a possibility of a WHA franchise in Vancouver."

"I'll have someone call you," Hatskin said.

A league executive called an hour later and said: "I'll have someone call you."

This time I asked: "Who?"

"Bernie Brown."

"Who's he?"

"He's the owner of the Philadelphia Blazers."

Brown, who owned a large trucking company in Philadelphia, phoned to say if we were interested in buying his team, we'd have to act quickly: A group in B.C.'s Fraser Valley, whom he'd visited recently, was about to put a deposit down.

That Sunday, on my way to New York, I met Brown and Blazers president Dick Olson in Toronto. After four hours' bargaining, we couldn't come to terms. Tuesday, Olson phoned to say he wanted to negotiate some more. Bill Sleeman and Vancouver lawyer Frank Murphy went to see where Olson and Brown were coming from. At that point, they wanted

$2.8 million, which we thought was a reasonable opening price. Reasonable because the faltering Vancouver Canucks had sold recently for $11 million and, despite their poor performance, had a season's-ticket waiting list of five thousand fans. If the WHA prospered, in three or four years we might have an asset worth as much as $10 million. We didn't hear from the Blazers' owners for five days; we learned later that our tentative offer was being shown around to other prospective buyers in Indianapolis and Milwaukee. Meanwhile, I'd hopped a float plane to Victoria to pay my first call on the new NDP government of Dave Barrett. Jack Wasserman, my friend at the *Sun*, had called the premier, who put me in touch with resources minister Bob Williams. An East-Sider like me, Williams was responsible for the Pacific National Exhibition, which ran the Coliseum where the Vancouver Canucks played. In our twenty-minute interview, he told me there was no reason why the Blazers couldn't play there too.

Thursday, we phoned Bernie Brown in Philadelphia to warn him that he had until 5:00 P.M. the next day to agree to a deal—"or we pull out." Confident—over-confident—we arranged to have a Neonex-manufactured mobile building moved to a central downtown corner as a ticket office and had printers on notice to churn out applications for season's tickets. Friday, Bill was back in Philadelphia, still negotiating. Saturday night, Mary and I were having a steak at Hy's Encore when we were interrupted by a flurry of phone calls from Bill. The Blazers wanted to change the deal. It took two hours to sort things out by long-distance from the restaurant.

Sunday, Bill and our lawyer Frank Murphy were in Chicago for a session with league president Dick Olson.

Monday, in Philadelphia, we were about to sign an agreement when it fell apart over last-minute details. We'd agreed to pay $2 million for the team, but with $1 million up front and the rest in five years. Now, Brown wanted the remainder in three years. The deal collapsed.

Tuesday, Bill and Frank were bargaining from scratch, when Frank discovered that neither playing coach Johnny McKenzie nor high-scoring centre André Lacroix could be moved from Philadelphia without their approval. That sounded like the final straw to me; our negotiators flew back to Vancouver.

Wednesday, we tried one last time. "Look," I told Brown,

"we've done sixty-nine deals and don't want this one to fall apart. If you come to Vancouver, I guarantee you that, on any kind of a reasonable basis, we can have a deal."

Thursday, Dick Olson was in Vancouver, carrying Bernie Brown's power of attorney. A phone poll of WHA owners agreed to transfer the team from Philadelphia. And the Blazers' owners accepted our cash offer—for $1.9 million, but only if they could guarantee us all of the players, especially McKenzie. By 10:30 that night, McKenzie and the team's general manager, Phil Watson, were in my office.

There were nineteen of us in six different offices at Neonex headquarters. We bargained half the night away, with lawyers and accountants haggling, secretaries typing, and Maureen cooking bacon and eggs for everybody. The major sticking point was McKenzie's contract. At 4:00 A.M., he and Dick Olson arrived from another office to report that we had a deal—$100,000 for three years of his services as playing coach. An hour later, we signed the agreement to buy the franchise, twenty-eight Blazers, and the rights to sixty protected players.

That morning, I went to see John Cleghorn of the Mercantile Bank (who's now president of the Royal) and only then arranged to borrow the $1.9 million. That's what you call faith. One of the side benefits of the deal was that we could attribute a high percentage of the purchase price to the value of the players' contracts and write that amount off in taxes. The write-off was based on a Revenue Canada ruling the Bronfmans had got a few years earlier on how they could treat their Montreal Expo players for tax purposes.

We all adjourned that afternoon to the International Suite at the Bayshore Inn to announce that Vancouver had its second major-league hockey team. We promptly challenged the NHL Canucks to a best-of-three series with the proceeds to minor hockey. The Canucks replied that they'd be glad to have us play two exhibition games against their number-one farm club in Seattle.

It was the only acquisition we'd ever made that every executive in Corporate Office unanimously approved—even one of our conservative vice-presidents, Bud Eberhardt. Not knowing if it was the right acquisition for a public company like Neonex, we bought the team privately. But we all became hockey fans; I went to every home game when I was in town. Soon everybody in Corporate Office was getting so involved with the Blazers that I saw a conflict with the time they were spending on the hockey team, which was a division of one of my private companies. With its apparent initial success—ticket sales booming and visible support from local fans—our outside Neonex directors voted to put the team into the public company.

We did well for a newcomer in a two-team town: Even though our first-year attendance at the Coliseum averaged little more than 8,000 in the 15,000–seat arena, it led the league. We had a tie-in with our Overwaitea supermarkets, giving away tickets to customers buying a certain amount of groceries. Wilf Ray went from communicating the financial details of Neonex deals to promoting the Blazers with firemen's hats on the ushers and fire engines running around the Coliseum with their lights flashing and sirens sounding. Denny Boyd, who had left the *Sun* to work for CJOR, handled media relations. He always seemed a little embarrassed about it. One day Denny accepted a delivery for Wilf at the Blazers office. Opening the box, he discovered three Rudy Vallee–type megaphones in bright Blazers orange. When Wilf walked in, Denny said: "Your hats have arrived." During the games, Wilf would run around the rink with those megaphones and have a spotlight pick out women fans as he gave them roses. With all that, the Blazers still ended up second-last in the league. The Houston Aeros won the championship with the help of Mark and Marty Howe and their dad, Gordie, who'd come out of retirement at forty-seven to become the WHA's Most Valuable Player. But there were signs of trouble in the WHA. The New York Raiders, for instance, had to change their name to the Golden Blades and finally to the Jersey Knights after bad debts forced them to flee to a New Jersey suburb of Philadelphia.

I continued to be hopeful about the league as long as I stayed away from the chaos of the owners' meetings. They were almost a total waste of time, but always entertaining; you'd never go to a nightclub if you could attend those meetings. Oh, there were some solid people there. The Bassetts and the Eatons of the Toronto Toros. Howard Baldwin of the New England (later Hartford) Whalers, who ran it for the Aetna group of insurance companies and was the most all-around, able executive in the league; he still operates the

Whalers in the NHL today. Ben Hatskin ("Benny the Hat") of the Winnipeg Jets had an interesting past, which included running a nightclub in Winnipeg ("I make mistakes," he'd say. "I once fired Barbra Streisand; she was plain-looking and I didn't think she had much of a voice"). Ben may not have been well-educated but he was an astute chairman who did more for the WHA than anyone else. And then there were guys like Bill Hunter ("Wild Bill" Hunter, he was called) of the Edmonton Oilers, one of life's most unforgettable characters. Bill, a dynamic salesman, enthusiastic and emotional, gave reporters at a press conference announcing his team a typical interview:

Reporter: Do you expect to make money this season?
Hunter: I expect to lose a few dollars.
Reporter: How much is a few?
Hunter: None of your [bleeping] business.
Reporter: How will you get your players?
Hunter: Steal them!
Reporter: Will you hurt the NHL?
Hunter: Here's a red-haired [bleep] who doesn't give a [bleep] about the [bleeping] NHL.

At the league meetings, he'd get so excited that after proposing a motion and hearing it discussed for an hour, he could become passionately opposed to it and vote against his own proposal. Sometimes, to get attention, he'd stand on the table and lecture the rest of the owners. He often had to when the meetings collapsed into shouting matches: "Shut up, you can't vote because you're not up to date on your financial obligations." "I am so—the cheque's in the mail." Guys would walk out, angrily. After the first couple of years, the list of owners current on their franchise dues grew shorter and shorter. The weak franchises started to fail and there were financing costs to prop up the league and the inevitable litigation expenses. Carl Eller, a businessman who owned the Phoenix Roadrunners, once made a dramatic speech in which he said: "For the money I've lost on the Roadrunners, I could have built a hospital, named it after my wife, and given it to the people of Phoenix." After attending a few of these meetings, which were like a circus, I decided I couldn't afford the time and left it to Bill Sleeman to represent us.

My Life in Sport

Eventually the meetings were held at the Airport Hilton in Chicago, the most central location for owners spread across the continent. We did manage to convince them to come to Vancouver once for the league's annual convention. They were intending to hold it in Honolulu, where we didn't even have a franchise. We put them into the best suites in the Bayshore overlooking the harbour and had them all picked up in limousines to come to my house in the British Properties.

We went into the second season hopefully. Realizing that Johnny McKenzie was not the right coach, we approached Joe Crozier, whose contract was about to expire with the Buffalo Sabres of the NHL. Joe had worked for our radio station, CJOR, and had a good reputation as a coach. The first thing he decided was that the Blazers had no talent; we'd have to sign some high-profile juniors. His scout in Buffalo had been Al Miller, one of the best in the business. Now, working for us, Miller went after a junior player from the Saskatoon Blades whom he figured could be better than Bobby Orr. The big, quick defenceman was Pat Price of Nelson, B.C. He was only nineteen, under-age by the NHL's draft rules, which the WHA ignored. Price had taken the Blades to the Memorial Cup, was voted best defenceman in his league, and was about to play with Team Canada against the Soviets. As the top draft choice of both major leagues, he was going to be pricey, but Joe Crozier wanted him.

Crozier and Bill Sleeman went to Calgary for the Memorial Cup weekend to meet Price and his agent, lawyer Dave Schatia of Pro-Am Sports Consultants of Montreal. Agents had become important, and expensive, factors in pro hockey since the launch of the second league. Pro-Am was concerned about the financial stability of the WHA, so Joe and Bill had to do a strong selling job, competing against the Washington Capitals of the NHL. "We'll charge you more to have him go to the WHA—for the risk and the lack of credibility," Dave Schatia said. Bill ended up offering Price $1.3 million over five years, the largest rookie contract in the history of the sport.

I was in Calgary at the time and happened to run into Bill, who told me about the basic agreement. "Bill, do you think it's the right thing to do?" I didn't know if the deal was good, bad, or indifferent.

"It's what all the hockey guys say will make our team."

It was big news. We thought we had the world by the tail. Wrong.

Part of our agreement with Pat Price was to give him a new $27,000 red Ferrari Dino 246 FT every two years (supplied by Jim Pattison Leasing). That summer Price was ticketed for speeding at more than a hundred miles an hour through Nelson and, another time, he and the Ferrari wound up in a ditch. The sportscar had several thousand dollars' damage; he was okay. But then he really did injure himself—twisting his ankle when he tumbled off his tall platform shoes. I can still recall my first sight of him in the Coliseum: I saw a fellow hobbling around on crutches and then realized that this was the guy we'd paid more than a million dollars for. Somehow that scene symbolizes the Vancouver Blazers for me.

Pat Price never did deliver. Joe Crozier accused him of fooling around, and later that first season assistant coach Andy Bathgate—once among the top dozen scorers in the NHL—said: "Joe, we've got to dump the kid. He's just not worth the money." At season's end, the New York Islanders were still interested in him, for some reason. Bill Sleeman told his agent: "Pat deserves to be in the NHL. He's free to go to the Islanders." Price fled to New York for only half a million over five years and then didn't make the training-camp cut; he wound up on New York's farm club in Fort Worth, Texas. The Islanders gave us $70,000 to release him and he gave us back the Ferrari.

Things didn't get any better for the Blazers. Crozier, who threatened and cursed his players, was reduced to teaching two defencemen to sharpen up their style by holding either end of a ten-foot two-by-four and skating backwards. Meanwhile, the Canucks had magically improved, and we were now getting attendance of only about six thousand to a game, which meant a loss of more than $1 million on the season. (The league as a whole had lost roughly $15 million.)

By then, we had a partner in the Blazers. An unhappy partner named June Sifton of the Winnipeg Establishment Siftons, who owned the *Free Press* and part of the FP Publications chain. I was in the Velvet Glove restaurant in the Winnipeg Inn when a Toronto lawyer (now Senator), Jerry Grafstein, came over to say: "There's a lady that wants to meet you." It was June Sifton, who said she was interested in buying half of the Blazers. The board agreed to sell her 25 per cent, for $750,000. But by the end of the '74 season, she sent her lawyers to see us, demanding that we buy her out. They refused our offer of $450,000, so she stayed in. Later, when she refused our call for more cash, her equity in the team went down.

But we needed her approval when, in the third season, we decided to move the Blazers to Calgary and rename them the Cowboys. Calgary was economically hot at the time and the city and the province indicated they'd soon be building a new rink to replace the Stampede Corral, less than half the size of the Coliseum in Vancouver. Meanwhile, we could charge higher prices at the Corral and have a fuller-looking arena. June Sifton agreed; she was on the receiving line with Bobby Hull and me at the cocktail party where we announced the move to Calgary. In the 1975–76 season, with Joe Crozier continuing as general manager and coach, the team tightened up and actually made the playoffs, finishing fourth overall in the WHA. But we still lost about the same amount of money as we had in Vancouver. When we made another cash call on June Sifton, she refused again; her equity dropped to about 8 per cent. Should we carry on? Sell? Fold? There was some serious talk in the hockey world about the possible merger of the two leagues the year after next. If we held on, we might be able to sell the team as it moved to a bigger city, or the other WHA clubs might pay us for deciding to stay out of the new, merged league. Bill Sleeman's last year of involvement with our team was spent at the league level helping devise a strategy of merging with the NHL and saving our investment.

Among the new WHA owners was Nelson Skalbania, the high-flying Vancouver real-estate speculator. He'd acquired the Edmonton Oilers from a group that included surgeon/entrepreneur Dr. Charles Allard, Zane Feldman, and Bill Hunter. Then he brought in a partner, his Edmonton financier friend, Peter Pocklington. Nelson got so caught up in hockey that he quickly bought the league's Indianapolis Racers out of receivership for $1—and later signed a Brantford, Ontario, kid named Wayne Gretzky to his first professional-hockey contract. In 1977, Nelson and Bill Sleeman were at a crucial league meeting to discuss the potential merger. Everyone knew that only a few of the WHA teams would be accepted for entry into the NHL; those clubs agreed to pay the ones that were rejected $1.4 million apiece in compensation—all of it in promissory notes over five years. That wasn't enough for us; we figured our operating losses were on the books for $2 million. Bill called Nelson out of the room. "Look, Nelson, you've got all kinds of property kicking around. Find a piece of property of yours that's free and clear and appraised at $2 million. Then you take our notes from your league partners for $1.4 million, and we'll have a deal."

"Terrific," Nelson said. "That's the way to do it."

They returned to the meeting to announce that the Blazers problem was solved in a side agreement between Pattison and Skalbania.

But when our appraiser went to see the Edmonton property Nelson had chosen for the transaction, he said it was worth only $1.6 million.

"That's no problem," Nelson said. "I've got another piece worth about $400,000. I'll throw that in."

In fact, our appraiser thought the second property was worth $600,000. We had what looked like a good deal.

Until Harold Ballard of the Toronto Maple Leafs soured it. Ballard wanted nothing to do with a merger. He led a small but powerful group of NHL dissenters who buried the idea that year.

There was a sequel. Less than a year later, Nelson called Bill to say: "Remember that piece of Edmonton property I was going to give you in the deal?" The piece our appraiser thought was worth only $1.6 million. "I just want you to know I sold it for $3.3 million." Well, I never did have much luck with the Blazers.

After Ballard killed the merger, the burning question became: What should we do now? Bill Sleeman told me that any alliance between the leagues was at least two years away, during which time we'd lose at least $1 million. And a combined league wouldn't grant a franchise to Calgary. "My recommendation," he said, "is to liquidate it."

We did, in August 1977, swallowing an overall loss of $6.5 million. As it turned out, not only was the WHA a bad investment for us and June Sifton, but also for most of the other owners in the league. The press release announcing the Cowboys' death ended with the prophetic line: "We hope that at a future date, when circumstances permit, Calgary will be part of major league hockey." In '79 the leagues merged, with Quebec, Winnipeg, Hartford, and Edmonton joining the NHL's seventeen franchises. A year later, when Nelson Skalbania bought and moved the Atlanta Flames, Calgary finally made it into the National Hockey League. We helped Nelson finance the Flames. I was in a hotel in St. Paul, Minnesota, when he called late one night in 1980. He was really up against it, needed some money by the morning to close the $16 million deal—could I help? Sure I could, and he paid us back. We never intended to make any money on it, but I was glad to help him.

Another day, the same year, I was in my office at 11:30 when Nelson Skalbania called again. "Jimmy, I'm going to buy the Canadians." The Vancouver Canadians of the Triple-A Pacific Coast baseball league, the farm club for the major-league Milwaukee Brewers. "We're going to apply for a big-league franchise and I'd like you to come in as a fifty-fifty partner."

If we'd made one mistake buying the Blazers, we were about to make another. "How much money do we have to put up?"

"I don't know," he said. "Don't worry about the money. Molson's will put up all the money." Molson Breweries had been involved with the Vancouver Canadians since 1978 when it acquired promotional rights to the team.

"How long have we got to decide?"

"I gotta know by noon."

"Okay," I said, "we'll go with it." Like that. Didn't know the price, didn't know where the money was coming from. What I did know was that our big domed stadium, B.C. Palace, was about to be built and Vancouver had a reasonable shot at getting a big-league baseball franchise. And historically, when you bought a minor-league team, you got the territorial rights to a major-league club.

The next morning, Bill Sleeman checked out the deal. Nelson told him that he was buying the club for two-thirds non–interest-bearing notes due in two years and one-third cash, which he'd arranged to borrow from the bank. All we had to do was guarantee half the loan and the notes; the team earned a couple of hundred thousand a year to service the debt.

Bill reported back to me: "We're on the hook for a loan for $750,000 U.S. and a couple of million dollars' worth of notes. Skalbania will be in charge and we'll sit and wait and may get a major-legue team."

About a month later, when the contract arrived for signing, I noticed that Molson's, not Nelson and us, had first refusal on all the TV rights for any big-league franchise in Vancouver. When I phoned Nelson about it, he said: "Look, just sign the deal and if you want out of it in thirty days, I'll take you out."

"No, I told you we'd do the deal. I don't like it, but we're in."

We weren't in for more than two months when the team needed more money. Nelson's financial problems had started to surface and he couldn't make the third payment. His share was slowly diluted until late '82 when we had to stop being a silent partner and take over the Canadians entirely. Interest rates were about 22 per cent, the Canadian dollar was down, and we weren't making much money from attendance at the games because of rain-outs. Bowie Kuhn, the American baseball commissioner, came to visit in Vancouver and reassured me that we had a decent chance for a major-league franchise. Someday. But not as soon as everyone hoped. Early on, we met with Bob Lurie, chairman of the San Francisco Giants, who wanted $40 million and the right to keep a piece of his team and be its president. That was $5 to $10 million more than we were willing to pay. It would have cost us $18 million just to get out of the Giants' lease with Candlestick Park. And Lurie was using the threat of a move to any viable city to put pressure on the city of San Francisco to build a new baseball stadium. No deal. Over the years we also made some serious calls on the Cleveland Indians and the Minnesota Twins to see if they were interested in coming to Vancouver, but nothing came of that either.

For two years we were the sole, reluctant owners of the Vancouver Canadians. I didn't hold out much hope for Vancouver's getting a franchise in the foreseeable future—still don't. Then the president of an Eastern-based brewery approached us to buy a minority share in the team. After telling him we didn't generally take minority partners, we began negotiating with the company—which was Molson's, part of the same Molson Industries empire that had bid against us for Maple Leaf Mills fifteen years earlier. We decided to sell, believing it would be better for the team and for the fans in Vancouver if the Canadians were owned by a strong national company with marketing expertise.

After unprofitable experiences with the Canadians and the Blazers, we were relieved to be out of the sports arena. As for our getting involved in it again someday, with a major-league team—well, in the deal business you never say never.

CHAPTER TWELVE

My Life in Management

One of the few times our hockey team really came through for us was in a game against the Winnipeg Jets in early 1976. We'd brought some of the key people in our companies to Calgary for a management conference. Bill Sleeman took coach Joe Crozier aside and said: "All of our executives are here. Try to win, but at least don't embarrass yourself." Our Calgary Cowboys won, 5-0. The team was part of our image problem in those days as shareholders took potshots at Neonex International for its continued weak performance. The conference in Calgary was one of our solutions to getting the public company back on the tracks. In mid-December '75, I'd left the office and stayed home to do some hard thinking about how to make Neonex more effective. The day after Christmas, I called Maureen Chant and said: "I've got a wonderful idea. We're gonna have a conference called 'Partners in Pride' for our top people and we're gonna have it in Calgary on January 6. I want everybody there. What do you think?" After she recovered, she started organizing a conference to be held eleven days later.

Maureen hadn't been back with me very long at the time. In 1974 I'd come to realize just how valuable she was in helping me run Neonex smoothly. That was the year she left me. She came to me one day to say that she had a chance to start a Christian-education school at the Glad Tidings Temple. I tried to talk her out of leaving. Anyway, she went, and on her first day at the school, she knew she'd made a mistake. But she organized the school for 133 kids from grades 1 through 12—and it's still going today as part of the Pacific Academy in Coquitlam, B.C. Meanwhile, I went through three secretaries in about nine months. Bill Sleeman finally said: "There's nobody who's going to replace Maureen. Why don't you get her back here?" I did, and she was back in time to pull together our first Partners in Pride conference.

We invited seventy of our senior and middle executives for one day's discussion about the directions their companies were heading and the opportunities they could see. In style, that conference at the Calgary Inn was like (but a little staider than) the ones that have followed every year since. We had motivational presentations and I showed the group a tall silver trophy—the President's Trophy—that would be awarded the following year to the president of the company or division who had best guided his management and staff to financial success. There were displays of our recreational vehicles outside the hotel; a woman dressed up as a Town Crier let people know what was happening; and the Calgary Stampede Band made a surprise appearance. We relaxed over dinner, which featured elaborate ice carvings and a harpist playing background music. At a casino night with cotton candy and balloons, dealers in cowboy gear handed out play money to be traded for prizes. And everyone went home with a souvenir—an Olympic coin set. There was even some unexpected drama: One of our mobile-building executives who said he'd got stuck in the elevator arrived late at the morning session; he was furious when Maureen made him cool his heels outside until after lunch. Our corporate policy is not to allow latecomers into any meeting.

The whole idea of Partners in Pride was to bring together the presidents and senior executives of our diverse companies. Get them to know one another as part of a larger corporation, a group with shared interests and objectives. And trade ideas to improve their own businesses and their colleagues'. It proved to be inspirational; it charged our batteries. The conferences later grew into three-day extravaganzas with special guests and themes. The following year in Los Angeles, the first prominent speaker appeared unannounced (as they all do): Presidential candidate Ronald Reagan got a standing ovation when he walked in to talk about the free-enterprise system. In the years since, we've heard from politicians as different as former Republican president Gerald Ford and former NDP premier Dave Barrett. And from nine other celebrities, including a couple of folk philosophers: Bob Hope ("Jim Pattison is sort of a Lee Iacocca with frostbite"); and my 77-year-old mother, Julia Pattison, who spoke about our theme of commitment and sacrifice by describing the adversity that prairie pioneers faced in the old days. Conference themes have ranged from the upbeat "You Gotta Wanna" to the recession-inspired "Do More with Less." And the locations have run the gamut from the Canyon Country Club in Palm Springs, California, to the Island Hall in Parksville, B.C. The executives participate by presenting elaborate sketches, with costumes and special effects, that tell their corporate stories entertainingly. I wind up each conference with a speech about my current interests and corporate philosophy. Scattered throughout the three days is the sheer fun of car rallies, barbecues, and bowling tournaments, sometimes even large-scale professional musical productions with high-kicking chorus girls.

An important guest at the second Partners in Pride conference in '77 was Ted McDowell, deputy chief general manager of credit at the Toronto-Dominion Bank. He's been the only outsider to attend every one since, from his time as the bank's senior lending officer to his current role as vice-chairman. Recalling that glitzy Los Angeles conference now, he tells people: "I'd never seen anything like it." Ted McDowell realizes the value of the conferences as the only real opportunity our executives have to understand the reach of the company and to raise issues that affect them individually and as a group. He once compared the Jim Pattison Group to "an anthill with a lot of satellite colonies. It's almost like a seething mass of ideas, and from anything I've seen at the Partners in Pride conferences, every one of these people can be likened to soldier ants—highly protective, intensely loyal, totally dedicated to the success of the Group as a family unit."

Ted McDowell has been a vital part of our success since 1975. That's when I first took him and two regional TD officials on a flying visit of all our properties in North America.

My Life in Management

The three-day tour stretched 6,600 miles, from our recreational-vehicle plants in California and Oregon, through B.C., and across the Prairie provinces to Toronto. (In Edmonton, I had our two large rented chauffeur-driven limousines drive up to an A&W for an in-car lunch.) Like me, Ted came from Saskatchewan (he was born a year later than me on a farm near Mossbank) and went into business without a university degree, joining the bank straight from high school. An old friend of Fred Vanstone, our vice-president of finance, he developed confidence in our operation and turned out to be the best thing that ever happened to us. More than once in those early days, he'd reassure me, in his slow and careful way: "Look, when we give this kind of support to a private operation like yours, consider that a very strong vote of confidence." Among the good advice he's given me over the years (and I wish I'd paid more attention to it) was to stay away from a hockey team like the Blazers because "professional sports is a game for the very wealthy entrepreneur." Nobody has made a greater contribution to this company than Ted McDowell.

Ted made that 1975 familiarization trip with us in our second Learjet. We'd just bought it after deciding that the company was spinning its wheels, it wasn't making any money—nothing was happening. I told Maureen: "We're not getting anywhere; go buy us a Learjet. We're gonna change the management style of the company. Everybody will deal directly with me from now on, and I'm going out in the field with the plane—to all our divisions from one end of the country to the other."

Maureen located a used Lear which we financed with the Bank of Denver. If I ever fell in love with a piece of equipment, it was that Lear 25B. We ran that baby night and day. If there was a problem at Acme Novelty, I was on the plane to Edmonton. Trouble at an RV factory down south? I was in California. I went to every Overwaitea store in B.C. every year. An executive jet like the Lear is no longer a frill for a far-flung corporation like ours. One survey showed that ninety-four of the top hundred among *Fortune* 500 companies had company-owned planes. Some years we fly it a quarter of a million miles, the equivalent of about ten times around the world. We've since moved up to a 1980 eight-passenger Lear 35, which cost about $2.8 million Canadian. It cruises at 520 miles an hour, with a maximum cruising speed of 550—faster than a Boeing 737—and can fly non-stop from Vancouver to Toronto in four hours and ten minutes with two pilots and a full baggage load. Under good conditions, it can land on a three-thousand-foot runway. Its seats fold down to make three beds, a phone aboard allows us to communicate anywhere in the world, and there's a sign that says: *If you wish to smoke, please step outside*. Our chief pilot, Mag Steinsvik, was a commercial fisherman like his father before joining the U.S. Coast Guard air/sea rescue service. He also runs *Nova Springs*, our eighty-five-foot motor yacht. She's a refined wooden beauty, with a hull of Honduras mahogany planking, teak handrails, and an oak interior. Her spotless engine room, for two 650-horsepower, 12-cylinder GM diesel engines, has plush white carpeting. We built her for $1.5 million to entertain clients and guests—an unbelievable eighteen thousand of them from May '84 until the end of Expo.

After the first Partners in Pride conference in '76, I had Maureen look for a company house in Palm Springs where we could entertain bankers, investment dealers, customers, and owners of companies we were interested in buying, and meet with our directors and, from time to time, our operations people. Winston Churchill claimed Marrakesh was the finest resort on the globe; I checked it out not long ago, and in my opinion that Moroccan city just doesn't compare to Palm Springs. It's my favourite spot in the whole world. In the desert, ringed by mountains, with an average daytime high of 88 degrees, cool nights, and only 5.39 inches of rain a year, it has more golf courses than anywhere else in the world and more than seven thousand swimming pools. In '76 we found the first of three places we've had overlooking the Canyon Country Club golf course, close to the airport. We began to fly in bankers from New York, Los Angeles, Toronto, and Vancouver to let them relax and play golf and learn more about us. (I can't imagine worse punishment than golfing; one of the two times I've played, the president of the Bank of B.C. shot a 78 to my 146.) When we started holding the Pride conferences down there, we bought a bigger house where up to 120 guests can dine on the lawn. The picture window in the living room looks out over a bubbling pond, an outdoor whirlpool, and a swimming pool surrounded by palms and grapefruit trees—all of it facing the greens of the golf course. Maureen runs the house, with the help of a housekeeper and a daily gardener, and my assistant Enzo maintains it and makes sure our limited-edition Cadillac, Lincoln, and Dreamer truck are operating. If you ever hear I've sold that house, you'll know I'm broke.

I started running Neonex on a day-to-day, hands-on, tire-kicking basis. One of our long-time directors, Bob Halliday, says I practise what the *In Search of Excellence* authors call management by wandering around—decentralized management where I get out and see our people, trying to make myself available to them. That all began a dozen years ago. First of all, I got rid of the system of group vice-presidents I'd created. They were just one unnecessary level of bureaucracy between me and the executives running the companies in the field. Instead of reporting to the vice-presidents, the operating people now had direct access to me. As a result, I came to know all of the companies and their senior management much more intimately than I ever had before. I let one group V/P go, transferred Stan Whittle back to Neon Products as president, and asked Harry Dunbar to get Neon's accounts into shape (one of my biggest disappointments was when the Harry, a hard-working team player, left two years later to manage a large carpet-manufacturing company in New Zealand). And I put Bill Sleeman in the deal-making business as vice-president of corporate development.

Bill was at a Young Presidents' Organization meeting in '76 when he heard a well-known American business consultant, Curt Symonds of Financial Control Associates, talking about a concept called Return on Invested Capital. ROIC, as he described it, was a way of comparing one business to another with a common yardstick. Bill came back to the office full of enthusiasm for the idea—we could use this means to measure the performances of our very diverse companies— and suggested I listen to Symonds's lecture the next day. "We won't wait till tomorrow," I said. We took Curt Symonds for dinner at Hy's Encore that night and hired him as a consultant. We still call him in for refresher courses.

ROIC became the cornerstone of our new philosophy of operating Neonex and, later, the Jim Pattison Group. A division's contribution to the Group is its operating profit, calculated before income taxes and interest on its debt. When you run any business, there are certain assets employed—such as receivables, fixed assets, inventories, goodwill—and on the other side there are such liabilities as payables owing. The difference between these total assets and operating liabilities is your invested capital. Return on Invested Capital is the measurement of your contribution divided by the invested capital employed in the business. It's the return you get on your assets without considering the money you've borrowed. That gives you a new concept of profit. For each division, we determine what a reasonable return on our investment is. It's what we call our hurdle rate, or objective. The objective differs for each division, depending on the nature of its business. We're prepared to accept a lower return on investment in a stable, low-risk industry like billboard advertising, but we'd set a higher objective for a division in an industry that's more cyclical, less stable, and higher-risk, like recreational vehicles.

The second principle of our philosophy is Market Share. We believe that if we can serve our customers better, everything else will follow. And we don't know how well we're serving them unless we know how many customers are buying our products and services. Market Share is a measurement of how much of the market you're capturing from competitors. A satisfactory and growing share of the market should ensure the long-term health and prosperity of a division. Finding the figures to calculate it can sometimes be difficult. For our car dealerships, we get information on how many new cars are sold in the Greater Vancouver market every month and measure our performance against that total. Polk, a Toronto industrial-measurement agency, offers monthly statistics on how many new lease cars the provincial motor-vehicle branches handle. But for a business like Ripley's Believe It or Not! museums, where there's nothing equivalent to compare them to, we draw up charts on admissions each quarter related to the historical pattern. However we get the information, it allows us to understand how each company performs within its own industry and in the marketplace, and how it might take better advantage of market trends for future growth.

Eventually, we introduced a third standard of performance for our companies: quality—quality products and services, quality working conditions, and quality people who bring it all together. It's a subject I'll discuss in another chapter.

My Life in Management

Return on Invested Capital, Market Share, and Quality—these three tenets have become our corporate gospel. Those are the targets for all of our presidents. From the start, our managers know where the pins are and it's up to them to try to hit them to the best of their ability. Taking into account the industry competition, economic conditions, and other variables—those factors under their reasonable control—we ask them to manage their individual companies effectively and profitably. And in their own way. There's only one direct order I give each of our new executives when they join us: "I don't want you to lie, cheat, or steal. Don't do anything that you don't want to see on the front page of *The Globe and Mail.*" We want executives who are self-motivated, who don't look for excuses, who do act like entrepreneurs. You have to offer people independence. You hire competent managers, then give them a job to do and the freedom to do it. How can you hold them accountable for their companies if you don't let them run them? I like a quote by American general George Patton: "Never tell people how to do things. Tell them what to do and they will surprise you with their ingenuity." When Nick Geer joined us several years ago as senior vice-president, he began telling our company operators that he wanted things done his way in tax matters. I took him aside and told him: "If they want your help, they'll call." The presidents will call on us if there's a major strategic decision to be made—a division wants to branch out into a different line of business, move into another country, or make a large acquisition. To reward their independent initiative, we have a formal bonus system for operating managers based on their total performance. And every couple of years, I bring in a compensation consulting firm to do a complete review of the senior positions of each of our divisions and compare them to a survey of leading Canadian corporations in comparable industries. Of course, if your managers don't perform—if they don't live up to the performance standards—then they have to be replaced with people who will. But I've always been up front about warning the presidents of problem companies. Sometimes we even warn their employees publicly, as we did on the front page of the 1986 edition of our corporate newspaper, *The Jim Pattison GroupNews*, which goes to outsiders as well as employees: "The economy of Canada, and in particular Western Canada—where we operate many of our companies—has undergone a significant change in the last few years. As a result, we have two or three divisions that are not showing a satisfactory return on our investment. And these companies (or part of them) will be closed or sold if they cannot regain their competitive position and produce an acceptable profit. We will continue to support those divisions and management that are showing a satisfactory result." Within a year, we'd sold or shut down several divisions.

Today, the parent company is Jim Pattison Industries Ltd., a private corporation, and the individual companies are its divisions. Our structure combines the benefits that flow from a large corporation with the autonomy and flexibility of a small company. The Corporate Office (not the *Head* Office) operates as a cost centre; it doesn't run any of the divisions. Its role is to decide what we want to own, who should run it, and what level of compensation the top people should receive —and then help them by offering the benefits of our collective size and strength. As a Group, we can open doors, can secure better lines of credit than an individual division might be able to get on its own. Every fall we agree with each division on a business plan. The Corporate Office goes to the bank annually to negotiate credit lines for the Group as a whole, then each division gets its own line based on our agreed-upon forecasts and requirements. A division is expected to live within its line of credit as if it were an independent business.

To keep tabs on the divisions' progress, we ask them for monthly financial statements. In the car business, there's a rule that no used cars should be held over ninety days, so I like to watch those figures every week. We do an annual audit of all divisions. And we have divisional meetings every quarter—a practice we began in '75. They've become my highest priority; I never miss them. At first, the Corporate Office staff and I went out into the field for each of these meetings to talk to the presidents and their managers on location across the continent. Until Expo, we had two meetings a year in the field and two in our Vancouver boardroom. Maureen Chant organizes the divisionals and Bill Sleeman chairs them.

Of the slim staff of seventeen in Corporate Office (which includes our chief pilot), seven attend the meetings; they've been with me anywhere from seven to twenty-five years. Bill, who's now vice-chairman of Jim Pattison Industries (and, besides me, the only inside director), is there in two roles. He's our deal man, in charge of acquisitions and divestitures; although we're often interchangeable when it comes to deal-making, he usually handles the fine details of negotiating. At the quarterly meetings, Bill is an effective presence. Always well-tailored, with a puff handkerchief complementing his tie, closely cropped silver hair, and a strong, sun-reddened face, he speaks quietly yet forcefully. Nick Geer is chairman of Great Pacific Capital SA, a wholly owned subsidiary of Dallas-based Great Pacific Holdings (a wholly owned subsidiary of Great Pacific Industries Incorporated, a public corporation). Nick is a tall forty-five-year-old, educated in English public schools. Bill and I decide *what* to do and Nick figures out *how* we do it. With his broad background in tax matters (he's a governor of the Canadian Tax Foundation), he handles all the tax work for Corporate Office and does tax overviews for the divisions. And he's involved on the money side with corporate secretary Rose Andersen and corporate controller Len Westfall. Rose is also Corporate Office manager, hiring and firing staff, and the closest thing we have to a corporate treasurer. She holds the purse strings; if any division is having a problem with bank lines, for instance, she deals with it. Len, soft-spoken and detail-oriented, is the front-line numbers man. He prepares all the corporate financial data and oversees the audits of all the divisions in North America. And Dan Johnsen operates Jim Pattison Developments, which develops potential sites and external projects as well as handling all our internal real estate, such as the car-company sites, sign-company plants, and our warehouses.

In recent years, we've also set up a system of group presidents: Les Landes of the Jim Pattison Communications Group, Don Connors of the Automotive Group, and John Seebach of the News Group. They're operating presidents who run their divisions, look for new opportunities, get the synergies of their groups going, and represent our company within their industry. For example, the hard-working and highly regarded Les Landes is reponsible for four individual communications divisions: electrical signs, outdoor advertising, transit advertising, and broadcasting. Many of those divisions have their own presidents: Bob Sinclair of Trans Ad in Toronto; Gordon Chamberlin of Cummings Signs, based in

Brampton, Ontario; Doug Eddy of Gould Outdoor Advertising in Southwestern Ontario; Morris Proskow of Hook Outdoor in Alberta; and Bob Smart of Seaboard Advertising in Vancouver.

Unlike the group–vice-president system I once created, the group presidents haven't become a layer of frustrating bureaucracy; the managers of the divisions always have access to Bill Sleeman and me if they think we can be helpful. Bob Sinclair of Trans Ad can pick up the phone and call us from Toronto anytime. But this access to us doesn't dilute the direct operating authority of the group presidents. (During my three full years at Expo, many managers went directly to Bill because they didn't want to bother me; without him and the people at the Corporate Office, I could never have taken the job the premier of B.C. asked me to.)

Presidents of the divisions and their key managers attend the quarterly meetings along with the group presidents. These meetings usually take half a day per division. Generally, the executives are remarkably frank about their progress and hard on themselves for any lack of it. As the president of one Canada-wide company reported at a divisional in early '87: "Our financial performance was dismal and the results produced were disappointing." And the president of another national division said: "At this meeting a year ago, we said that we expected an average year with some nervous moments and disappointments, but by the time '86 rolled to an end, we would have something to celebrate. Well, it took some December brinkmanship to do it." He gave his division an A for achieving a 78 per cent increase in his ROIC, but only a C—for plant expansion. And '87 would be a difficult year, he predicted. "Our strategy will be to wheel and deal and grab anything we can. I don't like it, but it seems like the only game in town."

"I understood that the initial numbers for the year were very disturbing," Bill Sleeman remarked. "They were scary. We're probably 30 per cent down for January."

Bill asked the president about potential competitors in the industry. The president reported a one-day-old rumour that two partners in a competing company had a falling-out.

After hearing from the division's other top managers, Bill said: "Your results are first-class. After a big increase in your ROIC last year, you beat it marginally. You're up in profits.

My Life in Management

Having such good assets managed by such good people, it's too bad you can't double your plant capacity."

Nick Geer then dealt with the division's Market Share, which was over 96 per cent nation-wide. "Congratulations," Nick said. "Not only on the bottom line but control of the asset side."

After Len Westfall handed out the ROIC graph, which showed a steady rise since '82, I spoke for the first time: "That's one of the best pictures we've ever seen."

I usually sit back and listen hard at these meetings. The Corporate Office people have their own areas of expertise, where they raise specific points, and everyone has the chance to ask general questions. "I'm interested," I told this divisional president. "Your bank loan's pretty high. Why is that?"

"It's capital expenditures."

"How do you handle going over your bank line?"

"You live within your lines," the president said.

Summing up, I said: "It's a first-class performance." Then I took the opportunity to chat with one of the division's managers, who held a part-time political office in the town where his company operates. I hadn't seen him for several months and was interested in his community: "What's the biggest problem you've got in your area? . . . How many policemen do you have? . . . How many women on the force? . . . You use volunteers—what do they do?"

Tough questions get asked at these quarterlies. "Your own sign at the airport is probably the worst sign in Canada," I told one sign-company president. "I would recommend that if you're going to advertise yourself, you do a better job. Do you agree?" The president replied: "Yes, I do. The signs aren't up anymore." Or Rose Andersen might ask: "Why aren't you paying off your term loan?" And get the answer: "We anticipate that we have to make a significant payment in March on our taxes and may come into heavy capital expenditures at the same time."

And sometimes the sessions just break down into a bit of good-humoured banter. Expressing concern about one division's bank line, Rose asked a visiting manager: "I'd like to do some work on this; are you staying in town this weekend?"

"What did you have in mind, Rose?" I wondered aloud, to general laughter.

"As chairman," Bill Sleeman said, "I'm going to have to ask for some decorum on behalf of Rose."

I attend another series of quarterly meetings with the same mix of hard business questions and pleasant personal relationships. Great Pacific Industries Inc. and the current parent company, Jim Pattison Industries, have five members of their boards in common. All but one of them—John Coleman—were on the board of Neonex, when it was a public company. The others are Mark Kaplan, Bob Halliday, Edward Meyer, Bill Sleeman, and me.

Mark eventually became president and chief executive officer of Drexel Burnham, which grew out of Burnham & Co., the New York investment house that he was representing as a lawyer when it helped us take over Neon Products in 1967. He left to become president of Engelhard Minerals, which was one of our co-investors in the Neon takeover. Now fifty-seven, he's with the influential New York-based law firm of Skadden, Arps, Slate, Meagher & Flom, the home of Joe Flom, whom Mark helped us negotiate with in getting an out-of-court settlement of our Maple Leaf Mills lawsuit with Bruce Norris.

At sixty-seven, Bob Halliday is supposedly semi-retired, spending several months a year in Palm Springs. He left Boise Cascade in '69 to help found Princess Cruises, which Pacific & Orient acquired. He then ran Equity Corporation with my old friend (and early Neonex director) Mike Dingman; later, they created Wheelabrator-Frye, the huge U.S. conglomerate. Five years ago Bob and a friend launched Franchise Finance Corporation, a real-estate syndicate with $1 billion worth of assets under management. His questions as a director, asked in his barrel-chested voice, are never easy. When we called in auditors to attend a recent Great Pacific Industries board meeting, he asked them bluntly: "Any pressure on you from management?"

Ed Meyer is the sixty-year-old chairman, chief executive officer, and part owner of Grey Advertising, a global advertising firm based in New York, which regularly ranks among the top ten American agencies in billings ($2.1 billion in '86). Ed is one of the highest-paid advertising executives in the world, if not the highest. A friend of Mark's, he became a Neonex director in 1974. Ed is more knowledgeable on more subjects than almost anyone I know. A recent article in *Fortune* on the reading habits of chief executives showed just how well-rounded he is: Some of the recent books he'd read were *Competitive Strategy*, by the Harvard Business School's Michael Porter; *Reagan's America*, by historian Garry Wills; *The Counterlife*, a novel by Philip Roth; and several other novels by such women writers as Ann Beattie and Amy Hempel. After one of our recent board meetings, I went with him on a tour of a Palm Springs supermarket; strolling down the aisles with him as he talked about the products was an instant education.

John Coleman is retired as a banker but active as president of his own consulting firm, J.H.C. Associates of Toronto, and as a director of many major corporations. At one point a few years ago, he was on twenty-four boards, including Chrysler, Colgate Palmolive, Thomson Newspapers, and the Royal Bank, where he was once deputy chairman. I first enticed him on to the board of Crush International in the mid-'70s. Recovering from a gall-bladder operation, he promised his wife he wouldn't accept any more directorships. But after I met the Colemans at their Toronto apartment, I sat down at his wife's piano and started playing. Then she played. And we became very friendly. After I left, John told his wife, "I'd like to go on his board; I like him," and she agreed. As a director of Great Pacific, he talks straight to me, telling me what he thinks from the viewpoint of his wide background.

John Coleman tells me he likes being on our board because it's so different from some of the others he's on. ("I was at a meeting of one board that lasted for three hours," he's said, "and two of those hours were spent looking at a video presentation of one of that company's old branches. Many of the directors were literally asleep.") There's no chance to sleep when our directors get together. John and Bob Halliday are the current audit committee for Great Pacific Industries. The questions they asked at one audit meeting were typically penetrating. Bob: "That to me doesn't make a bit of sense; what are you trying to say?" . . . John: "You *do* have liability insurance?" . . . Bob: "That's fine and dandy, but it happened and you had a policy in place—what's wrong?"

We run tight board meetings, discouraging private conversations while a speaker has the floor. The meetings usually last no more than a few hours now, though in past years they'd run for twelve and fourteen hours a day; for a couple of days at a stretch during our crisis years, we wouldn't see the sun. We once held a board meeting in a motor home that moved from town to town. For some meetings we brought in management consultants to give us advice; one guy told the directors they didn't need a library—just tear out the key pages of a book and file them. The whole tone was different in those days: At one meeting the directors asked such brutal questions of a chief financial officer that he was in tears. We weren't such shrinking violets then.

Because the Jim Pattison Group is such an assortment of companies, we try to give employees a sense of group identity. *The Jim Pattison GroupNews* is one of the effective vehicles we use. It chronicles our business year, reports media comment about us, underlines our corporate goals, quotes employees on such themes as innovation and service, and runs hundreds of employee photographs. And because it offers a full-colour pictorial rundown of all our companies, we use the *GroupNews* as a quick way of introducing ourselves to potential clients or the management of companies we're interested in buying. We also promote the idea of belonging to a group by encouraging our divisions to get involved in the GO program—Group Opportunities, which means buying and selling skills, goods, and services from one another. When these sales are made on a competitive basis, they strengthen the Group. For example, Overwaitea may buy electrical signs from Neon Products, the Canadian Fishing Company advertises on CJOR, and many of the divisions lease cars from our car-leasing companies. And every year we revise our corporate audio-visual which tells employees and customers our story with split-screen images and upbeat music. We even have the Jim Pattison Group song, like Japanese corporations do. Here's a sample of the lyrics:

> Together we got a good thing goin',
> Our best goes into every day's work done,
> Growing together, stronger than ever,
> Partners in Pride
> And we've just begun!

The highlight of all our group activity is the annual Partners In Pride Executive Conference, in alternate years

My Life in Management

between a small one for only the most senior executives and a full one that includes their key executives. I can still remember when Nick Geer joined us in '81 and went straight to one of the conferences in Palm Springs. There he was, an Englishman in a pinstripe suit, and all of a sudden people were glad-handing him and slapping buttons on him. By the end of the third day, he was standing on top of a table, covered in buttons, and singing a promotional song at the top of his lungs.

The conferences have themes, which I talk about in my wind-up speech to reinforce them as group goals. In '80 the theme was "We're halfway there"—halfway to our objective of $1 billion in sales. And when we reached that amount right on target five years later, it was "We've just begun."

Everybody attending the conference takes part in the skits that summarize their divisions' stories. The professionalism that these amateur performers bring to their productions always surprises me. In '87, the executives from Ripley's Believe It or Not! (which we'd bought three years earlier) opened theirs with a fake Movietone newsreel that entertainingly described the history of Robert L. Ripley. They followed up with a live performance that featured president John Withers stumbling around in a torn shirt as the adventurer Ripley during a jungle scene, and guys in glittering gold bowlers, light-up bowties, and mammoth cigars for a boardroom scene. Despite all the highjinks, they conveyed the flavour of the Ripley's operation and the current concerns of its managers ("It's time to do Niagara Falls. We built the show in 1964 and it's done really well. But there's no question about it—it's certainly old-fashioned"). In the usual question-and-answer session afterwards, they enlarged on those concerns: the problem of dreaming up another TV show to follow the Ripley's series with Jack Palance; the difficulty in finding interesting new exhibits for the museums; and the shortage of good locations ("Niagara Falls is perfect for us," John Withers said, "because the average stay is one night").

For this conference, we took over the Delta Inn in Penticton, B.C. Outside, our sign divisions put up big neon signs announcing our presence and the Automotive Group had enough new cars on show to stock a small car lot. Inside, Overwaitea and Save-On-Foods set up enormous bins of cashews, licorice, and Smarties with scoops for people to help themselves, and the News Group had a roomful of racks of paperbacks and magazines for the taking. The halls were thick with displays from the divisions—including a shrunken head from Ripley's and a computer updated every ten seconds to show how Canfisco's fish-canning lines were doing.

The guest speaker makes his surprise entrance at a Saturday-night dinner. Some of our previous speakers have been Dr. Henry Kissinger; Alexander Haig, who'd just been fired as American secretary of state; Bob Waterman, co-author of *In Search of Excellence;* and Donald Macdonald, chairman of the recent Royal Commission on the Economic Union and Development Prospects for Canada, speaking on free trade. In '87 we heard an American viewpoint on the free-trade talks from Walter Mondale, the former American vice-president who ran against Ronald Reagan for the presidency ("I do not anticipate industry-specific or country-specific protective measures," he said).

(Gerald Ford spoke on world affairs and the State of the Union in '79, warning against the excesses of government: "A government big enough to give us everything we want is a government big enough to take from us everything we have." We've seen one another several times since then. He and his wife have invited Mary and me to one of their recent wedding anniversaries and we've been to their home in Vail, Colorado. The Fords have a place at the Thunderbird Country Club in Rancho Mirage, near Palm Springs. When Wilf Ray, Maureen, and I went over to talk to him about speaking at the Pride conference, we weren't impressed by the size of the swimming pool we saw. Until we saw his golden retriever jump into it and Gerry said: "That's the dog's swimming pool.")

One night of the conference is reserved for nothing but fun. At the latest conference, Jimmy's Jamboree was a circus setting in a Penticton hall, with hot dogs and hamburgers, beer and wine, a fortune teller, jugglers, and carnival games. All ninety of us were dressed up in costumes. There were clowns and convicts, Satans and Roman senators, Bedouins in headdress, and judges in wigs. Bill Sleeman was a caveman with a necklace of dinosaur teeth, Nick Geer a robed monk, Rose Andersen a nun, and Ted McDowell, the vice-chairman of the Toronto-Dominion Bank, a pirate. I was a jester, with bells on my cap and curls on my shoes. And I was the favourite victim for the dunk tank. I sat on a stool over the tank while a chosen few tossed balls at a target. Although Ted McDowell missed on his try, several of our managers took very careful aim and dunked me squarely, bells and all, into the cold, deep water.

* * *

Clarence Heppell strolled around that evening dressed as Superman. The president of Overwaitea Foods has won our President's Trophy twice. It's awarded on the basis of Return on Invested Capital, Market Share, sales, employees' pride in performance, and administrative performance. He's only one of many who have won the trophy, all of them people we've seen grow along with their divisions. Clarence's running of Overwaitea and its subsidiary, Save-On-Foods, really defines the management philosophy we've tried to instill in all our executives. Along the way, he's created one of the fastest-growing and most innovative supermarket chains on the continent. A who's who of the food business from across North America and Europe has made pilgrimages to B.C. to study the success of his Save-On-Foods super stores.

A year older than me, a farmer's son from B.C.'s Fraser Valley, Clarence started working part time at an Overwaitea food store at fourteen and went full time for $16 a week after high school. At twenty-one, eight years younger than any other Overwaitea manager, he opened the company's first store in Campbell River, B.C. During the first five years of his marriage, Clarence worked fourteen hours a day, seven days a week, unloading trucks, cleaning bathrooms. He was a good administrator, an idea man in merchandising, a popular manager with his staff. Shortly after Neonex acquired Overwaitea in 1968, he'd worked his way up to assistant general manager and, in '73, I appointed him president.

I made it clear to Clarence that the business was his responsibility, not mine; he had absolute freedom to operate. We'd support him with the money to grow. And did Overwaitea grow. It pioneered discount supermarkets in B.C. through Prairie Markets and then Your Mark-it Foods. In the late '70s, Clarence began to notice a new trend in B.C., where lifestyles shift as rapidly as they do in California. It was one thing to see people buying fresh produce from roadside stands in the summer, but why, he wondered, were they driving out to those same stands to buy imported bananas in the winter?

And he watched the excitement in the eyes of food shoppers at Vancouver's bustling new Granville Island Market. As Clarence has told journalists, "We in the industry were making a terrible mistake. We'd built rectangle boxes as stores and forgot about service. There was no life in our stores. Grocery shopping was pure drudgery, but families could have a real outing when they bought fresh products at the farm gate. And our eating habits had changed: We'd stopped smoking and started drinking skim milk and eating less beef." The average Canadian today eats 495 pounds of fresh produce compared to an American's 325.

In 1982, the first Save-On-Foods store with all the bells and whistles opened in the Greater Vancouver suburb of Coquitlam. It was a new kind of supermarket. Natural light flooded in from the ceilings. The produce was beautifully displayed out front to suggest the freshness of a farmer's market. And the store was divided into distinct areas that looked like individual stalls: a smokehouse where shoppers could watch the sausages being made; an old-fashioned kiosk deli where the staff was only a few feet away from the customer; a self-serve bakery with the bakers in full view. There were 500 different bulk foods, including 15 kinds of tea and 55 bulk spices—250 lines of produce, many of them exotic items from places like Thailand and Morocco. And 200 flavours of yogurt spread across sixteen feet of display. All of it at discount prices. As Clarence saw more women joining the workforce, younger people forced to live at home and take lower-paying jobs—and a resulting increase in shift work—he recognized the need for one-stop shopping. So he extended hours from 8:00 A.M. to midnight and opened large bookshops in his stores, snack shacks with stand-up fast foods for workers just off shift, and the first drugstore and full pharmacy in a B.C. supermarket. Save-On-Foods stores are super supermarkets: The original Coquitlam location has expanded to become the province's biggest, at 86,000 square feet. And after having only a small percentage of the market in the province, our Overwaitea chain is now battling for leadership.

Clarence Heppell's management of his staff of 4,500 is just as significant in his success as his administration of the fifty-seven stores. He's Clarence to everyone, including the stockboy who's just started. Even though Overwaitea is a private company, he travels around B.C. every year to tell every employee exactly how the company has performed: sales, market share, even profits—the same figures he gives to me. Clarence is not Superman. He makes mistakes, like spending $1 million on an oil-painting promotion that flopped. But he admits his errors. While he thrives on the autonomy we allow our operations people, he never gets swell-headed and sure that he has all the answers. When Clarence visits each store at least once a year, he asks one important question of every employee he encounters: "How can we run this company better?" It's the same question I've kept asking in the more than twenty-five years I've been managing my own business.

CHAPTER THIRTEEN

Liquid Assets

The story on the business pages of *The Toronto Star*, May 1, 1976, was headlined: "Smiling Jim Is Buying Again." "After keeping a relatively low profile for the last couple of years," the article reported, "Neonex last month began buying heavily into shares of Crush International Ltd. Neonex has paid something like $14 million for about 34 per cent of the Toronto-based, multinational soft-drink company. Neonex spokesmen insist they do not plan a takeover in the style of the '60s."

Not in the style of the '60s, by exchanging shares. But we did take over the public company that made Orange Crush one of Canada's more famous exports. Neonex had lost $1.14 million in '75, while at first glance Crush looked nicely profitable. Net earnings of $5.3 million on revenues of about $62.5 million, returning about 14 per cent on its total assets. With virtually no debt, and about $12 million cash in the bank.

Crush was an old established Canadian company, even though its roots were in the United States. A Chicago chemist had created Orange Crush in 1916 from water, sugar, and the crushed skin, seeds, and pulp of oranges. It was the best-selling soft drink on the continent throughout the 1920s, advertised with Norman Rockwell paintings in magazines like

The Saturday Evening Post. But "the best drink on earth," sold in a dark-brown ribbed bottle, went flat during the Depression as Coke became the soda pop of choice. Its popularity revived during the Second World War, when it made big profits and came to the attention of the Canadian financier E.P. Taylor. At the time, Taylor was building Canadian Breweries into the largest brewing group in the world and just establishing an investment company called Argus Corporation. He bought Crush in 1945 without realizing the reason for its heavy wartime sales: It was a sweet beverage during a period of sugar rationing. Sales died after the war. Taylor wouldn't invest any more money in Crush, but he allowed a Montreal fellow named John M. Thompson to try and make a go of the company. Jack Thompson made a couple of important changes: He got rid of the chewy pulp and put the soft drink in clear bottles that showed its bright orange colour. Although the Argus Corporation sold the company in '59, Jack stayed on. Through the next decade, sales climbed again and Crush bought Hires Root Beer, Wilson's, and Pure Spring. Its executives offices were in Evanston, Illinois, run by president Louis Collins who'd moved south in '48 to market Orange Crush in the United States. By the time we got interested, it was still a distant fifth in the $15-billion-a-year American market (after Coke, Pepsi, 7-Up, and Dr Pepper). But the company had strong Canadian sales—with 10 per cent of the market—and sold its products in sixty countries, particularly in Central and South America, the Middle East, the Caribbean, and parts of Africa. Having the trademark for a soft drink, and selling the concentrate to bottlers around the world, can be a highly profitable business.

We first looked at Crush International in 1969, before our attempted takeover of Maple Leaf Mills. I approached Jack Thompson, who was then Crush chairman, about merging his company with Neonex. I liked Jack. Well-bred, he was well-connected in Toronto's senior business community. He'd married the daughter of Bill Horsey, the president of Dominion Stores, which was part of E.P. Taylor's Argus empire. Jack was a strong-willed fellow, absolutely loyal to the people around him. And he said he wasn't interested in doing a deal with me. The 22 per cent controlling interest of Crush was then held by the Horsey family.

"Well, why don't you come and get to know us?" I asked

Jack. "Come on the Neonex board. You get to know us, we'll get to know you." He agreed, became a director, and, at our invitation, he also put one of his Crush directors on the board of Maple Leaf Mills during the several months we had control of that company. Jack was a strong supporter of mine during the darkest days of Maple Leaf.

Over the next few years, I kept my eye on Crush International. During that time, Grant Horsey, who was Jack Thompson's brother-in-law, had surprised him by selling the Horsey family's controlling interest to the McConnell family estate in Montreal. John Wilson McConnell (founder of St. Lawrence Sugar Refineries and owner of *The Montreal Star*) had left hundreds of millions of dollars in the family's Commercial Trust, which had investments in the FP newspaper chain, Canadian Pacific, and the Bank of Montreal.

One day in 1976, Bob Deyell, an investment dealer with Burns Fry, flew in from the east to see us. He was in Bill Sleeman's office and I was leaning against the door when he asked: "How would you like to buy control of Crush?"

"Yes, Bob, we would," Bill replied, "but it's our understanding that it's not for sale."

"Not even Jack Thompson knows this." And Deyell went on to tell us that the Montreal lawyer supposedly managing the McConnell family estate really wasn't in charge of it. As we heard the story later, the lawyer had invested a lot of McConnell money in a joint venture with a Belgian firm to build a cement plant in Virginia and started construction before the legal agreement had been signed. Then the Belgians backed out and he was left with egg all over his face. The estate lost confidence in the lawyer and hired two young go-go money managers to replace him. But the lawyer was still seen to be managing the estate. Bob knew the two guys who were really running it, and knew they were questioning the McConnells' majority position in Crush.

"Are you sure?" Bill asked.

Bob thought he even knew the exact price per share it would sell for.

"Bob," I said, "we want that stock."

Of course, we didn't have any money and the stock might cost us as much as $20 million. Fred Vanstone, our vice-president of finance, went to Toronto with me to see his banking friend Ted McDowell, the Toronto-Dominion's chief lending officer. It was a Saturday, and Ted and his wife were curling that morning, so we had to meet him at our hotel at 8:00 A.M. before their match. Telling Ted we had a terrific opportunity, I said that if he lent us the money, we'd give the TD the Crush stock for security and sell off enough of the Neonex companies to start repaying the loan immediately. "And we'll have it all paid off in eighteen months."

He took it to the TD's loan committee, and they worried about what would happen if we had to sit in a minority position for a long time. But committee members agreed that, if worse came to worse, the block of shares could command a nice premium over its market value because we were buying at a good price. We got the money. A little later I took Ted and his wife to dinner at Toronto's La Scala and presented him with a can of Orange Crush with an orange-string bow around its middle. He kept the can for ten years until it started to leak. After we got control of Crush, I gave him a more tangible sign of our appreciation—the Crush account. When Russ Harrison of the Canadian Imperial Bank of Commerce called me and asked if we could let our Maple Leaf Mills bygones be bygones and keep the Crush account with his bank, I resisted. I felt I had a moral obligation to move it to the TD, as they had financed our buying of the stock.

The day we bought the shares from the McConnell estate, I flew from Montreal to Toronto to tell Jack what we'd done. I hoped he was as pleased as he said he was. I joined the Crush board, which included an incredible cross-section of well-established Toronto businessmen. Along with bank directors and former Conservative cabinet ministers were Yip Mackay of Pitfield Mackay Ross (now Dominion Securities); Don McIntosh, a director of the Argus Corporation; and the legendary Nelson Davis, who had a privately owned conglomerate with more than $200 million in annual sales. I still have a photo of all the directors in their grey or black suits and me in my checked jacket.

That was the beginning of a wonderful friendship I had with Nelson Davis until his death in 1979. He was about seventy when I met him, a sly old fox, small and red-faced, and one of the richest men in Canada. All I knew about him at first was what Jack Thompson had told me and what I'd read in Peter Newman's *The Canadian Establishment*. How he had four houses with five unlisted phone numbers, six cars, eighteen servants, twenty boats, and his own private eighteen-hole golf course where Arnold Palmer came to play. We had certain other things in common: He didn't swear, wasn't a drinker, loved classic cars (1904 Royce, 1933 Alfa Romeo), was the son of a man (an Ohio manufacturer) who was deeply involved in religion, acting as the deacon of a Congregationalist church. N.M. Davis Corporation had fifty companies, everything from Admiral Acceptance and Automobile Transport to Talon Construction and Yonge-Blythwood Realty.

I met him for the first time at a meeting of the Crush board in Chicago when he asked me to ride with him to the airport in a chauffeured limousine. Later, as we got to be friends, he asked Mary and me to come for a two-week holiday with him and his wife, Eloise. I said we'd go, but for only a week. The trip began with a Crush directors' meeting in Ireland, where Nelson was on a long-distance telephone call to Canada what seemed like every hour, helping Conrad Black take control of Argus Corporation. Then we went on to the Sacher Hotel in Vienna, where he said: "I'll look after everything." All Mary and I did was show up. I didn't know how people spent money until I met Nelson Davis. A Mercedes limo picked us up and took us to this hotel where the rooms were full of original oil paintings and sculptures, Queen Anne furniture, and duck-down quilts. My room rate was $450 (U.S.) a night; his was $600. We stayed in another fancy hotel in Germany where I actually thought I was reading the currency wrong. I looked at the price of our elegant suite in this hotel and asked the front desk: "Excuse me, but would you just tell me what the exchange rate is here?" And I had got it right. Then I had to go to the Vienna Opera one night, where Nelson had a box in the Opera House. I was doing all these things I'd never done before in my life. I'd never been to the opera, let alone an Italian one. I'd never paid those kind of hotel rates before. And he took us to palaces and churches and to Salzburg to study Mozart —I mean, he was a high-class individual. I loved Nelson, but I hated what I was doing. Meanwhile, his wife, a lovely woman, would go out and buy a $2,000 dress for dinner. Mary might spend maybe $200. At one point we went down the Rhine in a Russian hovercraft with the limo following along. Kings don't live better than Nelson did. After a week of this, when he asked me to come back to England with him, I said: "I've got to get out of here, Nelson. I've got to go home and make some money."

During the few years I knew him, he used to ask me to stay at his $12 million house whenever I was in Toronto—which I did a couple of times. We spent New Year's of '79 together at my place in Palm Springs. I think it was the last trip he took. In March, he was found dead in his swimming pool in Phoenix, Arizona.

Nelson was an influential member of the board of the Canadian Imperial Bank of Commerce. He once told me that the events leading to the 1961 merger of the Commerce and Imperial banks happened right in his living-room. And he was a Commerce director in '69 when the bank called my loans during the Maple Leaf Mills affair He was at a party for the American ambassador one night when Maple Leaf's co-owner, Jack Leitch, and his lawyers and a couple of associates stood in a corner and discussed how to deal with Jimmy Pattison. And within a couple of months of our meeting each other, Nelson Davis told me: "If I'd have known you in those days, Jimmy, you would have never had a problem with the bank."

In 1976, when I was trying to repay our bank loan with the TD and raise cash for more Crush shares, I told Bill Sleeman: "We're going to start at the bottom of the deck with our companies. Ted gave us eighteen months. I'm giving you a maximum of one year. I'd really like to see us do it within nine months. Let's get on an airplane and start selling $20 million worth of companies."

It took us about a year. By June '77 we'd sold Bazaar & Novelty, our eastern carnival-supplies merchandizer, for about $2 million; Associated Helicopters of Edmonton for $4.5 million; and Fabco Leasing (by then, one of the West's leading modular-building suppliers) for $10 million. That broke the back of our loan. When Ted McDowell saw us repaying so quickly, he offered us another $10 million to buy more Crush stock, although we never did get the total investment up to $30 million. Eventually we asked Ben Boyle, TD's president, on to the Crush board, along with Neonex International directors Mark Kaplan, Bob Halliday, and Bill Sleeman.

In '77 we acquired 50 per cent control of the Crush stock, and I became more involved as majority shareholder. What I discovered didn't delight me. Both chairman Jack Thompson and president Lou Collins were near retirement and their heir-apparent to run the company was executive vice-president Don Ottaway, an engineer by background. He was based in Toronto, at the head office, but the operational headquarters were in Evanston, Illinois, which is where we thought Ottaway should have been. We knew that the U.S. market share was small: For one thing, they didn't have any bottlers in New York or Florida. Our highest profile in the market came as a gift in 1977 when the Denver Broncos of the National Football League fought their way to the Super Bowl on the strength of their defensive team—dubbed "the Orange Crush" for the colour of its jerseys and the toughness of its players. The publicity was so effective that a grocery chain in New York sent its own truck to pick up Orange Crush because it couldn't wait for regular delivery; another chain in Chicago featured a huge display of Crush; and across the United States people held Orange Crush parties. In Denver, sales doubled, the company ran out of more than a quarter of a million Crush T-shirts, and the Colorado governor declared Orange Crush Day while drinking a bottle of you-know-what. That year we increased our advertising and public-relations budget by about 20 per cent to nearly $20 million. But that was a blip in our history, which ended when the Broncos lost by an embarrassing 27-10 to the Dallas Cowboys before a record television audience of 103.5 million.

Although Jack Thompson's approach to business and mine were usually in tune, occasionally we'd have our differences. A case in point: We were in Dublin at a meeting of the Crush board (it met outside Canada once a year), when Jack, as chairman, told the board he wanted the company to branch out into a new field and buy a California winery. Jack was a wine connoisseur, and he had Lou Collins on his side, but as major investors we didn't think a winery was a good fit with Crush. At the meeting, Bill Sleeman said he thought the price was too high; the owner was going to retire and we had no expertise in the wine business; and the winery made red wine when white was all the rage. Jack, seeing that Bill was starting to sway even his loyalists on the board, adjourned the meeting and said we'd reconvene later that day at Dromoland Castle four hours away where we were to stay. During one of the stops on the bus ride to the castle, our woman tourist guide took Bill aside and said: "Mr. Sleeman, do some of the people on the bus ever dislike you! I've been overhearing them and it sounds like war. I thought you were directors of the same company." But by the time we reached the castle, Jack's lobbying hadn't changed the majority of directors' minds, so he withdrew his recommendation to buy the winery.

During the next couple of years, I was also bothered by circumstances beyond the control of our management. Outside North America, we were becoming wary of the hit-and-miss nature of the international business; during the war in Angola, for instance, we were shut out of the country. In the United States, two companies were taking dead aim against our orange and root-beer products. General Cinema Corporation had acquired the licensing rights to the Sunkist label and introduced Sunkist Orange as a strong soft-drink competitor; in 1979 it stole half the American market for orange soda. (In contrast to Orange Crush, it was marketed so well, from a standing start, that R.J. Reynolds bought Sunkist Soft Drinks in 1984 for $57 million, leaving General Cinema with an after-tax of $37 million.) The widespread A&P supermarket chain began selling its in-store root beer through bottlers. Meanwhile, the big guys, Coke and Pepsi, were stepping up the pace in their cola wars, trying to make the other guy blink. Between them, they controlled 58 per cent of the market. Philip Morris, a powerful marketing company, bought 7-Up in '78. And Dr Pepper, after a decade of growth, had doubled its share of the market and tripled sales, pulling almost even with third-place 7-Up.

In all of this, we were like a minnow swimming around in a tank of sharks. In '79 our net income was $6.1 million, up only $100,000 from the previous year. John Coleman was so unimpressed after attending his first meeting of the Crush board that he said: "I think you should sell the company." And Mark Kaplan, our New York director, was urging us to get out because of our low market share. I was in Palm Springs one day in 1978 when out of the blue I phoned Dr Pepper's chairman, W.W. Clements. "Foots" Clements (he had big feet) was a real individualist and one of the nicest people I've known in business. A tall guy with a friendly face and a salesman's personality. Totally honest, plain-spoken, he'd started as a route salesman with the company in 1935 and worked his way up from the bottom. At sixty-five, he not only drank Dr Pepper, he ate and lived it. I went down to see Foots in Dallas with the idea that we might be just as interested in buying his company. Their product was a strange one. Its nineteenth-century creator had named the drink for a Texas doctor whose daughter he wanted to marry (the tactic didn't work) and it had twenty-three secret ingredients that gave it a slightly medicinal taste ("People never knew whether to drink it or rub it on," Foots used to say). The company had recently gone through some good years with its "America's Most Misunderstood Soft Drink" and "Be a Pepper" ad campaigns. But Dr Pepper was looking to increase its marketing power by acquiring a company like Crush to broaden its reach.

Nothing much happened in my first meeting with Foots. But as time passed, he displayed an interest in acquiring Crush. In '79, after Jack Thompson resigned, I became chairman, chief executive officer, and, by that time, 64 per cent owner. Then one of the major New York investment bankers approached us. Mark Kaplan, who was on the Crush board, had received a call from a friend, a senior partner at Goldman Sachs. John C. Whitehead was among the most respected names on Wall Street (he'd later be President Reagan's deputy secretary of state). Whitehead said Goldman Sachs had someone interested in buying Crush: Procter & Gamble, the giant manufacturer and marketer of consumer packaged goods with such household names as Crest, Crisco, Ivory, Tide, and Folger's. P&G's sales then were $10 billion a year. The corporation spent nearly half a billion dollars annually on television—as much as the next two biggest TV advertisers combined. It had such clout that it could buy a small tissue manufacturer, Charmin Paper Mills, and turn it into the best-selling bathroom tissue in America. P&G hadn't bought a company to get into a market since 1963, when it acquired Folger's coffee. Why was it interested in going the acquisition route now? The talk in the trade was that the company had been trying for years to perfect a powdered carbonated soft drink that it could distribute through its own sales force, bypassing the independent franchisers who market ordinary soft drinks.

Wall Street investment analysts were saying that the drink-powder research was obviously running into problems.

I consulted with one of our directors, John Coleman, who said he didn't think we owed Foots Clements anything. Now we would see what Procter & Gamble had to offer.

After giving P&G some background on Crush, we arranged to meet at Chicago's central O'Hare International Airport with two of their representatives from the head office in Cincinnati and two Goldman Sachs bankers from New York. From the start, we agreed that the Canadian operations of Crush would not be sold because there was some concern about Ottawa's Foreign Investment Review Agency (FIRA) and, anyway, we wanted to keep Canada for ourselves. At the meeting in a hotel room at the airport, the P&G reps presented us with an initial offer, then left the room so the Goldman Sachs pair could negotiate with us.

"We've got nothing to talk about," I told them. "We'd start entertaining something at $50 million [U.S.] or more, but nothing below."

One of the Goldman Sachs guys went to confer with the P&G delegation. He came back to announce: "They'll talk in the low 40s, but not $50 million."

Goldman Sachs said we should leave it with them; they'd get back to us. The whole meeting took no more than an hour.

Industry journals were pointing out that Procter & Gamble was trying to buy Crush to get a toehold in the soft-drink market with a respected international trademark. "P&G is bidding for the vehicle through which it might apply the technological work it has been doing on carbonated drinks for possibly the last ten years," reported *Advertising Age*.

The following week, the investment bankers kept phoning us with slightly increased offers from P&G. "Don't bother phoning us back," I said. "I told you we'll seriously consider $50 million and take it to our board, but anything less than that, forget it."

Sure enough, they did come back to us and say: "It's too much money, but we'll pay $50 million."

This time we met company officials and their lawyers in another central location, St. Paul, Minnesota, to do a preliminary agreement. It covered the sale of Crush trademarks, inventories, and receivables minus the payables. We'd get to keep the Canadian operations and the $35 million in funds that by now had built up in Crush International.

Because we were both public companies, the preliminary had to be announced. It was big news in the American soft-drink business. The day in May 1980 that it hit *The New York Times* and *The Wall Street Journal*, I got a call from Foots. Dr Pepper had expressed strong interest in buying Crush, but until this point there'd been no serious negotiations. The next day Foots flew up to Vancouver. Over dinner at the University Club next door to our office, he said he'd give us a written offer for $52 million U.S.

After Foots issued a press release reporting his offer, P&G's in-house lawyers phoned me angrily, arguing that we had a preliminary agreement with them. Our legal advice was that we weren't bound by that agreement. Preliminary agreements are merely agreements to agree; we almost never have a lawyer draw one up. I told P&G that Crush would be holding a board meeting in the hotel at O'Hare Airport and they could be there along with Foots Clements. P&G was threatening to sue us, but agreed to make another presentation to us. Meanwhile, in a slick but warm way, Foots made a first-class case to our board of directors about why Dr Pepper was such a wonderful company—and then increased his offer by $1 million. He was followed by Tom Laco, a Procter & Gamble group vice-president who arrived with his lawyers and said curtly: "Our legal opinion is that you're bound by our preliminary agreement, but your legal opinion is different. We want to get on with the business side, and rather than go through the courts to stop any deal you might want to do with Dr Pepper, our offer is: Whatever Dr Pepper has offered you, we'll go $1 million higher."

That meant their offer was now up to $54 million.

Several of the directors got excited, suggesting that we call Foots and then P&G back in for counter-offers. But I said: "We're more than satisfied with the price we're getting, but we do have an obligation to Procter and Gamble. They finally came up with our price of $50 million. Our last offer from Foots was $53 million. I think the fair way to do things is go back to P&G and ask them to match it."

Tom Laco listened quietly as I told him that we'd been acting in good faith and were prepared to sell at the price Foots Clements offered. By this time, my heart was with

Foots, and if it hadn't been for what I considered our moral obligation to P&G, I'd have liked to see him get Crush. But it was in the best interests of the bottlers to have the company in stronger hands.

Foots was disappointed but took it with his usual spirit: "We're getting our sales organization off their cans and going to work doing a selling job on our bottlers," he told reporters. Six years later, a couple of unknown Dallas bottlers, on their way to creating the third-largest soft-drink company in the United States, bought A&W Brands Incorporated, 7-Up, Squirt & Co., and—for $416 million—Dr Pepper.

That wasn't our last good deal with Procter & Gamble. In Canada, our Crush operations were soon focused strictly on the business of selling concentrates. We'd already got rid of a Montreal bottling plant for a good price; in 1982 we sold off our Toronto and Ottawa plants to 7-Up, who became our bottlers. The following year, 7-Up approached us to buy our Canadian concentrate business—offering us almost double what P&G had been willing to pay for it in an offer the year before. But, in our original deal, P&G had bought the Crush trademark rights for Canada, giving us a licensing agreement to sell the concentrates in this country. We kept telling 7-Up that any arrangement with them would require Procter & Gamble's approval. When we eventually did agree on a price for the Canadian business, 7-Up went to P&G for its blessing. That renewed P&G's interest in us.

"You made us an offer a year ago," Bill told Tom Laco, "and it was totally unacceptable. 7-Up have offered us a price that is acceptable. But if you're telling me you won't approve the licensing agreement for 7-Up, you're welcome to step in their shoes. But this may come as a shock to you: It's nearly twice as much as you offered. You're welcome to confirm the price with 7-Up." He did.

When he and Bill met at the O'Hare hotel this time, Laco said: "I've got to hand it you people. We paid a very stiff price for the U.S. and international business. But we expected that when you wanted to sell Canada, we'd get it at a reasonable price because we owned the Canadian trademark."

The sale of the U.S., international, and Canadian operations of Crush gave us a bankroll of more than $100 million. By the end of 1986, we would double it, to nearly $200 million—a stake that has given us the security to get involved in a whole bunch of fascinating ventures.

CHAPTER FOURTEEN

Maybe in Error, Never in Doubt

Those seven exciting years of the Orange Crush scenario unfolded at the same time several other dramas were keeping my life interesting. A Catholic bishop once said: "The man who makes no mistakes does not usually make anything." Doers make mistakes. And we made some good ones during the late 1970s. We took flyers in real estate and oil and gas and none of them really worked out. They ended up costing us many millions of dollars. And then there was silver, where I made and lost a small fortune and still came out a winner—by accident.

Starting in '77, we had more freedom to take calculated gambles, to risk more money, to slip and fall and pick ourselves up again. I was now the sole owner of all the companies that once came under the umbrellas of Neonex International and the original Great Pacific Industries. GPI, which operated only the car-leasing companies in Toronto, Calgary, and Vancouver, had gone private in '76. And just around the time we were gaining 50 per cent control of Crush, we had taken Neonex private. Yet even that decision, which turned out to be a wise one, had its initial problems. It should have been simple, but there were a few dissident shareholders and they forced us into a court case that led to a landmark legal decision.

In '75 we'd started increasing our stock position in Neonex. A kitty of more than $2 million in cash from the sale of CFRW, the Winnipeg radio station, along with surplus funds from the original Great Pacific, helped us buy shares that were trading as low as $1.04. We acquired 46.5 per cent of the stock. At the time, our plan was simply to increase our position, gain control of the company, but not necessarily go private. In fact, the directors didn't make up their minds to buy back all the shares until the day we announced our intention in August '77. Investment analysts couldn't seem to make head or tail of what we'd been doing in recent years—buying a hockey team here, selling a helicopter company there. By privatizing, we decided, we could reduce our overheads and have the independence to do exactly what we wanted, to buy anything from a baseball team to a struggling airline. Among the reasons we'd give shareholders in a management proxy circular:

> While it is difficult to predict the future earnings prospects of the Corporation's continuing operations, the price/earnings ratio being accorded to the common shares of Canadian and United States conglomerates on North American stock exchanges trading at yields higher than those of the Corporation indicate that the trading price of the Corporation's shares may show little change in the near term. . . . With the general decline in equity markets in the North American continent and the decline in the market value of the Corporation's shares, there is now little prospect for the Corporation raising additional capital or financing future acquisitions from the issuance of securities to the public.
>
> The Corporation will be relieved of the expenses inherent in maintaining its status as a public company with shares listed on two stock exchanges in Canada and the reporting requirements of the Securities and Exchange Commission of the United States.
>
> The Corporation will be encouraged to make business decisions on the basis of longer-range objectives and opportunities without concern for the possible adverse effect from time to time on short-term earnings.

Maybe in Error, Never in Doubt

Let's see if the shareholders want to sell out to us, I suggested to my associates. After making the decision one morning, I polled the Neonex directors an hour later on a conference call and got their agreement. Then we issued a press release announcing our plan to merge Neonex with Jim Pattison Ltd. to create a private company.

Our vice-president of finance, Fred Vanstone, quarterbacked the privatizing process with the stock exchange, the lawyers, and the accountants. My mind was still preoccupied by the continuing court battles with Jack Leitch in the long-running Maple Leaf Mills lawsuit. To finance the buying of shares, we had $11.6 million of our own cash and money borrowed from the bank; none of Neonex's funds or credit was used to do the deal. We valued the shares at $3, believing this was a decent premium over the $2.50 at which the stock was then trading. Shareholders had the option of selling their stock at $3 or taking 5.5 per cent redeemable non-voting preference stock worth $3.

Only 11,000 of the 3.9 million publicly held shares were converted into the preference stock, which had a low dividend payout. A large majority of the shareholders—84.4 per cent—agreed to sell at $3. But about thirty of them, holding a total of 120,000 shares, filed notice of dissent, protesting that the offer wasn't high enough.

They took their case to the B.C. Supreme Court. In early '78, the court ruled that companies wanting to buy out minority shareholders must prove that what they're willing to pay for the shares is fair and equitable. This contradicted previous practice where the shareholders had to prove in court that a company's offer was unfair. "Three dollars may represent the fair value of the shares," the judge said, "but the dissenters should not be compelled to accept Pattison's assurances on blind faith and untested evidence." Placing the burden of proof on us, he ordered a trial to determine whether our $3 offer was fair.

We appealed but never went to trial. The key dissidents were Bill McCartney of Red Deer and Bert Sladden of Calgary, the two biggest shareholders of Travelaire Recreational Vehicles, which Neonex had bought in '69 and sold back to them five years later. They had more than 85,000 shares of Neonex from the original acquisition. Bill Sleeman knew them well. After the Supreme Court decision, he happened to be meeting them on another matter when the case came up in conversation.

"Come on, Bert," Bill said to Sladden, who was taking the toughest stance, "tell me why you think this deal is unfair. You've got something in your craw." Bill was sure he knew what the problem was.

Neonex owned a mobile-housing plant in Calgary which sat on a valuable piece of land right on the Trans-Canada Highway. Although the market value of the real estate was between $5 million and $7 million, we had it on our books for a much lower figure. If we ever sold it, we'd get up to $7 million over our book value. And Bert Sladden didn't think we had taken that into account when we set the value of the Neonex shares we wanted to buy from him.

The first thing Bill pointed out to him was that, whenever we sold the property, we'd have to pay capital-gains tax. Sladden said he'd forgotten about that.

Offsetting that, Bill said, there was $15 million worth of goodwill on the left side of the balance sheet. "So the number is still back to $3 or less per share."

It was like a light bulb going off in Sladden's head. "I'd just taken your book value per share and added the market value of this land and came up with something like $4 a share," he said.

Admitting that a new trial could cost the dissidents plenty in legal fees, Sladden was agreeable when Bill said he'd recommend that they get the $3 a share offered a year and a half earlier, plus interest at prime rate for that period, plus their current legal expenses. The final total was above $3 a share but nowhere near the $4 they wanted. I agreed to the deal, and we withdrew our appeal.

On November 1, 1977, Neonex International was amalgamated with Jim Pattison (British Columbia) Ltd., a wholly owned private company. If we wanted, we could hold our next annual meeting in an elevator. Now all we had to do was keep the TD's Ted McDowell happy.

Investment Reporter, a Toronto investment newsletter, remarked after the privatization of Neonex: "It seems to us to symbolize the end of that brief era when any company with a name ending in '-ex,' '-ics' or '-tron' was assured of some following (however fickle) with a certain segment of the investing public."

Maybe in Error, Never in Doubt

* * *

In the inflation-driven late '70s, it seemed like everyone in Western Canada, including your dentist and your cabdriver, was in the real-estate market. The West Coast had two of the most prominent Canadian players in the game: Nelson Skalbania, whom I got to know through my dealings with the Blazers and the Canadians; and Jack Poole, president of Daon Development, which was quickly on its way to amassing more than $2 billion in assets. After meeting Jack at the Young Presidents' Organization (which I reluctantly had to graduate from, at age fifty, in 1978), we'd been involved with him in our short-lived joint venture in mobile-home communities. Every time we met, Jack would say: "You should take a percentage of your assets and get into the real-estate business, Jimmy." What finally triggered our entry into the field was the availability of one of Jack's own key executives, George Flanigan. He'd been running Daon's B.C.–Washington–Oregon division. But Jack and his executive vice-president, Bill Levine, were restructuring the company on a product rather than a geographical basis, which meant that Flanigan would have to move to Calgary. Wanting to stay in Vancouver, he came to see me instead. His message: "Give me two years, put in this much equity, and I'll show you how to really make money." Flanigan had an engineering background; I checked him out with Jack, who recommended him.

We hired him in '80, though we didn't really get rolling in real estate until the following year. Because we were newcomers, George Flanigan recommended that we do joint ventures with experienced people who needed a financial partner. That wasn't our normal style of doing business, but I agreed. Well, we did thirteen deals, and of the nine that were joint ventures, only one worked out. They were a mix of industrial, commercial, and residential projects—land to be developed for residential housing; warehouses; a minor shopping centre; and small office buildings (in Seattle, Vancouver, and Calgary). All but one of our partners were modest entrepreneurs/developers and some medium-sized companies like the well-respected Narod Construction, our partner in Seattle. The exception was Block Brothers, controlled by the Reichmann brothers, with whom we developed residential property on Vancouver Island which we still own. We got into the market at the very peak in '81; within a year, interest rates were rocketing to 22 per cent and the economy was going into the tank. Everybody in real estate was hurting, including Narod and Daon, which the year before had posted revenues of nearly $700 million.

It was a good lesson about the importance of having strong partners. Next time, I told myself, go into real estate with someone as strong as or stronger than yourself. Next time, I'd like to go in with someone as strong as a CPR. Because we were left on the hook: Our small joint-venture partners couldn't shoulder their share of carrying costs and development. We owned 100 per cent of the problem, had to pay every nickel of the debt. It's taken us from 1982 until today to work our way out of it, and we're still not finished. We either sold land off at big losses or completed the development and sold at a loss. On one deal we did make $4 million: a Calgary office building at 8th and 8th, which sold before the economy crashed. George Flanigan left us, amicably, in '83. Since then we've developed two shopping centres in B.C., with Overwaitea and Save-On-Foods as the anchor tenants. And while they've been good deals, they weren't profitable enough to help us recover the tens of millions we lost on the real-estate roller coaster.

There are certain businesses that lend themselves to joint ventures. Oil and gas is another one. We went into that field with people who were less than expert, we didn't know what we were doing ourselves, and it was all handled so badly that we deserved to lose money. We were just plain dumb on this one.

Iain Harris, who managed our investment in oil and gas, had an interesting background. Master's degree from the London School of Economics, MBA from the University of Chicago ("I firmly believe, having been through some of the best education in business, that I am not a better businessman for it," he says). Then assistant to the president of the Glengair Group of Toronto (now Jannock Limited), one of the few early Canadian conglomerates, which controlled both Atlantic Sugar and Canada Brick. Joined Glengair in '70, just when conglomerates were going out of fashion. Impatient, he leaped to Molson Industries as manager of financial analysis for its head-office control group and wound up as controller of the eastern division of Molson's Beaver Lumber. I came to know Iain when he became finance director for a Neonex company, Acme Novelty in Edmonton, as it was going sharply downhill. When Acme died, I brought him in as vice-president of finance for our private company and then, when Neonex went private, he took the same position in the new Jim Pattison Group.

Iain took the lead in oil and gas. A local promoter and friend, Izzy Wolfe, identified a petroleum situation in Kansas which he thought was full of promise. Putting together a group of investors, he approached us. The industry was booming at the time and, though we had no experience in it, Iain liked the deal because it involved a relatively diversified drilling program—we didn't have to bet a lot of money on one hole. There were several low-risk wells and, while the potential of each one was also limited, there'd be enough winners—in theory. In practice, that was wrong: You could lose money in low-risk ways just as easily. We went in with Wolfe, some Calgary investors, and the petroleum company in Kansas.

Our investment was $2.5 million. The oilmen hit just enough to tease us. But it was all over within a matter of months. We hadn't properly assessed the risk or our partners' abilities. The potential of the play they'd promoted was wildly overstated and the costs much greater than they'd projected.

Iain came to see me one day. "Listen, that two and a half million bucks is in big trouble," he said, "and it's probably going to be worthless." It was.

At the end of the year, when I gave him his bonus, I said: "It isn't as much as it might have been, and I think you know the reason why."

Everybody can make a mistake. It depends on how it's made and whether a person has the ability to learn from it. In a case like this, I never blame the individual for the error; it's the company's responsibility. Iain didn't go out and make that investment on his own. He came to me and I said, "Go ahead." And within a few years, Iain Harris would more than offset any of his mistakes by making our airline fly.

There's no one else to share any of the responsibility for my less-than-sterling performance during the Great Silver Bubble. I had a lot of solid advice to get out while the getting was good, but I ignored it. And it was only the action of my administrative assistant, Maureen Chant, that let me come out of the silver escapade with my skin.

For years, off and on, I'd been playing the stock market with mixed success. I began as far back as 1955, playing the penny stocks after I'd earned $52,000 in one year as sales manager of Aristocratic Cookware, teaching salesmen how to direct-sell pots and pans. In '66, before we took over Neon Products, I invested in pricier stock. My car business was quiet so I took a few hundred thousand dollars in cashflow from our group of companies and split it with my financial people, Harry Dunbar and Bud Eberhardt, to manage. The three of us kept track of the stocks and invested independently. It was a lively trading market, a lot smaller than it is now, and we played good-quality stock. Sometimes we bought through the Dean Witter brokerage office in Hawaii because it took nine or ten days for our cheques to clear the bank. I'd mail our payments to Hawaii on time, but the cheques would have to clear through the American and international banking systems before reaching my bank. That allowed us to play on real margins.

We were always competing with one another, meeting once a week to compare notes on what we'd bought and how we were doing. I remember Harry announcing one day that he'd bought heavily in Eastern Airlines at $98. "Well, as a matter of fact, so did I," Bud said. "And," I said, "so did I." Suddenly about three-fifths of our portfolio was tied up in Eastern; we quickly flew out of it.

We were trading so fast and furious that our local broker, a novice with Merrill Lynch, made more money with us in about four months than most of the rest of his colleagues made in a year. It all came to an end when our attention shifted and we went after Neon in '67.

For the next ten years, I fooled around with penny stocks—as a hobby, because I sure wasn't making any money at it. In January '78 I decided to switch to the commodities market. More than thirty commodities are regularly traded, everything from hogs and cattle to cotton and frozen orange juice—and, of course, gold and silver. It's a fast-track market. I've read that at least 80 per cent of commodities investors lose, but there's big money to be made on a relatively small stake. I started with copper and lumber, then traded in soybeans, pork bellies, and copper before falling in love with silver.

They call silver the restless metal; it has a long, volatile history. Egyptians knew about it as far back as 4000 B.C. and for the first three thousand years considered it more precious than gold. Although gold gets all the press today, silver has been the currency of choice of most people around the world for centuries. For good reasons: There's more of it than gold, it's half the weight, and almost as easy to make into coins and jewellery. While silver doesn't have quite the glitter of gold —it's much cheaper per ounce—it's increasingly considered a good hedge against inflation (in India, it's been hoarded for centuries). And silver is a more practical metal than gold. About 40 per cent is consumed in photographic films and papers; it's also used in medicine and the arts and in such products as batteries and conductors in the electrical and electronic industries. Silver is almost always in short supply, with the annual demand exceeding new production. The United States, as a major consumer, needs more than 160 million ounces a year but mines only about 40 million. Some of the shortfall comes from recycling, from the melting of coins, scrap, and the recovery of silver used in photography. The rest comes from the other big producers in the western world, including Canada and Peru, which have traditionally had a surplus of silver, mining about the same amount each year as the United States.

When you speculate in commodities like silver, you're not buying shares in a corporation the way you are on the stock exchange. The initial idea behind commodity trading was to allow farmers to sell their crops at a guaranteed amount well before harvest, and to protect manufacturers against future price increases. Some of the commodity contracts are on a cash basis for immediate or forward delivery. But most are in the form of futures contracts: to either receive or deliver certain quantities of commodities on a fixed date in the future, at an agreed-upon price—regardless of whether the market for the commodities increases or declines between now and that date. It's not a new concept: The Japanese were doing something similar in the 1600s and there were futures contracts being traded in major European and North American cities in the mid-1800s.

The people who contract to buy or receive are holders of

"long" contracts while those who sell or deliver have "short" contracts. As a speculator, you never handle the actual commodities; you're dealing in pieces of paper. A commodities exchange acts as a clearinghouse to ensure that the buyers and sellers—the longs and the shorts—fulfill their contracts. The open, competitive bidding that goes on there is classic free enterprise. The two major North American clearinghouses are the New York Commodities Exchange (Comex) and the Chicago Board of Trade. In commodities, unlike stocks, you pay cash up front, settling your accounts each day. If you don't pay, you can't play. But one attraction of commodities investing is that you can buy or sell contracts on a very low margin at a fraction of their nominal value. So a trader has enormous leverage: If you put down only 4 per cent of the total price of the commodity a 4 per cent move upwards can double your investment.

Yet you have to consider commodities trading much riskier than playing the stock market and be prepared to lose your money. It's not a game for triflers: You better pay very close attention to commodities prices. They can fluctuate wildly, reacting to unpredictable events like a war in Central America or the blowing up of a bridge in Zaire or Zambia.

Or the Hunt brothers in Texas.

My fate in the silver market ultimately depended on the incredible dealings of Nelson Bunker Hunt and W. Herbert Hunt. They were billionaires, the sons of American oilman H.L. Hunt, once reputed to be the richest man in the world. After inheriting some of their father's fortune, the boys made more money in the oil fields of Libya until Colonel Qaddafi nationalized their holdings in 1973. Looking around for new fields to conquer, Bunker Hunt discovered silver. I met Bunker once casually at a commodities seminar in Dallas and really enjoyed his down-to-earth, human qualities. He apparently loves to trade commodities.

Bunker, joined by brother Herbert, began buying silver and by the end of '76 owned at least one hundred million ounces, worth around half a billion dollars. Two years later, the Hunts had hooked up with princes of the royal family of Saudi Arabia. By the time I got into the market, their combined buying power was starting to send the price of silver surging.

I'd formed a little company called Jim Pattison Ltd. and

put $25,000 in to invest in commodities. The deal I made with myself was that if and when I lost my original stake, I'd quit. I didn't want to risk a lot of money. Maureen Chant was to handle the accounts with brokers like New York's Drexel Burnham and Conti Commodity Services and Vancouver's International Futures, whose Graham Dallimore first got me into copper. It was up to Maureen to let me know when the $25,000 was all gone. As we went along, I'd tell her: "Let's buy soybeans, or short copper" and then she'd give the order to the broker and keep track of my profit and loss. As it turned out, she had to watch the market constantly, checking prices throughout the day. After one of my big early losses (about $250,000 in soybeans) I went to New York to find an expert and was directed to Norton Waltuch, who ran Conti's office there and was purported to be one of the world's largest commodity traders. As I began to do a lot of business with him, I came to have the highest respect for him, both personally and professionally. We're still friends and I continue to deal with him today.

Before long, I was making more on commodities than I was losing; as I got caught up in the excitement, the fun of the trading, I made the accounts larger and larger.

By the end of the first year, my initial investment of $25,000 had shot up to $800,000.

Precious metals—platinum, gold, and silver—were hot. The media reported that some people were rushing out to have their silver vases and candlesticks melted down. Others were taking millions of dollars from their bank accounts and out of mutual funds to climb aboard the gold and silver bandwagons. Soon I was trading precious metals in London and Hong Kong too so I could trade around the clock; some nights, I'd wake up at three in the morning to call London.

In August '79, trading in silver by big players like the Hunt brothers caused a sudden leap in prices and scared the Chicago Board of Trade. Afraid that the Hunts and their associates might demand delivery of their contracts and put a squeeze on the silver supply, the exchange set its first-ever "position limits" on the number of silver-futures contracts a trader could own.

By the end of 1979, my $25,000 investment was worth about $25 million.

Early on, I'd got on the copper train and stayed long; in

a single day, I held 1,400 copper contracts. My position in copper was so big at one point that I had a profit of $14 million. But eventually, most of the money was in silver, which had leaped to $28 an ounce by December '79.

After a while, the millions started to be meaningless. I'd be down $2 million yesterday, up $3 million today, up $5 million tomorrow—and in U.S. dollars too. I'd get to the office early enough to be there when the commodities markets began opening at 5:30 A.M. my time. At first, I was through with my trading by 8:00 A.M., but as the pace quickened and the millions mounted, silver in particular kept interrupting my regular business day, sometimes every half-hour.

Around Christmas that year, I actually took physical delivery of two million ounces of silver. The standard contract covers delivery of five thousand ounces of silver that's 99.9 per cent pure or, as traders say, .999 fine or triple nine. Although you can pay a premium and get the silver in ingots as light as one ounce, the standard bar weighs one thousand ounces. But you don't pick up the metal and take it home; it's stored in secure warehouses. While there were some tax advantages in taking delivery of the silver, by this time I was so in love with the soft, white, lustrous metal that I wanted to actually own some of the bullion. I sent Maureen to the Conti office in New York to conclude the transaction. Not that she ever saw the actual silver; she simply got the ownership certificates for the two million ounces. The commodities brokers had her sign two hundred certificates that were numbered to match the labels on the bars of silver. Once signed, the certificates became negotiable; if she'd lost one, they would have been as good as cash to the finder. The stack of silver certificates was so heavy that the shoulder strap of her purse broke. Because she was doing a twenty-four-hour round trip, Maureen knew she'd fall asleep on the plane home. Nervous about losing the negotiable notes, she wrapped them around her waist under her clothing and kept her arms crossed protectively over them all the way to Vancouver. For good reason: They were worth at least $60 million.

Not everybody was as excited about the silver market as I was. One of our directors, John Coleman, the former chairman of the Royal Bank, was sitting in my kitchen about this time and suggested that I should take $4 or $5 million out of

Maybe in Error, Never in Doubt

my trading accounts, just in case the market crashed. I said I would; I didn't. We met again in the Westin Hotel in Toronto. Discussing silver's continuing climb, he said: "This is fantastic. How long can this go on? Many stories like this have had a very unhappy ending."

"The way I figure it," I said, "as long as we have inflation, the price of silver won't go down."

I'd been up about $50 million when I talked to our auditor, Don Selman, who's always given me good advice. He told me to take my profit and run. "Why stay in? It's such a big profit. Think of what you can do with a $50 million capital gain—the acquisitions, the good investments you could make." He pleaded with me to sell at least half my earnings.

I was stubborn. My plan was that if I hit $100 million, I'd cash in my chips and buy a big new executive jet.

One Monday morning in January, I arrived at the office to discover that the price of silver had reached an astronomical $50 an ounce; a year earlier, it had been $6. My little nut of $25,000 had grown into a mighty $78 million cash.

I didn't have much time to celebrate. That month, there were disturbing signs that the game was winding down—signals I chose to ignore. The other major futures exchange, Comex, also set position limits which prevented speculators from holding more than five hundred contracts in the month when delivery could be made. But prices continued to jump even higher; on January 18, they peaked at $50.35, nearly nine times the level they'd been at a year earlier. Three days later, the Comex board declared an emergency and announced that trading was now limited to liquidation of existing positions. That sent the price of silver plummetting the next day to $34 from $44. And it wouldn't stop falling until the end of March, when it bottomed at $10.20.

I started losing heavily. That's when I was plain stupid. If I'd have shorted—sold—when silver was falling out of bed so fast, I would still have made a fortune. Along the way, I did sell some: When the price dropped to the $40 range, I got rid of a significant portion of my holdings. But when the price hit $30 and then $16 and $10, I kept jumping right back in, buying more silver, figuring that what had fallen would rise again. And it did briefly, but ultimately it crashed.

At the beginning of March, just after our Partners in Pride conference, I took Mary down to Palm Springs for a few days' rest. I'd already been getting margin calls from my brokers—calls to settle up my accounts with them. After I left, Maureen had to keep fielding those calls. She sat on the phone in the boardroom of Corporate Office, talking to the brokers, then phoning me for instructions. Every day I told her to put up more cash. She soon realized that I had no intention of selling; I was going to hang in there in the hope that silver would rise once more. Meanwhile, our millions were flowing away as fast as snowmelt down a mountainside. The pressure on Maureen was intense.

Finally, within a couple of days, she phoned me in Palm Springs and announced: "This is our last margin call, Jimmy. This is it; I don't have any more money to make any more margin calls. There's no more cash."

So it was all gone, all $78 million.

"Do it," I said. "Shut down our positions."

I got out of the silver market, after learning the hard way that what goes up comes down. That night, I didn't sleep well, realizing I had lost all that money in a matter of days. But that was the only night's sleep I missed. After that, I told myself: *Let's get on with it.*

I was all right by the time I got back into the office. That day, I was running through my bank accounts when I spotted $6.6 million that I didn't know I had. There was no indication where the money came from. Calling Maureen in, I asked: "Where's this six-point-six from?"

"Well," she said. "I didn't tell you the exact truth. I hid that money. Because as long as you knew you had it, you'd still be meeting your silver margin calls."

What a pleasant surprise.

The Hunt brothers and their Arab partners were in the tank, with the Hunts alone losing an estimated $1.75 billion. Not everyone suffered; logically, if the silver buyers—the longs—had lost, many of the short sellers must have won. For instance, a lot of the precious-metals dealers had profited when the bubble burst. Armand Hammer, the controversial eighty-one–year–old chairman of Occidental Petroleum in Los Angeles—and an old rival of Bunker Hunt's—told a press conference that by going short in the silver market, he'd made a windfall profit of $119.6 million.

And thanks to Maureen's looking after my hide, Jimmy Pattison of Vancouver, British Columbia, could take some

Maybe in Error, Never in Doubt

comfort in the fact that he had made a profit of $6.6 million playing the silver market.

My company has been in commodities ever since, with an in-house professional trader or two following the markets for me. I like commodities: You can make money whether the market's going up or down—in good times or down times. It's fast. It's all cash. And, on balance, I win.

One of my other losses in 1980 was the day-to-day presence of my best friend, Wilf Ray. From the time he was our advertising manager at the Bowell McLean dealership and continuing through his work as director of corporate communications for the Jim Pattison Group, he and I were a good combination. Wilf was one of the family. I was enormously disappointed in the way we parted company. For a few months in mid-'80 he was on a hectic round of travelling, photographing all of Oral Roberts University in Tulsa, Oklahoma; on a month-long tour of Mainland China as official photographer for the Full Gospel Businessmen's Fellowship; then three days to put together an audio-visual show to present to Fellowship delegates in Los Angeles. And on to Gimli, Manitoba, to help stage one of our executive meetings. Two weeks later, during a church service, he had what was diagnosed as a mild heart attack. His wife told me the doctors wouldn't allow any visitors. Although I waited to hear when I could see him, word never reached me and Wilf never called. At Christmas I sent him a gift of salmon with a card saying that I missed him and quoting one of his favourite passages of Scripture, Romans 8:28: "And we know that all things work together for good to them that love God, to them who are the called according to his purpose." But Wilf put the fish in his freezer without finding the card. We finally met the following February, when I offered to give him an easier job while he was recuperating. Nothing came of it; I kept him on salary for a year, until September. I figured he wanted to take life a little easier, away from me. He moved to Maple Ridge, outside Vancouver, became an alderman, and went back into real estate. He continues to do his gospel-music program every Sunday on our radio station, CJJR. We've seen each other only a few times since. I've always felt badly about Wilf; I really love the guy.

CHAPTER FIFTEEN

I Get Religion

In January 1981, I was driving to Squamish, a town about fifty miles up the coast from Vancouver, on my way to look at a possible site for an Overwaitea food store. The highway to Squamish winds along the ocean shore, hugging the mountains that rear straight up from the edge of the road. It was a Saturday afternoon and traffic was light. Ahead of me I saw a boy on foot, pushing a bicycle. I stopped the car, got out, and asked him: "You got a problem?" He'd hit a rock that had fallen from the cliffside; his bike was damaged. We loaded it in my trunk and I drove him to his home in Britannia Beach, a few miles away. "Nice bike," I said, making conversation.

"Oh, yeah, the best bike I've ever had."

"What kind?"

"It's Japanese. This is my third bike, but this is the very best one."

After dropping him off, and as my '81 Buick began climbing the first long hill out of Britannia Beach, I thought about what he'd said. That kid loved his Japanese bike. I remembered when Japan used to export almost nothing but shoddy imitations of North American products, symbolized by the cheap toys that would fall apart after a few hours' play. In recent years, the Japanese had been quietly, thoroughly rebuilding their reputation. I pulled out the calculator I'd got

I Get Religion

for Christmas. A Sharp. Japanese. I remembered that Wilf Ray had wanted to buy a fancy new camera for his communications work, a Nikon—the finest camera in the world, he said. Japanese. I glanced at the three expensive Swiss watches I was wearing; they were all showing different times. Even re-setting them every day, I never had the right time. And I'd read about how good the Japanese Seikos were. Three motorcycles roared by me—*wham wham wham!* They reminded me that the Japanese had about 90 per cent of the motorcycle market. I'd bought a new boat recently and needed an outboard motor; somebody told me to get the top quality—from Japan. When I'd gone into a music store in Palm Springs the year before, looking for a new organ, the salesman said Yamaha was the best there was. Videocassette recorders: The Japanese had virtually the whole market. They were leading the rest of the world in TV sets, radios, radial tires, even tractors—29 per cent of the tractors in the United States were made in Japan.

On the way back to Vancouver, I thought about all this some more. The Japanese didn't have much of an effect on most of our company. They didn't make recreational vehicles over here, didn't distribute magazines, didn't get involved in the soft-drink business. The one area they did touch us, though, was automobiles. And I knew from firsthand experience how good they were in that field. One year earlier, after being raised on General Motors cars all my life, we'd opened three Toyota dealerships in Greater Vancouver. We became the first master dealer with branch operations in Canada. In the next few months, as I saw the figures coming through for the Toyotas we were selling, and noticed how few repairs they needed during their warranty periods, as compared to GM vehicles, I couldn't believe it. They were so much less expensive and their quality was so much higher. At that time, 64 per cent of all North American-made cars would have a mechanical defect in their first six months, compared to only about half that number of Japanese-made cars. In our experience, where GM would have to spend $331 to fix a car under warranty, Toyota would spend only $31. American semi-conductor computer chips had failure rates five to six times greater than Japanese ones. North American TV sets had 50 per cent more repairs throughout their lives than Japanese sets.

The same month as my reflective drive along the Squamish highway, I went to Japan. I was there trying to find out the secret of how a people who'd once been the world's purveyors of junk had become internationally synonymous with quality products. After opening our Toyota dealerships, I went to visit Toyota's corporate office in Nagoya, south of Tokyo.

And it was there that I got religion.

I met Eiji Toyoda, chairman of Toyota Motor Corporation, Japan's largest and most successful corporation. I'd met him twice before, when he visited Canada and came to my home. He's a member of the Toyoda family, which runs an interlocked empire of textiles, steel, and automotive-related companies, the Toyota Group (the soft "d" was hardened for North American consumption). Toyota had its beginnings in a textile company founded by Sakichi Toyoda, an inventor sometimes called Japan's Thomas Edison. Now, although the family business is mosily owned by banks and insurance companies, eleven Toyoda cousins operate it.

"Mr. Toyoda," I asked through interpreters, "would you please tell me, while I have this very important opportunity, what is the secret of how you've captured market after market, particularly in consumer goods, in North America and around the world?"

The chairman replied: "There is no secret. The whole of Japan has a strategy, a national strategy of commitment to quality."

How, I wondered, did they teach their more than a hundred million people about quality? The answer is: "One by one." And it begins with students who learn about it in their schools. Other key Japanese executives spelled out five keys to their system of maintaining quality:

1. Tally the defects in the system.
2. Analyse the facts of their tally.
3. Trace the defects to the source.
4. Correct the defects at the source.
5. Record what happens thereafter.

At age fifty-two, I had found religion. Not the spiritual kind, but a philosophy of running a business in the best interests of both the corporation and the employee. During my visit to Toyota's corporate office in Nagoya, I learned about Quality Circles (QCs). These are small groups of employees who meet voluntarily on a regular basis to identify, analyse, and solve quality concerns in their workplace. The Circles inspire teamwork and increase employee motivation and involvement. Trained in problem-solving and making presentations to management, employees grow not only as workers but as people. The theory is sound: It makes sense that the workers actually doing the job should know the best ways to analyse a process and correct any defects. And most employees have ideas about improving their workplace, and enjoy the recognition and personal satisfaction they get from seeing even the smallest of their good ideas bear fruit. Most people are motivated by more than just satisfying their basic needs. The psychologists call it "the desire for self-actualization," which is just a fancy way of saying we want to be all we can be.

At Toyota City, about forty miles from the wharves of Nagoya, there were forty thousand employees making Toyotas the year I visited Japan. In 1980, they had given management four hundred thousand written suggestions on how to improve quality and production in their plants—almost one a month from each employee. (By '85, they'd given ten million suggestions over three and a half decades.)

It all sounded great, but would it work in North America? In Japan, I heard about a corporation near Chicago that was using the Quality Circle concept. Motorola, which made the first television set I ever owned, had been taken over by Matsushita about five years earlier. Back in Vancouver, I called the company and told the president I was just home from Japan and wanted to know all about his QC program. Richard Kraft had been head of engineering for Motorola when the Japanese multi-national bought the factory with two thousand employees. At that time, there were 140 operating defects for every 100 Motorola TV sets produced in the plant. Matsushita sent in sixteen Japanese to teach Kraft, the new president, how to build quality into their products. The previous year—with the same workforce and management but a different management style—they were averaging only four to six defects per hundred Quasar and Panasonic TV sets. His warranty costs in '79 were one-tenth what they'd been before the takeover.

After hearing about a Sony plant that had opened two

and a half years earlier in San Diego, I called a Mr. Yamota, a senior executive for Sony in the States. He told me he had 1,775 employees in San Diego, with twenty Japanese supervisors but not one Japanese working on the factory line. And they'd just broken the record for all fifteen Sony plants in the world: They'd gone two hundred consecutive working days without a single operating defect in a Sony TV. That record beat Japan's six factories.

So it could be done.

A couple of weeks after returning from Japan, I introduced the concept at the Partners in Pride meeting in Palm Springs. I told our executives that we, the management, had to show the leadership in bringing Quality Circles to the Jim Pattison Group. "Give the employee a chance to suggest how we can improve. Don't take it as a criticism of your system. Say: 'It's a good idea.' " A big brass band marched into the conference and, to the tune of "Roll Out the Barrel," psyched up our people with the idea that "We are the difference."

I asked Stan Whittle from Corporate Office to organize the Quality Circle program. He attended workshops and called on experts before hiring a Thorne Stevenson management consultant with QC experience. Together they set up seminars to inform executives about the process and train employee faciliators and leaders in how to help create Circles in their workplaces.

Although the QC program has never been mandatory, we got up to a high of 125 Circles. They've all worked differently; some didn't work at all. In '79 we'd bought Canada's second-biggest electrical sign company, Claude Neon—repatriated it from American ownership—and many of its employees formed active Circles. But their styles of operating are diverse. One group in Montreal uses the pure approach of the original QCs. In-house leaders and facilitators help organize interested volunteers into a Circle. Its members learn how to quickly identify problems, define them, investigate all the relevant facts, analyse all the possible causes of the problems. And with data gathered and recommendations expressed, they go to work on a solution through consensus. Then they confirm their solution by gathering information that proves its effectiveness and finally present their recommendation to management. Another Claude Neon group, in Winnipeg, sometimes found it frustrating to spend three or four months trying to solve a quality problem. They agreed that their facilitator should meet with other groups in Regina and Saskatoon to come up with a variety of solutions and quicker ways of solving problems for more immediate satisfaction. In some divisions, like Neon Products, QCs have come and gone like the tide, depending on the enthusiasm of the employees and facilitators. In others, they've never even started. The reaction of unions has ranged from attempts to block QCs or passive support—some union leaders see them as a management tool to take advantage of workers. Middle management doesn't always like them either because they give employees the chance to change policies the managers have established.

For the first three years, the Quality Circle program cost us $1 million annually. But the return on our investment is tremendous. The first of our divisions to prove the concept was EDP, the Vancouver computer company. Instead of forming the classic focused Circles, its staff held quality meetings with representatives from each department. Before those meetings, the accuracy of EDP's computer-services material was only 78.5 per cent; in less than a year, it was 97.7 per cent accurate. Courtesy Chevrolet Oldsmobile in Vancouver had a problem with used cars that weren't being properly inspected. The QC brainstormed and came up with a checklist that, because of its thoroughness, increased the service department's revenues by $140,000 in one year.

But Quality Circles work just as effectively for employees as they do for management. Their recommendations have resulted in new safety equipment in our factories; staff training in the life-saving cardiopulmonary resuscitation method; and even reductions in a plant's shift work. At Mainland Magazine, a B.C. news distribution company we acquired in 1980, everybody in the plant wanted to reduce the workload on the assembly line. Managers had spent three months trying to solve the problem. Handed the challenge, the Circle spent just one weekend coming up with an ingenious solution that cut its two daily shifts down to one. Nobody lost a job: The extra people were absorbed in other parts of the company.

The QC process keeps evolving. At Overwaitea Foods, where it was tough to get groups of shift workers together regularly, the process was changed to allow employees to

226   *Jimmy: An Autobiography*

write down their ideas about improving the products and services they provide and the environment where they work. And they can get directly involved in implementing their solutions and receive recognition on a local and company-wide basis.

Overwaitea named its program "Excellence and Employee Participation." Whatever you want to call the Quality Circle concept, it's employee involvement. And—with a real commitment from management—boy, does it work.

Sadazo Yamamoto, the president of Toyota, visited Vancouver not long after we became Toyota dealers. I had him and a dozen other of his company officials over to the house for dinner. Aside from Susumu Yanagisawa, president of Toyota Canada, few of them knew much English. They were very formal at first, but I'd asked Maureen Chant to write some verses that we could all sing together. By the end of the evening, we were all gathered around the organ singing lines like:

> In 1957 you shipped
> The first two cars;
> You're shooting for a million,
> We're shooting for the stars.

We got into Toyotas because the Japanese company's Quality Circles were producing some of the most reasonably priced reliable cars in the world. *Consumer Reports'* auto-testing chief says: "Model for model, the Toyota products have been the most consistent for having good records." Even so, when the Toyota zone manager approached us and offered three exclusive territories, it wasn't an easy decision. We had an enormous IOU with General Motors; we'd been a faithful GM dealer for nearly two decades. But we knew the world was changing and we just weren't participating in half of the automobile market. Toyota, the best and biggest of the Japanese car-makers, was coming on so strong that in a couple of years they wouldn't need us. After checking our GM agreement, our lawyers assured us there was no legal problem to taking on competing dealerships. We called the franchise Jim Pattison Toyota because our name was synonymous with cars in Vancouver and we didn't want any subterfuge by concealing the ownership. Later, General Motors asked us to change the name; we declined.

We'd warned GM ahead of time about our involvement with Toyota. On a plane to Hawaii, I met vice-president and general manager Dick Colcomb and told him we were thinking about getting involved with the Japanese. "Go ahead," he said; it didn't matter to him. But afterwards the Canadian headquarters really raised Cain with us. They sent a national vice-president of sales and the zone manager to see us after the fact. We had a very testy time with them. I wrote a letter to GM Canada that I never mailed. After I read it to them over the phone, they asked me not to send it. We made peace. And in the next few years, General Motors and Toyota got together in a joint venture to make the Nova and other cars in California.

Interestingly enough, it wasn't until GM had talked about cancelling our franchises that I realized one of my life's ambitions: to become a Cadillac dealer. During my days at Bowell McLean, I hungered to someday have my own dealership where I could sell these luxurious automobiles. When I opened my own business, I'd talk to anybody I could in GM about handling Cadillacs. But not until Bow Mac went broke years later—and after our run-in over the Toyota dealerships—did GM give me the Cadillac franchise.

By the time I began handling the big, beautiful Cadillacs, the handwriting was on the wall. As early as 1980, the trend was towards smaller and fuel-efficient vehicles, and the Japanese and other foreign auto-manufacturers were going to get increasingly bigger pieces of the North American market. When I'd opened my first GM dealership nearly twenty years earlier, General Motors, Ford, and Chrysler held a commanding 86 per cent share of that market. Quietly, in '66, the Japanese carmakers slipped past the Germans into second place, behind the Americans, in global auto production. By '80, we were being rocked by new energy crises and, within a couple of years, fuel-efficient Japanese vehicles were flooding into North America. Production on this continent fell while Japan became the leading automotive manufacturing centre in the world. In '86, the North American manufacturers' share of the pie was down 15 per cent on their own turf; imports had 30 per cent of the passenger-car market in Canada.

One of the most significant trends of the last few years

has been transplants—vehicles built in North America by such foreign manufacturers as Honda, Nissan, and Toyota. A dozen new transplant facilities are being built or are already operating on this continent with a combined capacity of five million units. Another trend is the captive import. Deciding to join 'em if they couldn't beat 'em, the Big Three American car-makers are marketing the Chevrolet Sprint, the Pontiac Firefly, and other cars built by Japanese manufacturers. In the last three years, sales of these captive imports have more than doubled.

But you don't have to look to the States to see what immense changes are occurring in the automobile industry. In Canada, GM has just created a separate new dealer network selling only imported cars—including South Korea's subcompact LeMans and several vehicles from Japan's Isuzu. It's the first new franchise that GM has offered in three-quarters of a century. Meanwhile, car-makers from around the globe have jumped head-first into the Canadian market, which is the world's seventh largest. The first big Japanese investment was the $200 million Honda assembly plant in Alliston, Ontario; the Accords started coming off the line in late '86. In the next couple of years, Toyota will be opening a $400 million facility at Cambridge, Ontario, and Hyundai of South Korea a $325 million plant in Bromont, Quebec. Meanwhile, GM is teaming up with another Japanese company, Suzuki, to produce cars in a $500 million joint venture at Ingersoll, Ontario.

On its own, General Motors is investing $5 billion in its Oshawa, Ontario, Autoplex, which will be the largest and possibly the most sophisticated automotive complex on the continent. American Motors has a $750 million plant in Bramalea, Ontario, that rolled off its first vehicles in the summer of '87.

All this competition has some attractive spin-offs for the consumer. It's been a long time since a manufacturer could say, as Henry Ford once did, that his name on the cars is the warranty. Chrysler Canada extended power-train warranties on its '87 models to seven years and about 110,000 kilometres. Ford and GM Canada were offering six-year, 100,000-kilometre coverage. The moves were an obvious marketing strategy to battle imports like Mazda and Honda, which offered better coverage but for only five years.

I Get Religion

For the Jim Pattison car divisions, the competition spells opportunities. We recently bought two established Toyota dealerships and a Hyundai franchise on Vancouver Island and opened our first Nissan dealership, in Vancouver. Nissan—Japan's number-two car-maker—was reluctant to come to North America at first, but now it's a serious contender. Our Nissan location sits across the street from Jim Pattison Pontiac-Buick-Cadillac, our Main Street dealership where we've doubled the sales volume in the last year. Don Connors, head of our Auto Group, figures the car business is heading for the biggest war ever in the next three years: If every plant runs close to capacity, there'll be as many as five million more vehicles for sale on this continent than there will be buyers. For us, as Canada's largest automotive retailer, it's a terrific opportunity. As Don told our latest Partners in Pride conference: "We think there'll be more opportunities in the next three years than we've seen in the last twenty-six."

There are some striking parallels between the automobile and airline industries, besides the obvious fact that both are in the transportation business. The airlines are also going through a period of overwhelming adjustment—deregulation, rationalization, realignments, mergers. The future is up for grabs as competitors fight for customers. In my experience, there's another parallel: We've come to realize how the employees on the firing line in both industries can make or break a business. From Toyota, we learned that employees who want to do their best can transform a company. In the case of our airline, AirBC, we learned that employees who understand that their interests and their employer's are mutual can save a company.

A young guy who understood this was Rick Hedley, a customer-service agent with AirBC in Victoria and the head of his union local. One November night in 1982, he literally saved the airline.

AirBC had its beginnings three years earlier, when we bought a twenty-year-old float-plane operation called Airwest Airlines. The owner, Norm Gold, was the first in the world to put Twin Otters on floats and the first to start a harbour-to-harbour air service between Vancouver and Victoria. But he later faced competition when West Coast Air Services also began flying that route. Meanwhile, Gold was having serious labour problems with the Teamsters Union. With the joy going out of the business, he found a buyer: Cromarty Holdings, a group of Alberta and B.C. financiers. But the day before the parties were to look over the final agreement, an Airwest plane crashed in Vancouver's Coal Harbour, killing eleven people; Comarty backed out of the deal. The airline was getting the nickname "Scare West." Gold, who was shaken by the accident, was even more convinced about getting out. I got a call from his accounting firm, Ernst & Whinney: "Do you want to buy an airline?"

They knew we were interested, because we'd made an approach through them to buy Airwest the year before. One reason for our interest in Airwest was because its president, Dick Laidman, had run Pacific Western Airlines for nine years. Our interest in the airline business itself had been piqued in '76 when Pacific Western Airlines moved its head office from Vancouver to Calgary. Bill Sleeman and I felt that PWA would now pay less attention to B.C., which would open up a business opportunity. We'd also approached West Coast Air about selling, but Cromarty Holdings beat us to it after its deal with Airwest fell apart.

Our own multi-million-dollar deal with Airwest almost collapsed several times over issues worth only a few thousand. Norm Gold was a tough negotiator. He, Bill, and an Ernst & Whinney accountant named Nick Geer bargained over such little details as the number of hours flown on an engine since its last servicing. One argument over an engine was actually decided on a toss of a coin.

We bought Airwest—with its twenty-four planes, hundred employees, and president Dick Laidman—in March '79. To make sure Corporate Office staff knew something about the airline, I insisted that all executives and secretaries fly it the week before any divisional meeting (and give me their boarding passes as proof). One of our early decisions was to upgrade Airwest, putting on two pilots per flight, instead of one, and improve service without worrying about initial profits.

Our idea all along was to create a new third-tier carrier and eventually a strong regional airline. The vision was to fill the void between the jet service of PWA and the top-of-the-line DC-3 or Twin Otter of the float-plane operators. It's an expensive vision because to service routes effectively in moun-

I Get Religion

tainous B.C., you need pricy, medium-sized, pressurized planes.

The second company we went after was Pacific Coastal Airlines, which offered commuter service between Vancouver and Vancouver Island and the Queen Charlottes. Next, Trans-Provincial Airlines of Prince Rupert, which covered northern coastal points and southern Alaska. Then Gulf-Air Aviation, a scheduled-service carrier based in Campbell River on Vancouver Island, which also gave us the licences for Haida Airlines and a subsidiary, Island Airlines. We bought all of them from their grassroots owners-operators, except Trans-Provincial, which was in receivership.

We over-bought: if it flew, buy it. Things got so crazy that one day I was looking out the window of my sixteenth-floor office and saw a float plane taking off from the harbour. "Who's that operator?" I asked Iain Harris, our vice-president of finance.

"Tyee."

"Why don't we buy 'em?"

"It's rumoured that West Coast has already bought them," Iain said, "but I'm not sure if the deal is firm."

"Find out," I said, "and if it isn't, offer them $100,000 more."

"I'm not sure we need it," Iain said. He called Tyee's lawyers, and by the time they called back to say West Coast wasn't doing the deal, we were no longer interested. (Afterwards, Tyee launched a suit against West Coast's owners and approached us to act as a witness in the case.)

We finally got West Coast Air, which, as well as going head to head against us in passenger service, was also the largest and oldest charter and freight operator on the coast.

The buying spree lasted nineteen months. By November '80, we had 423 employees and 20 different kinds of aircraft: 104 in all—floats, wheels, and amphibians. There were fourteen de Havilland Twin Otters, three Turbo Beavers, thirty-three piston Beavers, and nine single Otters; four Britten-Norman Islanders; one Grumman Turbo Mallard, two Turbo Goose, two piston Mallards, and five piston Goose; sixteen Cessna 185s, one Cessna 182, and seven Cessna 180s; three Beech 18s; three Douglas DC-3s; and one Piper Apache. Somebody told me we had more planes than Air Canada.

We kept Trans-Provincial as a separate operation and

blended the rest to form AirBC. It was a real dog's breakfast. Rationalizing the companies, we had to deal with several different unions, some with a history of wretched labour relations. We cut the staff to 140, including half the pilots. The company, which had cost us $28 million to create, was highly leveraged; we'd borrowed $17 million from the Bank of B.C. Interest rates were now over 20 per cent. And we had a cost structure that was too expensive for the current economic conditions. The recession was slamming British Columbia. Our best clients—forestry, mining, and the provincial government—were in sharp decline.

(The B.C. government had backed us at our federal hearings to establish what was essentially a monopoly airline situation. Not long after, an AirBC Twin Otter went down in Victoria without any injuries. But on board were two mayors and a provincial cabinet minister, Pat Jordan, who made headlines by swimming to shore; she'd been a competitive swimmer in her youth. I phoned her up and apologized for the incident.)

The people running AirBC were airline veterans, among them chairman and CEO Rusty Harris, a former executive vice-president and chief operating officer of PWA. They wanted to build up the airline at a time when we had to pull in our horns. Their ambitions were grand: At one point they bought a forty-eight–seat Hawker Siddeley 748 in Singapore, repainted it, and then we sold the thing without putting it in the air. In the first year, we lost $3 million—a huge amount for a company whose revenue base was no more than $18 million. So I put Trans-Provincial's president in charge of AirBC, but he was soon in over his head. That's when I turned to Iain Harris.

In early '82, Iain left Corporate Office to take over the management reins of an airline that was hemorrhaging cash. As well as harbour-to-harbour float-plane trips, we'd inaugurated flights between the Vancouver and Victoria airports. In desperate efforts to increase traffic, we reduced the one-way fares by 24 per cent for one month and weekend returns by 35 per cent. On the day we bumped up the number of inter-city flights to eight from six, we even offered a fare of ninety-nine cents (the Canadian Transport Commission, frowning on that, ordered us to suspend flights on the route for one day). Overall, as the economy worsened, our scheduled flights

I Get Religion

were down to fifty from seventy; fifteen of our thirty-five aircraft were parked. We were on our way to losing another couple of million dollars in our second year.

Then Iain Harris came to us with a business plan that made sense. To create a profitable airline, we had to get off the water and invest in bigger, wheeled prop planes like the fifty-passenger de Havilland Dash 7s. Our largest aircraft at the time could carry only nineteen people.

But I sure wasn't about to invest $5 million per Dash 7 unless we could get a guarantee of labour peace for five years. To borrow more money for a sick company, I needed the peace of mind of a long-term no-strike contract. It wouldn't be easy. The unions were already upset. Early on, we'd given employees a 10 per cent pay increase outside the contract and later had to ask to drop wages back to the original level. Throughout '82, Iain had laid off ten pilots and half of our maintenance workers and was asking employees to take more pay cuts. There were two key unions at the time: the International Association of Machinists and the Canadian Brotherhood of Railway, Transport and General Workers (CBRT). The Machinists represented maintenance and ramp-service workers and dock attendants. The larger CBRT represented everyone else but the head-office staff. The CBRT was reasonable, the Machinists weren't.

I have mixed views about unions. I've seen union leaders who are a disgrace to their members. Some are neither responsible nor realistic—they're so political that they forget what they're supposed to be doing, which is to represent the best interests of the workers. They don't understand that unless employees help the business make money, they don't have any job security. Capital does not flow to a company that does not offer a decent return. The most irresponsible leader I've met in organized labour was a one-time representative of the Machinists' local at AirBC. When I told him the company was losing a lot of money and we needed some help or we'd have to shut it down, he said he couldn't care less. On the other hand, another Machinists' leader at a different time, Dave Chapman, was a reasonable, honest guy; even though we had a strike during his tenure, I had the highest respect for him and eventually hired him to handle union relations out of Corporate Office. Now, in large part, I feel management is to blame for many of the bitter attitudes that exist in B.C. between companies and unions. I've sat in the same room with a lot of management people who are so anti-union that they're not realistic either. They're the kind of employers who make unions necessary at times.

The president of the CBRT Local 235 was the kind of leader who gives unions a good name. Rick Hedley was a thirty-seven–year–old customer-services agent for AirBC in Victoria. He was active in the union and the NDP, but reasonable—a good, sound person I trusted. His union was a member of the Canadian Labour Congress and in November '82 he'd recently returned from a CLC convention that had taken a strong stand on giving no concessions in contract bargaining. I wanted his local to give us a five-year contract guaranteeing labour peace at the airline. The CLC was adamant that unions could not sign an agreement for longer than three years. Our dispute went public in mid-November when *The Vancouver Sun* quoted me as saying: "Unless we get an understanding with the unions, we will shut AirBC down. We're not bluffing. We can't lose money month after month, year after year. We need some understanding shortly, a firm answer within weeks. We do not intend to carry it through the winter."

I wasn't bluffing. I'd invited Rick to my office to tell him that things weren't just adding up financially and, without any concessions from the union, the airline was closing. He told me later that he left that meeting certain that AirBC was doomed.

It seemed to be, even though Iain Harris had told me that the workers represented by the Machinists were prepared to decertify their union and reorganize under the more moderate Operating Engineers, who didn't belong to the CLC. And petitions showed that employees were almost unanimous in their support of a five-year agreement. But the problem was that the company couldn't get any commitments from the CBRT bargaining agents. "That's too bad," I told Iain. "We're going to close it down unless we can get five years." Iain went to Ottawa to inform the chairman of the federal Air Transport Committee that we were about to make some tough decisions but we'd dismantle AirBC in a responsible manner. Closing down would be costly. Because there were

I Get Religion

no immediate buyers for most of our aircraft, we'd have to store them in a desert climate down south.

On November 30, we had scheduled a meeting of the AirBC board where I was sure we'd agree to close the company. It would be followed by a meeting that night to give employees the news. Bill Sleeman, meanwhile, was trying to find a last-ditch solution. "What if the CBRT guys gave you their personal word on the five years?" he asked me. When I agreed, he had Rick Hedley come in for a meeting that day: "Look, I know Jimmy would far sooner build the airline than liquidate it. I'm of the opinion that he'll accept the word of your guys if most of them will agree to labour peace for five years." Rick said he'd try; he'd ask some of his members to get up at the meeting that evening and talk about commitment to the company.

As local president, Rick Hedley didn't have authority to sign a contract. So, Bill was on the phone trying to get commitments from the senior CBRT executives. Regional vice-president Bill Apps was taking a hard line. At 4:00 P.M., AirBC chairman Mel Cooper (who owns Victoria radio station CFAX) called the board meeting to order. Iain Harris reluctantly recommended that the company terminate operations. Most of our discussion was about the wording of the press release announcing the closure. At 6:30, we were back in my office. Mel said he thought we owed it to the union to let them know what we were doing. Bill Apps was having dinner at home when we called; he suddenly realized that we hadn't been bluffing. "Could you phone me when you get to the hangar?" He was going to talk to the senior union people in Ottawa.

Time to go tell the employees. We all piled into my car—Iain, Bill, Mel Cooper, Maureen Chant, and Chuck Conaghan, our labour-relations consultant. It was a lousy rain-drenched night. The AirBC hangar brimmed with about a hundred pilots, flight attendants, mechanics, and ground crew, many of them from out of town. They were expecting the worst. Still trying to pull it out of the fire, we met Rick in an office upstairs. He said that while it would be up to his members to commit to five years with no strikes, he'd offer us his support at the meeting.

Bill and Iain were on the phone to Apps again. Rick talked to him too, underlining the seriousness of the situation. Then Rick and I went downstairs, where television cameras crews were setting up while I waited impatiently for Bill and Iain to finish their conversation with Apps. Maureen finally went up with a message for them: "If you guys aren't down here in sixty seconds to say this thing is resolved, I'm going to announce the company will be liquidated." They got off the phone. Apps had just got agreement from Ottawa headquarters that the union would give us a three-year contract with no strikes. And based on my belief that Rick could deliver his members for the other two years, Bill and Iain gave me the "Okay" sign.

I announced to the employees that we'd reached agreement with the union. There were cheers. Rick got up and talked about his commitment to them and AirBC. Then I asked them to indicate their support for an additional two years of labour peace. They erupted in applause and hoots of approval. As chairman Mel Cooper said: "Tonight was the beginning of a new AirBC. We're making the move into the Dash 7s. We need everybody in this room with us. We're not looking back."

It was an emotional moment. Afterwards, I turned to Mel and said with a smile: "An hour ago, we were closing a business down and parking the planes in the desert. And now we've just committed to spending millions more on new aircraft. Well, that's the way she goes."

We got a three-year contract with wage freezes and a no-strike clause. "The purpose of this agreement," it began, "is to promote the interests and general welfare of the employees of AirBC who wish to cultivate a spirit of harmony and understanding with their employer, founded upon a basis of equity and justice."

I believed in Rick Hedley's honesty and sincerity. Up in the office, he'd given me his hand and said: "All you can count on is my word." He kept it. He saved AirBC. It wasn't Jimmy Pattison, it wasn't Bill Sleeman or Iain Harris. It was Rick Hedley who saved that airline. And he's still working for it in Victoria and is still president of Local 235 of the union.

After that, we took off. AirBC bought its first Dash 7, a repossessed second-hand model picked up in Spain. Iain, meanwhile, was trying to make a commercial arrangement with Canadian Pacific Air Lines. Our timing was terrific. CP's president, Dan Colussy, had come from Pan Am in the

I Get Religion

States, where a concept called "hub and spoke" had taken hold: Small feeder airlines were the spokes around the hub of a major airline. He agreed to let AirBC take over CP Air's Vancouver-to-Victoria service, which we understood was losing $3 million a year running jets between the two airports. In '83 we became its feeder airline, timing our flights to connect with CP's schedule in and out of Vancouver. All of a sudden, we had a new lease on life. A year later, our passenger loads had risen 90 per cent.

Iain, meanwhile, had been looking at other short-haul routes in B.C. that could be better served with more efficient aircraft flying more often. But the current regulatory environment, with its stringent conditions, favoured existing carriers. In May '84, the federal government announced deregulation. No longer would there be restrictions on when, where, how, or what an airline could fly in Canada. AirBC began service to the B.C. Interior and began making money. We introduced thirty-six–seat Dash 8 turbo-props in Western Canada and took on PWA with cost-cutting and extra services. Today, AirBC is the largest commuter airline in the country, carrying almost 700,000 passengers. But as Iain Harris says, "everything we've got here was by digging, clutching, clawing, and grabbing."

The Canadian airline industry had its biggest shaking-up in 1986. Despite the success of the relationship, AirBC was starting to see constraints in its links with Canadian Pacific. As we looked for further growth into its regional routes, CP was reluctant to deepen its involvement with us without some ownership. CP approached us a couple of times, wanting at least the right of first approval if we sold the company. Yet we were hearing strong rumours that CP and PWA were talking of a merger. It would be a logical fit—and if it happened, where would that leave us?

We'd already sold Trans-Provincial Airlines to its employees. Iain Harris came to me with a pitch to sell AirBC. The time had come, he said. CP was convinced that in order to compete with Air Canada, it had to be more equal, in the size of its network and the frequency of its service. Both major airlines were also realizing the importance of expanding to communities beyond the mainline points—which meant control of and commercial agreements with commuter airlines like ours that have lower cost structures. In the deregulated industry, we had to have strong alliances with one of the two large carriers; we couldn't survive as an independent. So we might as well sell when we had a possibility of two buyers.

I was reluctant, but I listened and asked questions, and finally said: "Bring me a deal." CP had already approached us twice to buy equity in AirBC. We arranged to meet them again on a Thursday in late November '86. On the Monday morning of that week, Air Canada's chairman, Claude Taylor, called me and expressed his interest in buying AirBC. It was pretty apparent that Air Canada—which relied so heavily on PWA and its affiliate, Time Air—could use a company like ours. "You'd better get out here right away," I told Taylor. "We're considering doing something." He sent two senior finance people out to Vancouver that evening and by 10:30 A.M. Wednesday we'd hammered out an interim agreement. Air Canada bought AirBC for $26.4 million; we made a profit of $15 million. In the more than two hundred deals we've done, we've never dealt with more efficient and decisive people than those at Air Canada. It was a real pleasure to do business with them. Although Crown corporations generally have a poor public image, Air Canada—with its professionalism—may be one of the few exceptions to the rule.

The following week, in an announcement that surprised a lot of people, PWA reported that it was buying Canadian Pacific for $300 million. The companies would merge under the name Canadian Airlines International. In hindsight, it made sense: PWA may have been a regional carrier, ranking third in the number of passengers, but it was the most profitable airline in Canada and had ready cash from a recent sale of aircraft and a leaseback deal.

The Air Canada connection has already been good for AirBC—which is challenging Canadian Airlines' lock on regional air services in Western Canada. Under the presidency of Iain Harris, who stayed with the company, AirBC will more than double the size of its fleet with $160 million worth of sixteen regular and stretch Dash 8s to expand current routes and begin new ones.

Much as I miss AirBC, I'm glad to be out of the airline business. The transformation of the industry has been swift and total. When '86 began, there were seven fractured regional and national carriers, dominated by Air Canada, which had no alliances with commuter airlines. Today, there are two national carriers much more equal in strength, each with its own commuter network, and a third national airline, Wardair. Our timing was perfect. From now on, it's going to take the big boys with their deep pockets or dedicated industry veterans like Max Ward to make a major Canadian airline fly.

CHAPTER SIXTEEN

"Park Your Cadillacs"

After years of having our Partners in Pride Executive Conference in Palm Springs, we were holding it for the first time at home. It was a cool, wet Vancouver weekend in March 1982. Maureen Chant passed out umbrella hats, although it actually snowed. The conference wasn't quite as fancy as it had been in past years. Our visiting senior executives stayed at the Holiday Inn. Instead of importing a Gerald Ford or Henry Kissinger, we had British Columbia's NDP Opposition Leader, Dave Barrett, as guest speaker. We'd invited Premier Bill Bennett too, but his people didn't want him appearing at the same three-day meeting as his opponent. No car rallies or chorus girls. For fun, we took everyone in buses on a progressive dinner that began at Bill Sleeman's house and ended up at mine. For excitement, we flew the executives up the Fraser River on AirBC float-planes and took them in our recreational vehicles on a tour of a new Overwaitea store. The one posh event was the President's Award dinner at The Mansion, Hy Aisenstat's classiest restaurant. But by then the mood of the group was definitely downbeat.

I'd just given my annual theme speech. I hadn't told anyone, not even Bill or Maureen, what I was going to be discussing that year. My wind-up at these gatherings had

"Park Your Cadillacs"

happen. And to enlist their help in solving problems where they should be solved."

I defined the new attitude: If an expenditure isn't vital to making a profit, eliminate it, or at least control it tightly. Our priorities would be slashing inventories and receivables. We'd be cancelling newspaper and magazine subscriptions; tightening up on telephone costs; even watching our stationery expenses. And I hit them with a warning: "The Jim Pattison Group is in a healthy financial position and we intend to keep it that way. We will not give sustained support to any weak branches, divisions, or companies. We will shut them down, liquidate, or sell any if we have to. We cannot and will not allow them to pull down or jeopardize the overall strength of our Group and its employees."

When I finished, there was dead silence. The executives' faces showed shock and disbelief. Maureen was crying. Afterwards, she said she was thinking, *I've worked for this man for twenty years and I don't know him.* I walked out of the Terminal City Club ahead of everyone else. As I marched down the street to the Holiday Inn, no one walked with me. People straggled behind, silently. Only Ted McDowell, as our banker, was pleased: "That sure took some steam out of their sails," he told me. But at the hotel, Clarence Heppell of Overwaitea remarked to Ted and a group of executives: "You know, I fully endorse what Jimmy's doing." As it turned out, so did most of the other executives.

Monday morning, I had a public-relations firm prepare a press release about our personal restraint program. It got national coverage. CBC television phoned and asked: "When are you going to park your Cadillacs?"

Thinking fast, I said: "This afternoon at five o'clock. We'll all be at Jim Pattison on Main turning in our fancy cars." And on the national news, there we were, me in my Chevy, Bill Sleeman squeezing into a Pontiac 2000. We reaped so much publicity that every division got the message.

The crunch had come. Our regular office staff started work at 8:00 A.M. instead of 8:30. We abandoned our plan to renovate our thirteen-year-old Corporate Office. We flew in the economy sections of regular scheduled aircraft instead of the comfortable privacy of the corporate Learjet—which was a big shock to the system of our executives. We told our divisional managers that they had to improve their returns.

They could do it however they wanted. If they had to, they could ask employees for longer hours and wage concessions, close money-losing operations, or lay off staff. Employees in many of our divisions—AirBC, for instance—did agree to wage freezes or rollbacks. Over the next two years, the only operation we closed was one of our three Toyota dealerships, which had a bad location in Burnaby, B.C. The only company we sold was Crush Canada—first, its Ottawa and Toronto bottling and canning plants to 7-Up, and then Crush Canada itself to Proctor & Gamble. But in making our divisions more efficient—saving the body by cutting off the ailing limbs—we let one thousand employees go. The process was difficult, painful. And it was the first time in my twenty-one years in business that our company had fewer employees at the end of the year than at the start.

That year, Canada was weathering its worst recession since the Great Depression. With inflation and unemployment both high at the same time, we were in a period that the economists call stagflation. Primary industries like lumber, mining, and agriculture—the backbone of Western Canada—had to cut back as they felt the squeeze of a contracting economy. The petroleum industry was dying: Dome Petroleum was virtually bankrupt; the monster oil-sands projects in Alberta and the natural-gas fields in the Arctic were abandoned. We hadn't misread the warning signs.

Fortunately, we had gone into the recession in good shape. We'd sold off the bottom 20 per cent of our companies in the late '70s, and Crush International in '80. We'd also converted our cash into American currency when the Canadian dollar was much higher than today.

Throughout that first tough year, only four of our divisions lost money: CJOR, the airlines, recreational vehicles, and some of the car business. We may have bought too many airlines too fast and made some dumb moves in our oil and gas investments. But we were diversified enough in our markets, we cut our overheads deeply (by the tens of millions), and our employees were productive. As a result, we had our most profitable year ever in 1982.

That allowed us to diversify even further in the following year, buying half a dozen new companies for a total of $17 million. At the beginning of '82, we'd bought Toronto-based Trans Ad, Canada's largest transit advertising company. We then acquired another, small transit-ad company; minor outdoor-advertising plants in B.C. and Alberta and a major one, Gould Outdoor Advertising of London, Ontario; National Advertising, a Montreal sign manufacturer; and a Vancouver Chevy-Olds lease fleet.

We had our next Partners In Pride on Vancouver Island. Though we brought in a high-profile speaker, Alexander Haig, I still maintained the bread-and-water basics of the '82 conference. The theme was "Do More with Less." We met at a motel on the highway in Parksville, which at least had better weather than Vancouver in spring. The Corporate Office people served hamburgers and hot dogs. And on St. Patrick's Day we dressed up in Paddy hats and vests and went bowling.

As economic conditions improved, we continued buying—a real stew of companies, including *Beautiful British Columbia* magazine from the B.C. government, six sign companies, and the Vancouver Canadians baseball club. But the biggest departure was our move into the food-processing business: Berryland Canning Company (the country's biggest fruit-canning operation), Mrs. Milne's Cannery, Fraser Valley Frosted Foods, and the Canadian Fishing Company (Canfisco).

We tend to be a bit of a contrarian; we don't usually run with the herd. When we acquired Canfisco, everybody was down on the fishing industry. So we got it at an attractive price. Of course, it would have been even more attractive if we hadn't let it go to auction.

After the Vancouver office of Coopers & Lybrand brought us the Berryland Canning deal, we let them know we were in the market for other opportunities. A few months later, one of the partners, Gary Powroznik, called Bill Sleeman to say he knew that Canfisco, a well-managed company, was for sale. Its American parent, New England Fishing, was bankrupt and a Seattle trustee in bankruptcy was selling off its assets. Bill knew that B.C. Packers, among others in the West-Coast fishing industry, was losing money. But strictly out of politeness, he agreed to discuss Canfisco.

Gary Powroznik had worked with his father, a commercial fisherman, and knew the business. He took Bill to meet Canfisco's chairman (who retired soon after) and its president, Doug Souter. Realizing at once they were quality people, he listened to their story. The Vancouver-based company, operating since 1906, had a fleet of more than a hundred company-owned and contract vessels. Each year it harvested thousands of tonnes of salmon, herring, and other species for Canadian consumption and international export. It marketed under the brand names Gold Seal, Red Seal, Tea Rose, and Ocean Spray. With a quarter of the Canadian canned-salmon market, it was the country's second-largest salmon-processor. Under a confidentiality agreement, we looked over the company's books. Canfisco's most recent net earnings were only $199,000, but the year before they'd reached about $3 million. There was no long-term debt.

Bill wanted me to get to know the chairman and Doug Souter, whom I liked from the start. Ten minutes after meeting them, I surprised Bill by announcing: "Bill tells me he likes what we see and we want to buy the company. So what do we do?"

Sam Rubenstein, the trustee in bankruptcy, said he wouldn't recommend to the court any offer less than $22 million.

Bill told him he'd heard that Jimmy's friend, financier Joe Segal of Vancouver—who has owned the Zeller's, Fields, and Marshall Wells chains—had offered Rubenstein $10 million "and that's probably what it's worth."

Rubenstein came down to $18 million, cash. In a series of meetings, we offered $12.5 million and he countered with $15 million, which he was prepared to recommend as a solid offer. Rubenstein had admitted there was nothing to prevent us from going directly to the court with a proposal. Bill then offered $13.5 million and got the trustee to agree that he wouldn't actively oppose that figure in court.

But what we didn't understand is that the U.S. rules of bankruptcy require publication of an offer like ours. As we suspected, the public notice brought other contenders for Canfisco out of the woodwork. One was Ocean Fishing, a local family-run operation, and the other was Ron Stern, a lawyer with Vancouver's Shrum Liddle Hebenton, who was representing a group of native fishermen. The three competitors would have to meet in Seattle court where we could bid up each other's offers.

I consulted with Bill Sleeman and Nick Geer, our in-house financial expert, to discuss how high we should bid over our last $13.5 million proposal. Nick said $16.2, Bill $18.5. We weren't going to let Doug Souter down. He and

"Park Your Cadillacs"

his people wanted us to get control of the company and no matter what it took, we'd buy it.

In January '84—about eight months after we first heard of Canfisco—we were in a Seattle courtroom, where the judge turned the auction over to Sam Rubenstein. It was tense. Bidding opened at $13 million and, after the first round or two, the three groups were bidding in increments of $300,000 and $500,000. At about $15 million, Ron Stern dropped out. In the high $15 millions, the Ocean Fishing family group started slowing down, the father and three brothers huddling over every move. They'd spend a couple of minutes deciding whether to raise their bid; I'd take only a second to top it.

We got the company for $16.1 million. "If you'd taken my advice," Rubenstein said afterwards, "you could have got it for $15 million"—the price he'd been willing to recommend to the court.

But it was still a good deal for us. The Canadian Fishing Company has turned out to be an excellent acquisition, increasing its earnings every year. We'd bought it because of the high regard we had for its president, Doug Souter, and his team. They've more than lived up to our expectations. And Doug later took on the responsibility for Fraser Valley Foods, the canning and frozen-food operations we've just recently sold.

By the end of 1984, I was breathing a lot easier. Despite the recession, we'd had our three best years ever—they were so good I'd gone out and bought a Lear 35 jet for $2.8 million. And our pot of cash from the sale of the international and Canadian operations of Crush was invested outside Canada in a finance company that was becoming more and more profitable.

In early '81, I'd asked Nick Geer to look for opportunities to invest the $80 million we'd got from selling Crush. One possibility was to create an offshore institution that was close to a bank in operation. After investigating financial regulations in several places around the globe, including Hong Kong, Singapore, and the Caribbean, he identified Switzerland as the strongest contender.

Switzerland was stable, had an attractive domestic tax structure, and was home to a large pool of sophisticated financial people we could draw on to run our company. It was also the world's traditional money capital. The Swiss have been involved in international finance since the eighteenth century. It wasn't until the twentieth—when the currency of their neighbours collapsed after the First World War—that their politically neutral nation became the legendary safe haven for foreign funds. And in the worldwide banking crisis of the 1930s, Switzerland established rules on bank secrecy that prohibited outsiders from getting information on accounts in the country's banks.

Nick was working with Harold Nelson, the Royal Bank manager who'd given me the loan that allowed me to open my first car dealership twenty years before. Harold had retired early in Dallas; he continued to live there after we made him director of Grantison Holdings, the company that initially held the Crush money. From his banking days, he knew Dr. Erik B. Gasser, general manager of J. Henry Schroder Bank AG in Zurich. Dr. Gasser was one of Nick's contacts when he went to Switzerland to talk to government, tax, and banking authorities. They welcomed him so warmly that Nick told me, "It's the only time I've heard a government official say 'I'm here to help you'—and mean it." When I arrived later to look over the situation, I was being cautious. As I'd told Harold, "I want you to look after this money so I can sleep nights. I don't care so much about the return; I just don't want any risk involved with it." Advising us on the tax implications was Bert Stitt, a partner in the Canadian branch of Baker & Mckenzie, the largest American law firm specializing in tax.

Switzerland looked ideal for our purposes. It soon became clear that we'd be creating a near-bank, or a bank-like finance company. Because of reciprocity rules between Switzerland and Canada, we couldn't found a full-fledged bank—which prevented us from taking deposits from the man on the street or issuing debentures of our own to borrow money. But we could lend money and deal in financial instruments with relatively low risk.

"Okay," I told Nick, "let's do it. But if we're gonna do it, we need somebody with a banking background to be involved." In the fall of '81, in the lightly taxed canton of Zug, we incorporated a company that eventually became known as Great Pacific Capital SA. Nick became chairman. To run

Great Pacific, we hired Sid Spiro, who'd been a vice-president of the Bank of America when we borrowed from that bank for our recreational-vehicle business in the United States. Sid, who had a Swiss passport, operated Great Pacific by remote-control from his base in Seattle for about a year until Guy Krug became managing director. Guy had been senior vice-president with American Express International Banking Corporation. A U.S. citizen living in London, he was married to an extremely attractive and vivacious French woman named Beatrix. They didn't have to move to our office in Zug, which is a pretty little town but about thirty minutes from Zurich. By then we had a favourable tax ruling from cantonal officials in Geneva, which became Great Pacific's new headquarters.

By June '82 we'd moved a little over $90 million (U.S.) to Switzerland. Starting slowly, we made some low-risk Eurodollar loans to multinational corporations. After relocating in Geneva, Great Pacific also began underwriting in Eurodollars and entered the private-banking world of money management. One of the first underwritings we did was the first foreign-targeted U.S. Treasury note issue. It was a nice beginning for a small Canadian company. We were one of eleven co-managers in a bidding syndicate led by Credit Suisse First Boston, one of the dominant lead managers in Swiss underwriting. Among our partners were Lloyds Bank International, Lehman Brothers International, and Hambros Bank. In the last half of '84, we underwrote $48 million in twenty-four issues totalling $1.5 billion. And by year's end, shareholder funds totalled $123.3 million.

By that time, the lead managers were starting to call and invite us to participate in their issues. In June '85 Great Pacific Capital became manager in a $1.3 billion underwriting led by Merrill Lynch for John Deere Credit Company. Guy Krug pointed out in our annual report: "As the credit rating of the issued notes depends on the quality of the underwriters, the Company was pleased to be invited to participate in a group comprised of many of the world's leading financial institutions."

We were also generating a lot of fees, commissions, and other income, mostly from our portfolio-management services. Today, more and more of our income is coming from this managing of other people's money, which is a high-quality cash stream. We operate on a boutique basis compared to the major Swiss banks. Because our senior people know every one of our clients, we can offer very personal service. To take the risk out of a client's portfolio, we do a fair bit of work in securities options, puts, and calls.

In a presentation to our latest Partners in Pride conference, Nick Geer played the role of the interviewer, asking Guy Krug: "Why would a customer choose us to manage his funds rather than go to one of the more recognized Swiss Banks?"

Guy's reply: "Great Pacific Capital caters to high-net-worth individuals looking for sophistication and service. In the U.S., the financial boutiques have taken most of the money-management business away from the commercial banks. The reason is that the financial boutique, because it's smaller and more flexible than a big bank, can show a higher return on funds managed. . . . For example, in today's market we invest heavily in bonds denominated in strong currencies such as the Deutschemark, the yen, and the Swiss franc. We also invest in equities in the stock market in weaker currencies such as the U.S., the U.K., and Canada. We like those markets, because a weak currency tends to help in the national market by reducing foreign competition. However, we don't want to lose in the exchange markets what we make in capital gains in the equity markets. So we'll use a package of currency, futures and options, stock options, and other techniques—such as borrowing in the same currency we're investing in—to eliminate the currency risk. We'll also use stock options to eliminate or reduce market risk."

That same Partners in Pride skit explained broadly how we handle a new client. Harold Nelson strolled on stage in a Stetson and cowboy boots as a Dallas millionaire meeting Guy and his manager Roland van der Haegen.

Guy: Mr. Nelson, welcome to Great Pacific Capital! Can we help you?

Harold: Yes, I'd like to open one of those Swiss bank accounts I've been reading about in the papers.

Roland: Well, Mr. Nelson, we don't take an account from just anybody. Who referred you to us?

Harold: My cousin, J.R. He told me he's had an account with you for years.

Guy: How did you get this money, Mr. Nelson?
Harold: What difference does it make to you? I thought in Switzerland you didn't care where the money came from.
Roland: That's not so, Mr. Nelson. We're a member of the Swiss Bankers Association and we're committed to certify that we know who the client is and that his money was earned honestly. And we take these rules very seriously.

We believe that at the end of '86, with $240 million (U.S.) in assets, Great Pacific was Switzerland's largest bank-like finance company that's not attached to a major financial institution. It's opened doors for the Jim Pattison Group in Europe, giving us access to about two hundred banks and brokers that do business with us on a regular basis.

We have nineteen employees in the financial centre of Geneva, overlooking the lake. Our directors, along with Nick, Guy, and me, are: Donald Etienne, a partner in the Geneva law firm Etienne, Blu, Stehle, Manfrini; Dr. Erik Gasser of J. Schroder Bank; Dr. Jürge F. Geigy, former treasurer of Ciba-Geigy, now a member of the executive committee of Bank Julius Bär & Co., Zurich; and Dr. Max R. Wehrli, a partner in the Zurich law firm of Homburger, Ackermann, Muller, Heini.

As chairman, based in Vancouver, Nick Geer monitors the company's progress on a daily basis. Every morning he uses his computer to access the figures for all the securities the company deposits in the two main security clearinghouses in Brussels and Luxembourg. He gets a daily print-out of our Geneva or New York bank accounts and a list of every transaction. On the phone to Geneva two and three times a week, he also travels there about five times a year. Distance doesn't mean anything any more in this business: Between the phone and the Fax machine, it's as if Geneva is next door. I fly over for all the board meetings, where our policy is decided, and attend the quarterly divisional meetings, in Geneva, Vancouver, Toronto, or wherever. I also see the complete portfolio-management report weekly and short versions of the monthly statements.

We're the majority shareholder in Great Pacific Industries, the corporate parent of Great Pacific Capital. In '81 we'd tried to turn Industries into a private company with an offer to the minority stockholders of $22 a share. Under the Canada Business Corporations Act, we needed 90 per cent of them to acquire the remaining minority through the courts. The Post Office went on strike, so we couriered the information to all the shareholders we could locate, advertised in the newspapers, and tried to phone everyone holding more than five hundred shares. Battling us was Stephen Jarislowsky, the Montreal investment counsellor who'd later lead the well-publicized fight on behalf of minority shareholders for control of Canadian Tire in 1986. Jarislowsky (whose firm is reported to manage or advise on about $8 billion worth of pension-fund cash) and a group of associates owned some of our shares and had no intention of selling. In the end, we did acquire 89.1 per cent of the minority stock—0.9 per cent away from our target. Needing 4.2 million shares, we were just 12,000 short. We returned all the stock to the minority shareholders. Since then, we've acquired more shares to bring our position up to 83 per cent. But at this time, I have no thought of making another offer to take Great Pacific Industries private. I'm as content as Stephen Jarislowsky, who said not long ago: "I think it is a good company."

Just when you believe your life's in good order, as I did by 1984, something happens to shake you out of your smugness. In July, Mary and I got a call that our daughter Cindy and her husband, Al Kilburn, were under house arrest in Uganda.

Mary knew how bad conditions were in that African nation in the wake of Idi Amin's reign of terror. Two months earlier, she'd gone there with Cindy, who was trying to form a children's choir to raise money for orphanages in Uganda. Five years after Amin fled to Saudi Arabia, the country still had a lot of mercenary activity in the bush and thousands of homeless and parentless children. A layman named Ray Barnett had spoken about their plight at Glad Tidings Temple, the Pentecostal church Cindy and Al attend in Vancouver. Ray, from Northern Ireland, ran a Christian human-rights group called Friends in the West. He was looking for volunteers to help him help those kids. Cindy volunteered, and together they formed a group called Ambassadors of Aid, which got support from several different churches. Cindy agreed to lead a team to Uganda to create the fund-raising choir.

She lived in a place in Kampala with a broken toilet, only occasional electricity, and no running water. Mary stayed about three weeks. Cindy, who remained there with a missionary named Dorothy Williams, began auditioning hundreds of children. Though she had her Grade 9 in piano, played clarinet and harp, had sung in a choir, taught Sunday school, and had been a critical-care nurse, it was the first time she'd ever attempted anything like this. Working out of the Makari Full Gospel Church, she found and trained thirty-one children, aged five to twelve. Preparing for their overseas trip, she had to plead with the Minister of Internal Affairs to get passports for them because the passport officers wanted bribes.

During her visits to some villages, Cindy would sometimes wind up hiding under her bed as rebel gunfire erupted around her. In July, her husband came to visit; they'd been married only a year. She'd lost fifteen pounds from her slight frame. On their way to a choir practice one day, Al took some pictures of malnourished children to show church people back home. Suddenly, as they drove off, about a hundred men in army uniforms surrounded them, yelling and jumping on their car. The soldiers took them to army headquarters where plainclothes officers grilled them and seized their passports. Refusing to believe Cindy was a missionary, they locked her and Al in a barred holding room, under guard. When the young man posted at the door asked her about the electric piano she was holding, Cindy played the only song she could think of: "Jesus Loves Me." Finally, another official interviewed them rudely, insinuating that Al must be a mercenary. He released them after about seven hours, but kept their passports.

Under house arrest—unable to leave the country—but free to move around, they approached the British High Commissioner, a woman, who told Al: "You're lucky to be alive. They're not going to kill your wife, they're going to kill you." Cindy and Al managed to call Ray Barnett in Vancouver, who let Mary and me know what was happening. We were plenty worried. I called the Canadian government in Ottawa for help, but in the end we had to rely on Ray. He was a good man to rely on; he'd been in Uganda during the Amin regime and once helped publicize the case of two Russian Pentecostal families who were holed up in the U.S. Embassy in Moscow; they were allowed to emigrate to the West. At our urging, Ray began making plans to fly to Uganda.

Meanwhile, a Ugandan woman in the Makari church was making a fuss about Cindy and Al with her husband, who was a cabinet minister. Six days after the arrest, Ray Barnett arrived unannounced at Cindy's place in Kampala. He told them he had people waiting outside the country to help them escape, if necessary. Ten minutes later, the Minister of Internal Affairs showed up to lift the house arrest. The first thing he said to Cindy was: "How can someone so small get into so much trouble?"

In September, Cindy was in Kenya with the choir just before its tour of North America. My assistant, Enzo Centrone, and I were in Switzerland when I decided to visit Cindy. I played my trumpet in a black Pentecostal church in Kenya while the people clapped to the beat. Then Cindy, Enzo, and I spent a couple of days in Tanzania's Serengeti National Park. It was the most spectacular trip I've ever taken: elephants, giraffes, forty lions, some of them feeding on a zebra kill, and a huge herd of migrating wildebeests as far as you could see. At one point we had a friendly argument; my daughter told me that lions could climb and I assured her they couldn't. A little later, we spotted a lioness in a tree and Cindy says she thought, *Oh, thank you, Lord.* We had a good time together.

I helped finance the tour when Cindy brought the children to sing in California, Western Canada, and throughout Britain. One day I'd just finished a meeting with Mayor Tom Bradley in Los Angeles on Expo business when someone said: "Jimmy, come back here and listen to these children sing." It was Cindy's choir. They raised about $80,000 on that trip, and two more choirs have come to North America since. In all, they've funded six orphanages in Uganda.

I had something else to worry about in 1984. For the last three years, I'd been chairman of what was now called Expo 86. It had mushroomed into a much more ambitious world's fair than anyone had imagined when Premier Bill Bennett first asked me to become chairman. With construction already under way, it was quickly becoming a full-time job. I had to make the hard decision to leave the running of our company to our executives and jump into Expo with both feet.

Just to make things more complicated, I was considering another corporate decision. I might have to sell my B.C. news distribution company, Mainland Magazine, because it was affecting my role with Expo and the image of the world exposition. Some people in the community were accusing me of distributing pornography. After the fair ended, I would still be dealing with some of the consequences of that charge.

CHAPTER SEVENTEEN

The Porn Debate

Two feminists told a special federal-government task force that Jimmy Pattison owned a company that was dealing in pornographic publications. In the British Columbia legislature, a female NDP member called me a "peddler of hard-core pornography." And the B.C. chapter of the Congress of Canadian Women wrote Vancouver city council to say that "the fact that [Pattison] panders pornography gives a signal to the rest of society that pornography is acceptable."

Those charges against me flared up in April 1984, a politically sensitive period just two years before Expo 86 was to open in Vancouver. As the provincial government's choice as chairman of the world exposition, I was in full view as a public servant. In my new role, I couldn't act like a private businessman whose corporate dealings affected my own reputation and no one else's. If my image suffered, so would Expo's.

The issue surfaced during the Vancouver hearings of the Fraser Committee on Pornography and Prostitution. Chaired by a local lawyer, Paul Fraser, the federal committee was created by the Trudeau government. Its seven members included the dean of law at the University of Calgary, a former Montreal police chief, and a vice-president of the Canadian Civil Liberties Association. In early April, they were meeting at the Hotel Vancouver when two women criticized me for my part in distributing magazines they claimed were pornographic.

Kit Stevenson of the University Women's Club of Vancouver told the committee: "Mainland Magazines, which distributes more than 250 pornographic magazines, including some depicting incest and rape, is owned by Richards Enterprises of Vancouver, which is wholly owned by Pattison Enterprises." Her description of Mainland's ownership was about as accurate as most of the charges against the company.

She was followed by Donna Stewart of the North Shore Women's Centre, the wife of a minister and a veteran campaigner against pornography. "It is not the so-called Mafia we have to fear," she said, "it is the respectable businessman. There may be a Mafia element in this, but what we do have to fear is when the chairman of Expo, who presents himself as a respectable businessman and who is closely related to the Social Credit government, turns out to own a company that distributes this [pornography]."

The Vancouver newspapers were on strike, but *The Globe and Mail* reported: "Expo Chiefs Firm Deals Porn, Women Say." The link between me and Expo was too obvious a target for the media to resist. I had to act so the controversy wouldn't embarrass the world exposition.

I'd heard these kind of charges before. "Pattison Porn Peddler," shouted a headline in a community newspaper in '83, when I was about to buy *Beautiful British Columbia* magazine. The acting mayor of a Greater Vancouver municipality had accused me of denying my background as a churchgoer and family man to be a dealer in pornographic publications.

The same year, I received a statement on pornography from Anglican archbishop Douglas Hambidge. His Greater Vancouver diocese had formed a task force on the issue and sent me a copy of a message from Anglican bishops across Canada. It ended: "As we endeavour to combat this pernicious influence in our midst, we must challenge those who profit from the multimillion-dollar pornographic industry. This includes retailers, distributing agencies, and those involved in the production of such materials." Not long after, I met the archbishop at one of the dinners I organized to bring Christians and Jews together in mutual understanding. I said I'd like to talk to him about the statement he'd sent. When he came to see me, I explained how complicated the periodical-distribution field actually is. By the time I finished, he said he understood the scope of my problem and reported later that he felt very good about our meeting.

At the time, Mainland Magazine Service, operating in the Lower Mainland market, distributed more than twenty-four million units of consumer magazines, paperbacks, and periodicals annually. We handled eighteen thousand different titles a year. The adult men's magazines represented 1.8 per cent of the overall magazine units we sold. In our overall business, they accounted for only 1 per cent of total unit sales and 4 per cent of total dollar sales. So the obvious thing for us to do was to simply stop distributing any publications that could even in the slightest way be considered sexually offensive. But if we did that, I told Archbishop Hambidge, I might as well sell Mainland and get out of the business.

Periodical publishers deal with international distribution companies who deal with regional wholesalers like Mainland who deal with local retailers. There are about five hundred publishers who have their products handled through only sixteen major American and Canadian distributors. These distributors control the business. The same company that supplies Mainland with *Ladies' Home Journal* also supplies *Penthouse*. The distributor of *Vogue* and *Glamour* also handles *Playboy* and *Oui*. If we were to tell Curtis Circulation Company of New Jersey that we'd no longer distribute *Penthouse* (which is a legal product in Canada) to our retailers, Curtis could put tremendous pressure on us in terms of *Ladies' Home Journal* and the rest of its line. International distributors could easily put us out of business in six months. They could deliver the product late, ask for cash in advance, and ultimately find another wholesaler in our area who would distribute their entire line. We'd be squeezed by the retailing side, too. If Mainland told store-owners that it was no longer handling any of the adult magazines, they'd go to our competitor in Vancouver who could offer them everything.

Now, there's another argument that has to be made: censorship. Do you really want a wholesale distributor to be deciding what you read? If there's a market for a legal product, our job is to distribute it. Some adult magazines may offend me personally, but then so may *Sputnik*, which is a Russian *Reader's Digest;* during the Soviet Union's invasion of Afghanistan, we may have wanted to pull that publication off the shelves, but we had no right to. I might not have liked the cover of *Maclean's* when it showed a Santa Claus carrying a gun to illustrate a story on war toys. It caused a big fuss: Some retailers wouldn't display it; others wanted to. Was it Mainland's role, if we disagreed with the cover, to refuse to distribute that issue to our customers? We can't allow our personal biases to limit what the general public has a legal right to read. In many parts of the country where our news-distribution companies operate, there are no competitors to offer any material that we personally might not want to distribute. But even if there were other wholesalers in an area, we can't act as censors. Once you start, where do you stop?

I disapprove of cigarettes because they're a proven cause of cancer. Because we own the Overwaitea supermarket chain, should I impose my will on everyone else and refuse to sell cigarettes in those stores? I also disapprove of people getting drunk. Should we have got out of the airline business because they serve liquor on airplanes and some people abuse it? Because I go to church, should I refuse to distribute *Penthouse* in places like Inuvik and impose my personal views on an oilman or construction worker who wants to read it up there? And because I also personally dislike the actions of the most radical environmentalists and extreme anti-nuclear protesters, is that a good reason for our news-distribution companies to refuse to distribute their literature?

Not even the feminists agree on censorship of pornographic material. Lynn King, a feminist lawyer in Toronto who's been active in the fields of family law reform and women's crisis centres, has written: "Censoring pornography is like using an Aspirin to cure cancer: it might ease the pain, but does not eliminate the disease, and may well have serious side effects." As she points out, "Freedom of expression is a fundamental right only tentatively secured and ought not to be dismissed lightly, especially for at best a doubtful result." Another feminist, the writer June Callwood, was one of two women who started Nellie's hostel for women in Toronto, which has sheltered more than eighteen thousand women in crisis. Yet on the subject of pornography she says: "I believe that censorship will change nothing for the better and has the potential to make matters worse. . . . Legislation designed to suppress what one group considers to be unseemly can always be interpreted to stamp out what another group does not like."

One of the submissions to the Fraser Committee on Pornography and Prostitution was made by the Periodical Distributors of Canada, a national association of wholesalers of magazines and paperback books, including our distribution companies. The association had recently done a survey of three hundred Canadian women's leaders. Many of them were active in such organizations as the National Committee on the Status of Women; others were influential members of such professions as journalism. The survey showed that 62 per cent of the women would approve the removal of sanctions against sexually explicit material from the Criminal Code—providing the sanctions against violent pornography were maintained. And 69 per cent had no objections to sexual explicitness in periodicals or films "as long as they portray consensual adult behaviour and are free of violence."

People wonder where I—a businessman and a Christian—personally stand on the issue of sexually explicit publications. I don't read them, I don't like them. But as long as they're legal products and conform to community standards, my personal opinion doesn't matter. A Canadian evangelical magazine, *Faith Today*, asked me recently if my corporation was my form of Christian witness. I'm sure I surprised the interviewer by saying: "Not at all. I run my business on a very businesslike basis . . . on what I consider to be sound business principles, as would be normal. My business is my business. I never let politics or religion affect my business knowingly. If I did, I wouldn't distribute Communist books. I don't agree with Communist ideas, but if people in a free society want to write about Communists, then we distribute [them] if the public wants them. So you let the market decide." Or you let the elected authorities, who represent the public, decide.

The people who run Mainland Magazine are good, Christian people. John Seebach, head of our whole News Group, went to Bible College; his brother is a missionary in Los Angeles' Watts ghetto. Norm Reeve, vice-president of operations, is the son of an Anglican priest. Marcel Leroux, the controller, is an evangelical Roman Catholic. But whatever their faith, they shouldn't have the power of censorship. Nor should the people who operate the other divisions in the Jim Pattison News Group: Gordon Birk of Mountain City News in

Hamilton; Steve Senuck of Provincial News in Edmonton; and Ken Gibson of Valley News on Vancouver Island.

These wholesale distributors are only one link in the chain that puts adult magazines and paperbacks into the stores. When we got into the news-distribution business with Provincial News, about the only adult magazine we handled was *Playboy*. At the time we also owned Reimer Express of Winnipeg. Our associate in the trucking company was the very religious Reimer family. Don Reimer came to me once and said they were concerned about the fact that we distributed *Playboy*. I asked him: "How does it get here, Don?" He replied: "Well, we deliver it to you." And I asked: "Well, what's the difference between us delivering it to a store or you delivering to us? The day you quit delivering it, maybe we'll consider not distributing it." I never heard from him again on that subject. The Mainland Magazines of this world are only part of a network that includes the advertisers in the magazines, the publishers, the international distributors, the federal Customs officials who decide what the Canadian public should read, the trucking firms that deliver it, the wholesalers who distribute it, the retailers who sell it, the customers who buy it.

I've heard the argument that Section 159 of the Canadian Criminal Code specifically refers to those who distribute and circulate obscene written matter. The question that has to be asked: Who defines what's obscene? The wholesale distributors? It's not as easy and clear-cut as my critics would like to believe. Even the judges of the Supreme Court of Canada have a hang of a time deciding on a legal definition. The Criminal Code has had the same definition of obscenity for more than three decades—yet during that whole time, the Court has never come up with a unanimous decision in an obscenity case. In the lower courts, judges in different provinces have given contradictory decisions when they were considering exactly the same piece of alleged pornography. A case in point is the December 1984 issue of *Penthouse*, which had a photo-essay of nude and semi-nude women bound with rope and hanging from trees. Some people considered the pictures, taken by a well-known Japanese photographer, as fine-art studies; they'd already appeared in an issue of *Photo Magazine* that was distributed in Canada without any complaints from the public. The issue of *Penthouse* in question had been approved for distribution in Ontario by a panel of experts, the province's Advisory Committee on Contemporary Literature—a community-standards committee of private citizens established at the suggestion of Ontario's Attorney General. The magazine had also been cleared by Canada Customs. But, after some complaints, Perrin Beatty, then Canada Customs minister, closed the border to any further copies of that issue of *Penthouse*, saying: "This sort of material has no place in Canada." And Metro News of Toronto was charged with distributing that issue, which was ruled obscene. In 1986, Metro's conviction by a district court jury was upheld by the Ontario Court of Appeal. Yet in early '87, Judge Gerald Jewers of the Manitoba Court of Queen's Bench ruled that the same issue of *Penthouse* was not obscene. The photos were not an undue exploitation of sex or violence, the judge said in finding Canadian News Company of Winnipeg not guilty. And in Montreal, an obscenity trial on that issue ended in a hung jury, with no decision.

Judge Stephen Borins of the York, Ontario, County Court has pointed out the unfairness of convicting distributors when there's doubt whether material is obscene or pornographic. In 1984, as he acquitted a dealer charged with possessing and distributing obscene videotapes, the judge said: "To condemn people to the stigma of a criminal conviction for violating a standard they cannot understand, construe and apply is a serious thing to do in a nation which, by its recent Canadian Charter of Rights and Freedoms, has affirmed its dedication to fair rights and due process."

Obviously, the politicians can't decide what's obscene either. The Liberal-appointed Fraser Committee came out with a two-volume report that included many recommendations that seemed generally reasonable to wholesalers. Then in '86, the Conservative government—ignoring most of those recommendations—introduced an anti-pornography bill that created more problems than it was trying to solve. Critics said it was so loosely worded that a photo of a man and a woman kissing could be considered illegal. The government went back to the drawing board and one year later presented a new bill that received both praise and criticism. Even opposition politicians supported some of its major provisions: for example, one that would impose up to five years in prison for possessing or distributing violent or sadistic pornography;

and another that would impose up to ten years for trafficking in porn material featuring anyone under eighteen. But the opposition attacked details of a new category of legal but controlled material called erotica—which they claimed was so narrowly defined that *Playboy* could be banned. Even some important women's groups criticized the proposed bill. One of them was the National Action Committee on the Status of Women, which represents about three million women in 479 organizations, including YWCAs, several churches, and the women's caucuses of the three major political parties. The NAC's president, Louise Dulude, said the bill's measures were too broad: "The bill still suggests that sex is bad."

For many years, we believed that if Canada Customs allowed a periodical into the country, it was considered a product that could be legally distributed and sold. But, as we've discovered, Customs doesn't look at every publication that might be pornographic—for various reasons, including a shortage of staff. And, as recent court cases have shown, even getting a publication cleared by Customs doesn't necessarily protect a wholesaler from prosecution. That puts the onus on the wholesaler to become an expert in pornography when the courts and politicians can't agree on what porn is. In December 1986, the Periodical Marketers of Canada (the new name of the Periodical Distributors) argued this point in a brief to federal justice minister Ray Hnatyshyn:

> The provinces spend a great deal of time and money regulating film distribution, articulating standards and in general protecting the legitimate film industry from obscenity prosecution. It seems unfair to the periodical distributors that the province on the one hand refuses to devote any resources to giving any guidance to distributors of periodicals yet claims the right to then prosecute responsible people who must on their own attempt to cope with an indefinite standard. The fact is that the federal authorities have assumed the burden and surely it is not unfair for an accused to reasonably rely on the approval by those authorities. We are not here speaking of publications which might slip through the Customs screen. Publications such as *Penthouse* are actually submitted to the Prohibited Imports Branch

prior to any attempt to import. The problem is that there seems to be no other body with the requisite degree of expertise and credibility upon whom the responsible distributors and marketers can rely. It is in the highest degree unfair that *federal* legislation require that publications be submitted to approval by *federal* officials and then permit the prosecution by provincial authorities under other *federal* legislation of persons who have relied upon that approval. This state of affairs is wholly mystifying to responsible business people and tends to bring the administration of justice into disrepute.

The pressure was on. I heard reports that some people in local Pentecostal churches believed I was compromising my faith by distributing adult magazines. One Sunday after the Fraser Committee hearings, my wife and I had gone to Glad Tidings Temple to be met by TV cameras and women wheeling baby buggies as they handed out pamphlets listing provocatively titled magazines that Jim Pattison's company supposedly distributed (checking the next day, I found that Mainland didn't handle most of the titles mentioned). My wife urged me to sell Mainland Magazine. "Why don't you get rid of it?" Mary asked. "Your reputation as a Christian is at stake."

"If we don't own it, it would probably be a lot worse," I argued. "Selling is the easy way out of this. That isn't the solution. What we need are responsible distributors who care about the community and are prepared to balance freedom of speech with community standards and good taste."

But in early May '84, after studying Mainland's operations, talking to community leaders, and considering my options, we decided to sell—only in the best interests of Expo, which didn't need another controversy. As I announced to a news conference: "During the past week I have carried out an intensive examination of the operations of Mainland Magazine Service. I have consulted with church leaders, women's organizations, industry representatives, and the top seventeen senior executives of the Jim Pattison Group in the Vancouver area. I have been troubled to learn that some of the publications handled by Mainland, which happen to represent a very small proportion of the company's total product

The Porn Debate

line, are offensive. In examining some of these publications myself, I too have been offended." But I also pointed out that because governments have failed to produce any clear definition of obscenity, "magazine wholesalers are forced to try to act as self-censors, a role for which they are not qualified." I went on to say that as chairman of Expo 86, "I cannot own a company that is in a controversial issue like this. If it wasn't for Expo, I would attempt to bring the church, women's groups, wholesalers, and the government together to see if we can improve the standard."

Even though we intended to sell Mainland, I gave reporters my recommendation for an agency that would help any future owner: a review board, similar to Ontario's, that would screen the so-called adult magazines and keep the worst of them off the racks.

We decided to give a kick-start to the idea of a review board. The next day, we held a meeting of B.C.'s wholesale distributors, municipal politicians, and my critics: the heads of several churches, including Archbishop Hambidge, and women's groups, among them the Status of Women and the University Women's Club. Donna Stewart and Kit Stevenson, the women who'd criticized me at the Fraser Committee hearings, were there. We proposed a board that would be funded by the distributors but operated at arm's length by private citizens knowledgeable about community standards. There was general approval of the idea and all seven of the province's major distributors agreed to support it. Afterwards, the archbishop told me: "It's a step forward." And later he told a reporter: "I thought it was a victory not only for the church, but for Jimmy."

We presumed that the board should be under the auspices of the provincial government, who would appoint the members. But Attorney General Brian Smith said he'd prefer it to be a self-policing body along the lines of the B.C. Press Council. In the legislature, the NDP's Rosemary Brown reported that several years ago our news-distribution company in Hamilton (Mountain City News) had twice been convicted of distributing obscene material. She didn't raise the issue of how difficult it is for the government and courts—never mind a distributor—to determine what's legally obscene. "In view of this record," she asked, "will the Attorney General advise why he continues to promote a self-policing model for this peddler of hard-core pornography?"

Brian Smith replied that he wanted a body that could operate without a lot of government regulation and bureaucracy. "Mr. Pattison has tried to do something about this. He's tried to bring about some consensus on the part of church groups and women's organizations to recommend that we have a review panel. I welcome that recommendation."

Vancouver's city council didn't welcome our decision to sell Mainland Magazine; we were damned if we did and damned if we didn't. I got a phone call from Mayor Mike Harcourt (who has since become the provincial NDP leader) urging me to keep the company in my hands. In a memo to aldermen, the mayor said: "While I welcome Mr. Pattison's concern over the distribution of this very offensive material, the proposed sale of his agency to another party is not going to eliminate or reduce the offence. Consequently, I have been discussing with Mr. Pattison the alternative . . . of establishing an independent review board which would advise on which publications are so obscene and offensive that they should not be distributed."

What the mayor and other people were telling me is that Mainland was in responsible hands; if I sold it, the new owners might be less concerned with controlling pornography. That wasn't so far-fetched. The news-distribution business in North America had its share of bad eggs. Our vice-presidents Bill Sleeman and Harry Dunbar and I had met one group in the business that made us literally fear for our lives.

Several years earlier, we'd tried to buy a Canadian news-distribution company from its American owners. For obvious reasons, I'm not mentioning their names. I sent Harry down to the States for a first meeting. They told him the story of how they'd forced a wholesaler in another U.S. city to sell out to them: A woman picked the man up at a Las Vegas gambling table and took him up to his room—where they got incriminating photographs they threatened to show to his wife. More frightening was their account of getting rid of a relative they wanted out of the business by arranging for the guy to fall off a boat. Bill went to see them later and said the price they wanted for their Canadian wholesale operation was way too high. They warned him that if we ever tried to take

The Porn Debate

control of it or compete with them, they'd make sure that our non-union trucking firm, Reimer Express, would be unionized in no time flat. "Whatever you've heard about us, you can assume it's correct," they told Bill. "If you and your people want to stay healthy and wealthy, stay out of our area." Bill flew back to Vancouver on the next plane and announced to me: "There's one thing I guarantee you: If you want to get involved in this deal, I'm not going to have anything to do with it." A month later I went to see the Americans myself. I was met at their door by two guys with guns on their hips. The owners told me about a stockbroker who'd lost them a lot of money and was found under a bridge with his stomach full of rat poison. They also asked me if I liked my children. I was scared and decided Bill Sleeman had been right; I got out of there fast and I've never seen them since.

In '84, when we decided to sell Mainland, we had a very respectable buyer in mind: Vandella Enterprises, owned by our former vice-president of finance, Fred Vanstone. We signed a preliminary agreement. But Mainland was in the middle of a price war with its competitor, Vancouver Magazine Service, which had affected our earnings picture; the deal didn't close. Meanwhile, the new Conservative government had announced that it intended to rewrite the laws on pornography. And the review board that I'd proposed was now in operation. Taking all those factors into account that fall, I decided to keep the company and wait and see what the future would bring. Archbishop Hambidge approved of my decision to stay in the business. "The easy way out would be to sell," he told a journalist later. "You can't attack things from the outside. Jimmy couldn't criticize the business if he weren't in it. He has to take the harder road."

As it turned out, the independent, three-member review board got off to a good start in November. The chairman was Jillian Riddington, who'd attended the board's organizational meeting and presented a brief to the Fraser Committee. Jillian, a former vice-president of NAC, had her master's in sociology from the University of British Columbia and had worked at Vancouver's Transition House for women. The other members were Gwenith Ingham, a member of the Anglican Church task force on pornography; Graeme Waymark, a Vancouver school trustee; and an alternate, Karen Phillips of the Port Coquitlam Women's Centre. Today, the board includes Jillian, Karen, and Gary Mavis, former director of the Vancouver Crisis Centre; the alternates are psychologist Derryl Goldenberg and author Jan Drabek.

The members work out of offices supplied by the Attorney General's department. Every Wednesday, wholesalers send the board an average of sixteen adult magazines and receive a report on them by the following Monday. Jillian Riddington spends about sixteen hours a week reading every word of every magazine. Members can approve a magazine totally, approve it subject to the removal of certain pages, or reject it entirely. The board—which decides on the basis of two out of three votes—tends to turn down material more for violent content than for consenting sex between adults. There's a lot of room for subjective judgement. As the chairman has pointed out, "The Criminal Code isn't that clear on the matter of pornography." The board takes note of guidelines from the B.C. Attorney General's department, which are used by Crown counsel in deciding whether material is liable to prosecution under the Criminal Code:

1) Sexually oriented material involving violence, coercion, compulsion, force, bodily harm or threats or fear of bodily harm, or other similar acts;
2) Sexually oriented material involving young persons;
3) Material involving acts of bestiality;
4) Sexually explicit material in which one person is represented as the parent, child, brother, sister, grandparent or grandchild of the other person;
5) Sexually oriented material involving excreta;
6) Material involving acts of necrophilia.

"Sexually explicit" means graphic representations of human sexual activity, and "sexually oriented" includes not only graphic representations of human sexual activity but also salacious representations of human nudity. "Young persons" are those under eighteen years of age. It is noted that the categories may not be exhaustive, and that material which is to be used for research purposes, and material with literary or artistic merit is exempt. Sexually explicit material is not to be sold or displayed in establishments which permit the entry of young persons, and should not be displayed so as to be in public view from outside the store.

To avoid giving the offending magazines free publicity, the review board doesn't give their names to the media. But it does mail the list of names to Canada Customs; the Corrections department, for guidance in prisons; the B.C. Attorney General's special projects division, which sends the list to every police department; a dozen community groups; and any other group that requests it.

Between the board's launch in November '84 and the end of '86, it received 1,314 magazines for review. It cleared 748 of them for distribution, recommended that pages be removed from 271, and rejected 295 outright. It only recommends; the wholesale distributors can decide to ignore the board. Mainland Magazine follows its recommendations to the letter. But the Attorney General's department recently prosecuted our competitor, Vancouver Magazine Service, for distributing obscene materials: four magazines the board had rejected entirely and a fifth which had some offensive material the board had recommended deleting. The magazines were *Oui Letters*, *The Canadian Key*, *Adam Film World Guide 1986*, *Velvet Bonanza*, and *Live*. They contained articles or scenes of coercive sex, sado-masochism, incest, bondage, degradation, and humiliation.

That trial, which showed us that the review board is working, raised some interesting points. The court heard that the B.C. board had rejected as many as 35 per cent more publications than the similar advisory committee in Ontario. The chairman of the Ontario committee was the distinguished writer Arnold Edinborough, who runs the Council for Business and the Arts in Canada. His committee had actually approved all five of the magazines that Vancouver Magazine Service was charged with distributing in B.C.

Ontario and British Columbia are the only two provinces with advisory bodies on print pornography. We haven't been successful in our attempts to interest the Alberta government in helping our Edmonton-based company, Provincial News, set up a review board there. But, across Canada, the problem isn't anywhere as bad as it was: Sales of adult magazines generally are about half what they were six years ago. Of course, that's because of the increasing popularity of sex on videotape. We had an opportunity not long ago to buy a video company and the financial projections were terrific. But the first question I asked was what percentage of items the company distributes were blue movies. Over half, they told me. Forget it, I said.

The porn issue died down after the review board went to work. But, then it reared up again two years later, after Expo ended. The University of British Columbia had asked me to accept an honorary degree. I appreciated being recognized by my alma mater, by the university I'd never officially graduated from. In late '86, I agreed to accept the degree at the spring convocation.

What I didn't know was that, while the vast majority of UBC's eighty-seven Senate members approved my award, Senate chairman Jean Elder had resigned in protest. And four other academic women on the Senate had sent a letter of protest to UBC president David Strangway. Their charge: The university was honouring a man who distributed pornography. In her letter of resignation, Professor Elder wrote: "While it is certainly true that anyone may be in business within the law, to honour persons engaged in businesses which exploit and humiliate women seems more than I can countenance." A student senator said she would urge students, professors, and others to support protests against me at the convocation ceremonies.

One day just before Christmas, I told my old friend Bob Wyman, chancellor of the university, that I was very reluctantly thinking of turning down the degree. It looked like some of the women senators and students were going to cause a great furor and I didn't want to ruin the convocation for the graduates and their families. I didn't care as much about the effect a big demonstration would have on me—I've been criticized publicly before. But I sure didn't want to see a graduation ceremony disrupted by bullhorns and pickets. Bob and President Strangway both strongly urged me to reconsider; they didn't want me to back off because of the protesters.

The next day, I wrote a letter to the president: "Further to our telephone conversation, I just wanted to drop you a note to confirm that after serious consideration I would like to have my name withdrawn from the list of those to receive an honourary degree from the University of British Columbia. Would you please advise the selection committee of my decision and let the members know of my personal appreciation. The nomination was an honour in itself."

President Strangway later sent me a letter expressing the university's "deep regret" and enclosing a copy of the tribute that would have been read if I'd decided to accept the honourary degree, after all. After mentioning my involvement with Expo, it ended: "Your personal contributions, usually unheralded and unannounced, have been the backbone of many a philanthropic campaign. For these you sought no reward. In deciding that you would not accept the honourary degree offered by the university, your primary concern was to avert the disruption at the graduation for students and parents. It is your stated view that UBC is a precious resource to the people of this province; your personal decision reaffirms your commitment to this province."

CHAPTER EIGHTEEN

Expo

Back in 1981, just when I was seeing signs of a deepening recession, B.C.'s premier, Bill Bennett, asked me to take on the chairmanship of what was then called Transpo 86. It was to be a modest little specialized world's fair celebrating transportation. The job was going to be part time—"an hour on Friday afternoons," he said. A friend strongly advised me not to accept the position. I'd known Ray Smith, the president of MacMillan Bloedel, ever since we met at a reunion of the Kitsilano Boys' Band twenty years before. Ray told me the story of how his father had ruined his health when he helped produce the 1954 British Empire Games in Vancouver. "Please don't do it, Jimmy," Ray said.

But when the premier of your province asks you to perform a public service, you consider it seriously. I agreed to be a part-time, unpaid chairman for two years. The job grew like a bad weed as the fair ballooned into a $1.6 million World Exposition. For thirty-six months I did almost nothing else. I left the overseeing of our companies to good people in Corporate Office and to the individual presidents—who have always had the autonomy to operate the companies in their own way.

Expo was born in 1978 when Grace McCarthy, then British Columbia's minister of travel industry, was in Britain promoting tourism and looking for ideas to help celebrate Vancouver's Centennial in 1986. Lunching with B.C.'s Agent General in London, Lawrie Wallace, and Patrick Reid, president of the International Bureau of Expositions, she wondered if the city could host a world's fair that year. Told that Japan had first call on an '86 Exposition, she began lobbying the bureau until the Japanese agreed to hold theirs a year earlier. Expo 86 was Grace McCarthy's initiative. She would be its unwavering cheerleader. But the politician who really deserves unequivocal credit for the success of the fair is Premier Bill Bennett, who made the hard calls to keep it alive when it wasn't popular politically. He first announced it in 1980 as Transpo 86, an $80 million exposition with the single theme of transportation—an appropriate one because it would be a hundred years since the CPR reached the West Coast tidewaters to link Canada coast to coast. Unlike the universally themed Expo 67 in Montreal, where every nation built its own distinctive pavilion, Transpo would be a special-category fair, which would provide prefabricated buildings to participants. It would rise on 173 acres along the north shore of False Creek in downtown Vancouver. At the same time, the premier announced that the B.C. government would build a $126 million domed stadium in the area and a $135 million trade and convention centre on Vancouver's nearby harbour waterfront. A new $854 million rapid-transit system—SkyTrain, as it was later named—would link outlying municipalities with central Vancouver. And, after the world's fair, the Expo site on False Creek would become one of North America's largest urban-redevelopment projects.

For a while, the fate of what was now called Expo 86 had been uncertain. The Trudeau government, remembering the astronomical costs of Expo 67 in Montreal, had no desire to help finance Bill Bennett's fair. In late '81, the provincial government, reeling from the recession, had announced it would not be building the convention centre on the harbour. All of Expo's costs were being reconsidered. At one point, weighing his options, the premier asked me bluntly: "Jimmy, how much for a shlock fair? What's the minimum we could get away with?" But by the following April, he could announce that Ottawa would be funding a combined convention centre, cruise-ship terminal, and national pavilion at Expo—

the $144.8 million Canada Place, to be built on the same waterfront site the province had wanted to develop.

So, there we were, with a board of well-connected directors who didn't know a thing about world's fairs and with a glorified used-car salesman as chairman. The management we hired would have no background in international expositions. And there was no history to call on: You couldn't transfer the experience of a fair in another country at another time to one in Vancouver in 1986. But my first major problem as Expo chairman was the in-fighting between us and B.C. Place, the provincial Crown corporation in charge of the urban-redevelopment project. B.C. Place was Expo's landlord on the downtown site. And because its senior executives wanted to begin planning for office towers and apartment buildings, there was constant conflict over the landlord-tenant relationship—everything from our plans to erect permanent structures to the placement of retaining walls. The B.C. Place chairman was the respected Alvin Narod, the recently retired owner of a major contracting company, who'd spent eight months negotiating the purchase of the False Creek site from Marathon Realty. The president was Gil Hardman, the former vice-chairman of the Mobil Land Development Corporation in the United States. They were tough-minded men and they had their own board of directors to answer to. But just before the Stadium at B.C. Place opened in '83, Alvin Narod died and wasn't replaced. My term as Expo chairman was at an end. The job was taking increasingly more of my time—the one hour a week was a bad joke now—and I had no intention of staying on. When I reported my decision to Bill Bennett, I advised him to get a full-time chairman for the fair and make him chairman of B.C. Place too, dealing with only a single board of directors.

A week after I'd announced my decision to resign, the premier was entertaining the governor of Alaska on my boat. Bill Bennett sat with me in the lounge and said: "If I can't ask people like you to come and help me, people who made money and became successful in this province, who can I turn to?"

"You're absolutely right," I said. "I'll do it."

I spent the next two months in the B.C. Place offices and made what might have been one of my most important contributions to the exposition: I arranged through the government to put two Expo directors on the B.C. Place board and four B.C. Place directors on the Expo board so we could all start working together. The animosity that had built up between us disappeared within a few meetings. And I fired Gil Hardman. Though he had a lot of strong qualities, he was always fighting with Expo and the city of Vancouver. We replaced him with Stanley Kwok, an architect, a gentle-spirited team player who was chairman of Expo's design committee and a director of B.C. Place.

During Christmas week, I moved into Expo's headquarters, into a small room next to the fancy office that Mike Bartlett had as president before I'd fired him (even his wastebasket cost $125). By now, the world's fair had two themes, transportation and communications, and everything else had swollen way beyond Transpo's modest beginnings. As our board had recently announced, the exposition now would cost $800 million and it would incur a deficit of $311 million. But a Currie, Coopers & Lybrand report estimated that Expo would generate $2.8 billion worth of economic activity in B.C. along with $400 million in federal taxes and $172 million in provincial taxes.

Throughout 1983, the mood of the province was tense. The Social Credit government had introduced a tough package of twenty-six bills that cut social programs, skinnied down the civil service, and placed new controls on unions. By November, the labour movement came close to calling a general strike. And at Expo, we were starting to accept low bids from non-union contractors.

That was a sharp about-face for us. From the start, I'd wanted to strike a deal with B.C.'s unions. In '82 I'd gone to the office of Roy Gautier, president of the B.C. and Yukon Building Trades Council. Gautier is a strong, businesslike, intelligent Scot. "Look, we've got to have labour peace at Expo," I told him. "And we've got to be assured that it's going to get built on time, and to do that we can't risk any labour disruption. What we need is a no-strike agreement until the fair's built. And for that, we'll do a deal with the unions: It will be an all-union site." While he didn't give me any encouragement that a deal was possible, he didn't say no. And later the Expo board voted 14 to 1 in favour of a union-only project.

But the '83 provincial election changed everything. With the Socreds solidly back in power on a program of restraint, the government still wanted a no-strike guarantee from the unions but let Gautier know that the Expo site would be open to non-union bids. Bill Bennett and his cabinet were about to play hardball and the world's fair would become their playing field. The decision to take that stance had repercussions that continue to this day in B.C.

The issue first came to a head the following March. A Fraser Valley contractor named Bill Kerkhoff, whose company was firmly non-union, won a contract to build a $19 million condominium project in the False Creek area within view of Expo. The site became the scene of confrontations between union and non-union workers, with the building trades fined $30,000 for ignoring court orders. In a television address March 17, Premier Bennett announced "a new reality" in the province: "My colleagues and I in government want jobs for all British Columbians whether they belong to a union or not." Saying that he still wanted peace at Expo, he gave me ten days to make a deal with the unions.

Roy Gautier was willing to compromise—up to a point. He'd sign a no-strike deal and accept a very limited number of non-union workers on the site. But they had to be paid the same wages and benefits as union men; for example, the package for a carpenter amounted to $22.73 an hour. I knew the government would never go for that. After a week's bargaining, I reported to the government that we'd made no progress in our talks. On April 10, we had one final day-long meeting, this time with the premier's advisor, Norman Spector. But the government refused to accept the union's proposal for what it called a "fair wage" for all.

The next day, I summarized my thinking and gave my recommendation in a document to the premier. We'd had $114 million worth of contracts on hold for three weeks, I told him, and they couldn't be delayed more than another week with any guarantee of completing the fair on time and on budget. A major meeting of Expo's commissioners general, representing countries and corporations, would be held in early May and some participants could withdraw their commitment to the fair if there was no labour agreement by then. I questioned the wisdom of any settlement enforced by government legislation. "In my opinion," I wrote, "a unilateral legislated agreement will increase the financial risk, reduce foreign participation, jeopardize our ability to open on time, and is therefore not a sound option." If Expo closed down on April 18, the write-off would be about $80 million, plus some lawsuits—compared to about $950 million if we tried to struggle through to the end of '85. I admitted that cancelling the exposition would be "an international embarrassment to the government and people of British Columbia" and damage the province's investment potential for years to come. "Having said all that, I would rather suffer the embarrassment now, as bad as it might be, than have to cancel a year from now, be held to ransom by labour, or be unable to open on time."

My recommendation to the premier: "Cancel Expo 86 unless a settlement that ensures construction labour peace is accepted by the Building Trades Council."

I wasn't bluffing to scare the unions or shock the provincial cabinet; I meant every word of my report.

The shock waves resounded for the next two days, as Bill Bennett met with Roy Gautier, the cabinet argued, and the premier finally announced that the government would pass legislation ensuring that there would be no labour disputes at Expo.

In this hostile atmosphere, I continued to negotiate with Roy. I'd come to know him and respect him; we once took my boat up Indian Arm outside Vancouver, where the former carpenter started talking about the teak and mahogany on the *Nova Springs* and what it had been like to work with wood for twenty-five years. Now, with the threat of legislation hanging over us, he and I finally came to an agreement: The minimum-wage scale for all work on the site would be based on the federal fair wage rate of $15.25, adjusted for inflation to just over $19 an hour.

But the cabinet, in its wisdom, vetoed our deal. In early May, the government introduced changes to the provincial Labour Code that would allow it to split up construction sites "of special economic importance" into zones that would effectively limit the unions' right to refuse to work alongside non-union labour.

There was one more major attempt to reach agreement. Graham Leslie, the deputy minister of labour, who used to bargain with Vancouver's municipal unions, brought Roy and me together in June for around-the-clock sessions. Again, we fashioned a deal that we thought would fly: Its main feature was a wage of $18.73 an hour for all construction at the fair. The only catch, which I thought we could sell, was that the union wanted this rate to apply retroactively to an Expo contract already signed with Bill Kerkhoff, the controversial non-union contractor who was paying his workers a lot less than that. I drove out to Chilliwack to see Bill, who agreed to the stipulation in the best interests of Expo.

Again, the cabinet wouldn't accept our deal; for one thing, they wouldn't use Bill Kerkhoff as a sacrificial lamb. The government announced that a fair-wage rate of $15.25 would apply to all non-union construction. Finally, tasting defeat, the unions agreed to exempt the Kerkhoff contract from any wage settlement if we'd agree to the $18.73 rate for everybody. Mike Bartlett and I both recommended acceptance. But it was too late. A majority of the Expo board refused to go along with that compromise. The federal government and the city of Vancouver each had three appointees on the board (though one of Vancouver's had died); the other seven directors were named by the province. And the government's representative on the board, tourism minister Claude Richmond, presented a strong case to make sure the board understood the government position. Labour minister Bob McClelland was there to support Claude. Then, in a move that ended all discussion, the government passed its special legislation, which ultimately separated Expo into about two hundred distinct economic zones—union and non-union projects.

Throughout all of this, I was acting in good faith with the unions, but neither they nor I ever knew where the pins were; the government kept moving them. The premier, looking at the bigger provincial picture, had a different agenda. Yet, in the end, I thought that Bill Bennett did exactly the right thing for B.C. because it ushered in a whole new tone to provincial labour relations. Of the last batch of contracts Expo awarded in the final few months of construction, 70 per cent went to non-union contractors. Overall, though, 70 per cent of the fair was built by union workers. It created 9,250 construction jobs over three years. I was out on that site every day, and while there was the odd skirmish between the two sides, the rank-and-file guys got along fine. They built

Expo well, on time, and $17 million under budget. But it's probably true to say that the confrontation between government and labour over Expo helped polarize the province even further, hardening the government in its position and weakening B.C.'s labour movement.

During my three years as full-time chairman, I'd do Jim Pattison Group business myself only if it didn't steal much time away from Expo. Like the day in 1985 I got a call from Peter Ackerman of Drexel Burnham Lambert Inc., which has become one of Wall Street's most important investment bankers. Peter, senior vice-president of high-yield and convertible bonds, is the right-hand man to Mike Milken, celebrated for his popularizing of the high-yield bonds known in the trade as "junk bonds." The details of the transaction Peter was pitching show just how much the deal business has changed—how sophisticated it's become—since I first got into it nearly two decades ago. Milken, based in Los Angeles, had a group of about one hundred investors across North America that would commit to buying high-yield bonds to finance hostile takeovers of large corporations. Canadian members of the investment group included Edgar Kaiser, president of the Bank of British Columbia; the Belzberg brothers, whose First City Financial of Vancouver has become a major player in corporate takeover attempts; and the Reichmann brothers of Toronto, who are the world's largest office landlords and who were about to take over Gulf Canada. Milken's idea was that the investors wouldn't have to pay for the bonds unless the takeover actually happened. But just for committing themselves, they'd get a fee—maybe 0.75 per cent of their investment (in a typical deal, the Bank of B.C. was to get $750,000 for putting up $100 million). This investment group became powerful enough to finance billion-dollar takeovers, something that none of the individual members of the group could do on its own. One of their bids was to back a raid on Unocal Corporation, America's twelfth-largest major petroleum company, by the legendary T. Boone Pickens, chairman of Mesa Petroleum Co., its largest independent oil company. Pickens is the slight, sandy-haired Texan who took strong stock positions in bigger oil companies like Gulf, threatened to take them over, and made hundreds of millions of dollars as he chased them into a merger or a major restructuring from which he profited (he and his partners made $760 million pre-tax profit by selling their Gulf stock to Chevron Corp.). He may look unsophisticated, but he knows his onions. As he says with a twang in his voice, "We didn't just get off the watermelon wagon yesterday."

Peter Ackerman called us to put up $40 million in the Unocal takeover attempt, which we did through a Bank of B.C. nominee and a couple of other names that Unocal wouldn't recognize. We made our initial commitment to Peter for Pickens in one minute over the phone. Pickens had taken a big position in Unocal. But in a loud, public corporate battle, its president fought him off and Pickens lost his bid to take over the company. The members of his investment group (which included us) shared in $83 million in commissions and fees. (*The Vancouver Sun* carried a story on the Unocal fight that mentioned the Belzbergs and the Bank of B.C. as a couple of Pickens's partners, but because we'd used nominee names it didn't identify us.) Another way deal-making has changed over the years: During the whole takeover attempt, I never even met Boone Pickens. Still haven't.

A little later that year, the Unocal deal put me in an interesting position in my role as Expo chairman. There was a meeting in Vancouver of the commissioners general of all the pavilions. The American commissioner general, Ambassador Fred Hartley, also happened to be the same chief executive officer of Unocal who was trying to beat back T. Boone Pickens and save the company. One afternoon during a lunch on my boat, the *Nova Springs*, he was angrily telling the story of the Unocal takeover attempt and railing against Boone and his backers. I couldn't let him continue. "I'm one of the guys who helped finance the takeover, Fred," I told him. He was visibly taken aback, and stayed very unhappy for a few hours. That night, during dinner, he came to me and said: "Let's put that behind us."

I fired Mike Bartlett as Expo's president in June '85—for his lavish spending and his insensitivity to the demands of a public corporation. Three months later, I was the permanent president as well as chairman. There just wasn't time to find anyone else with the fair opening in May. Mike wasn't the last person to be let go. One month after the fair began, somebody estimated that forty senior executives had been fired or quit. Contributing to that total was the fact that as we got closer to opening day, many people's jobs came to a natural end. But the other reality was that in a fast-track project like an exposition, people either had to prove themselves quickly or expect to be dismissed. I wasn't the hatchet man for everyone who got fired. Chris Wootten, who was in charge of Expo's entertainment program, had a good reputation as a manager in local arts circles and I kind of liked him. When he was let go in August, there was a fuss in the press. But his superior, Jeff McNair, made a strong case on why Chris wasn't right for the job. Then on New Year's Day, 1986, I fired McNair, one of the last of Mike Bartlett's senior associates from Canada's Wonderland.

The minute I took over as full-time president, I clamped down on costs. At a public corporation like Expo, it's everybody's money and everybody's your boss. And the way some people had been spending that money was totally unacceptable. I'd seen a vice-president take a taxi for a two-block trip on a nice day, another executive make an out-of-town taxi trip that cost $475. Or a guy earning more than $100,000 a year charge us for his lunch in his office because he was working over the noon hour when his secretary, making $20,000, had to pay for hers. I took away every executive's signing authority, refusing to let any expenditure go for payment unless I'd approved it. That meant everything, from the million-dollar construction contract to the $10 lunch. Every vice-president had to have a purchase requisition order signed by me before he or she could even get a purchase order. That continued until the various managers could prove to me they had good judgment and I understood what was going on in detail. I had seven hundred big signs made that read: *Let's be remembered by this* [an Expo symbol] *not this* [a dollar sign]. *Every penny counts. Is your purchase absolutely necessary?* Eventually I ran contests every Friday afternoon, with prizes for employees who could suggest ways to cut costs. I'd give them a trip to San Francisco on my jet or dinner for twenty on my boat. There'd be prize draws just for the people who showed up at these weekly staff meetings. We'd bring in special guests to give pep talks—Bobby Ackles, general manager of the B.C. Lions, spoke about winners. And it all worked: One receptionist, for example, suggested that we should use the regularly operating Expo shuttle buses to pick up mail instead of hiring so many couriers; she saved us $13,000 a month.

My biggest job at Expo was to listen. To get out of my ninth-floor office, wander around where all the work was being done on the floor below, ask questions, and listen to the answers. I'd stick my head in the mail room and ask a clerk: "What are you working on?" Ask a secretary: "What's the biggest problem you've got today?" Or check with the switchboard operator about the volume of calls she was getting that day. Answering phone calls was something I insisted on with all our executives. That was one of the problems with Jess Ketchum, our first vice-president of communications: I had many complaints that he didn't return his calls. While liking him personally, I had so many complaints about him that I couldn't stand it. I replaced Jess with George Madden, who was a good communicator with a calm approach and a healthy sense of humour as he dealt with the world's media. George returned his calls. So did I, including the calls from kooks. It's simple politeness as well as good sense. People deserve an answer quickly, even if they may not like the one they get. And they may have something important to tell you. Before Expo opened, when I went out to community meetings around the province, there wasn't a single time that I didn't come back and change a policy because I'd learned something, listening.

Sometimes I didn't like what I heard. We got criticized soundly for awarding our largest contract, for about $75 million worth of souvenir sales, to Specialty Manufacturing, a company linked by common ownership to Ace Novelty of Seattle. Not only was it an American firm, but we found out much later—after we'd awarded the contract—that it had been convicted of defrauding the New Orleans world's fair in 1984. Ace paid an official of that fair $25,000 under false pretences to get a souvenir contract. Our board of directors hadn't wanted to deal with Americans in the first place. We tried very hard to get Woodward's—the respectable, deep-rooted, locally based department-store chain—to take the entire contract. Because the souvenir field is a cash business that requires big inventories, and because we could get the best returns at the least risk with one supplier, we didn't want to piece out the contract to several companies. But neither Woodward's nor anybody else wanted to assume the whole contract. So we settled for Specialty Manufacturing, which through Ace Novelty had experience with world's fairs. We signed our contract in June '84, while the New Orleans fair was still on. Months later, Ace was charged with fraud and later convicted. I doubt whether our directors would have signed if Ace had been convicted before we gave them the contract. But from our point of view, the contract with Specialty turned out be excellent. They did a first-class job and there were no scams. We had excellent co-operation from the provincial and federal governments on the continuous monitoring of the Ace contract.

We got some more criticism from Canadian manufacturers when Specialty said it would be importing an extra 1.2 million T-shirts from Korea. In the end, it did end up using domestic suppliers for some of the shirts. We had a policy to buy Canadian and in particular British Columbian whenever feasible, but I was more concerned with the Canadian customer than I was the Canadian supplier. If an overseas manufacturer couldn't supply a cheaper T-shirt, that was too bad. Our number-one responsibility was getting Expo visitors the best value possible.

That was one of the considerations when it came to the involvement of the Jim Pattison Group at Expo. At the time, the Group owned more than thirty different companies doing business in B.C.—including the biggest commuter airline, sign company, auto dealership, and magazine distributor. As tourism minister Claude Richmond told the B.C. legislature, "It's very difficult to do business in this province without running into a company that is owned by Mr. Pattison." Now, if Neon Products bid on a job at the fair and came in $100,000 lower than any competitor, should the taxpayer suffer and pay more because I'd been asked to be chairman of the world's fair? Not only that, should the employees of the Jim Pattison Group be penalized because of my involvement? That's silly. Expo leased cars and bought magazines, signage, and computer services from our companies, and placed advertising with one of our radio stations and outdoor-advertising companies. But if I wanted to tally up whether we made money on the fair, I'm sure I would find that, overall, we didn't. If you total the three full years I spent away from my business, as well as the important deals I didn't do during that time, we'd come up on the loss side of the ledger. One of the major opportunities that slipped through our fingers because of my absence was a $105 million investment in the takeover of an American company, which we should have had.

Other Expo directors, performing a public service for no remuneration, were in the same position. For instance, Clark Bentall of the Bentall Group, whose Dominion Construction of Vancouver is one of the premier contractors in Canada. Because Dominion offered the best bid on the B.C. Pavilion complex, it won the job. Naturally, the directors realized that, with their broad corporate involvements, there had to be rules covering any potential conflict of interest. At our second board meeting, we began planning regulations that would prevent directors from sharing in any decisions that could benefit them. The conflict-of-interest guidelines, which we followed to the letter, were drawn up in '83 by a former justice of the B.C. Supreme Court, Kenneth Fawcus. They were model guidelines, according to our vice-president of law and general counsel, Russ Anthony, who'd worked on the Canadian Constitution. When Russ joined us, we told him to assume that a Royal Commission would someday examine Expo's finances; he'd better make sure that every contract could withstand a public inquiry. His department researched conflict-of-interest guidelines for Crown corporations throughout North America; ours were supposed to be the best and most comprehensive of them all. Our board members had to make full disclosure of all companies or directorships that could give rise to conflicts. Each year they had to list areas of potential conflicts and complete supplementary forms if there was any change during the year. If conflicts arose, including those involving close family members, directors had to detail them in writing. And of course they had to leave the room during any discussion of their companies' bids on Expo contracts. Every potential conflict-of-interest case was forwarded to Judge Fawcus for his opinion.

Even so, there was a storm of protest when the Jim Pattison Group's *Beautful British Columbia* magazine bid successfully against two other local firms to publish the official Expo guidebook. I wasn't involved in any of the deliberations leading up to the board's decision. But I've since been told that the directors had a long debate about whether they should *not* give *Beautiful British Columbia* the contract—unless its bid was very much better—because of the possible embarrassment it would cause me. Apparently, they decided it was the best deal that followed the specifications, Judge Fawcus agreed, and the hang with the chairman's embarrassment.

The board was always a strong one. In its final form, it had seventeen members as well as me: Walter Badun, chairman of Penreal Advisors Limited; Clark Bentall, chairman of the Bentall Group; Peter Brown, president of Canarim Investment Corporation; Herb Capozzi, director of Capozzi Enterprises; Ray Dagg, president and general manager of Target Media Incorporated; Don Hamilton, president of General Communications Corporation; Lucille Johnstone, president and chief operating officer of Rivtow Straits Limited; Dr. Norman Keevil Jr., president and CEO of Teck Corporation; Lyall Knott of Clark, Wilson, Barristers and Solicitors; Stanley Kwok, president of B.C. Place; Allan Laird, chairman of Hastings West Investments Limited: Keith Mitchell of Farris, Vaughan, Wills & Murphy; John Newton, president of J.F. Newton Limited; Patrick Reid, Expo's commissioner general; tourism minister Claude Richmond; Robert Roddick of Roddick and Peck Barristers and Solicitors; and Alison Robinson, an active civic worker.

I never knew there were people who gave so much of their time and interest to a community project like Expo. The directors spent thousands of hours over six years. Not only did they attend monthly board meetings—which eventually became weekly (every Monday at 7:00 A.M.)—but they all sat on time-consuming committees, some of them on two or three. The board and the committees set policy; it was my job to execute the policy whether I liked it or not. The committee system, which I instituted, gave the board hands-on involvement in the fair. The negative was that the directors sometimes got involved in operations rather than policy-making and monitoring. All of the board members, except Patrick Reid and Claude Richmond, were unpaid volunteers. In their dedication, they were a terrific example to Expo's employees and the volunteers. (As for Claude, once in a while you get lucky, as I did when the premier made him Minister Responsible for Expo. Claude Richmond's intelligent support made my life as chairman so much easier.)

No director gave more of her time or contributed more to the fair than Alison Robinson—nobody, including Jimmy

Pattison. From a philosophical point of view, we couldn't be farther apart; she was an appointee of the NDP mayor and I'm a small-c conservative. Among the board members, she was my biggest headache, sometimes phoning me three times a day with things to improve Expo. But the people of B.C. and Canada owe Alison a great debt of gratitude.

We called on other people in the business community with special expertise to handle specific tasks. One of them was Mel Cooper, chairman of AirBC, who in the summer of '85 became vice-president of corporate sponsorship. We already had some spectacular financial support from Canadian corporations. The first two to become official sponsors were those transportation giants, Canadian National and Canadian Pacific. Then we started attracting a roll-call of household names: General Motors, Imperial Oil, Coca-Cola, Labatts, Kodak, Xerox, McDonald's—thirty-four official corporate sponsors in all. Building on the early work of the team led by Don McConachie, vice-president of marketing and corporate participation, Mel's mission was to keep the momentum going until the day the fair opened. He was right for the job. As *The Financial Post* described him at the time: "The owner of Victoria radio station CFAX, Cooper is the epitome of hard-sell and professional enthusiasm. He offered to work without salary (as Pattison is doing) but Expo will insist he be paid." I told Mel that he'd have to spend only a three-day week at Expo; for a year and a half, he worked enormously long hours raising money from corporations. In his first month, we had a two-hour meeting where I took him through every single account he thought we could sell. "Okay, bottom line," I said finally. "How much are you going to bring in?"

He was hesitant to commit.

"I want to know," I pushed.

Finally, he gave me a figure.

"*That* is the number," I said, and then turned to our dedicated vice-president of finance. Dennis Burdette, and told him to write it down. "But just in case Mel forgets what he said today, every Monday morning he's going to tell me how much he owes me."

And at our weekly management meetings, I'd ask Mel out of the blue: "Well, Mel, how much do you owe me today?" He'd give me supporting documents to show which corporations had come aboard since the last meeting. Two weeks before Expo opened, he still owed me a couple of million. Over the weekend, he'd concluded a deal with Hasbro Incorporated, the big American toy-makers, who sponsored the Expo Centre. On Monday morning, I asked Mel: "How much do you owe me?"

He fumbled with the papers in front of him. "I'm having a little difficulty finding the number."

I waited impatiently.

"Oh, I found it." He stood up, walked the length of the boardroom table, and slapped the papers down in front of me. "Jimmy Pattison," he said, "you owe *me* half a million dollars." Striding away, he asked, "Now, can I go home to Victoria?"

"No," I said. "There's still more money out there."

The final total of corporate involvement at Expo, everything from straight money to services, was $174 million.

Attracting national participants was the job of the Expo commissioner general, who was well liked and respected by his peers and had a long association with the International Bureau of Expositions. He and his team, which included his deputies, Bob Dawson and Claude Servant, originally had a target of twenty foreign countries. They got fifty-four, including, for the first time, the superpowers of the Soviet Union, the United States, and the People's Republic of China on the same world's fair site in North America. Occasionally, at the suggestion of the commissioner general I went along on the foreign trips. Overseas, I found some good people in External Affairs who were co-operative and supported our objectives. Once I was flying in from Germany to meet the commissioner general in Russia. I can still remember being in the Frankfurt airport, sicker than I'd ever felt in my life. I don't know what it was, but I went into the men's washroom, laid down on the floor in front of the toilets, used my bag as a pillow, and stayed there until the Aeroflot flight was leaving. Once in Moscow, I revived. It was winter—it's always winter in Moscow—and by the time I left, the Jim Pattison Group was the official sponsor of the Canadian Embassy hockey team. The staff asked if we'd finance them for their games against the other embassies. We shipped them new helmets, pads, gloves, and uniforms with "Jim Pattison" on the front and the Expo symbol on the back. They sent us a thank-you letter saying they did well in their diplomatic league.

The Russians, meanwhile, were still deciding what they wanted to do with their pavilion at Expo. We met their officials in a spartan room in a building across the street from the Kremlin. During our conversation, one Russian said they wanted to have a restaurant in their pavilion but didn't want to run it themselves.

"Why?" I asked through an interpreter.

"Because," he replied, "we don't want to deal with your unions."

And, in fact, a fellow from Chilliwack operated their restaurant.

On another trip, I was with the commissioner general and Claude Richmond in Prague to sign up Czechoslovakia as a participant. It was 10:30 in the morning when we met the Czech Minister of Transport and his party for the formalities. Afterwards, our hosts served us glasses of a lethal drink they call *becherovka*. The stuff was supposed to be good for the stomach. It tasted awful, so strong that it felt like it was tearing your throat out. After about three toasts, I was starting to sweat. Then they gave us demitasses of Turkish coffee, so syrupy that a spoon could stand up in it. Claude, who likes to kid, said: "This is the first coffee I've ever had that not only hits the spot, it removes it." And: "I thought coming all the way from Canada, you'd serve us something strong." Humour doesn't always translate well. "Oh," the Minister of Transport said, "*slivovitz!*" And he poured us some of that colourless plum brandy that's like drinking straight alcohol. I counted thirteen toasts that day during business hours. In the evening, guests at a mime theatre, Claude and the commissioner general fell asleep. At Expo, the Czechs were superb, not only in creating their own pavilion but also in producing a witty history of transportation at The Roundhouse and contributing to the Telecom Canada Pavilion, the Via Rail exhibition, and even the Pavilion of Promise, which celebrated Christianity.

I made eight trips to Communist countries and, of them all, I found Cuba had the friendliest and happiest people. I was pushing to have Cuba at Expo, knowing that the possibility of a visit from Fidel Castro would get the Americans' attention, sell a lot of tickets, and garner worldwide publicity

At the very least, we hoped to get their best baseball team for what might be an Expo-sponsored true world series involving Japanese, Americans, and Canadians. We flew down to Havana in my jet and the Cubans greeted us at the airport with rum daquiris and soldiers carrying sub-machine guns. What I found fascinating was that the streets of the city looked like the world's biggest used-car lot. Aside from late-model Russian Ladas, Havana was full of DeSotos, Chevys, and Edsels from the '40s and '50s—no new American cars since the revolution in '59. The government people were gracious, putting us up in a faded Spanish-looking mansion in the diplomatic quarter, complete with a cook to serve us breakfast. The next day, we were meeting in the Ministry of Transport when one official surprised me by asking if I'd be interested in getting involved in a joint venture with the Cuban government. They'd done their homework: At lunch one day, a key government fellow said he'd read the section about me in Peter Newman's *The Acquisitors*.

While the commissioner general was negotiating about Expo, I flew a Cuban tourism official named José Rodriguez to Varadero Beach, a beautiful twenty-kilometre peninsula of powdery white sand in northern Cuba. After the revolution, the houses seized from wealthy Cubans and Americans had become tourist villas. Now the government wanted to build resort hotels there—maybe with me. On our flight back, I told José I'd be willing to finance half the cost of a hotel if the numbers were right. But I needed a firm contract. "Capitalists like me are very worried about the Communists. It's very important when we sign a contract that it's good."

We left with nothing decided about Expo, but I'd promised to send a team of Pattison Group people back within five weeks. I paid a second visit there myself with some of the best architecture, construction, and hotel consultants in North America to look at building a hotel complex at Varadero. The irrepressible Claude Richmond came along too. One morning he looked up at the ceiling in the house he was staying in and said: "If you're there, my shower's broken." When he returned later, it was fixed. On this trip, I met the vice-president of Cuba, Carlos Raphael Rodriguez. He was seventy-one years old. He'd gone up into the mountains with Castro, instructed him in the ways of Communism, and helped him organize the revolution. I was impressed by the fact that

Rodriguez had a television set in his office that let him watch American programs by satellite. "I'll show you what's on in New York," he told me, and turned on the CNN cable network to monitor the news.

Our group took the two-and-a-half-hour drive out to Varadero a couple of times in a van, swimming in the bathwater-warm Caribbean, and talking to Cuban people, asking questions and seeing how they lived. At the resort, our consultants saw problems with the project. Later, after we'd returned home and they gave us a thorough written report, I made one final trip to Havana to tell the Ministry of Tourism that I wouldn't be doing a joint venture with the Cuban government. The infrastructure that tourists in western countries demand—especially good shopping—just didn't exist in Cuba.

The Cubans did come to Expo, even if they didn't bring their baseball team or Fidel Castro. They did the best they could with the money they had, but their little pavilion was probably the poorest on the site.

Wherever I went, I paid my own way—all my expenses as well as the entertaining of eighteen thousand people on our boat and the cost of the many Expo trips in our Learjet. My most effective travels for the fair were the visits I made in the Lear to the volunteer Expo community groups across the province. They were our biggest success story because once British Columbians caught the excitement, they became the fair's best supporters and salespeople. They created their own Expo projects which gave them ownership of what had originally been thought of as a strictly Vancouver event. A woman named Maire Shaw did an extraordinary job of organizing these ninety-six volunteer committees outside Vancouver. At one point, Mike Bartlett wanted to cancel the volunteer program. But after I made a couple of trips on my own, I called Bill Bennett and said: "There's something out there in the small towns that's for real." I took the premier's right-hand man, Bud Smith, and deputy-premier Grace McCarthy to Prince Rupert to show them what was happening. Beforehand, I went to the beer parlour to talk to the working guys, where I heard honest-to-goodness opinions about Expo. Knowing what was on people's minds, I was ready for the meeting in a hotel banquet room. After the formal speeches, I opened it up to questions from volunteers, local politicians, service-club members, and the general public. It was on that trip I decided I needed a speechwriter and asked a senior writer on staff, Diana Barkley, to take on the task. When she protested that she wasn't qualified, I said: "Listen, you don't know how to write speeches, I don't know how to give them—we'll learn together." The speeches would always begin by saying Expo would lose between $300 million and $400 million at the gate, which would be paid by provincial lottery funds; the few times we left that out, the first question from the audience was always about the money.

I must have made more than seventy trips. It wasn't unusual to have six hundred or more people come out to hear about Expo. In Lillooett one day, they were celebrating Judge Begbie Days in western garb. I emerged from the jet in a bowler hat and gambler's shirt, playing my pocket trumpet. About a dozen cowboy kidnappers ordered me to get on a horse. I hadn't ridden in a quarter of a century; they had me get on the horse backwards and a picture of me wound up on the front page of *The Vancouver Sun*. These out-of-town visits gave me the heart to keep going. I could sit in Vancouver all day grinding out the grief and the problems and then fly up to a Fort Nelson or a Fernie and hear the positive, involved support of the people, who soaked up news of the fair like sponges.

In Vancouver, meanwhile, we were holding pre-Expo community meetings every second Friday morning for everybody from groups of cab drivers to clergymen. About three hundred at a time would gather in the Big House in the Folklife area to hear about their specific interests from fair officials. We'd stay there for a couple of hours until every question was answered. And immediately follow up on any legitimate criticism, no matter how mild.

One of our best decisions—one strongly recommended by Mike Bartlett—was to open up the Expo Centre a year before the fair began. Seventeen storeys high, the mirror-like steel geodesic dome, fondly referred to as the Golfball, was an instant landmark. With its huge OMNIMAX film screen and three revolving theatres, the popular Centre gave people a preview of the flair and fun we were promising. It was a good staff training ground for the main event and set a standard of excellence in the public's eyes.

By late '85, a good feeling about Expo was beginning to build in B.C. Our problem was to sell it to everyone else, especially the Americans, who'd seen two of their recent world's fairs end disastrously. Knoxville's in '82 had forced the Tennessee city to increase taxes by 8 per cent to pay off a $76 million debt; New Orleans in '84 went bankrupt with a $100 million debt and five million fewer visitors than forecast. They gave the whole exposition movement a black eye. Neither of those fairs was backed by senior governments and neither attracted much corporate or international support. We had both the provincial and federal governments behind ours as well as the legacy of Expo 67 which suggested that Canadians really know how to do this sort of thing. And from the early days, when Britain signed on and Queen Elizabeth II visited Vancouver to invite the world to Expo 86, there was the expectation that we'd attract several dozen international participants.

But we needed more than all that. This was a one-time, five-and-a-half-month happening; there was no second chance. We knew we had to attract visitors from long distances. Knoxville had an attendance of 8.5 million from a population of 73 million within eight hundred miles; New Orleans 7.2 million from a pool of nearly 50 million. Within eight hundred miles of Vancouver, there are only 12.6 million people —and we were hoping for 13.75 million visits. Knowing that, we'd done the most extensive market research in the 150-year history of world's fairs. If I came out of Expo learning anything, it was the importance of doing good research. We interviewed people in small focus groups in Alberta, eastern Canada, and down to the Pacific coast. What we discovered shocked us: Visitors wouldn't come to our fair unless there was another reason for travelling to Vancouver. Californians, for instance, wanted to see red-coated Mounties and rugged mountains; the last thing they wanted to see was a lot of other people. So, our California TV commercials featured a Mountie and B.C.'s natural beauty—and, oh, by the way, come to Expo 86. It was one of sixteen different commercials we produced to focused audiences (in Quebec, we conjured up the magic of Expo 67). They were the cornerstone of the continent's largest single marketing campaign ever, a $90 million effort by Expo and our corporate sponsors.

When I became president, I discovered the astonishing fact that there was nothing in the budget for advertising in the United States. We called the ad agencies in and told

Expo

them to get moving on it with about $10 million worth of TV commercials, magazine ads, and 130 newspaper supplements. We paid for journalists from the States and fifty other countries to make pre-Expo familiarization trips. And—one of the most inspired moves—we asked the people of the province to give us the names of friends and relatives they'd like to visit Expo and we'd have the premier send personal invitations on their behalf. The "B.C. Invites the World" direct-mail campaign distributed 1.5 million letters. It not only helped convince thousands to come, it also took some of the pressure off the hotels because the visitors stayed with the friends or relatives who'd invited them.

In the year leading up to the fair, we also got some great free publicity—well, at last it was free for Expo. Glancing through an American paper one day on the jet, I read that Sotheby's would be auctioning the Rolls-Royce that John Lennon had owned for eleven years. After the Beatles and the Rolling Stones used it for touring, Lennon donated it in '77 to the Cooper-Hewitt Smithsonian Museum of Design in New York, which was selling it to raise money. The '65 Rolls Phantom had a psychedelic paint job, all swirly floral patterns. *What a terrific exhibit to attract the kids to Expo*, I thought. With all due respect, not all of the pavilions at a world's fair are always entertaining. Expo had to be fun; here was a chance to lighten things up and still be faithful to one of our themes, transportation. And think of the publicity. Now, I didn't expect to use taxpayers' money to pay the couple of hundred thousand it would probably cost. I decided to go to Sotheby's in New York myself and buy it through Ripley's Believe It or Not!

I'd attended only a few auctions. The first was after my mother called me up after my father's death and told me that a rare '39 Packard V-12 was being auctioned in Vancouver (Dad had sold Packards). I outbid the Rothmans Craven Foundation at $20,000. Then at a black-tie auction in the ballroom of the Bayshore Inn, I spent $1,000 on a puppy. I'd had dogs all my life and my latest one had just been killed. I thought the auctioneer said the dog was a male Labrador. It turned out to be a female golden retriever. Mary was so mad at me for getting another dog for her to look after that she wouldn't speak to me on the way home; I had to drive with the pup on the lap of my tuxedo, worried that it was going to wet me. We still have Brackenhollows Tewkesbury the Third ("Tookie"). And then I'd bought the Canadian Fishing Company at a court auction, paying about $1 million more than we could have got it for if we'd listened to the trustee in bankruptcy. As Ted McDowell of the Toronto-Dominion says, "Jimmy's so competitive, he should never go to an auction."

I talked to Ted before the Sotheby's auction and arranged for a letter of credit from the bank for $350,000 to $400,000. Ripley's president, John Withers, figured the Lennon car was worth, at most, $50,000. But there was a reserve bid of $210,000 and I was prepared to go as high as $500,000.

At the Manhattan auction house, they gave me a green Sotheby's paddle for bidding. I had three competitors: two anonymous people calling in their bids by phone and the world's biggest Rolls-Royce dealer at the front of the room. I was out on the floor, too, with John Withers, in the rear, my back against the wall. The bidding started quickly, but by the time we got up to about $800,000, there were only the Rolls dealer and me left. I never hesitated. When the total hit $1 million, the audience started cheering our every bid. When we topped $2 million, it was deathly silent. Maureen Chant, my protective assistant, was in the audience, her head in her hands. "He's going to buy the darn car," she whispered to her seatmate. I did—for $3.1 million Canadian. That was the highest price that had ever been paid up to that time for any car, much less a used one (the following year, a '31 Bugatti Royale went for $6.5 million U.S. to a Texas real-estate developer).

We got a tidal wave of publicity. The story was on "Entertainment Tonight" and other network television, in *People* magazine ("Baby, You Can Drive My Car But It'll Cost You"), and in newspapers around the world. A Czech publicist came to Expo and the first thing she wanted to see was the Lennon car she'd read about in the Communist newspaper in her little town back home. The British asked to have the Rolls outside their pavilion, which is where it stayed until Bill Bennett Day when I donated it to the province and it was moved near The Roundhouse. It's now on display at the Historic Transportation Centre in Cloverdale, B.C.

Throughout the pressures of 1985, I also had a family problem on my mind. My daughter Cindy was expecting for the first time—twins—and she was having a bad time of it. Five months pregnant, ten pounds overweight, she spent a couple of weeks in hospital with a toxic condition that caused severe nausea and vomiting. Then one Sunday not long after, she had to leave church because of a piercing pain in her leg. When she went to hospital to have the foetal heart rate monitored, she happened to mention the pain to a nurse, who called Cindy's obstetrician. Luckily, he was right there doing his rounds. He diagnosed it as a clot in one of her veins, a potentially fatal condition. She went back to hospital for six more weeks. I was in Europe when all this happened; for the first week, I was phoning her several times a day.

Her delivery, by Caesarean section, went well. But in the middle of the night, she began throwing up and had a seizure. Her body was so full of toxins from her troubled pregnancy that she stopped breathing. A resuscitation team had to revive her. I came to see her the next day. The drapes were drawn in her room. She was under sedation, intravenous tubes were stuck in her, and she looked awful. "Boy, Cindy," I said quietly, "we nearly lost you." And then she changed the subject.

She spent another two weeks in hospital before going home with her healthy twins—Mary (after her mother) and Chandos (after my father). They're all doing fine.

By the beginning of 1986, the success of the Expo Centre, the eagerness of our volunteer community groups, the magnitude of our marketing campaign, and the advance publicity from the journalists' familiarization trips were all paying off. The public was enthusiastic as the media grew excited about Expo, predicting that it would restore some of the lustre that world's fairs had lost in North America. Our season-ticket sales soared.

But two months before the fair opened, we had a bout of bad press across Canada as landlords of low-priced downtown East-Side hotels evicted their tenants to make room for Expo visitors. I was sympathetic to the plight of the poor and elderly people who were being forced to find other quarters. For years I'd played my trumpet down on Hastings Street for the Pentecostal Mission. In fact, the Mission was just across the road from the Downtown Eastside Residents Association (DERA), whose organizer, Jim Green, asked me to come and see what the hotel-owners were doing. It was a provincial-government problem, not Expo's, but I went and walked through the area. There were about five hundred people being evicted from hotels and rooming-houses that were really awful. I liked Jim Green; he's a bright guy. But he was so politically opposed to the Social Credit government that he lost a lot of his effectiveness. I offered to go to Victoria to talk to the government as a private individual if the Expo board didn't want to become involved. And I did let the government know that, though the majority of residents being kicked out were not on welfare, there were some who could not help themselves.

One night I joined Jim Green and Mayor Mike Harcourt at a forum to discuss Expo's impact on the downtown East-Side residents. The Ukrainian Hall was full of senior citizens, native people, the handicapped. As I was speaking, an egg smacked me squarely on my temple. I smiled, but continued talking, the yolk dripping down my cheek. It was thrown so hard that it left a welt. My first thought was that the guy was an excellent shot. Then I wondered if there were more eggs coming. Just then, a second one sprayed me as it hit Jim Green. Jim apologized to me, and some of his people washed off my car, which had been smeared with eggs and scratched with a key or nail that caused $1,000 damage. I decided not to lay charges against two men whom police had arrested.

Fortunately for those evicted, the province had an on-going housing program and there were enough places for them to go. Although the media didn't follow up, in some cases the dispossessed people were far better off, thanks to the efforts of organizations like DERA. But for a while, because of the national publicity, Expo had egg on its face.

CHAPTER NINETEEN

A Year to Remember

It rained May 2, 1986. All of the early criticism of Expo, the nay-saying and doom-crying, was drowned in a sea of celebration. The world's media were in love with us. And so were the people from thirty-nine countries, every province, and every state who had bought advance tickets. We'd already pre-sold fifteen million visits—and I was predicting that we'd hit twenty million. The $1.6 billion exposition had sixty-six governments involved in eighty pavilions, theatres, and plazas. There were one hundred and ten places to eat. Fourteen thousand live shows, most of them free, from street entertainers to big names like Bill Cosby and Julio Iglesias, the world's best-selling singer. And more than two hundred and fifty performances at an off-site World Festival produced by Ann Farris Darling, who'd managed to lure the La Scala opera company and the Kirov Ballet in its first North American appearance in two decades. Fourteen specialized periods mixed new technology and nostalgia in displays and demonstrations of the fair's themes, transportation and communications. The Expo site itself, under creative director Ron Woodall's imaginative direction, was a crazy-quilt of colour and light; as Ron liked to say, "There's an awful lot of fun here and it's all my fault."

The staff of the fair and the international participants had been pushing night and day to make sure everything was ready for the opening. I'd driven through the grounds in my red Pontiac convertible at 5:30 that morning, making notes: Garbage cans need emptying; somebody's left a hose lying around. We had a quick staff briefing where I pointed out the trouble spots, sounded my trumpet, and yelled: "Charge!" At the gates, I greeted a couple I'd met in the B.C. Interior—they'd been on the road from Newfoundland for seven weeks—and had asked to be the first into the fair. My first stop was at the pavilion of my birthplace, Saskatchewan. The first province to sign up, it led the others in spirit and commitment to the fair (at one point during Expo, it held the world's biggest reunion when twelve thousand natives of Saskatchewan threw a party at B.C. Place Stadium). Then I went on to the British Columbia Pavilion, and by car to the spectacular sail-topped Canada Pavilion on its separate harbour site. There, the Prince and Princess of Wales—Charles and Di—were joined by Prime Minister Mulroney and his wife to officially open the national host pavilion.

Although most of our staff were already suffering from Expo burnout, it didn't show as we watched the Royal Couple cut the ceremonial ribbon. Bill Sleeman was there as a director of the Canada Place waterfront complex; I spoke briefly to him about business for the first time in three weeks. But my mind was preoccupied with security. One of my biggest fears was the threat of terrorists at the fair. On hand were 250 Mounties and city police in plainclothes and uniform. It all went like clockwork. But I was on edge, impatient. As I told a reporter, "I'm going back to work as soon as I get outta here."

After lunch with Soviet officials, I started walking the grounds, listening to comments from fair-goers. We did the first of our exit surveys that were conducted on all but the last three days of Expo, polling between five hundred and a thousand people daily. I told the staff, "I don't care how old people are or where they come from. I want to know where the hot dogs are cold, where the washrooms are dirty—and we'll fix them. Every single day, we're gonna make Expo better." Every night George Madden would compile a list of complaints from the Expo Information phone system and the guest-relations office and deliver them to the 7:00 A.M. operations meeting. That's where all the problems were dissected and solved.

A Year to Remember

That first afternoon, nearly seventy thousand people attended the ceremonies in the B.C. Place Stadium where Prince Charles opened the world exposition. Mary was with me, and my good friend Mike Dingman and his wife, Betsy, who were staying with us and had met Charles and Di the day before on a ferry trip from Nanaimo. And one of the real thrills for me was that my eighty-six-year-old mother was there and would later manage to see a lot of the fair.

At one point, when Premier Bennett was speaking, tourism minister Claude Richmond whispered to me: "Get up, Jimmy, they're giving you a standing ovation." I was so tired and so focused on what still had to be done that I hadn't even noticed. Afterwards, Liberal leader John Turner said, "That will be the highlight of your life, Jimmy." But at the time, though I was grateful, I didn't even have a moment to think about it.

From the start, we were an artistic and entertainment success and attendance was better than anyone had expected. But as the numbers started rolling in, we began to realize that the $311 million deficit we'd predicted could easily skid out of control to $405 million. At first we were happy about the high rate of season's pass-holders—35 per cent—but it proved to be a problem. Although they attended the fair an average of 13.5 times, per capita they spent far less on food, rides, and merchandise than those holding one- and three-day passes.

Yet I knew we had to increase costs in at least one major area: entertainment. The budget wasn't big enough to provide the fun and free entertainment that was vital on the site. Even though revenues were down, the last thing you do is hurt your product; you only try to improve it.

Decreased revenues, increased budgets: We had to cut our overhead immediately. One way was privatizing all the restaurants and other concessions, allowing outside entrepreneurs to run them instead of us. It lowered our projected earnings but also reduced our risk and overhead. The other way was to cut our operational costs. Three weeks into the fair, I told every vice-president that we had to trim 10 per cent off our overhead and our employee count. There was no negotiating. "I want you to think of this as your money," I told them. We were soon running with only about four thousand on the Expo office payroll, roughly two thousand fewer than when we'd opened.

The people who stayed were generally superb. I was surrounded by three women who exemplified the quality of the staff. Kathie Moseley was my secretary, hard-working, efficient, and unflappable on the firing line. The equally cool-headed Fran Steed handled complaints and requests—anything from bikers who had their Harleys towed away to people who wanted to peddle things at the fair (like buffalo chips, which were flat fried bread slices coated with sugar and lemon, and which we didn't handle). And Jane Butler, our bubbly manager of guest relations who was also responsible for VIP services, helped train three thousand volunteers and two hundred hosts and hostesses on staff who spoke thirty-four different languages. They described themselves as the Official People Department of Expo 86. According to our surveys, the staff and volunteers were by far the most popular attraction at Expo. Next on the list was the cleanliness of the site. That was the department of Bjarne Christensen, director of design, signage, and grounds, working with assistant manager John Mitchell. They'd remove as much as 150 tons of garbage a day. And the site, although it was built on two miles of seawater frontage, was so clean that I never once spotted a scavenging seagull.

The Jim Pattison Group has since hired about ten people who worked at the fair. Fran—who'd been such a big help to me—became an administrative assistant with our Automotive Group. I hired Jane to work on human resources, Quality Circles, and employee-involvement programs. Bjarne is working for Neon Products. Communications vice-president George Madden is general manager of CJOR and CJJR. Oh, and at a post-fair liquidation auction I bid $53,000 for Expo Ernie, the exposition's little robot mascot, who's as busy as ever in Corporate Office for promotions and charitable functions.

If the people I worked with at the fair were a good half of the pleasure I had there, the other half were the fair-goers I was privileged to meet. The folks who came up to me with a smile to tell me how much they enjoyed the dazzling sights and sensations, like the magical smoke-and-mirrors show at the GM Pavilion's Spirit Lodge, the most popular on site. (On the other hand, our exit surveys showed the U.S. Pavilion had the highest disappointment rating.)

I also had the pleasure of meeting scores of prominent politicians, business people, and celebrities. Among the snapshots in my mind are the opening days with the Prince and Princess of Wales. They were a sensation wherever they went. I'd met him years before at the Calgary Stampede and was impressed by his quick intelligence and general attitude. At Expo, I probably talked more to Princess Diana, who was very gentle and soft in spirit. To co-ordinate their tour, I brought in Maureen Chant from Corporate Office, who was always at least one step ahead of their schedule to prevent unwelcome surprises. On their one day off, when they wanted to evade the media, we put them in my dog van. I have a Chevy van that I use only to take my golden retriever, Tookie, down to the beach or to bring into work. And that's what Their Royal Highnesses used to slip away to take a private jaunt to Vancouver Island where they met Galen Weston of George Weston Limited (Prince Charles plays on his polo team in England).

The young Princess Diana was quite a contrast to Princess Margaret, a much more worldly woman. Princess Margaret is well informed and interested in life. And a good sport. When she visited Expo, I took her out on the *Nova Springs*. We had photographers on board, but she had her own little camera and took pictures of the harbour, the Coast mountains, and even the boat. When I played the organ for her, she asked me not to do "The Red River Valley." So as the Princess was about to leave, I started playing the tune and people sang along until she came over and said: "Isn't that dreadful?"

One of the most impressive people I met at the fair—and probably in my life—was Margaret Thatcher. After flying in on a Concorde, the British Prime Minister had a private meeting for nineteen Canadian business people, including me. She spoke about the world economy, opportunities in Britain, Ronald Reagan, and voiced her concern that the industrialized nations should avoid protectionism. I met her a couple of other times, when her knowledge of world economics and politics staggered me. She is one tough, smart woman. After that gathering at the Hotel Vancouver, I walked away thinking that I'd never met anybody with quite her combination of qualities. In one of her speeches, she said: "It was Britain's good fortune to put Vancouver on the map two hundred years ago. Now we're putting Britain back on your map—as a source of ideas, a centre of new technology, a reliable trading partner, and an active friend." As a direct result of her encouragement to look at business possibilities in Britain, I flew over there on a scouting mission after Expo.

I have more mental snapshots. We took American vice-president George Bush out on the boat and he insisted on looking at all the staterooms and going through the white-carpeted engine room. A tall, good-looking fellow, full of energy, he struck me as the consummate American politician. Lee Iacocca visited at a time when the media were trying to promote him as a presidential candidate. The Chrysler chairman, who'd recently overseen the restoration of the Statue of Liberty, arrived with his attractive new wife. She was a live wire, with a lot of punch. "Peggy," I said, "tell me about yourself."

"Well, I'm a tobacco farmer's daughter and I was a flying waitress for ten years and I decided to go to work for the Statue of Liberty Committee, just as an ordinary worker. And when they had the dedication on July the Fourth, I found myself standing between the vice-president of the United States and Lee Iacocca. Who would have believed it?"

Surprisingly enough, I didn't talk cars with Lee Iacocca. But I did ask him about the biggest problem he faced in his business. "The number-one problem in my job," he said, "is to get people to understand that their jobs are at risk." We had lunch aboard the *Nova Springs* on a beautiful summer day; later, he sent me an autographed copy of his best-selling autobiography. Lee was just what I'd visualized: strong face, good sense of humour, a very human guy.

Malcolm Forbes was all that I ever imagined and far more. One of the world's richest men, the publisher of *Forbes* magazine roared into Vancouver on one of the seventy motorcycles he keeps in his homes around the world. He has, among others, a palace in Morocco and a château in France, where he flies his hot-air balloons. He arrived after a tour through the Rockies with ten other bikers, all of them in red T-shirts emblazoned with the *Forbes* slogan, "Capitalist Tool." He lives a storybook life: After driving in on his Harley-Davidson, he had a 727 pick him up and fly him to New

York. During the several times we saw each other, he kept encouraging me to make a decision that would have forever shaped my future.

Malcolm Forbes was in town a month after one of the most astonishing political announcements British Columbia had heard in years. Everyone, including me, had assumed that Bill Bennett intended to use a successful Expo 86 as a launching platform to propel him into another term as premier. On May 22, I was in a meeting when my secretary, Kathie Moseley, came in to announce that the premier was resigning. I was startled: We'd been together on many Expo volunteer-committee trips and he'd given me no indication, in his speech or manner, that he was even thinking of quitting. A couple of hours later, I saw a big scrum of television cameras and radio mikes at the Expo office. Somebody said the reporters were there to ask me if I'd be a candidate for leadership of the Social Credit party. The question was strictly out of left field. It honestly hadn't even dawned on me to consider the option.

I was with one of our politically active directors, Alison Robinson, and George Madden. "What do I tell these people?"

"What's your interest?" George asked.

"No interest. But I haven't really thought it through."

George advised me to say: "The answer is no, I'm not interested, but I would never say never to anything."

That was enough to encourage endless speculation in the media, and elsewhere. Two days later, I was in bed on a Saturday morning when the phone rang. A very senior cabinet minister was calling: "Jimmy, we've carefully analysed who's available and we think that you're the person to be the next leader of the party. And we don't think there'll be any problem with the nomination if you run."

After we discussed the other potential candidates, including Bill Vander Zalm, I told the caller that I'd carefully consider it.

If I did decide to run, I knew that the first person I'd call for advice would be one of the most impressive Canadian politicians I've ever encountered: David Peterson, the Liberal premier of Ontario. I'd met him on several occasions during Expo and each time I came away with higher regard for his sincerity and intelligence. That evening I discussed the offer with Mary, who'd been living patiently with all my absences because of Expo and with the fact that, in recent years, I'd been a target because of my high visibility. That day I swam and swam in my pool and that night, trying to make up my mind, I didn't get much sleep. The next morning, Mary had gone early to church. She'd left a note: "Go for it." I couldn't believe it.

It wasn't my first offer to enter politics. But I've never felt the need to join any political party, much less represent one. My dad always wanted me to go into politics. "Jimmy," he'd say, "one day, I think you should run for mayor of Vancouver." He was a Liberal and so, growing up, that's what I was. I even voted for Trudeau the first time in '68. When I felt the Liberals weren't paying enough attention to Western Canada, like a lot of business people I began to vote Conservative. But although I think Joe Clark is a decent fellow, I wasn't keen on him as leader of the country.

Provincially, I've always been a Social Credit supporter. Having said that, I've never looked on the New Democrats in B.C. as quite the monsters that some people did. When Dave Barrett's NDP government came into power in '72, I made a speech in Victoria that urged the B.C. business community to be reasonable and understanding—instead of knocking the socialists, let's try working with them. Dave himself is a first-class man. I have great respect for his sincerity and integrity. He came from the same side of town as I did, the East End. We couldn't be farther away from one another politically, but I like him personally. (This isn't the strangest pairing of a socialist with a capitalist in the car business: I read recently that Lenin was a great admirer of Henry Ford.) In '75, when the Socreds defeated the NDP, I offered Dave a job in Corporate Office, doing any number of things. He didn't accept, but I later hired one of his appointees, Jim Rhodes, who'd run a successful Crown corporation, B.C. Petroleum. Because of his political background, Jim had a hard time getting work so I used him on special projects for several months. In 1982, I invited Dave Barrett to address our Partners in Pride conference. He spoke on the evils of capitalism and the ways free enterprise was destroying itself—drawing several good questions. When he stepped down as party leader two years later, I asked him to run our Quality Circle program; he had a master's in social work and

A Year to Remember

was good with people. Not interested in that, he did bite when CJOR's manager, Harvey Gold, then offered him a job as an open-line radio host (he left recently to pursue a career in federal politics). To this day, I consider Dave Barrett a good friend.

The only time I've ever tried for any public office was in the '60s when I ran for the board of the Pacific National Exhibition in Vancouver; I lost. My first real political involvement was in '66, helping in the provincial campaign of Les Peterson, the Socred Minister of Education and Labour, and his new running mate, Grace McCarthy. I donated some money and supplied them with some convertibles. They both won their seats.

If I'd wanted, I might have been a Socred candidate in the next election. The premier, W.A.C. Bennett, called me one day to meet him in his suite at the Hotel Vancouver. I considered him, with the force of his personality and his strength of mind, one of the two giants of British Columbia: He and J.V. Clyne, chairman of MacMillan Bloedel, stood head and shoulders above everyone else. "Jimmy," the premier said, "we'd like you to run for the Social Credit party in the next election."

"Well, there'd only be one job I'd be interested in, ultimately, if I ran," I said. "I'd like to talk about future leaders of the party. Who might they be?"

We discussed Bob Bonner, the attorney general, whom he had a lot of confidence in but didn't believe had enough pizzazz; Phil Gaglardi, the controversial highways minister, who wasn't that popular with the cabinet; and newcomer Herb Capozzi, who had a high public profile.

"Herb Capozzi," the premier said, "doesn't know whether he wants to be a politician, a businessman, a sportsman, or a playboy. I don't think he's really going to be a factor."

He called me back a week later for my decision. I said no. At that point, I'd begun buying Neon Products stock. If I hadn't been involved in my first major takeover, I probably would have gone into politics.

A few years later, members of the Non-Partisan Association, a right-wing municipal party, were interested in having me run for the Vancouver mayoralty. The fact that J.V. Clyne was one of their supporters seriously influenced me. But I was having one of my regular weekly lunches with my old pal

Jack Wasserman, the *Sun* columnist, when he put everything clearly into context: "What happens if you *win*, Jimmy?"

I've had several encounters with the federal Liberals. In '67, a local senator, George van Roggen, asked if I'd help stage a dinner in Vancouver for Prime Minister Lester Pearson. My associates, Maureen Chant and Wilf Ray, had earned a reputation for mounting spectacular productions for groups like the tourist association. When they decided to create an elaborate show for the Liberals that involved dances from different eras, I was so sure it would bomb that I stayed in Hawaii. It was a wonderful success; "Proud Night for the West," said *The Vancouver Sun*.

I was much more personally involved in the Paul Martin campaign for the Liberal leadership a year later. This followed the Neon Products takeover when Paul Nathanson of the Famous Players theatre chain helped me regain my credit line with the Royal Bank. In return, he made me promise to help Martin. That's how I got to know Jack Austin well; in those days before he became a senator, he'd run unsuccessfully for the Liberals and now was working for Paul Martin in Vancouver. He got me together with Jack Gibson, a former Liberal MP, and George McKeen, son of the late Liberal senator Stanley McKeen. The four of us underwrote the B.C. campaign for Martin. I helped organize a 1,200-seat dinner for him, drove him around to coffee-party meetings, even found rubbers for him when it was raining. Ahead 2 to 1 in the early polls, Paul Martin got beaten by a dark horse named Pierre Trudeau.

In 1972, another dark horse was emerging on the B.C. scene. That election year, Dave Barrett's New Democrats were posing a distinct threat to twenty years of Socred government. Premier W.A.C. Bennett invited me and fifteen others to a dinner where he made a speech about how dangerous socialism was and how the province was in good health and good hands. The other guests—captains of industry, Vancouver Club types—spoke up to say what a good job he was doing, but I was silent. The premier noticed. "Jimmy, you haven't said a word. What do you think?"

"Mr. Bennett, sir, I don't agree with you that everything is good in the province. I think that you're in trouble politically. I think the message out there is negative."

He got mad and and gave me a lecture on loyalty and the need to support Social Credit as a party and him as premier.

"Well, you misunderstand me, sir," I said. "I'm just telling you that the tone out there right now is anti-W.A.C. Bennett."

I went home with my tail between my legs. The next thing we all knew, Dave Barrett was premier.

Now, nearly fifteen years later, I was being approached to run for the Socred party leadership and, with it, the premiership. Mary had given me her blessing to go for it. But my friend Ray Smith of MacMillan Bloedel—Ray Smith, who'd warned me about taking on the Expo chairmanship—called me when he heard the speculation and said: "Don't do it."

There were many reasons not to. One was Expo: To run for the leadership that summer, I'd have to leave the fair before it was finished. There was another, larger obstacle that I'd come to appreciate during my time at Expo: the enormous potential for conflicts of interest. With all the companies the Jim Pattison Group owned in the province, I would be in trouble every time I turned around as premier. Overwaitea is located in shopping centres, where provincial liquor stores lease space. AirBC handled an incredible amount of government traffic between Vancouver and the capital city of Victoria. Mainland Magazine tenders for contracts to distribute periodicals on the government ferry system. Our car companies sell and lease to the government. Neon Products bids on projects for Crown corporations like B.C. Rail and B.C. Place Stadium. *Beautiful British Columbia* continues to work very closely with the provincial tourism department, from whom we bought the magazine. CJOR carries government advertising. Trans Ad bids for transit-advertising contracts that cover every vehicle run by B.C. Transit, a Crown corporation. EDP Industries has had some computer business with the provincial government. Great Pacific Capital would like to do some business with the government. If I wanted to avoid any hint of conflict of interest, I'd have to sell every one of our companies except Ripley's Believe It or Not!

Selling, I'd be abandoning the people closest to me who had built the company over so many years. I'd already left them for three full years. And I was anxious to get back into the business world. At Expo, I'd had a taste of the public life. People considered me a semi-politician, and I had to answer to literally thousands, from cabinet ministers to special-interest groups like pensioners and the handicapped. And, as *Forbes* magazine would later quote me as saying: "Since working with the government, I've learned patience. But I don't like operating this slowly."

After considering the offer over the weekend, I phoned the cabinet minister and said, "No, thank you."

That didn't stop the attempts to convince me otherwise. For a few weeks my name kept surfacing in the newspapers as a possible candidate. During that time, Malcolm Forbes was one of the people urging me on. We were on the boat one night when he said: "Jimmy, run for premier."

"You're a smart fellow. Why don't you go into politics?" I asked.

"Well, I tried in New Jersey and failed miserably. I got soundly defeated."

But he kept pressuring me on the two other occasions we met: "After this, you ought to get involved in public life. If you go back to business, you're just another guy running a company. But in politics, you could do some good things. You'll never regret it."

Malcolm Forbes is a wise and knowledgeable person; he made me reconsider. Then a delegation of five Socreds, including cabinet ministers, came to see me. And they said, in effect: "Here are the polls. It looks like you have a chance of winning this thing without a lot of trouble." I had about a 50 per cent lead over the nearest contender, Bill Vander Zalm, who'd been out of the Socred government for a few years. Attorney General Brian Smith was second, followed by the premier's assistant, Bud Smith.

When I raised the issue of conflict of interest, there was a difference of opinion. Some in the delegation thought I'd have to sell our companies; others who were lawyers thought there might be a way of creating blind trusts. I didn't buy it, although I promised to reconsider. Which I did, for one night. The next day, I said: "Thanks, but I've decided against it."

Bill Vander Zalm won the leadership handily and succeeded Bill Bennett as premier.

I was approached later by both the federal Liberal and Conservative parties to run as an MP. I respectfully declined.

A Year to Remember

* * *

I continued to oversee the world's fair. The five and a half months were a blur as we went from success to success. In August, which was almost continuously sunny, we broke our original attendance target of 13.75 million. In September, when people expected the crowds to slacken, they held and built through October. The word of mouth had raced around the world. Some of the very top executives from American and Japanese companies started arriving in the fall. Meanwhile, all the local people who were going to savour the quiet off-months descended en masse. On the second-last day, 341,000 flooded the site. The final attendance was 22,111,578 visits.

And, best of all, we came in under the budget that we had committed to Premier Bennett and his cabinet and the people of British Columbia. The total deficit was $279 million—which was $32 million better than we'd promised the government.

There was other good news. As I told the Sales and Marketing Executives of Toronto in accepting their 1986 award on behalf of Expo, "The things I worried about most didn't happen. No terrorists. No labour stoppages. No serious bad weather. No financial surprises. And no scams."

At a news conference at 11:00 A.M. on October 13, the final day of the fair, I resigned as chairman of Expo and B.C. Place. That evening, after the official closing ceremonies, we threw a party in the domed stadium for the staff and volunteers; forty-two thousand showed up. I gave a speech thanking them. Then I went back to my Expo office, cleaned out my desk, and put my belongings in the car. A little after ten I came back to the stadium, worked my way through the crowd, saying goodbyes, and climbed to the second row from the top of the stands. People came up to have me sign their Expo passports, but most of the time I sat there alone. Looking down on the boisterous party, I was thinking that it could have been better organized, but I didn't spot any big problems. Overall, I was feeling good about the last six years. I'd done it, stuck with it through the hills and valleys. I was relieved. And very happy it was over. At ten to twelve, I walked out and drove home from Expo for the last time. I never went back.

It was time to make a buck for Jimmy.

CHAPTER TWENTY

Back in the Deal Business

A month after Expo's end, I was on the road, getting back into the business life I love, when the letter arrived at our home in West Vancouver's British Properties. The envelope, marked "Personal," was addressed to me. Because I was out of town that November day, Mary opened the letter and read it. The message was brief and brutal. The thrust of it was that somebody was out to kill me and, for a price, the letter-writer would give me the name of the person who was threatening to take my life. The price was $2 million. I was to signal my intention to co-operate by putting a coded notice in a newspaper classified section. Oh, and I better not go to the police.

It was all chillingly familiar. One of the prices of the high visibility I've had as a businessman, and for the past few years as a public servant, is extortion attempts. The most recent one was the tenth I'd received over the years. We—the police and I—take them all seriously. Sometimes the extortionists threaten me, sometimes my family. I've had twenty-four-hour surveillance on my mother and on my daughter Cindy, with police following her to the hospital where she was a nurse and keeping watch while she worked her shift. I try to keep the threats quiet—why frighten the family unnecessarily? But there are times when it's impossible to shield them from this kind of ugliness. Mary knew about a previous incident. She was home on Boxing Day, 1985, when I picked up the phone and heard a threat to my life unless I came up with $2 million. After a money drop was made, police arrested a man and a woman. Though the charges in that case were stayed for lack of evidence, the woman charged later went to jail after being convicted on a similar charge.

This latest attempt quickly grew nasty. While I was still away, someone threw a baseball-sized rock at our bedroom window, cracking the double glazing. Later, we had a disturbing phone call. A man with a gravelly voice laughed and said: "We're going to get you this time." From the first moment, we'd had police in the house with us at all times and private security guards patrolling the grounds. One night, after they spotted a man in our garden, he escaped in a car; it was too dark to see the licence plate. We have a large house—seventeen thousand square feet—but because it has a good security system, Mary wasn't particularly nervous. With her usual fatalistic view, she was less worried about the actual threat than she was bothered about having police with her wherever she went. "You're giving me a terrible reputation," she told the young plainclothes policemen. "People think I'm running around."

The police were with us for about three weeks. They were treating this extortion very seriously, for reasons I can't reveal. We put the ad in the paper. A second letter arrived, with instructions for the money to be driven to a Vancouver suburb and dropped. If I was afraid to come, it said, I could send my wife. Police made the drop. Soon after, they arrested and charged a nineteen-year-old man who allegedly acted as the courier in the extortion bid. At this writing, he was out on bail and the case had yet to be heard.

Like Mary, I believe you can't walk around living in fear twenty-four hours a day. In the words of one of my mother's favourite writers, James Russell Lowell, "Let us be of good cheer, remembering that misfortunes hardest to bear are those which never come."

The morning after Expo closed, I was in the Corporate Office of the Jim Pattison Group.

"I'm glad you're back," Maureen Chant said.

"I'm glad I'm back too," I replied, with a lot more feeling than those few words could express.

After spending an hour in the office, wading through a mountain of mail, I left for meetings around town. The next day, Mary and I and some of the family went to Palm Springs for a week's rest while I reflected on what I wanted to achieve with our Group over the next few years. I had a goal: to have us grow from the $1.4 billion in annual sales during Expo year to $2 billion by '89. (I'm not sure I agree with Peter Newman, who took note of that target in his *Maclean's* column and remarked: "That would put him in a similar league to the Eatons and Bronfmans—except that he earned every penny himself, instead of inheriting a head start.") My batteries recharged by the peace of the desert, I flew to Toronto for a meeting of the board of the Toronto-Dominion Bank. I've been in the air ever since, visiting our operations and looking for deals around the world, especially in the United States.

I did take a few days out of my schedule to check out my health after the hectic pace of Expo. At the Scripps Institute in La Jolla, California, I had a complete physical of my fifty-eight–year–old body. No guarantees, the doctors said, but things looked good. They put me on a treadmill and said I should collapse when the indicator reached 169; I got up to 170 before stopping. But my cholesterol level should be 190 to 200; it was 223. So, for about three weeks I quit eating eggs and red meat altogether, then tried to take them in moderation—which is hard, because I like steaks.

Our companies got their own physical. We called in the international management consultants, Booze Allen, based in New York, for an outsiders' view and a thorough evaluation of each corporate member of the Group. I already knew that I had come back to a pretty healthy business. We now ranked sixty-fourth in size among Canadian companies in *The Financial Post 500*, up ten places from the previous year. (When I told Bob Halliday, one of our directors, that our assets have never been in better shape, he laughed and said: "Maybe we better put you out in the boonies for another three years.") However, as I pointed out in the spring '87 edition of *The Jim Pattison GroupNews*, 1986 "was the first year in a long time that we didn't buy a significant company, but rather, sold off some assets."

Back in the Deal Business

All but one of them were companies that had failed to give us a decent return. We sold Vanguard and Frontier Manufacturing, our recreational-vehicle companies in Kelowna, B.C.; and Trans-Provincial Airlines of Prince Rupert, B.C. And we liquidated one of our recent mistakes, Mimic Systems of Victoria. Mimic had only joined us in '85 as the world-wide licencee of the Spartan, a micro-computer peripheral designed to let the Commodore 64 run the more powerful Apple software and hardware. We hadn't done enough research before getting into Mimic, and the management was inexperienced. In early '87, we continued to get rid of remnants of our real-estate holdings, including a shopping centre in Richmond, B.C., that we sold to Sun Life. Our fruit and vegetable canneries in B.C.'s Okanagan and Fraser valleys were having problems, partly caused by competition from American, European, and Third World products. It looked like a good time to get out. We did a deal with American-based Pillsbury Foods (the Jolly Green Giant people) to buy Fraser Valley Foods, which is in frozen foods as well as being the province's largest processor of agricultural products and Canada's largest fruit-canning operation. And we concluded negotiations with Air Canada to acquire AirBC, which had had a good year.

Meanwhile, we continued buying companies that were natural fits with our existing operations. Joining Trans Ad, Canada's largest transit-advertising company, were Trans Public, Quebec's largest, and Pillar Ad of Toronto, which markets advertising on parking-lot pillars. The Jim Pattison Sign Company acquired the eighty-year-old Martel-Stewart Limited of Winnipeg, an electrical-sign company that was a pioneer in shopping-centre and stripmall sign programs. On Vancouver Island, we acquired three new automobile franchises: Toyota and Hyundai dealerships in Duncan and Victoria's only Toyota franchise, Metro Toyota, which has one of the highest volumes of any Toyota dealership in Canada. And across the street from Jim Pattison Pontiac Buick Cadillac in Vancouver, we opened Jim Pattison Nissan. With these acquisitions, we became the biggest automotive retailer in the nation. In the broadcasting field, as well as Vancouver's CJOR and the new country FM station, CJJR, we now have three new radio stations and a TV station in the B.C. Interior: CFJC and CIFM of Kamloops, CFFM of Williams Lake, and CFJC-TV of Kamloops.

CJOR is currently our only trouble spot, but we've appointed a new general manager, George Madden, a broadcaster who worked with me as vice-president of communications at Expo. Our other operations have been doing well: The sign companies, for example, are expanding on all fronts; Overwaitea Foods recently added three hundred thousand square feet of floor space with four new stores in B.C.; Ripley's Believe It or Not! keeps opening new museum tourist attractions, the latest in Niagara Falls and on Bourbon Street in New Orleans; and under automobile-group president Don Connors, Jim Pattison Pontiac Buick Cadillac—Jim Pattison on Main—has been doing far better than it ever did when Bill Sleeman and I were overseeing it.

To get back into the deal business, to develop a strategy on acquisitions, I wanted to look around at what had been happening in the business world in the years I was away from it. Since Expo, my travels have taken me to Europe, East Asia, Mexico, and the United States.

I made one European trip to take part in an ultra-private financial conference, the first of its kind to be sponsored by the Swiss Bank Corporation, one of the Big Three Swiss banks. There were twenty-two representatives meeting in St. Moritz from around the world, including the heads of major multinational corporations and a former European president; I was the only Canadian. We discussed global economic issues, among them the ECU, the new currency unit of the European Economic Community. I came home to find that our Swiss-based company, Great Pacific Capital, had been dealing in some ECU bonds.

I've been to England a couple of times, following up on the interest that Prime Minister Margaret Thatcher inspired in me during her visit to Expo. With a healthy pound and a wave of foreign investment, Britain has been picking up. We'd done business there before, a successful money-management deal in '82 with Lord Tryon, who is one of Prince Charles's closest friends. They shoot pheasant together and fish during the summer on a river they lease in Iceland. Anthony Tryon, chairman of All Investments, is well-connected in the financial community through directorships in such firms as the merchant bankers Lazard Frères. Mary and I have since visited with him and his wife in the Grand Cayman Islands. When he stopped over in Vancouver in '84, I was so immersed in Expo that I asked Maureen Chant to take him on a tour of our locally based divisions. She drove him to the Neon Products plant and the Overwaitea Foods warehouse (whose sheer size impressed him). When she stopped to make a call from a McDonald's, they had hamburgers in the car. During Expo, Lord Tryon came to visit, and our manager of guest relations, Jane Butler, showed him around. He was interested in how we'd recruited volunteers because he was chairman of a committee to restore old London. Dealing with involved and influential Britons like Lord Tryon, I see a renewed vitality on my trips to England and fresh potential for investment possibilities.

During the fair, Lord Tryon was interested in touring the Republic of Korea Pavilion. The exhibit highlighted that ancient nation's extraordinary achievements in everything from land use to shipbuilding and auto manufacturing. General Tae Joon Park, chairman of Korea's Pohang Iron & Steel Company, had visited Expo and I was invited to his country in early '87. I flew into Seoul, which has exploded into a city of ten million, and found a South Korea that's quickly catching up to its historic rival, Japan. There are building cranes everywhere. Koreans seem to have the inborn energy, optimism, and discipline necessary to succeed in large-scale manufacturing. Once known mostly for their work in ceramics and textiles, they now have strong steel and shipping industries. Korea's massive conglomerate, Hyundai, had an overnight success with the Italian-designed Pony when it entered the Canadian market in '84. The Pony shook up our domestic automobile business, which had been concentrating on competition from Japan. As a new Hyundai dealer, I found it fascinating to meet company chairman Se Yung Chung, who'd recently been quoted as saying: "The workers understand that it is the duty of this generation to sacrifice for the good of the country." Korean wage rates are much lower than the Japanese, averaging about $4 an hour in heavy industry. I visited a new Kia Motors factory that builds cars and trucks. It runs twenty-two hours day, seven days a week. The workers, who do eleven-hour shifts, get time and a half for their three extra hours a day; in the six months since the plant opened, they hadn't had a day off. It's something to behold: These people don't walk, they run. The quality isn't as high yet as in Japan, but it's coming. And Korea is eager for certain foreign investment. With helicopters at our disposal and introductions to the very senior executives, I've never been treated better in all of my travels; even Nelson Davis couldn't have competed with their hospitality. I came home realizing that South Korea may have some significant problems —North Korea, American protectionism, and the continuing riots sparked by the country's univesity students—but economically speaking, it feels like the new Japan. I hope there may be some opportunities to deal with Korea in the future.

Mexico intrigues me too. In Hermosillo, about a hundred and fifty miles south of the Arizona border, I recently saw a new half-billion-dollar Ford factory that is the most automated car-manufacturing plant in the world. Except for its information system, I couldn't see a single piece of equipment from anywhere but Japan. Sixteen hundred Mexican workers, with no experience in the auto industry, operate the plant with no quality-control inspectors on site—and Ford is an industry leader in quality. Employees are organized into teams of fifteen and all workers have the right to push a button that shuts down the assembly line if they spot anything wrong. The American running the plant, who'd worked for Lee Iacocca at Ford, told me that so far he'd never seen more commitment to quality. When I visited, the Mexicans' wage-and-benefits package was $1.12 an hour. Ford is shipping the cars from Hermosillo up to the United States and Canada.

We've since sent consultants to Mexico to do a feasibility study on such things as production and shipping costs, locations, tariffs, and the factors involved in working with the Mexican government. Our idea is that if the conditions are right, the Jim Pattison Group might do some manufacturing in Mexico. My visits there and in East Asia have brought home to me once again the fact that some segments of North American industry are in serious trouble. As I told the Automotive Industries Association of Canada, during its annual convention in Las Vegas, "There's a whole new ball game out there. To stay in the game, this country must compete on price and the quality of the product."

The American economy, although it's under attack, remains attractive. Our Group has been doing business in the United States since 1971. We continue to like Canada as a place to invest, but this nation must become competitive for investors or capital will flow to countries that are politically safe and offer greater returns. Which is why we're looking hard at further opportunities in the United States, where the business environment is somewhat more hospitable. We're probably lagging behind other major Canadian companies that have diversified down south. There's a big attraction there because of President Reagan's new tax structure which is a lot easier on corporations—34 per cent per cent compared to Canada's 50. The American unions are generally more realistic. And on top of all that, you also have the benefit of the exchange rate on the dollar. We try to keep in touch with as many deal-makers down there as we can. Recently I spoke during a panel on human resources at a Los Angeles conference sponsored by the investment bankers Drexel Burnham Lambert. Among the twenty-eight hundred invited were many of the important American entrepreneurial CEOs and colourful corporate raiders, including Boone Pickens.

In our search for American investments, we've been following up every reasonable possibility, figuring that we can learn something even from prospective deals that don't go anywhere. That philosophy took me to Dallas not long ago to see Jimmy Ling, the one-time Merger King. We'd both witnessed enormous changes since 1970. That's when the crash of his conglomerate, LTV, had such a domino effect on the fate of other North American conglomerates, including Neonex International. Since then, he'd pursued several ventures that foundered and in '81 was struck by Guillain-Barré syndrome, a nerve-damaging illness that paralysed him everywhere but his left eyelid. He'd been in therapy for six months and still was in continuous discomfort; he had trouble walking. "Sometimes you're out of it and you don't know you're out . . ." he told me. "But I'm on the hunt again." We met in downtown Dallas, in his small Hill Investors office, bursting with books and mementoes—African masks, a Chinese abacus, his framed membership in the Young Presidents' Organization. At sixty-four, enthusiastic and energetic, Jimmy talked in his rapid-fire Texas drawl of complicated deals involving jet engines and oil and gas. Now he was trying to put together a syndicate to take control of a company whose only value, it seemed to me, was that it had $50 million in undervalued real estate. "You know, we're operators; is there anything there worth operating?" I asked him. We'd look at the numbers, I said, but we never did become part of the syndicate.

One of our possibilities in the States might be the opportunity to get involved again, in even a minor way, with the man who influenced me so profoundly—Mike Dingman. It's been a decade and a half since Mike resigned from the board of Neonex International. Close friends ever since, we've never had the chance to do any deals together. Throughout these years, I've often wished Mike had been around. Since the early '70s, he's done fabulously well. He and Bob Halliday created Wheelabrator-Frye, a $2 billion conglomerate that had more than a dozen straight years of ever-increasing growth and earnings. Its assets included the Pullman railcar empire. In '83 he merged Wheelabrator with the Signal Companies, which were in electronics, construction, real estate, and the aircraft-engine business, among many others. Mike's ambitions outgrew Signal. Two years later, he merged it with Allied Corporation to form the sixteenth-largest American industrial corporation. Then, when Allied-Signal's chairman, Edward L. Hennessy Jr., decided to spin off some operations he didn't want—including a health-care supplies company, a soda-ash mine, and a global engineering and construction firm—Mike volunteered to take them over in a new company. He became chairman of the Henley Group, which went public in '86 with a $1.2 billion stock common-stock offering. It was the biggest initial public issue ever made in the United States; *Fortune* called it one of the "deals of the year." Today, Henley has $7 billion in assets and a net worth of $3.8 billion—with no debt, $1.2 billion worth of cash in the bank, and $3.2 billion in revenues.

There's another side to Mike Dingman, which showed up when he backed the successful 1986 bid by Dennis Conner to regain the America's Cup in the world's premier yacht race. In a recent account of the financial campaign that sent *Stars and Stripes* to Australia, the American skipper describes Mike as a saviour—"the single most valuable relationship ever developed by Sail America in the hunt for corporate dollars." Mike set up appointments for Sail America with leading money men across the U.S. and was personally responsible for raising more than half the campaign's $15 million worth of corporate dollars. It helped that Mike is a sailor, but more important—as Dennis Conner points out—he's "on a first-name basis with almost every major CEO in the country and is personally a very generous and loyal man." I couldn't have said it any better myself.

As Mike says, "the difference today, Jimmy, is that we have the credibility we didn't have twenty years ago. And it's nice to be a partner." I'm hoping to spend one or two days a week in the States, sometimes working out of La Jolla, California, where Mike has his headquarters.

My ties with the U.S. deepened in the spring of '87 when I accepted a proposal to serve on an international council for the United States Information Agency. The invitation came from the agency's director, Charles Z. Wick, one of President Reagan's closest friends:

> The United States Information Agency is charged with the responsibility of telling the truth about America to the rest of the world. I am writing to request your assistance with this important mission.
>
> As Director of USIA, I serve as principal adviser on foreign attitudes to the President, the Secretary of State, and the National Security Council. It is important that my input be as complete and accurate as possible.
>
> After five and one-half years in this post, I have come to the conclusion that my responsibilities could be fulfilled more effectively, on behalf of the United States, if USIA had a private sector International Council of distinguished leaders, such as yourself. Although USIA has 211 posts in 128 countries, it would be of great service to our country if you and others like you, both in the United States and abroad, shared with USIA your views and opinions regarding perceptions of the United States abroad—as well as how we can better explain our role to the world.
>
> Dr. John Brademas, President, New York University, and Rupert Murdoch, Chairman, News America Publishing, have accepted my invitation to be co-chairmen of the council. The Honorable David Rockefeller, the Honorable Henry Kissinger, and the Honorable Jeane Kirkpatrick will serve as honorary co-chairs. Alexander Papamarkou has agreed to serve as Vice Chairman.

> We plan to meet approximately three times a year. . . . We expect top-level officials of the White House, State Department, Defense Department, National Security Council, and Commerce to meet with us. . . . This is a unique opportunity to work together for international understanding and world peace.

I was very pleased to accept.

I was also pleased to be able to perform a public service for Expo. It was one of the highlights of my career when Canada's Governor General, Jeanne Sauvé, recently made me an Officer of the Order of Canada.

In recent years I've decided to accept invitations to become an outside director of a few corporations. I'm a director of the Toronto-Dominion Bank, Crown Life Insurance Company, and the B.C. Resources Investment Corporation. In '87 I also joined the boards of two very different companies, Galveston Resources Limited and MacMillan Bloedel.

There was some surprise when I became a director of Galveston, which is controlled by the flamboyant Vancouver promoter Murray Pezim. Murray—whose aggressive promoting helped bring in the tremendously productive gold fields at Hemlo, Ontario—wanted to use Galveston to regain control of International Corona Resources of Toronto, which has extensive Hemlo holdings. Murray has contributed a lot to Vancouver's financial community, and in the last couple of years he'd suffered several reverses. It's easy to have friends when you're successful. But I've been down and had trouble finding people to support me. Even though I knew full well that people wouldn't understand why I did it, I accepted when Murray Pezim asked me on his board as a personal favour. After I agreed, he offered to donate $1 million to a charity of my choice—a very generous offer that I declined.

When chairman Adam Zimmerman invited me on the MacMillan Bloedel board, it meant being with some old friends on a more regular basis, including Russ Harrison, former chairman of the Canadian Imperial Bank of Commerce, and Ray Smith, chairman of MB. Ray and I go back to the Kitsilano Boys' Band and to the long-ago days I offered him jobs running our car and leasing companies, and the private company, Jim Pattison Industries. He turned me down both times, deciding instead to stay with British Columbia's largest publicly owned company. Ray Smith is proof to me that nice guys can finish first.

Now, approaching my sixth decade, when many chief executives are thinking about retirement, I get excited about the corporate mountains yet to climb, the horizons I haven't even seen. Recently some of our directors were discussing my future in front of me. One of them, older than me, said I should start selling off some assets to prepare for the time when I want to slow down and eventually retire. Mark Kaplan, who knows me well, said: "I don't ever see Jimmy quitting." He's right. As Mary, my family, and my best friends realize, business is my lifeblood.

In the months following Expo, we began preparing the Jim Pattison Group for another major leap in growth. Right now we're looking for the right opportunity in both Canada and the United States. Because prices are higher than they have been historically, we may have to be patient. But we're ready to move. If necessary, we believe we can handle an acquisition of up to $1 billion. That's a long way from the $40,000 I borrowed from Harold Nelson at the Royal Bank to get into business twenty-six years ago.

One intriguing opportunity that came our way in 1987 involved the company that we'd taken over briefly in 1969, only to wind up financially wounded: Maple Leaf Mills. Canadian Pacific Ltd., which now owned Maple Leaf, had put it on the block. On July 1, we were one of several bidders for the food-products corporation with annual sales of $819 million. We weren't going after it for the wrong reasons—like revenge. If we could acquire it at a reasonable price, the company would be a good investment. But an offshore buyer bid higher, and once again Maple Leaf Mills had slipped from our grasp.

No regrets. Neatly two decades ago we'd had to resort to trading our Neonex stock to acquire Maple Leaf. This time around we could take some satisfaction in the fact we could easily offer all cash—more than a quarter of a billion dollars.

CHAPTER TWENTY-ONE

You Gotta Wanna

When we held the official opening for my first car dealership in 1961, my mother showed up with a special present. She'd thought a long time about what she could give me that would be meaningful. What she offered me that night cost her nothing in cash, but it was priceless. Looking through her collection of favourite poetry, she came across a poem by James Russell Lowell. In a few words, it perfectly captured her philosophy of life, a philosophy she passed along to me:

> Life is a sheet of paper white
> Whereon each one of us may write
> His word or two
> And then comes night.
>
> Greatly begin! though thou have time
> But for a line, be that sublime,
> Not failure,
> But low aim is crime.

She had those two verses framed and presented them to me during the evening. I've treasured those lines ever since; for years, they were the only decoration to hang on my office wall, other than a framed copy of The Vancouver *Province*'s war-end edition that I'd sold on V-E Day during my teens. At our Partners in Pride Executive Conference in 1978—whose theme was "No Pain No Gain"—my mother was guest speaker. Along with describing the hardships of Saskatchewan's settlers, she elaborated on her belief that "low aim is crime." To me, it means that failure in life is not the mistakes you make as you attempt things; failure is when you don't try. I had one of our executives in not long ago and said, "Look, we're gonna knock this company out of the comfort zone. Things are moving along too smoothly these days. We're gonna go and borrow some money, do some deals, take some risks. Because we're too complacent. We can't take things for granted." I don't want to be that kind of person or have that kind of company. I don't ever want to reach a plateau and stay there. We have to aim high.

Over the years, I've collected lines of wisdom like the ones my mother gave me, sayings and verses that reflect my personal philosophy, sum up my business values, inspire me to reach beyond the easy goals. I share some with the people who work with me. They'll come in one morning to find a copy of a maxim or motto that's touched me and that mirrors my thinking. Most of us—me included—find it hard to express ourselves about our basic attitudes and beliefs. And anyway, there's not much time during a business day to talk about them. So these ready-made sayings are a kind of shorthand to communicate corporate values, like the little proverb I sent around at the beginning of '87:

A man lived by the side of the road and sold hot dogs.
He was hard of hearing so he had no radio.
He had trouble with his eyes so he read no newspapers.
But he sold good hot dogs.
He put up a sign on the highway telling how good they were.
He stood by the side of the road and cried "Buy a hot dog, Mister."
And people bought.
He increased his meat and bun orders.
He bought a bigger stove to take care of his trade.
He got his son home from college to help him.
But then something happened . . .
His son said, "Father, haven't you heard the news?

There's a big recession on.
The unemployment situation is terrible.
The energy situation is worse."
Whereupon his father thought, "Well, my son has been to college.
He reads the paper and he listens to the radio, and he ought to know."
So the father cut down on his meat and bun orders.
Took down his advertising signs.
And no longer bothered to stand on the highway to sell hot dogs.
And his hot dog sales fell almost overnight.
"You're right, son," the father said to the boy.
"We are certainly in the middle of a great recession."

Several of these sayings have meant a lot to me. They're the ones that I keep around my office as reminders or pass out to my associates:

And when you have reached the mountain top, then you shall begin to climb. Wilf Ray, one of my best friends for more than two decades, taught me that one. He found it in *The Prophet*, by a fellow Lebanese, the poet-philospher Kahlil Gibran. Wilf gathered what he called thoughts for successful living—pearls like "Most human beings live out their life as if it's a dress rehearsal" and "We are judged by what we finish, not what we start." To me, the Gibran quote is a classic that fits right in with the lines about aiming too low. Even though you may reach what some people think is the peak, I believe that you have to extend yourself and continue climbing. I've always set new targets for myself. Once, as a way of keeping score, my goal was to have the company make $25,000 a year. Then $50,000, $100,000—and $1 million. I keep moving our objectives. Measured against many business people, I don't feel that successful. Look at Armand Hammer of Occidental Petroleum: At eighty-eight, he's not only still climbing corporate mountains, he's moving them as he expands a company that's already the twelfth-largest industrial concern in the United States. And Ken Olsen, just a couple of years older than me, who in three decades took Digital Equipment Corporation from virtually nothing to $7.6 billion in annual revenues. *Fortune* recently named him "America's most successful entrepreneur" (and the magazine quoted some of the parables he writes and distributes to his senior managers). Compared to people like Ken Olsen and Armand Hammer, we've got a lot of catching up to do.

The trouble is that he was born on third base and thinks he hit a triple. There are people who inherit wealth and simply look after it like financial caretakers. Others who go and do something productive with their inheritance. And still others who think they've accomplished something simply because they have a ton of money thanks to an accident of birth. I've observed that few of the second generation in wealthy families ever reach very far beyond the security of their family fortunes and contribute to society by creating new ventures and new jobs. Of course, there are some notable exceptions—like the Bentall sons of Vancouver, Clark and Bob; Galen Weston of Toronto, who has done a spectacular job with the family baking and supermarket business; the Eatons, whose fourth generation, Fred, is doing well with the department-store chain in a difficult market; Ken Thomson who has continued to build and diversify his father's newspaper holdings; Conrad Black, who's creating his own media empire; and the three Sobey boys of Stellarton, N.S., who successfully operate a network of companies they actually call Empire, Inc. But, as I've mentioned, I met too many underachieving rich kids during my days at Bowell McLean. Years later, one of them came up to me in the Terminal City Club. It was my first day as a member and the first words I heard there were from this arrogant guy: "How did they ever let you in this club?"

Nothing in the world can take the place of persistence. Talent will not; nothing is more common than unsuccessful men with talent. Genius will not; unrewarded genius is almost a proverb. Education alone will not; the world is full of educated derelicts. Persistence and determination alone are omnipotent. Mike Dingman has that framed in one of his offices; at the time we were operating Neonex International, I had the message inscribed on a sign which still sits in my office. Those words sum up my mother. If there's one quality I inherited from her, it was persistence. Whatever else I may be, I'm determined. Once I get involved in a venture that I believe in, I won't quit. I've tried to encourage that attitude in the people who work with me. Wilf Ray was a good example. He once sent out an important press release with a couple of spelling errors that I spotted. "They're in the mail; we can't get them back," he said. "You'd better fix it," I replied. Wilf went to the main post office, where the manager told him our bag of mail was now Crown property and, anyway, there were so many thousands of bags that Wilf would never find ours. Determined, Wilf went upstairs to a room where the incoming mail was being sorted. Looking as if he worked there, he kept checking all the bags until he saw ours. Bringing it to the manager, he showed him the mistakes in the press release and convinced the fellow to let him take the mail bag back to our office. Persistence.

There's no limit to what a man can do or where he can go if he doesn't mind who gets the credit. More than ten years ago, Maureen had this line on the cover of her appointment book. It came in handy at Expo, where I put it on two signs, one facing me and the other facing whoever was in the office with me. When I started at the fair, I was horrified that many people who worked for Crown corporations and particularly for the federal government were less concerned about getting the job done than they were about who got the brownie points for doing it. Then one day I discovered I was beginning to think like them: "If we do this, are we going to be seen to get the credit? I want to make sure Premier Bennett knows that we did this." That's when I realized that I was catching the disease myself and hung the sign on the wall opposite my desk to make sure I didn't forget.

Nothing will ever be attempted if all possible objections must be first overcome. There is no perfect person, no perfect marriage, no perfect company, no perfect country, no perfect deal. Realizing that there's always a negative in doing a deal, you have to approach it positively: How can I get around the problem? That's the difference between people who do deals and those who don't. A senior Canadian banker once told me that in the whole of North America, there are only six hundred significant deal-makers—people who truly make it happen in the business world. To create good deals, you have to have courage with balance: the courage to take the risk and the balance to manage it successfully. If I wanted to drive fast, I'd do it on a nice dry four-lane freeway, not on a slippery one-lane mountain road. Of course, there's another crucial question to ask about any deal: If it goes sour, can you afford the risk? You don't bet the farm.

You Gotta Wanna

People are our most important asset. Or, to put it another way: *People make the difference.* You have to believe this if you want to run a company the way we do: offering people a tremendous amount of autonomy. We've used both those slogans at our Partners in Pride conferences. One of our guest speakers, Bob Waterman, co-author of *In Search of Excellence*, is a firm believer in those concepts. Discussing hands-off versus hands-on executives, he says: "Our cultural model of a boss is someone really involved, in control. But that doesn't get the most out of people in terms of productivity and initiative. . . . You need to pick good people, and you need to kick the tires every once in a while. And if something doesn't feel right, you've got to dig deeper." My sentiments exactly.

Maybe in error, never in doubt. The Jim Pattison Group has always been decisive; it doesn't take us long to make up our minds. We don't do a lot of fence-sitting: Should we? Shouldn't we? There's no doubt where we stand on an issue or a deal. But because we're not wishy-washy, we sometimes make mistakes when we move too fast. When a local producer, Jack Card, complained that Vancouver entertainers weren't getting enough bookings at Expo, we asked him to produce a song-and-dance show for our Partners in Pride conference when Bob Hope was a special guest. Jack did a good job, and when he came asking for financial backing to put together a troupe to tour Europe, we advanced him $225,000. The troupe wound up in Spain, broke, with neither the bookings nor the revenues they expected. When Jack Card requested more money, I shut them down.

You gotta wanna. Somewhere I picked up a card with that slogan and it instantly rang bells with me. We used it as the theme of our first big Partners in Pride Conference in '76. I believe *wanting to* is the most important quality a person can bring to business. I've always wanted to work hard; I hate holidays. Twenty years ago, Mary and I spent a month in the Caribbean with our friends Frank Baker and his wife, Dorothy. Aside from one week acting like a tourist in Spain and my post-Expo week of recuperation in Palm Springs, that's been it for vacations. I thrive on business. In the words of James Russell Lowell, the poet my mother likes: "There is no better ballast for keeping the mind steady on its keel, and saving it from all risk of crankiness, than business." It was during my days at the car dealership that I realized that no matter how smart a salesman is, how good a family man, how hard-working—if he doesn't have the overwhelming desire to achieve, he won't be a good salesman. Obviously, if you're looking for a director of your company, you consider a person with judgment and wisdom. But if you're trying to build a company, you need someone at the top who also has that intangible drive that springs from deep down—from the fire in the belly. You've gotta wanna succeed.

And as for me, after a quarter of a century in business, after doing more than two hundred deals, after more success than I ever dreamed possible, I still wanna.

Index

A.B. Balderston's, 32
Ace Novelty, 282–83
Ackerman, Peter, 279, 280
Ackles, Bobby, 281
Acme Amusements, 151
Acme Merchandise Distributors. *See* Acme Novelty
Acme Novelty, 112–13, 150–52
The Acquisitors (Newman), 289
Adams, Annie, 18, 19
Adams, Elmer, 38
Adams, Henry, 19
Adams, John, 38
Adams, Will, 30
Advertising Age, 201
Aetna Life, 160
AirBC 8, 138, 229–39, 313
Airwest Airlines, 229–30
Allarco Developments, 160
Allard, Dr. Charles, 160, 167
Alpha Tau Omega fraternity, 47

Altman, Jerry, 84–85
Ambassadors of Aid, 252–54
Andersen, Rose, 64, 79–80, 181, 183–84
Anderson, William M., 100
Anthony, Russ, 284
Apostolic Church of Pentecost, 21, 29, 31
Apps, Bill, 235–36
Ardies, Tom, 154
Argus Corporation, 193
Aristocratic Cookware, 60
Associated Helicopters, 115, 147, 197
Atlanta Flames, 169
Austin, Jack, 85
Automotive Industries Association of Canada, 316

Badun, Walter, 285
Baker, Frank, 64, 70, 78, 327

Bakker, Jim, 25
Bakker, Tammy Faye, 25
Baldwin, Howard, 163–64
Ballard, Harold, 157, 168
Bank of British Columbia, 66, 138
Bank of Nova Scotia, 49
Barkley, Diana, 291
Barnett, Ray, 252–54
Barrett, Dave, 87, 90, 148, 161, 174, 240, 304–305, 306, 307
Bartlett, Mike, 1–3, 275, 278, 280–81, 290, 291
Bassett Jr., John, 157, 160
Bates, Percy, 46
Bathgate, Andy, 166
Bawden, H.H., 125
Bazaar & Novelty, 151, 197
B.C. Resources Investment Corporation, 320
Beatty, Perrin, 262
Beautiful British Columbia magazine, 7, 16, 89–90, 245, 257, 284–85
Bell, Max, 89
Bellman, Bill, 84, 85
Bennett, Bill, 4, 272, 273, 274, 276–77, 290
Bennett, W.A.C., 305, 306–307
Benson, Edgar, 117
Bentall, Bob, 90, 325
Bentall, Clark, 77–78, 284, 285, 325
Bernard, Frank, 154
Berryland Canning Company, 245
Bigelow-Sanford Inc., 142
Birks, Peter, 62–63
Black, Conrad, 325
Block Brothers, 209

Board of Broadcast Governors, 83, 84, 85
Boise Cascade Corporation, 96, 97
The Boissevain (Man.) Recorder, 39
Bonner, Bob, 305
Borins, Judge Stephen, 262
Bowell, Mackenzie, 53–54
Bowell McLean Motor Company, 47, 53–67
Bowser, Ed, 101
Boyd, Denny, 87, 163
Boyle, Ben, 197–98
Bradley, Tom, 254
Brazier, Charles, 100, 105, 109, 140–41
British Columbia Television (BCTV), 84–85
Brown, Bernie, 160–62
Brown, Doug, 139
Brown, Peter, 139, 285
Brown, Ron, 59–60
Brown, Rosemary, 265–66
Buffalo Sabres, 165
Buhrke, Helmut, 10
Burdette, Dennis, 286
Burnham II, I.B. (Tubby), 99
Burnham & Co., 97, 98, 99, 101
Burns, Pat, 81–83, 85–86
Bush, George, 12, 302
Business Week, 148
Butler, Jane, 300, 315
Butler, Sir Michael, 148

Calgary Broncos, 159
Calgary Cowboys. *See* Vancouver Blazers
Callwood, June, 259–60
Calvary Temple, 45

Index

Campagnolo, Iona, 5
Canadian Airlines International, 238
The Canadian Establishment (Newman), 121, 196
Canadian Fishing Company, 8, 245–47
Canadian Imperial Bank of Commerce, 7, 116, 127–28, 131, 135, 139–40, 148–49
Canadian Radio-Television Commission, 86
Capozzi, Herb, 57, 157, 285, 305
Card, Jack, 327
Carmichael, Jack, 93
Carney, Pat, 100, 105
Castro, Fidel, 288, 289, 290
Cattermole, Ralph, 48, 49
Centrone, Enzo, 74–75, 254
CFFM radio, 313
CFJC radio, 313
CFJC-TV, 313
CFRW radio, 88–89, 153
Chamberlin, Gordon, 181–82
Chandler, Marie, 83–84
Chant, Bob, 71, 75
Chant, Maureen, 75–76, 88, 100, 109, 112, 116, 123, 136, 141, 160, 172–73, 212, 215, 216, 218–19, 243, 294, 301, 306, 315, 326
Chapman, Dave, 233
Chaston, John, 114, 144
Chippendale, Warren, 107
Christensen, Bjarne, 300
Christopher, Arthur, 95, 100–101, 103, 105, 109, 140–41
Christopher, Gordon, 95, 96
CHUM Ltd., 88
Chung, Se Yung, 315
CIFM radio, 313
C-I-L (Canadian Industries Limited), 49
CJJR radio, 55, 313
CJOR radio, 33, 55, 58, 82–89, 91, 153, 313–14
CKNW radio, 33–34
Clark, Joe, 304
Claude Neon, 7, 224–25
Cleghorn, John, 162
Clements, W.W., 199–203
Cleveland Crusaders, 160
Clyne, J.V., 139, 305
Cohon, George, 93
Colcomb, Dick, 227
Coleman, John, 184, 185, 199, 201, 216–17
Collins, Lou, 193, 198
"Colonel Flack," 58
Colussy, Don, 236–37
The Complete Encyclopedia of Hockey, 158
Conaghan, Chuck, 235
The Confessions of Klaus Barbie, The Butcher of Lyon (Wilson), 154
Congress of Canadian Women, 256
Conner, Dennis, 318–19
Connors, Don, 151, 181, 229
Consolidated Motor Company, 152
Consumer Reports, 226
Cook, Chuck, 87
Cooper, Mel, 235, 236, 286–87
Coopers & Lybrand, 107, 245
Cornett, Jack, 33

Cornfeld, Bernie, 137
Courtesy Chevrolet, 153, 154, 225
Crockett, Art, 129
Crossen, Jim, 83
Crossgrove, Peter, 94
Crown Life Insurance Company, 320
Crozier, Joe, 165, 166, 167
Crump, Dr., 50
Crush International, 148, 192–204
Cummings Signs, 181–82
Cunningham, Ralph, 84–85, 92
Currie, George, 139

Dafoe, John, 73
Dagg, Ray, 2, 285
Dallimore, Graham, 215
Dan McLean Motor Company, 50
Darling, Ann Farris, 297
Davidson, Gary, 158–59
Davies, Bob, 126, 135
Davis, Nelson, 194–97, 316
Dawnex Properties Ltd., 116
Dawson, Bob, 287
Dawson, Graham, 93–94
Dawson Developments, 116, 140
Delamont, Arthur W., 34
Deyell, Bob, 194
Dingman, Mike, 97–99, 101–102, 103–104, 105, 114, 121–22, 123–24, 128, 129, 130, 132, 139, 184, 299, 318–19, 325
Divine healing, 22–25

Dominion Construction, 77–78, 90, 284
Donaldson, John, 84, 85
Donner, Fred, 97
Doric Howe Motor Hotel, 119, 143, 144, 148
Downtown Eastside Residents Association (DERA), 295–96
Drabek, Jan, 268
Draper, Dawn, 84
Dubbs, Harvey, 36
Dueck Chevrolet Oldsmobile, 57, 71, 153
Dulude, Louise, 263
Dunbar, Harry, 80–81, 89, 98, 105, 109, 111–12, 116–17, 132, 140, 146, 148, 150, 154, 177, 212, 266
Dunn, Russell, 141
Dye, Kenneth, 4

Easton, Don, 141
Eaton, Fred, 325
Eaton, John Craig, 160
Eberhardt, Lawrence (Bud), 141, 148, 162, 212
Eddy, Doug, 182
Edersheim, Mark, 99
Edinborough, Arnold, 269
Edmonton Oilers, 160, 164, 167
EDP Industries, 146, 153–54, 225
Elder, Jean, 270
Eller, Carl, 164
Engelhard, Charles, 99, 104
Etienne, Donald, 251
Expo 86, 1–6, 254–55, 272–303
Eyre, Alan, 100, 153

Fabco Leasing, 119, 143, 148, 197
Faith Today, 260
Farrell, Gordon, 95
Fawcus, Kenneth, 284
Feldman, Zane, 167
The Financial Post, 6, 58, 125, 286
The Financial Post Moneywise Magazine, 66
Flanigan, George, 209, 210
Fleming, Ian, 99
Fleming, Willie, 78–79
Flom, Joe, 134, 184
Forbes, Malcolm, 302–303, 308
Forbes magazine, 302, 308
Ford, Gerald, 174, 188
Forge, Norm, 39, 41
Fortune magazine, 66, 67, 106, 185, 318
Fotheringham, Allan, 6
Fraser, Paul, 256
Fraser Committee on Pornography and Prostitution, 256–57, 260, 262–64, 267–68
Fraser Valley Foods, 8, 245, 247, 313
Full Gospel Businessmen's Fellowship International, 24, 219
Fullerton, R. Donald, 128–29

Gaglardi, Phil, 45–46, 305
Galveston Resources Limited, 320
Garbovitsky, Gregory, 34
Gardiner, Doug, 89, 101, 102–103
Gasser, Dr. Erik B., 248, 251
Gautier, Roy, 275–78
Geer, Nick, 179, 181, 183, 187, 230, 241, 246, 247–51
Geigy, Dr. Jürge, 251
General Cinema Corporation, 199
General Motors Acceptance Corporation, 71
GM Canada, 68
GM Motors Holding, 69, 71
Genstar Corporation. *See* Sogemines Ltd.
Gibran, Kahlil, 324
Gibson, Jack, 306
Glad Tidings Temple, 34, 64, 173, 252, 264
The Globe and Mail, 119, 179, 257
Godbout, Guy, 114–15, 142
Gold, Harvey, 305
Gold, Norm, 229–30
Goldenberg, Derryl, 268
Goldman Sachs, 200–201
Gould Outdoor Advertising, 182, 245
Goulet, Rudy, 151–52
Grafstein, Jerry, 166–67
Graham, Billy, 25
Grantison Holdings, 248
Gray, Abe, 93
Great Pacific Capital SA, 8, 12, 181, 248–51
Great Pacific Industries, 119, 137, 142–44, 148–49, 181, 184, 185, 251–52
Green, Jim, 295–96
Greenwood, Larry, 129, 130
Griffiths, Frank, 93–94

Index

Group Opportunities program, 186
Gulf-Air Aviation, 231

Hackett, G.O. Basil, 48
Haig, Alexander, 188, 245
Hall, Albert, 133, 148
Halliday, Bob, 96–97, 107, 109, 111, 122, 132, 140, 141, 177, 184, 198, 312, 318
Hambidge, Archbishop Douglas, 257–58, 265, 267
Hambros Bank, 249
Hamilton, Don, 285
Hammer, Armand, 11, 218, 324–25
Hansberger, Robert Vail, 96
Harcourt, Mike, 266, 296
Harding Carpets, 115, 142
Hardman, Gil, 274
Harris, Iain, 151, 210–11, 232–33, 235–38
Harris, Rusty, 232
Harrison, Russ, 129, 149, 195, 320
Hatskin, Ben, 160, 164
Hedley, Rick, 229, 234–36
Hennessy Jr., Edward L., 318
Heppell, Clarence, 189–91, 243
Hickok, Ray, 92
Hnatyshyn, Ray, 263
Hoguet, Larry, 99, 105, 109, 132
Hook Outdoor, 182
Hope, Bob, 174, 327
Horsey, Bill, 193
Horsey, Grant, 194

Housser, George E., 100
Howe, Gordie, 163
Hull, Bobby, 159
Hunt, Nelson Bunker, 214
Hunt, W. Herbert, 214
Hunter, Bill, 164, 167

Iacocca, Lee, 302
Iaccoca, Peggy, 302
Imbrex Limited, 112–13, 114–15, 137, 142
Ingham, Gwenith, 267–68
Investment Reporter, 208
Investor's Digest of Canada, 132
Israel, 27–29

Jarislowsky, Stephen, 252
Jenks, Frank, 58
Jewers, Judge Gerald, 262
Jim Pattison Automotive Group, 151, 181
Jim Pattison (British Columbia) Limited, 70–79, 207–208
Jim Pattison Communications Group, 181
Jim Pattison Developments, 116, 181
Jim Pattison Enterprises, 138
Jim Pattison Group, 1, 6, 7–8, 10–16, 27, 66, 152, 241–52, 283–84
The Jim Pattison GroupNews, 179, 186, 312
Jim Pattison Group song, 186
Jim Pattison Industries Ltd., 15, 180–81, 184, 321
Jim Pattison Leasing, 2

Index

Jim Pattison on Main, 79–81
Jim Pattison News Group, 151, 181
Jim Pattison Nissan, 66, 313
Jim Pattison Outdoor Group, 7
Jim Pattison Pontiac Buick Cadillac, 313, 314
Jim Pattison Sign Company, 7, 72, 313, 314
Jim Pattison Toyota, 226–27
Johnsen, Dan, 115–16, 181
Johnson, Daniel, 86
Johnstone, Lucille, 285
Jordan, Pat, 232
Jordan-Knox, Charles, 114
Jordan-Knox, Trevor, 114
Juneau, Pierre, 86

Kaiser, Edgar, 138, 279
Kaplan, Mark, 98, 134, 141, 184, 198, 199, 200, 321
Kapp, Joe, 78–79
Kaufman, Rex, 147
Keevil Jr., Dr. Norman, 285
Ker, R.H.B., 100, 105
Kerkhoff, Bill, 276, 278
Ketchum, Jess, 282
Kidd, Dr. Molly, 110–11
Kidd, Robert, 110
Kilburn, Al, 252–54
Kiburn, Cindy. *See* Pattison, Cynthia (Cindy)
King, Lynn, 259
Kingsway Motors, 46
Kissinger, Dr. Henry, 188
Kitsilano Boys' Band, 34, 64, 272
Knott, Lyall, 285
Koffman, Morley, 141
Kraft, Richard, 223
Krug, Guy, 249, 250, 251
Kuhn, Bowie, 170
Kwok, Stanley, 275, 285

Laco, Tom, 202–203
Lacroix, André, 159, 161
Lade, David, 37, 40, 41, 44, 45
Lade, Paul, 37
Ladies' Home Journal, 35
Laidman, Dick, 230
Laing, Art, 110
Laird, Allan, 285
Landes,, Les, 181
LaPointe, Audrey, 90
Lawrence, Ed, 148
Lehman Brothers International, 249
Leitch, Jack, 121, 123–24, 127, 129, 132, 133–35, 149, 197
Lennon, John, 293
Leslie, Graham, 277–78
Levine, Bill, 209
Lewall, Guy, 109, 123, 148
Lewtas, Jim, 126–27, 129, 135
Ling, Jimmy, 96, 106, 132, 137, 317–18
Lipp, P.J., 78–79
Lloyds Bank International, 249
Logan, Frank, 123
Long, Fred, 85
Long Jr., G. Roy, 47–49, 80
Lowell, James Russell, 311, 322, 327
Lurie, Bob, 170

Index

Luse Land and Development Co., 18
Luseland, Saskatchewan, 18

MacLachlan, G.M., 122
MacMillan, Dr. Harvey, 48–49
MacMillan Bloedel, 34, 320
MacNaughton, Angus, 141
McArthur, John, 46–47
McAuley, Blair, 88–89
McCall, Hugh, 70
McCarthy, Grace, 272–73, 290, 305
McCartney, Bill, 207
Maclean's magazine, 6, 82, 312
McClelland, Bob, 278
McClelland, Vern, 40
McConachie, Don, 286
McConica Bros. & Pattison, 19–20
McConnell, John Wilson, 194–95
Macdonald, Donald, 188
McDowell, Ted, 94, 174–75, 194–95, 197, 241, 243, 294
McIntosh, Don, 195
McKay, J. Stuart, 85
McKay, Yip, 195
McKeen, George, 306
McKeen, Stanley, 306
McKenzie, Johnny, 159, 161–62, 165
McKinnon, Neil, 127, 128, 129, 139, 149
McLaughlin, W. Earle, 102
McLaughlin Motor Car Co., 19
McLean, Dan, 50–51, 53–54, 59, 61–63, 68, 97
McMyn, Keith, 84
McNab, Doug, 144
McNair, Jeff, 281
McQueen, Rod, 94
Madden, George, 282, 298, 300, 303, 314
Maines, David, 25
Mainland Magazine Service, 8, 225, 255, 256–71
Mair, Rafe, 87
Major, Saskatchewan, 38
Malkin, J.P.D., 95
Maple Leaf Gardens, 157
Maple Leaf Mills, 7, 32, 120–35, 193, 321
Market Share, 178–79
Marshall Pontiac Buick, 69
Martin, Paul, 102, 306
Marwell Construction, 77–78
Mathews, Wilf, 71
Mavis, Gary, 268
Maxwell, Earl, 149
Medicor, 157–58
Meyer, Edward, 184–85
Mileti, Nick, 160
Milken, Mike, 279
Miller, Al, 165
Mimic Systems, 313
Mitchell, John, 300
Mitchell, Keith, 285
Mitton, Stuart, 109, 110, 111, 140
Moffatt, C.K.S., 33
Molson, Harold E., 95
Molson Industries Ltd., 124–27, 170–71
Mondale, Walter, 188
Moseley, Kathie, 303
Mountain City News, 153
Mowbray, Alan, 58

Index

Mrs. Milne's Cannery, 245
Mulroney, Brian, 4, 298
Munro, Scotty, 159
Murphy, Dennis, 158–59
Murphy, Frank, 160–61
Muzak, 83, 87–88

Narod, Alvin, 28, 274
Narod Construction, 209–210
Nathanson, Paul, 99, 101–102, 104, 306
National Action Committee on the Status of Women, 263
National Advertising, 245
Nelson, Harold, 69, 71, 248, 250, 321
Neonex International, 6–7, 106–19, 136–55, 205–208
Neon Products, 7, 49, 57, 92–105, 108–109
New England Whalers, 160
Newman, Peter C., 36, 312
Newmark, Alan, 99
Newton, John, 285
Nichol, Senator John, 100, 101, 105
Non-Partisan Association, 305
Norris, Bruce, 121–24, 126, 132–35, 156
Northern Paint, 110, 115
Northwest Sports Enterprises Inc., 157–58
Nova Springs, 176, 277, 280

Oakridge Securities, 48–49, 80
Ocean Fishing, 246–47
Olsen, Ken, 324–25
Olson, Dick, 160–62
"100 Huntley Street," 25
"Operation Peru," 48–49
Ottaway, Don, 198
Otto Manufacturing Enterprises, 118–19
Overwaitea Foods, 8, 10, 64, 109, 110–11, 115, 152, 189–91, 225–26, 314

Pacific Coastal Airlines, 231
Parent, Bernie, 159
Park, General Tae Joon, 315
Partners in Pride conferences, 61, 76, 172–75, 176, 186–89, 240–41, 327
Pattison, Chandos (Pat), 17–18, 19–21, 30–31
Pattison, Cynthia (Cindy), 63, 64, 66, 252–54, 294–95
Pattison, James Allen (Jimmy): and Mary Hudson, 38–42; early life, 17–42; family life, 63–67; management style, 145–48; 177–80, 181–84, 185–89, 222–26; musical background, 33–35, 38; on bureaucrats' spending, 3–5; on car leasing, 71–72; on cars, 44–45; on censorship, 258–60; on commodities speculating, 212–14; on conglomerates, 106–108, 137; on Cuba, 288–290; on expenditure control,

Index

Pattison, James Allen (Jimmy) (*cont.*)
  242–44; on the Expo Corporation, 1–5; on the Expo experience, 5–6; on Great Britain, 314–15; on Israel, 27–29; on Korea, 315–16; on the media, 90; on Mexico, 316; on partnership, 209–10; on Pentecostalism, 21–29; on pornography, 260–64; on the price of high visibility, 310–11; on running for political office, 303–308; on timing, 50; on unions, 233–34, 275–79; on the United States, 316–20; personal philosophy, 10, 65–67, 322–28
Pattison Jr., Jim, 42, 63, 66–67
Pattison, Julia (née Allen), 18–19, 27–28, 32–33, 174, 322–23
Pattison, Mary (née Hudson), 9, 38–42, 63–64, 136, 138, 304, 310–11, 312
Pattison, Mary Ann, 63, 64, 65, 66
Patton, George, 179
Pekarsky, Don, 28
Pemberton Securities, 143–44, 148
People magazines, 294
Periodical Distributors of Canada, 260, 263–64
Perot, H. Ross, 11, 66
Peterson, David, 93, 303
Peterson, Les, 305
Pezim, Murray, 320
Philadelphia Blazers, 159–62
Phillips, Karen, 267–68
Phillips, Lazarus, 102
Phoenix Roadrunners, 164
Pickens, T. Boone, 11, 279–80, 317
Pilgrim Products, 49
Pillars of Time (Julia Pattison), 28
Pocklington, Peter, 167
Poole, Jack, 116, 140, 209
Pooling of interests, 107–108
Pop Shoppes, 150
Porta-Built Industries, 119, 143, 144, 148
Pousette, Peter, 127, 139
Powroznik, Gary, 245
Prairie Market, 111
Prefontaine, Marcel, 143–44
President's Advisory Council, 79
Price, Pat, 165–66
Princess Margaret, 301
Proctor, Frank, 23
Proctor & Gamble, 200–204
Proskow, Morris, 182
The Province (Vancouver), 36–37, 69–70, 322–23
Provincial News, 115, 152–53, 269
Pryor, Sam, 126, 131, 133
PTL Club, 25
Pyrik, Ed, 153

Quality Circles (QC), 223–26, 242

Index

Ray, Wilf, 55–57, 70, 78, 81, 88–89, 98, 109, 113, 123, 124, 143, 163, 219, 306, 324, 325–26
Reagan, Ronald, 174, 301
Reay, Bill, 33–34
Regan, Don, 159
Reid, Patrick, 273, 285
Reimer, Don, 113
Reimer, Express Lines, 112–13, 267
Return on Invested Capital (ROIC), 177–78
Reynolds, John, 87
Rhodes, Jim, 304
Richmond, Claude, 2, 34, 278, 283, 285, 288, 289, 299
Richmond, Fred, 46, 69
Riddington, Jillian, 267–68
Riley, Wilson (Joe), 52, 54, 68
Ripley's Believe It or Not!, 7, 14, 178, 187, 314
Roberts, Oral, 23–27
Robertson, Harry, 17, 52
Robinson, Alison, 285, 303
Roddick, Robert, 285
Rodriguez, Carlos Raphael, 289–90
Rodriguez, José, 289
Rogers, D.P., 100, 105
Ross, Reg, 62
Ross, Sandy, 125
Rothschild Incorporated of New York, 28
Rubenstein, Sam, 246–47

Sanderson, Derek, 159
The Saturday Evening Post, 35

Saunders, Peter Paul, 85
Sauvé, Jeanne, 320
Save-On-Foods, 8, 10, 11, 189–90
Scallen, Tom, 157–58
Schatia, Dave, 165
Seaboard Advertising, 182
Seebach, John, 151, 260
Segal, Joe, 246
Selman, Don, 80–81, 95, 98, 107, 108, 116–17, 128, 217
Servant, Claude, 287
Shakarian Demos, 24
Shaw, Maire, 290
Short, Russell, 39
Shrum, Dr. Gordon, 153
Sifton, June, 166–68
Sifton, Victor, 89
Sinclair, Bob, 182
Skalbania, Nelson, 167–68, 169–70
Skiroule Limitée, 116–17
Sladden, Bert, 207–208
Sleeman, Bill, 73–74, 76, 118–19, 141, 142–44, 148, 156, 164, 165, 166, 169–70, 172, 173, 177, 182–84, 197–99, 207–208, 235–36, 241, 245–46, 266, 298, 314
Smart, Bob, 182
Smith, Brian, 265, 308
Smith, Bud, 308
Smith, Harvey, 100, 103, 108
Smith, Ray, 34, 272, 307, 320–21
Smythe, Stafford, 157
Snider, Francis, 39
Sogemines Ltd., 107
Souter, Doug, 245–47
Speaking in tongues, 21–22

Spector, Norman, 276
Spiro, Sid, 249
Stars and Stripes (yacht), 318
Steed, Fran, 300
Steinsvik, Mag, 176
Stern, Ron, 246, 247
Stevenson, Kit, 257, 265
Stewart, Donna, 257, 265
Stewart, Jack, 88
Stitt, Bert, 248
Strain, Matt, 39
Strangway, David, 270–71
Symonds, Curt, 177

Tallis, Cedric, 57
T.A. Richardson, 101
Taylor, Alan, 68
Taylor, Claude, 238
Taylor, E.P., 193
Thatcher, Margaret, 15, 301–302
Thompson, Jack, 141, 148, 193–195, 198–99
Thomson, Dick, 130
Thomson, Ken, 325
Thomson, W.E., 100
Time magazine, 119
Tithing, 27
Toronto-Dominion Bank, 7, 130, 139, 140, 320
Toronto Life, magazine, 130
Toronto Maple Leafs, 156, 157
The Toronto Star, 137, 140, 192
Toronto Toros, 160
Townsend, Doug, 10–11
Toyoda, Eiji, 222
Toyoda, Sakichi, 222
Trans Ad, 8, 182, 244, 313
Trans-Provincial Airlines, 231–32, 237, 313
Travelaire Recreational Vehicles, 119
Travelaire Trailer Manufacturing, 119
Trimble, Tiff, 88, 89
Triple E Manufacturing, 119
Trudeau, Pierre, 86, 117
Tryon, Lord Anthony, 314–15
Turner, John, 299
Turner, Ross, 109, 116, 132, 140, 141
TVS Group, 118

The Ubyssey, 44
Udall, W.V., 39
Umphrey, E.J. (Jeff), 58–59, 60–61, 69, 70, 71, 73, 76–78, 97
United Israel Appeal of Canada, 28
United Trailer, 115–16
United Way, 27
University of British Columbia, 8, 40, 44, 270–71
UniverSport, 112–13, 115
Unocal Corporation, 279–80
Upper Lakes Shipping, 121, 123, 124, 125–26

Vancouver Blazers, 157–69
Vancouver Canadians, 157, 169–71
Vancouver Canucks, 157, 161
Vancouver Junior Symphony, 34
Vancouver Magazine Service, 269

The Vancouver News-Herald, 45
The Vancouver Sun, 86, 87, 89, 100, 154, 234, 280, 306
Vandella Enterprises, 267
van der Haegen, Roland, 250–51
Vander Zalm, Bill, 303, 308
Vanguard Manufacturing, 152, 313
van Roggen, George, 306
Vanstone, Fred, 26, 148, 175, 194–95, 207, 267
M.S. *Victoria*, 48
Vincent, Robert, 122–23, 133, 134, 135

Wales, Prince and Princess of, 301
Wall, Don, 86
Wallace, Lawrie, 273
Waltuch, Norton, 215
Wasserman, Jack, 87, 90, 154, 161, 306
Waterman, Bob, 188, 327
Waters, Allan, 88, 89, 153
Watson, Phil, 162
Waymark, Graeme, 267–68
Webster, Jack, 58, 86–87
Wehrli, Dr. Max R., 251
West Coast Air, 231
Westfall, Len, 181, 183
Westminster Savings and Loan, 68
Weston, Galen, 93, 301, 325

Whitehead, John C., 200
Whittle, Stan, 100, 108, 148, 177, 224
Wick, Charles Z., 319–20
Williams, Bob, 161
Williams, Dorothy, 253
Willmot, Donald G. (Bud), 124–25
Wilson, Bobby, 154
Wilson, Jim, 111
The Winnipeg Free Press, 73, 89, 113
Winnipeg Jets, 160
Winser, Joan, 4
Withers, John, 187
Wolfe, Evan, 93
Wolfe, Izzy, 211
Wood, Bill, 153
Woodall, Ron, 297
Woodward, W.C., 95
Wootten, Chris, 281
World Hockey Association, 7, 156, 158–60
Wyman, Bob, 125, 148, 270

Yamamoto, Sadazo, 226
Young, Alex, 84
Young, Maurie, 93–94
Young Presidents' Organization (YPO), 92–96, 107, 116

Zimmerman, Adam, 320

ABOUT THE CO-AUTHOR

PAUL GRESCOE is co-author of *The Money Rustlers*, a bestseller about self-made millionaires of Western Canada. As an award-winning magazine journalist, he has written for *Canadian Business*, *Saturday Night*, and *Reader's Digest*. He lives in Vancouver, where he is corporate-communications consultant as well as an author.

SEAL BOOKS BRINGS YOU CANADIAN BUSINESS

Canadian business is big business and Seal Books is the publisher of books by and about some of the biggest names in Canadian business.

01779-5	The Acquisitors, Peter C. Newman	$5.95
42063-X	Ballard, William Houston	$4.50
42286-1	Claims: Adventures in the Gold Trade, Ken Lefolii	$5.95
42335-3	Contrepreneurs, Diane Francis	$6.95
42213-6	Controlling Interest, Diane Francis	$5.95
42197-0	Ford: The Men and The Machine, Robert Lacey	$6.95
42252-7	Jimmy: An Autobiography, Jimmy Pattison, with Paul Grescoe	$5.95
42235-7	Mind Over Money, Dr. Norm Forman	$4.50

Watch for the annual CANADIAN PRICE WATERHOUSE PERSONAL TAX ADVISOR by Richard Birch. Available each tax season from Seal Books for only $5.95

The Mark of Canadian Bestsellers

Seal Books Brings You Controversial and Timely Non-Fiction

LIFE WITH BILLY The harrowing account of Jane Stafford's abusive marriage and how it drove her to murder.
With Brian Vallee.   42239-X $4.95

RITUAL ABUSE: CANADA'S MOST INFAMOUS TRIAL ON CHILD ABUSE A behind-the-scenes look at the custody trial arising from allegations of satanism and sexual abuse. A precedent-setting case on child abuse in general.
By Kevin Marron.   42250-0 $4.95

NEVER LET GO: THE STORY OF KRISTY MCFARLANE
The story of a mother's courageous effort to save her teenage daughter from the streets. After two and a half years, the struggle ended in Kristy's death. Why?
By Tom MacDonnell   42261-6 $4.95

VICTIMS: THE ORPHANS OF JUSTICE A testimony to the families and victims of violent crimes. It is also the story of a fight to change a system that grants more rights to criminals than to victims.
By Jerry Amernic   41862-7 $4.50

The Mark of Canadian Bestesellers

SEAL BOOKS

Offers you a list of outstanding fiction, non-fiction, and classics of Canadian literature in paperback by Canadian authors, available at all good bookstores throughout Canada.

THE BACK DOCTOR	Hamilton Hall
THE IVORY SWING	Janette Turner Hospital
NEVER CRY WOLF	Farley Mowat
THE KITE	W. O. Mitchell
RITUAL ABUSE	Kevin Marron
ANNE OF GREEN GABLES	Lucy Maud Montgomery
BLOODSHIFT	Garfield Reeves-Stevens
LADY ORACLE	Margaret Atwood
BORDERLINE	Janette Turner Hospital
AND NO BIRDS SANG	Farley Mowat
STONE ANGEL	Margaret Laurence
STRAIGHT FROM THE HEART	Jean Chretien
BLUEBEARD'S EGG	Margaret Atwood
JOSHUA THEN AND NOW	Mordecai Richler
CONSPIRACY OF BROTHERS	Mick Lowe
A CERTAIN MR. TAKAHASHI	Ann Ireland
NO EASY TRIP	Jean Sonmor
A JEST OF GOD	Margaret Laurence
HOW I SPENT MY SUMMER HOLIDAYS	W. O. Mitchell
SEA OF SLAUGHTER	Farley Mowat
THE HANDMAID'S TALE	Margaret Atwood
THE CANADIANS (seven volumes)	Robert E. Wall
KING LEARY	Paul Quarrington
THE VIOLENT YEARS OF MAGGIE MACDONALD	MacDonald & Gould
THE DOG WHO WOULDN'T BE	Farley Mowat
WHO HAS SEEN THE WIND	W. O. Mitchell
HOME GAME	Paul Quarrington
CONTROLLING INTEREST	Diane Francis
DREAMLAND	Garfield Reeves-Stevens
JACKRABBIT PAROLE	Stephen Reid
NO FIXED ADDRESS	Aritha Van Herk
THE GOLDEN ROAD	Lucy Maud Montgomery
THE SUSPECT	L. R. Wright
DIVORCED PARENTING	Dr. Sol Goldstein
HUNTING HUMANS	Elliott Leyton
MECCA	William Deverell

The Mark of Canadian Bestsellers

For the millions who can't read Give the gift of literacy

More than four million adult Canadians can't read well enough to fill out a job application or understand the directions on a medicine bottle. You can help. Give money, volunteer with a literacy group, write to your MP, and read to your children.

For more information, contact:

Canadian Give the Gift of Literacy Foundation
34 Ross St., Suite 200,
Toronto, Ont. M5T 1Z9
(416) 595-9967

The Canadian Give the Gift of Literacy Campaign is a project of the book and periodical industry of Canada.